Ratings Analysis

The Theory and Practice of Audience Research

Second Edition

James G. Webster
Northwestern University

Patricia F. Phalen
The George Washington University

Lawrence W. Lichty
Northwestern University

LAWRENCE ERLBAUM ASSOCIATES, PUBLISHERS
2000   Mahwah, New Jersey   London

Lawrence Erlbaum Associates, Inc., Publishers
10 Industrial Avenue
Mahwah, NJ 07430

Cover design by Kathryn Houghtaling Lacey

Library of Congress Cataloging-in-Publication Data

Webster, James G.
Ratings analysis : the theory and practice of audience research /
    James G. Webster, Patricia F. Phalen, Lawrence W. Lichty. — 2nd ed.
        p. Cm. — (LEA's communication series)
        Includes bibliographical references and index.
ISBN 0-8058-3098-7 (cloth) — ISBN 0-8058-3099-5 (pbk)
1. Television programs—Ratings—Methodology. 2. Television viewers.
    3. Radio programs—Ratings—Methodology. 4. Radio audiences.
    I. Title. II. Series. III. Phalen, Patricia F. IV. Lichty, Lawrence
    Wilson.
HE8700.65 W42 1999
384.54'3—dc21   99-41179
                                                                          CIP

Books published by Lawrence Erlbaum Associates are printed on acid-free paper, and their bindings are chosen for strength and durability.

Printed in the United States of America
10 9 8 7 6 5 4 3 2 1

To

Debra Webster
John and Betty Phalen
Sandra Lichty

Contents

Preface

As we noted in the preface to the first edition, this book was written with two groups of people in mind. First, it is intended for anyone who needs more than a superficial understanding of audience research. This would certainly include many people who work in advertising, the electronic media, and related industries. For them, audience data are a fact of life. Whether they have been specifically trained to deal with research or not, their jobs typically require them to make use of "the numbers" when they buy and sell audiences, or make marketing, programming, and investment decisions. The second group includes those who are not compelled to use audience data, but who nevertheless should know something about it. In this group we would include academics, critics, policymakers, students of mass media and even interested members of the general public. For both groups of readers, we have tried to make the book as plainspoken as our subject matter allows.

None of that has changed in the second edition. But the world of audience research has changed since the first edition of this volume was published. Arbitron exited the business of local TV ratings, leaving the field to Nielsen Media Research, Birch got out of the business of ratings altogether, and the Internet arrived as an exciting new medium of communication and electronic commerce. Along with the Internet have come new companies intent on measuring the audiences of the World Wide Web. Moreover, as the media environment has become more competitive, audience ratings have become more and more commonplace in industry and popular press alike. All of these changes are, of course, reflected in the new edition.

The book is divided into three major sections. The first begins with a new introductory chapter providing an overview of audience research in its different forms, from academic studies to commercial audience measurement. In subsequent chapters we illustrate the major applications of audience research in advertising, programming, financial analysis, and social policy. The second section describes the nature of audience research data. It summarizes the history of the audience measurement business, the research methods most commonly used, and the kinds of ratings research products that are currently available. The third section discusses the analysis of audience data. It begins by offering a framework within which to understand mass audience behavior, and concludes with two chapters devoted specifically to the analysis of ratings data.

ACKNOWLEDGMENTS

We are indebted to many people for making this book a reality. First are those individuals identified in the original edition. Their contributions live on in this new work. Since then, many others have offered us their guidance and insights. They include Oveda Brown, Margaret Bustell, Tony Cardinale, Steve Coffey, Steve Carver, Ed Cohen, James Duncan, Bruce Hoynowski, Barbara Jarzab, Jack Loftus, Stacey Lynn, Laura Murray, Charles Marelli, Marla Pirner, Greg Pomaro, Jack Wakshlag, and Ned Waugaman. We are also indebted to countless others at different media and measurement companies for providing data and examples of how research is used. These include Arbitron, Nielsen Media Research, Media Metrix, NetRatings, SRI, The Tribune Company, Veronis, Suhler & Associates, and the several major trade associations. Much of what is good about this book is a credit to them. Anything that is bad we managed to introduce in spite of their help.

I

Applications

1

An Introduction
to Audience Research

Audiences are of critical importance to the mass media. They fund the industry by buying tickets, paying for subscriptions, and renting videos. More important, the media sell audiences to advertisers for billions of dollars. As a result, they are the prizes publishers and programmers constantly pursue in their quest to make money. But radio, television, and Internet audiences are elusive commodities. Dispersed over vast geographical areas, they remain unseen by the media and their advertisers. It is only through audience research that they become visible. This research, especially ratings research, is indispensable to the media's interest in building audiences and to society's interest in understanding mass media industries.

TYPES OF AUDIENCE RESEARCH

We begin by considering several broad categories of audience research. These categories do not exhaust the possibilities, nor are they mutually exclusive. They include many forms of research not discussed elsewhere in this volume. They are offered in this chapter as a guide to help the reader distinguish the various goals, assumptions, and methodologies of audience researchers, and to acquire the basic vocabulary of audience research.

Applied Versus Theoretical

Applied research is designed to provide practical information that can guide decision making. Oftentimes it describes some phenomenon of interest or illumi-

1

nates the consequences of following a specific course of action. For these reasons, it is sometimes called *action research*. Applied research typically focuses on an immediate problem or need. Rarely is there a pretense about offering enduring explanations of how the world works, although sometimes applied research offers useful insights for grander attempts at theorizing.

Applied research is the dominant form of audience study in media industries. In print media, examples include research on recall to determine whether people remember seeing an advertisement, copy testing to assess the appeal or informativeness of messages, and studies that describe the characteristics of people who read various publications. In electronic media, examples include survey research to assess the appeal of celebrities and popular music, auditorium testing to evaluate pilot programs, and ratings research to measure the size and composition of audiences. All of these studies have practical applications.

Another type of applied research sometimes treated as a distinct category is *methodological research*. This is, essentially, research on research. As we show in the chapters that follow, many audience research companies (e.g., Arbitron, Nielsen, etc.) rose to prominence by developing new research methods. Their business is selling a research product and, like any self-interested company, they engage in product testing and development. Methodological audience research might include questions like: "can we measure TV viewing more accurately?" or "how can we improve the response rate to our surveys?" or "can we design a better questionnaire?" The section on audience data in this volume addresses many of these issues and practices.

Theoretical research is designed to test generalized explanations of how the world operates. If the explanations, or theories, are consistently supported by evidence, they may have a broader usefulness than most applied research. Although sometimes done in industrial settings, theoretical research is usually conducted in the academic world. Examples include experiments dealing with the effect of watching violence on television, studies of why individuals use media, or analyses that explain how mass audiences are formed. These studies typically go beyond the practical and specific problems of individual organizations.

Neither applied nor theoretical research is reliably identified by the investigator's method. Surveys, experiments, in-depth interviews, and content analyses can all have either an applied or theoretical purpose. To further complicate matters, a specific piece of research could conceivably serve either purpose, depending upon who is reading the study and the lessons learned. This flexibility of application is a good thing, but it does mean the boundary between applied and theoretical research is not definite.

There is another distinction made in audience studies that overlaps with our discussion of applied versus theoretical work. In the early 1940s Paul Lazarsfeld, whom most regard as a founder of communication research, suggested distinguishing *administrative* from *critical studies* research (Lazarsfeld & Stanton, 1941). Administrative research focuses on making existing operations and institutions function more effectively. It generally accepts the status quo as a given and tries only to improve upon the system. Although all applied research has an administrative purpose, administrative research can also be theoretical. Kurt Lewin, another founder of communication research, was fond of saying, "Nothing is as practical as a good theory" (Rogers, 1994, p. 321). In fact, for the first half of the 20th century, much of what passed as communication theory was administrative in character.

Critical studies are harder to define. This research makes no pretense of being useful in an administrative sense, and many critical scholars would vehemently reject such use of their work. Rather, researchers who advocate a critical approach tend to stand apart from the status quo and ask questions like: "In whose interest is all this going on?" or "What do media mean to people?" Critical studies can certainly be based on empirical data, but they tend to be more self-consciously ideological than most administrative audience research. Whether they are "theoretical" in the way social scientists use the term is an interesting question, but one that goes beyond the scope of this book.

Quantitative Versus Qualitative

Industry researchers as well as academics often make a distinction between quantitative and qualitative research. However, there is a good deal of imprecision in how these terms are used, especially among industry professionals. A proper academic definition would say that *quantitative research* reduces the object of study to numbers. This allows for the use of statistics and facilitates the process of reporting results across large numbers of people—a process researchers call aggregation. *Qualitative research* produces non-numeric summaries, perhaps in the form of field notes or transcribed comments from an interview. Qualitative investigators delve into a topic in depth, though the generalizability of results is sometimes open to question.

Unlike the distinction between theoretical and applied research, here the categories of research tend to be associated with particular methods. Quantitative research relies heavily on surveys and experiments. For example, someone doing a telephone survey might ask whether a respondent agrees or disagrees with a list of statements. These answers are almost immediately converted to numbers. Similarly, an experimenter might quantify physiological responses, such as heart rates or eye movements.

Qualitative methods, such as group interviews or some form of observation, usually produce non-numeric results. However, this is where some of the confusion in terminology begins. To help identify patterns, investigators sometimes assign numbers to data gathered with qualitative methods. Thus the rich text of respondent interviews or field notes can be expressed in numbers that represent the prevalence of ideas or phrases. The methods are still qualitative, but the statistical analysis of the results resembles quantitative research. In fact, many qualitative researchers in academia would deny that these studies are qualitative at all. Academics often apply a more limited definition to qualitative research—one that includes ideological considerations and requires that the researcher acknowledge his or her influence on the data.

There is further inconsistency in how these terms are actually used in media industries: quantitative research takes on a narrower meaning, whereas the label "qualitative research" is affixed to many studies that are laden with statistics. At best scholars can try to understand conventions of categorization in the industry by offering a few examples and rules of thumb.

For most media professionals, quantitative research means audience measurement—it is all about knowing the size and composition of the audience. Industry researchers center their attention on some measure of exposure and a small number of audience characteristics that interest advertisers; accuracy and generalizability are the goals. It is this kind of information that drives media industry revenues. In the electronic media, the numbers are referred to as audience *ratings*. Ratings are of such overwhelming importance, that some textbook writers simply distinguish ratings from non-ratings research (e.g., Wimmer & Dominick, 1997).

In industry, qualitative generally means any research not focused exclusively on audience size and composition (e.g., age, gender, etc.). This might include studies that address less routine audience characteristics (lifestyles, values, attitudes, product purchases, etc.), or work centering on causes and consequences of exposure. While these data do not provide the hard audience estimates used to buy and sell media, they are, by a stricter academic definition, quantitative—they specify characteristics of interest reduced to statistical summaries. It seems that mass media professionals in the real world ignore academics' "proper" definitions.

There are truer examples of qualitative work in industry. One of the most common qualitative methods is the *focus group*. This involves gathering a small group of people and having an interviewer talk to the group at length about some topic of interest. Krueger (1994) defines a focus group as "a carefully planned discussion designed to obtain perceptions on a defined area of interest in a permissive, non-threatening environment" (p. 6). Participants in focus groups are often shown programming or products to start. Afterward a summary and interpretation of their comments are reported. This kind of research is a popular means to assess radio station formats, local news, program concepts, and a host of new products.

There are also examples of qualitative research in academic settings. One approach, which has gained popularity in the last two decades, is called audience *ethnography*. This is an umbrella term that describes several techniques. Some ethnographies are very much like focus groups. Others may try to introduce an observer into some place of interest, a homeless shelter or family setting, for example. Still other ethnographies require the investigator to immerse himself or herself in the site of study for months or years. This might require the researcher to live among the people being studied. The best ethnographies produce a depth of understanding hard to match with quantitative methods.

Syndicated Versus Custom

The final distinction that we will take up is the difference between syndicated and custom research. *Syndicated research* is a standardized research product sold to multiple subscribers. One of the preeminent examples is audience ratings. A single report serves all users in a particular market. Many companies offer syndicated services. Table 1.1 lists the major suppliers of syndicated audience research and their products.

This is not a complete list of all companies doing audience research. As commercial mass media have spread around the globe, many countries have developed their own domestic audience research services. Nor are these the only syndicated numbers that media professionals might encounter. There are comparative media reports that track advertising and the cost of reaching various audiences in various markets. There are organizations that audit the methods and circulation claims of the media. There are trade association reports and newsletters that offer data to a wide number of readers. All in all, the media industries are awash in numbers. Moreover, as the media environment becomes more complex, the ability to size up and use these numbers is increasingly important.

Syndicated research has several important advantages relative to other kinds of sources. Because the results of one study are sold to many subscribers, the cost to any one of them should be less than it would be if fewer organizations were funding it. Additionally, the same reports serve different clients, some of whom have competing interests, so research syndicators have an interest in being objective. The semi-public nature of the documents makes it harder for any one entity to misrepresent the research, while the standardization of report formats facilitates routine uses of the data. Though imperfect, syndicated data, like audience ratings, often become the official numbers used to transact business.

Custom research is tailored to meet the needs of a particular sponsor and may never be seen by outsiders. Sometimes clients buy customized research from specialists like news and programming consultants. Other times research is done entirely in-house. For example, major market radio stations that specialize in popular music conduct a kind of telephone survey known as *call-out research* to track public tastes. A sample of listeners is called and asked to listen to the *hook*, or most memorable phrase, of several popular songs. The station can then adjust its playlist based on the results. Similarly, in the late 1930s, CBS developed a device called a *program analyzer* to test the appeal of new radio programs. People were invited to an auditorium to listen to programs and vote at regular intervals on their likes and dislikes. TV pilots are tested in this way before they reach the air. Even long-running programs are often re-tested in what is called *mainte-*

TABLE 1.1

Major Suppliers of Syndicated Audience Research

Supplier	Service
AGB Media Services *www.agbms.ch/home.shtml*	Provides TV audience measurement using peoplemeters in more than a dozen countries worldwide.
Arbitron *www.arbitron.com*	The major supplier of radio audience ratings in more than 260 U.S. markets.
Claritas *www.claritas.com/*	Operates a system called PRIZM providing zip-code level data on demographics and lifestyles. Often combined with information on media use.
Information Resources Inc. *www.infores.com*	Conducts BehaviorScan study to match consumer buying habits with media use.
International Demographics Inc.	Produces the Media Audit, a syndicated study of local market media use and consumer information.
Marketing Evaluations Inc. *www.qscores.com/*	Publishes scores, called TvQs, that measure the public's familiarity with and liking of celebrities.
Media Metrix, Inc. *www.mediametrix.com/*	Operates a large panel equipped with PC meters providing data on Internet usage.
Mediamark Research Inc. (MRI) *www.mediamark.com/*	Publishes an annual survey of product usage and demographics, with broad measures of print and electronic media use.
NetRatings *www.netratings.com/*	Measures Internet use with a panel. Partnering with Nielsen Media Research to produce Nielsen/NetRatings.
Nielsen Media Research *www.nielsenmedia.com/*	The preeminent supplier of TV audience ratings in the United States.
Roper Starch Worldwide *www.roper.com/*	Publishes a number of surveys including Starch Readership Services, which measure recall of print advertising
Scarborough Research *www.scarborough.com/*	Provides local market reports on demographic, shopping, lifestyle, and media usage data.
Simmons Market Research Bureau (SMRB)	Publishes a national survey with demographics, product usage, and general measures of print and electronic media use.
SOFRES *www.sofres.com/*	A large international marketing research group providing audience measurement in Europe and Asia.
Statistical Research Inc. (SRI) *www.sriresearch.com/*	Provides radio network ratings in the United States. Conducts methodological research on audience measurement.
Strategic Media Research *www.strategicmediaresearch.com*	Provides telephone-based radio audience measurement called AccuTrack in selected U.S. markets.
Yankelovich Partners *www.yankelovich.com/*	Conducts many surveys including the Yankelovich Monitor, which tracks consumer social values and celebrity ratings.

nance research—measuring the appeal of various story lines, the strength of characters, and so forth. This device is also used by political consultants to measure the response to candidate speeches and TV debates.

Custom research may be of great value to the user but is of limited value otherwise. Obviously, the sponsors of call-out or program analyzer research would be loath to share the results with anyone outside their organizations. If custom research is circulated to a larger readership, it may be regarded with suspicion. Often the methods are difficult to verify, and it is assumed the sponsor has a self-serving motive for promoting the results.

Much research conducted in colleges and universities is customized, though it is generally referred to as original or *primary research*. If published in an academic journal, it is reviewed by other experts in the field, which provides some assurance that the authors used defensible research procedures. Occasionally, academics or university research centers are commissioned by the industry to do customized studies that may have greater public credibility.

It is increasingly common to see a kind of hybrid study that has attributes of both syndicated and customized research. Once research syndicators have produced their reports, they find themselves with vast stores of raw data. In an age of computers, it is simple to tap those databases to produce specialized reports. This is sometimes called a *secondary analysis* of existing data.

Examples of such hybrid analyses include studies of audience flow derived from the Nielsen Media Research database. Using original data, it is possible to track how viewers move from one channel or program to the next. As explained in chapter 3, this information can be useful to a programmer. Media researchers can also use these data to develop mathematical models of audience behavior. The Claritas company, for example, links census data to existing estimates of media use and can describe audiences by income levels and other lifestyle variables.

These hybrid studies have a number of advantages. They are certainly in the syndicator's interest since they can generate additional revenues while requiring very little additional expenditure. Clients may also find them cheaper than original custom research. Moreover, since the results are based on syndicated data, they have the air of official, objective numbers.

For all these reasons, secondary analyses of existing data can be enormously valuable. But they must also be done with caution and an understanding of what is sound research practice. Quite often, when data are sliced up in ways that were not intended at the time of collection, the slices become too small to be statistically reliable. We will have much more to say about the problems of sampling and sample sizes in chapter 7.

COMMERCIAL AUDIENCE RESEARCH

The type of study at the heart of this book is commercial audience research. Defining *commercial research* would seem a simple matter: it is research that supports commercial enterprises, usually for a price. Unfortunately, that definition is inadequate. As critical scholars are quick to point out, even academic research that appears to have the purest of motives is typically undertaken in service of institutional interests. Some organization, whether a university, foundation, or media company, is paying the bill—in effect, buying the research product. But does this make all funded research somehow commercial? For the purposes of this book, we offer a more specific description of commercial audience research.

The Characteristics of Commercial Research

Despite the universal recognition that research costs money, there are a number of generalizations that apply to commercial audience research. It usually has an administrative purpose, whether applied or theoretical. It is generally quantitative and often based on survey research, although independent consultants are sometimes hired to conduct focus groups. The term is usually applied to syndicated research, though large sums of money are sometimes paid for customized studies. It is usually focused on exposure to media and the business of audience measurement. And it is usually concerned with aggregates and not any individual audience member.

Most of these distinctions have been thoroughly reviewed in the preceding section, but the last point warrants special comment. Audience analysts are usually concerned with the behavior of large numbers of people. They probably don't care whether Bob Smith sees an early evening newscast but do care how many men ages 18–49 will be watching. This interest in mass behavior, typical of much social scientific research, is actually a blessing. Trying to explain or predict how any one person behaves, moment to moment, day to day, can be an exercise in frustration. After all, human beings are complex creatures with different moods, impulses, and motivations. Strangely, however, when the researcher aggregates individual activities, the behavior of the mass is predictable. And the business of selling audiences to advertisers is built on predictions.

This science of predicting mass behavior and audience characteristics has been called statistical thinking. It was developed in the eighteenth century by, among others, insurance underwriters. Consider, for example, the problem of life insurance. It is almost impossible to predict when any one person will die. But if the researcher aggregates large numbers, it's not hard to estimate how many people are likely to expire in the coming year. It is unnecessary to predict the outcome of each individual case to predict an outcome across an entire population. It is similarly unnecessary to know what every member of a ratings sample will do on a given evening to predict how many households will be using television.

One important consequence of focusing on a mass, rather than individuals, is that audience behavior becomes more tractable. Stable patterns emerge showing audience size and flow. Mathematical equations, or models, help researchers predict audience behavior. Some even posit "laws" of viewing behavior. These laws, of course, do not bind each person to a code of conduct. Rather, they are statements that mass behavior is so predictable as to exhibit law-like tendencies. This kind of reasoning is typical of commercial audience research and underlies many of the analytical techniques presented in the final chapters.

Whether this is the best way to study audiences is debatable, but, for the most part, that's the way commercial audience research operates. Leo Bogart, a well-known advertising executive and author of several books on the media makes the point directly: "The bulk of communication research is commercial research and is addressed to the question of measuring audiences, rather than to study of the process through which audiences reject or inject the information presented to them" (Bogart, 1996, p. 138).

Criticisms of Commercial Research

Commercial audience research is the subject of several criticisms which should be of concern to any thoughtful user. One is that it tells us very little about why people use mass media, nor does it explain the consequences of media use. These questions, the argument goes, ought to be the central concerns of communication research. They are certainly important, and it is true that audience measurement sheds little light on these questions. However, in defense of commercial audience research, most studies were never designed to answer such questions. Every type of research has limitations. It is the job of the user to identify those limitations and how to circumvent them.

Another concern with commercial audience research is that it reduces people to neat numerical summaries. According to critics, this has undesirable consequences. The first problem, especially with "official" syndicated reports, is that people will regard the numbers with undue reverence. Many published numbers are not as "hard" as an inexperienced user might imagine. Indeed, they are usually estimates. Here, again, it is up to the user to know the source of the numbers and what they mean. This demands considerable attention to critiquing the methods used to generate audience research reports.

A related problem stems from the fact that commercial audience research is a product. According to critics, the sellers of research skew their products in favor of client needs. In the words of an old proverb, "He who pays the piper calls the tune." There may be something to this, but it seems doubtful that companies selling audience measurement can drift too far from fairness and objectivity without risking their businesses.

The final concern, heard mostly from critical scholars, is that commercial audience research is an instrument of repression. The whole business of turning people into numbers so they can be bought and sold like any commodity is, at the very least, dehumanizing. By doing so, commercial audience research participates in the control and colonization of the masses. The validity of this last criticism seems to be in the eye of the beholder. Other academics have argued that audience research actually empowers audiences by giving them a voice (Webster & Phalen, 1997).

RATINGS RESEARCH

Audience ratings are the most visible example of commercial audience re-search. They hold a unique place in industry practice and public consciousness. Hugh Beville, a former network executive often referred to as the dean of broadcast audience research, observed the following:

> Ratings are a powerful force in broadcasting and telecommunications. They deter-mine the price that will be paid for programs and the pay that performers will receive. They govern the rates that advertisers will pay for 60-second or 30-second or smaller commercial units in and around each program. Ratings determine stations' audience and rank order in their market, and to a large degree they dictate the profitability of broadcasting stations and their value when they are put up for sale. The salary and bo-nus compensation of key network and station officials is also governed by ratings suc-cess. Ratings results ultimately determine whether top management and program and news management in television and radio broadcast organizations will retain their jobs, be promoted, or demoted. (1988, p. xi)

Not only is the industry preoccupied with audience ratings, but, unlike any other form of syndicated research, ratings have worked their way into popular culture. Almost everyone has heard about the Nielsens and formed some opin-ion about them. Larson (1992) argued:

> Most viewers know Nielsen only as the maker of the bullets that killed such shows as "Star Trek" and "Twin Peaks," but to think of its ratings exclusively in terms of their show-stopping power is to underestimate the depth of Nielsen's influence over the culture, content, and business of television, and therefore, over the evolution of our consumer culture itself. Nielsen *is* television. (p. 105)

While it's easy to get swept into overstatement, audience ratings are certainly a force to be reckoned with. Many people in the electronic media use the terms *ratings research* and *audience research* interchangeably, implying that nothing else matters. Since this book deals extensively with the analysis of ratings data, it seems appropriate to consider why ratings are such a visible and pervasive form of audience research.

It should be noted from the outset that we use the term *ratings* as shorthand for a body of data on people's exposure to electronic media. Strictly speaking, ratings are one of many audience summaries that can be derived from that data. Ratings research originated in the 1930s in response to the explosive growth of radio and industry's desire to turn broadcasting into a mass advertising medium (see chap. 6, this volume). Because the broadcast audience could not be seen, there was no credible way to determine who was listening to radio programs or the commercials they contained. Ratings solved the problem. To make people aware of this new service, C. E. Hooper, a pioneer of ratings research, deliber-ately publicized his *Hooperatings*. To this day, broadcast media are almost totally dependent on advertising revenues and in turn on ratings as the sole measure of the invisible audience. Ratings appear widely not only in the trade press but also in popular media.

The other key to understanding the power of ratings is to appreciate the sheer pervasiveness of broadcasting. Radio and television dominate the consumption of mass media in the United States and much of the world. Table 1.2 summarizes the number of hours the average American spends with each of several media in a year.

Some caution is in order when reading this table. While the numbers are presented as additive, media use sometimes overlaps leading to the possibility of double counting. These are also averages, so one person's profile might look different from the overall patterns presented here. Even so, the numbers are staggering. The average person spends more than 9 hours each day consuming media, with nearly 80% of their time spent with radio or some form of television. Other media pale by comparison. Old competitors for advertising dollars, like newspapers, are losing audience. New competitors, like the Internet, have a

TABLE 1.2
Hours per Person per Year Using Media

Medium	1990 Hours	1990 Percent	1997 Hours	1997 Percent	2002 Projected Hours	2002 Projected Percent
Television	1470	45.1%	1561	46.3%	1575	46.4%
Radio	1135	34.8%	1082	32.1%	1040	30.6%
Recorded Music	235	7.2%	265	7.9%	289	8.5%
Daily Newspapers	175	5.4%	159	4.7%	152	4.5%
Consumer Books	95	2.9%	92	2.7%	97	2.9%
Consumer Magazines	90	2.8%	82	2.4%	79	2.3%
Home Video	38	1.2%	50	1.5%	58	1.7%
Home Video Games	12	0.4%	36	1.1%	46	1.4%
Movies in Theaters	12	0.4%	13	0.4%	13	0.4%
Internet On-Line	1	0.0%	28	0.8%	49	1.4%
TOTAL	3263	100.0%	3368	100.0%	3398	100.0%

Note. Columns may not add up to 100% due to rounding. Adapted from Veronis, Suhler & Associates 1998 Communications Industry Forecast.

long way to go. It is small wonder that the electronic mass media figure so heavily in the public consciousness.

By extension, it is clear why audience ratings loom large for everyone connected with the electronic media. They are the tools used by advertisers and broadcasters to buy and sell audiences; the report cards that lead programmers to cancel some shows and clone others. Ratings are road maps to patterns of media consumption, and, as such, can interest anyone from a Wall Street banker to a social scientist. They are objects of fear and loathing and the subject of much confusion. We hope this book can end some of that confusion and enable an improved understanding of audience research and the ways it can be used. The book comprises three sections. The first reviews the users of audience research and how they look at numbers. The second considers audience data, reviewing the history, methods, and reporting formats of commercial research. The final section provides a way to understand and analyze audience data, including a general framework for explaining audience behavior and rather specific analytical techniques.

RELATED READINGS

Ang, I. (1991). *Desperately seeking the audience.* London, Routledge.

Beville, H. (1988). *Audience ratings: Radio, television, cable* (rev. ed.) Hillsdale, NJ: Lawrence Erlbaum Associates.

Ettema, J., & Whitney, C. (Eds.). (1994). *Audiencemaking: How the media create the audience.* Thousand Oaks, CA: Sage.

Krueger, R. A. (1994). *Focus groups: A practical guide for applied research* (2nd ed.). Thousand Oaks, CA: Sage.

Lindlof, T. (1995). *Qualitative communication research methods.* Thousand Oaks, CA: Sage.

Potter, W. J. (1996). *An analysis of thinking and research about qualitative methods.* Mahwah, NJ: Lawrence Erlbaum Associates.

Webster, J., & Phalen, P. (1997). *The mass audience: Rediscovering the dominant model.* Mahwah, NJ: Lawrence Erlbaum Associates.

Wimmer, R., & Dominick, J. (1997). *Mass media research: An introduction* (5th ed.). Belmont, CA: Wadsworth.

2

Audience Research in Advertising

Broadcasters sell audiences. Despite some appearances to the contrary, that is the most important activity of the business. Virtually all other actions undertaken support that function. Whether this is good or bad can be, and frequently is, debated. For now, it is sufficient to note that this is an essential characteristic of commercial mass media. Not only do traditional broadcasters sell audiences, but newer forms of electronic media, like cable, Direct Broadcast Satellite (DBS), and the World Wide Web, offer ways to reach them as well.

The people who buy these audiences are advertisers interested in capturing the attention of the viewer or listener in order to get across some message. It might be as simple as introducing people to a new brand or reminding them of an old one. It might involve trying to change their attitudes toward a person or product. Often it represents an attempt to influence behavior in some way. Whatever the purpose, the process requires that the advertiser gain access to an audience—if only for a moment. To do that, they are willing to pay the media.

Unlike the print media, which can document possible readership with more concrete figures on the number of issues sold, broadcasters must estimate who is out there listening—their audience has a unique, intangible quality. Advertisers' desire to buy audiences and broadcasters' eagerness to sell created the need to define the intangible, which brought the ratings services into being. Advertisers have the biggest stake in the audience measurement business and wield the most influence in shaping the form of ratings. Without advertiser support of electronic media, ratings would not exist in their current form.

13

The buying and selling of audiences occurs at many levels. There is a national marketplace dominated by a few broadcast and cable networks, syndicators, and major corporate advertisers. There are many local markets where individual stations sell to area merchants. And there are national spot and regional markets providing access to audiences in various geographic areas. This trade in audiences is organized by medium into radio, broadcast television, cable, and, increasingly, Internet. Table 2.1 illustrates the growth of these markets by summarizing the revenues that have flowed to each, in this multibillion-dollar business.

The characteristics of each marketplace affect how audience data are handled and the analytical techniques used. What follows is a description of the major markets where electronic media audiences are bought and sold. Ratings information available to buyers and sellers in each market appear in chapter 8 of this volume.

NATIONAL MARKETS

Broadcast and Cable Networks

The largest audiences and biggest sums of money are exchanged at the network level. Although the radio and cable television businesses sell national audiences through networks, the major broadcast television networks still have the largest audiences overall. For advertisers who need to reach vast national markets, network television has much to offer.

As a practical matter, the network television marketplace is divided into smaller markets called *dayparts*. The precise name and definition of each daypart varies from medium to medium and from time zone to time zone. A daypart is a portion of the broadcast schedule defined by time of day and program content. Because each designation is associated with specific audience characteristics, the various dayparts appeal to different advertisers and generate different amounts of money for the networks.

Prime time is the most important of the network dayparts. Unlike the official definition of prime time used by federal regulators, broadcast network prime time includes all regularly scheduled programs from 8:00 p.m. to 11:00 p.m. eastern standard time (EST), Monday through Saturday, and 7:00 p.m. to 11:00 p.m. on Sunday (EST). The networks have their largest audiences during this daypart and, accordingly, generate their largest revenues. This daypart has special appeal to advertisers who are trying to reach a wide variety of people across the entire nation. It is also the best time to reach people who work during the day. Access to this mass market, however, does not come cheaply, and the most popular prime-time programs are the most expensive.

Daytime is the second most lucrative daypart. For the networks, it extends from 7:00 a.m. to 4:30 p.m., Monday through Friday. The daytime audience is

TABLE 2.1
Advertising Revenues of Electronic Media[a]

Year	Radio[b] Network	Spot	Local	Television[c] Network	Spot	Local	Synd	Cable[d] Network	Spot/Local	Internet[e]	Total
1950	$132	$119	$203	$85	$31	$55	$—	$—	$—	—	$625
1960	45	208	402	820	527	280	—	—	—	—	$2,282
1970	49	355	853	1,658	1,234	704	—	—	—	—	$4,853
1980	158	746	2,643	5,130	3,269	2,967	50	50	50	—	$15,063
1985	329	1,320	4,915	8,285	6,004	5,714	540	612	139	—	$27,858
1990	433	1,626	6,780	9,863	7,788	7,856	1,109	1,802	737	—	$37,994
1995	426	1,920	9,124	11,600	9,119	9,985	2,016	4,036	1,648	—	$49,874
1996	465	2,093	9,854	13,081	9,803	10,944	2,218	4,876	1,899	267	$55,500
1997	498	2,407	10,741	13,020	9,999	11,436	2,438	5,754	2,172	907	$59,372

[a]Revenue in millions
[b]Radio Advertising Bureau
[c]Television Bureau of Advertising
[d]Cabletelevision Advertising Bureau, as published in CAB's *1998 Cable TV Facts*
[e]Internet Advertising Bureau/PricewaterhouseCoopers, reprinted with permission, ©1998 IAB
Fox was counted as syndication prior to 1990, and as network after 1990.
UPN & WB were counted as syndication from 1995–1997.

15

much smaller than in prime time and, with the exception of the early news programs, disproportionately female. It appeals most to advertisers trying to reach women, particularly women who do not work outside the home. Companies selling household products like soap and food frequently buy spots in this time period, paying far less than prime-time advertisers.

Sports is a daypart defined strictly by program content. The most important sports programming for the networks is coverage of major league games like those of the National Football League or National Basketball Association. These events attract disproportionately male audiences. That fact is suggested by the advertisers who buy heavily in this daypart, which include breweries, car and truck manufacturers, and companies that sell automotive products. The cost of advertising during sports programming varies widely, mostly as a function of audience size. The fee for a 30-second spot during the Super Bowl can exceed $1 million.

The news daypart is another market defined by content. It includes the networks' evening news programs, weekend news programming, and news specials and documentaries. Excluded from this daypart, however, are the morning news programs (considered daytime), and regularly scheduled prime-time programs like 60 Minutes. The news daypart tends to attract an older audience, which appeals to companies that sell products like headache remedies and healthful foods.

Late night runs from 11:30 p.m. (EST) until early morning, Monday through Friday. Its best known programs are The Tonight Show with Jay Leno, and Late Show with David Letterman, which have dominated the time period for years. Not surprisingly, the audience during this daypart is small and almost entirely adult in composition.

One of the most important markets from the point of view of public interest groups and government regulators is the children's daypart. Traditionally, this has included the Saturday and Sunday morning children's programs, a time period that critics once dubbed the "children's ghetto." It may also include weekday programming aimed at children. Although children watch a great deal of television at other times, from an advertiser's viewpoint, this daypart is the most efficient way to gain access to the child audience through broadcast television. The biggest buyers of time in this daypart are cereal and candy makers and toy manufacturers. The cost of a 30-second spot can vary widely, because demand for advertising time is seasonal. Leading into the December holiday season, a spot might cost three times what it would in later months.

Markets can also be defined by the calendar time frame in which buying occurs. Some advertisers purchase time well in advance of airdate and others purchase time a few months or weeks before broadcast. These different rounds in the buying process are called the upfront market, the scatter market, and the opportunistic market.

The upfront market is the first round of buying. Each spring and summer, major advertisers tell national media salespeople what kind of audiences they wish to buy in the upcoming television season. The network salespeople respond with proposals detailing the audiences they will sell and at what prices. The networks want maximum price for their audiences, while the advertisers want the most viewers for their dollars. To complicate matters, no one can know exactly which shows in the fall lineup audiences will watch, especially the new series. This market generates high-stakes gamesmanship, which David Poltrack (1983) described in detail. At the end of the buying, the major advertisers have committed to buy large blocks of network time throughout the coming year.

Although this method of buying ties up advertisers' budgets for months, it affords them access to the best network programs. Because these companies are making long-term commitments to the network, they are also likely to get time at more favorable rates than will be available later in the year. In fact, to minimize the advertiser's risk, networks often guarantee to deliver the audience estimates, even if that means running additional commercials, called *make-goods*, for free.

The scatter market operates within a shorter time frame. Each television season is divided into quarters. In advance of each quarter, advertisers may wish to buy time for specific purposes. Sometimes products are seasonal and don't require yearlong advertising. Others may require the purchase of additional network time for a limited campaign not envisioned during the upfront buying. Because advertisers in the scatter market have less flexibility and the networks have already sold much of their inventory, this market often finds the buyer at a disadvantage, which usually means higher costs. However, conditions in the scatter market could work to the buyer's advantage. Programs considered risky in the upfront market will have proven track records when scatter buying occurs, providing a safer investment for the advertiser. Additionally, if the networks have a slow season, rates could actually be lower in scatter than in the upfront market.

The opportunistic market occurs as the television season progresses. Although most network inventory is purchased during upfront and scatter markets, some is unsold close to the airdate. Deals negotiated early may fall through, due to changes in an advertiser's budget or implementation of new marketing strategies. Changes in network programming might also generate inventory. For example, a faltering series may be canceled or rescheduled, relieving advertisers of their commitments. Similarly, the network may preempt regularly scheduled programs with specials or special events. These scenarios leave holes in the network lineups and create opportunities for savvy buyers and sellers.

These developments could favor either the network or the advertiser. Buyers and sellers often use such opportunities to settle debts from past business deals. For example, a salesperson with opportunistic inventory might offer a low-cost spot to a particular buyer who has been an excellent customer. Or a buyer may purchase a spot to help the seller because the salesperson has given preferential treatment in the past.

Despite their clear domination of national television audiences, the broadcast networks are not the only way to televise a message across the country. Since the early days of television, an alternative delivery system has been developing. Cable television uses a wire to distribute signals, instead of broadcasting them through the electromagnetic spectrum. Cable originally supplemented the broadcast delivery system by routing signals to areas with poor over-the-air reception. As such, the early systems were little more than glorified antennas. In fact, cable was referred to by the acronym "CATV," for community antenna television.

After years of struggling with government regulators and much financial uncertainty, cable television has emerged as an advertising medium in its own right. Through technological developments like coaxial cable and fiber optics, systems can offer an abundance of channel space to programmers. That, in combination with the growth of communication satellites—which can send TV signals to many small and widely dispersed cable systems—has opened a door for new network services. The limits of the spectrum no longer constrain the number of television signals that can compete for the viewers' attention.

Since the late 1970s, a number of entrepreneurs have exploited these technological changes to create cable networks. Table 2.2 lists the top 20 national cable television networks ranked by the number of subscribers. Most of these services depend at least in part on advertising revenues to sustain their operations. Indeed, many are programmed to attract a particular kind of viewer—the kind that interests an advertiser. MTV is designed for teens and young adults; Nickelodeon for children. Other networks appeal to particular ethnic or cultural groups, such as Galavision, which is programmed for Hispanic audiences. In terms of program quality and access to the audiences that advertisers seek, cable television is increasingly indistinguishable from broadcast.

The two forms of distribution, however, are not completely equal. There are roughly 98 million television households in the United States, but even the largest cable networks reach nowhere near that number of households in their potential audience. Despite growth in the number of homes that subscribe, cable is used by only about 74% of all television households. Broadcast networks—especially the big four—are likely to attract larger audiences than cable.

Even though cable can't compete with broadcast networks in the size of audiences, they have developed successful strategies to position their services. Cable salespeople often concentrate on their potential to reach target audiences. One of three rationales is commonly used. First, because the growth of cable has reduced the time people spend with broadcast television, cable networks often position their service as a way to reach those lost viewers. The sales pitch is that broadcast networks underdeliver the audience, and that buying time on cable networks corrects that problem in a cost-effective manner. Further, it is argued that cable households, where broadcast underdelivery is the biggest problem, include the most affluent and generally desirable target audiences. Second, be-

TABLE 2.2
Top 20 Cable Networks*

	Subscribers (in millions)
Discovery Channel	73,471
ESPN	73,000
TBS Superstation	73,000
Turner Network Television	72,400
The Nashville Network	71,400
C-SPAN	71,400
The Weather Channel	71,000
Cable News Network	71,000
USA Network	69,677
Lifetime Television	69,500
Headline News	68,000
American Movie Classics	67,000
FOX Family Channel	66,900
A&E Television Network	66,880
Music Television	66,700
Nickelodeon/Nick at Nite	66,000
CNBC	64,000
The Learning Channel	64,000
QVC	63,010
VH1	61,600

*Source: National Cable Television Association, www.ncta.com, October 2, 1998.

cause many cable services cater to subsets of the mass audience, advertising on the appropriate services is considered a more efficient way to reach the kind of viewer an advertiser wants. Third, cable networks are often more willing to work with an advertiser to develop some special programming or promotional effort. This can sometimes enhance the impact of the advertising.

Although television networks presently command much of our attention, it is worth remembering that the first networks distributed radio programming. Radio networks were permanently established by the late 1920s, along with many of the practices and traditions that are a part of network television today. In fact, radio networks have been an important social and cultural force in American life. Despite radio's rich history, television has moved to center stage and garnered the lion's share of advertising revenues. Nevertheless, radio networks are still viable and offer advertisers another way of reaching a national audience.

There are more than a score of national radio networks, but most are controlled by a handful of companies. The original radio networks, now more than 70 years old, and important radio program syndicators dominate the business. Disney/ABC and Westwood One are among the most important networks. Each offers several services, including news broadcasts, music formats of various types, talk and sports talk programming. Syndicators, although not networks per se, provide specialized radio formats via satellite to a large number of stations all over the country. Syndicated programs featuring well-known personalities like Rush Limbaugh and Don Imus can be carried by hundreds of stations simultaneously. Many music and talk formats are delivered to stations including all types of popular music, call-in sports, and political conversation. News-gathering organizations, such as Associated Press and United Press International, provide network services, as do cable services CNN, Fox News, and ABC's ESPN.

Syndication

Broadcast stations are in constant need of programming. Even network affiliates have large blocks of time they must program themselves. As a result, broadcasters acquire programming from different sources. One such source, particularly relevant to a discussion of advertising, is *barter syndication*.

Barter syndication has fairly straightforward origins. Basically, advertisers found they could use a station's need for programming to get their message to the audience. All they had to do was produce a program, place their ads in it, and offer it to stations free of charge. Stations found this attractive because they got new programs with no cash expenditure, and could even sell some spots in the show if the program's original sponsor did not use them. In the 1980s, with the advent of satellite program distribution, this simple idea gave rise to a rapidly growing new advertising marketplace.

Today, barter syndication works like this: A distributor that produces programs or owns the rights to existing programming approaches local broadcasters and convinces the stations to carry the show. Sometimes this is an *all-barter* arrangement, meaning the station gives all available airtime to the syndicator for sale in the national market, and sometimes it is a *cash-plus-barter* deal. Under this latter arrangement, the station actually pays a fee for the program, in addition to accepting ads placed by the distributor.

The terms of a deal are determined by the syndicator prior to placing a program in the marketplace. At the beginning of each calendar year the trade publications print lists of these arrangements, just before the National Association of Television Programming Executives (NATPE) conference. It is at this conference that programs are marketed intensely to potential buyers, especially from medium and smaller markets. Table 2.3 reproduces part of this list for the

TABLE 2.3
Major NATPE Clearances*

Half-hour strips	Distributor	Terms	Markets/ Clearances	Premiere
Hollywood Squares	King World	Cash-plus	100/80%	Sept.
Judge Joe Brown	Worldvision	Cash-plus	n/a/70%	Sept.
Match Game	Pearson	Cash-plus	64/66%	Sept.
Hour strips				
Donny & Marie	Columbia	Cash-plus	185/97%	Fall
Forgive or Forget	Twentieth	Cash-plus	65/70%	June
Howie Mandel	Paramount	Cash-plus	151/90%	June
Love Connection/ Change of Heart	Telepictures	Barter	71/79%	Sept.
Magic Hour	Twentieth	Barter	72/75%	June
Maury Povich	Universal	Cash-plus	125/90%	Sept.
Roseanne	King World	Cash-plus	140/90%	Sept.
Half-hour weeklies				
Almost Live	Litton	Barter	135/85%	Feb.
Better Living With Carrie Wiatt	Kelly	Barter	61/63%	Sept.
Bill Franks ForeverYoung	Litton	Barter	n/a	Sept.
Gravy U.S.A.	Litton	Barter	n/a	Sept.
Malibu, CA	Tribune	Barter	80/74%	Sept.
News of the Weird	MG/Perin	Barter	n/a	Sept.
Hour weeklies				
Acapulco H.E.A.T.	Western	Barter	n/a/60%	Sept.
Air America	Pearson	Barter	81/75%	Sept.
The Crow	PolyGram	Barter	60/70%	Sept.

Note. Reprinted from *Electronic Media*, 1/26/98, p. 4, by permission. © 1998, Crain Communications, Inc.

1998 NATPE convention. The barter terms may change, depending on market demand, but this list gives a good indication of the syndicators' asking prices. Individual barter contracts may also require stations to broadcast a program in a specific daypart. This is typical of popular programs, like *Wheel of Fortune.*

In addition to the terms of sale, Table 2.3 contains an estimate of the number of markets that have already purchased (or cleared) the programs. The more stations that acquire a program, the larger the potential audience. If one station in every market agreed to air the program, the distributor would, hypothetically, have the same reach as a major television network. As a practical matter, once a program is carried on enough stations to reach 70% of U.S. households, it is sold to advertisers much the same way that network time is sold.

Just like the networks, barter syndication firms go to national advertisers and their agencies to sell time. They sell in the upfront, scatter, and opportunistic markets, and may even guarantee audiences like their network competitors. In fact, advertisers may look upon barter syndication as a supplement to their purchases of network time, or as a substitute. Sometimes program environments not offered on traditional broadcast networks are available through barter. For example, game shows, talk shows, and science fiction programs like *Star Trek* are available mostly through syndication. Still, the major attraction of barter is participation at a reduced cost.

Despite these similarities, buying time in barter syndication is not comparable to network advertising. Many programs, especially those produced for first-run syndication, are sent to all stations in the country at the same time, and at least run on the same day. But other types of programming, off-network syndication, for example, may be on the air at different times in different markets. A syndicated program shown once a week might even appear on different days.

Barter syndication and similar options for advertising to national or regional audiences are certain to grow. Satellite communications have made the rapid, cost-efficient delivery of programming feasible, creating, in effect, ad hoc networks. Station managers can receive these syndicated program feeds, perhaps even preempting more traditional networks. Assuming there is an effective way to buy and evaluate the audiences, advertisers are likely to use these alternative routes for reaching the public. Such ever-changing syndicated networks are also likely to pose some of the most interesting challenges for audience analysts.

LOCAL MARKETS

Broadcast networks reach national markets by combining the audiences of the local stations with which they affiliate. Similarly, national cable networks aggregate the viewers of local cable systems. But representatives of an individual station or cable system can sell audiences to local advertisers who want to reach their markets. These audiences are attractive to businesses that trade in a concentrated geographical area, and to national or regional marketers who want to place advertising in specific markets. The former create a market for *local sales;* the latter take part in the *national spot market.*

Broadcast Stations

The physics of broadcasting determine the geographic limits of a station's signal. In light of this, the FCC decided to license radio and television stations to specific cities and towns across the country. Larger population centers have more stations. Naturally enough, people spend most of their time listening to stations in close proximity because they can receive the clearest signal and can hear programs of local interest. In television, the major ratings service uses this geographically determined audience behavior to define the boundaries of a local media market area. Nielsen calls these markets *designated market areas* (DMAs).

Appendix A lists the 210 U.S. television markets designated by Nielsen. There are even more radio markets. In both cases, market size varies considerably. New York, for instance has nearly 7 million TV households, whereas North Platte has fewer than 20,000. Buying time on a major station in New York might deliver more viewers to an advertiser than a national cable network. Conversely, many small-market radio stations might have audiences too small for a ratings company to economically measure. This point is best illustrated by the fact that regular radio ratings are available to approximately 3,000 of more than 12,000 stations in the country. But those stations that are measured constitute more than two thirds of all radio listening.

These vast differences in audience size have a marked effect on the rates local broadcasters can charge for a commercial spot. The price of a 30-second spot in prime time might be $400 in Des Moines and $4,000 in Detroit. Other factors can affect the cost of time, too. Is the market growing or has it fallen on hard times? Is the population relatively affluent or poor? How competitive are other local media like newspapers? Even things like a market's time zone can affect the rates of local electronic media.

Another thing that varies with market size is the sophistication of ratings users and the volume of audience information they must interpret. The audiences in many radio markets are measured just twice a year. In major TV markets, however, audiences are measured continuously. In addition, there are more advertising dollars available in major markets. Consequently, buyers and sellers of media in those markets tend to be more experienced with and adept at analyzing ratings information.

In most markets, the major buyers of local advertising include fast-food restaurants, supermarkets, department stores, banks, and car dealers. Like network advertisers, these companies often hire an advertising agency to represent their interests. The agency can perform a number of functions for its client, from developing a creative strategy, to actually writing copy and producing the ads. Most important in this context, the agency's media department will project the audience for various programs, plan when to run ads, buy time, and evaluate whether the desired audience was delivered. Smaller advertisers, or those in smaller markets, may deal directly with the local stations.

Because of the different types of people involved, the process of buying local time varies from market to market. It might involve an intuitive judgment by a merchant that buying a certain number of ads on a local station will generate extra business. In fact, many small radio stations and cable systems sell without using any ratings information. Increasingly, though, the process depends on the use of ratings.

Although specific terminology may differ across organizations, the purchase of local time generally works like this: The advertiser or an agency will issue a request for *avails*, asking what spots are available for sale on local stations. Avail requests typically specify the kind of audience a buyer wants, the dayparts they wish to buy, and their budget. Station salespeople will respond by proposing a schedule of spots that will deliver some or all of the desired audience. At this point the buyer and seller negotiate differences over the projected audience and costs. When the parties reach an agreement, the buyer will place an order and the spots will air. After the campaign has run, the next available ratings information is used to determine whether the expected audience was actually delivered. As in network buying, this last stage in the process is called *post-buy analysis*.

National and regional advertisers also buy spots on local stations. A snow tire manufacturer might want to advertise only in northern markets. A maker of agricultural products might wish to buy time in markets with large farm populations. Such national spot buys constitute the largest single source of revenues for many TV stations. The question is, how can so many local stations deal effectively with all these potential time buyers? It would be impractical for personnel from thousands of stations to contact every national advertiser.

To solve this problem, an intermediary called a *station representative* (or *rep firm*) serves as the link between local stations and national advertisers. Rep firms for both television and radio are located in major media markets like New York and Chicago. Television reps usually have only one client per market, to avoid conflicts of interest. Radio reps may serve more than one station in a market, as long as their formats don't compete for the same audience. Rep firms vary in terms of the number of stations they work with, and the types of services they offer. Some firms provide stations with research services or advice on their programming. Most important, though, reps monitor the media buys that national advertisers are planning and try to secure some portion of that business for their stations.

The local sales force at a station and the salespeople at the rep firm under contract with the station are essentially selling the same commercial time. This can cause some conflicts. Local advertisers could be shut out of a daypart because national advertisers secure the inventory, or vice versa. In Las Vegas, for example, local businesses pay a premium to advertise in early news programs to reach visitors deciding where to go for the evening. This means that national advertisers cannot purchase time in local broadcast news without paying very high rates. Instead, they may turn to cable television to reach those audiences.

Cable Systems

Cable now offers local advertising. Usually this means inserting a local ad in a cable network program, but it could also mean sponsorship of locally produced programs. There are two limitations to this process. First, cable systems can't reach every member of the available audience. And second, a technology limitation complicates ad insertion. This difficulty is being solved with digital insertion technology, but it will be some time before all cable systems have this capacity. The market for local cable audiences is further hampered because ratings for local cable services are unavailable in most DMAs.

In a way, cable system advertising is not just local, it's ultra-local. In TV markets with several cable systems, it's possible for an advertiser, for instance a small merchant, to run a spot in only one or two communities. Similarly, because cable franchise areas—almost by definition—conform to governmental boundaries within the market, cable seems a likely venue for political advertising. When several cable systems coordinate their efforts, rather precise and varied geographic coverage of the market is possible. This potential is being exploited more and more as cable rep firms develop.

INTERNET

New modes of communication no longer conform to the local-versus-national distinction that traditionally defined media markets. In the last decade, advertisers have recognized a new opportunity for reaching audiences: The World Wide Web. According to the Internet Advertising Bureau (IAB), yearly advertising expenditures on the Internet reached $267 million in 1996 and $907 million in 1997. This explosive growth creates the need for audience information to support the sale of advertising. In fact, just as the development of commercial audience research for radio and television was driven by advertiser needs, audience measurement on the Web is being shaped by those who want to purchase its "audiences."

The Internet audience research business is developing along the same lines as broadcast audience measurement. Concepts like reach, frequency, shares, in-tabs, and weighted samples are used to summarize and evaluate the research data. Like their broadcast counterparts, Web sites are represented in the advertising market by rep firms that provide a variety of services. Foremost among them is soliciting advertising revenue for Web-site clients.

There are, however, major differences between broadcasting and the Internet affecting how audiences are tracked. Some people spend a great deal of time on the Web at work, but capturing this business usage is difficult. Research technology requires that software be downloaded onto a computer, which creates privacy concerns for businesses. Without this capability, a huge segment of the Internet audience remains invisible.

Another major difference is that Web-site operators can generate their own audience research data from actual records. A Web-page server can place signatures, called *cookies*, on the hard drives of all computers that access a page. Each time a user visits the site, a log records it. Data from the logs can then be summarized to give advertisers usable information about who saw their advertisements.

But the convenience of this type of measurement is offset by several problems. First, some users block the placement of cookies on their computers, so their usage is not counted. Second, if people share a computer, there is no way to identify who is viewing the Web page. Third, this type of data generally only logs how many *hits*, or requests for the site, the page received. Advertisers are more interested in who sees their *banner advertising* and who clicks on the ads to get more information. Data on hits is less useful than a statistic like *unique visitors*, which reports the number of different users visiting the site. And fourth, there is potential for inflating the number of hits unless a third party audits the data. A major print auditor, the Audit Bureau of Circulation (ABC), has begun to offer its service to Web-site operators, but the need for an objective third-party provider of audience data has spurred the development of new research services as well.

These audience measurement services use samples to estimate Web use. The first two companies to offer this kind of measurement were Media Metrix and RelevantKnowlege, which merged in 1998. The newly formed company, Media Metrix, Inc., sells *clickstream* data that represent a clearer picture of Web audiences to advertisers. A panel of participants agree to download tracking software onto their computers, which keeps track of all activity on the Internet as well as the usage of software programs installed on their computers. The data are sent back to the research provider electronically, or they are downloaded onto a floppy disk and returned via mail. This methodology resembles the television peoplemeter. Users identify themselves when they log on to the computer and then verify usage at regular intervals. Nielsen launched its panel survey to measure Internet users in March of 1999. Their venture is a partnership with NetRatings, an already-established Internet audience research firm. Although it is impossible to predict exactly what the Internet audience measurement business will look like in a few years, it is certain to include the traditional broadcast audience research providers.

Web audience measurement presents difficult challenges for research firms, perhaps most notably the problem of definition. Should users be counted if they simply see a page, or only if they take some action such as clicking on an advertisement? This is similar to the question of audience exposure (introduced in chap. 1 of this volume). What constitutes exposure to a message? Internet technology allows advertisers to track a behavioral variable unavailable in the traditional mode of broadcast delivery—the choice to request more information. This may drastically change the definition of "viewership" that has survived for so long in the broadcast measurement business. With some methodologies (the passive household meter in particular), viewership is assumed to occur if the TV set is on. With the Internet, audience members are more active in choosing content and interacting with it. Information such as the click rate will indicate to advertisers and Web programmers the items of content most interesting to users.

Another unique problem with Web measurement is *caching*, or saving Web content onto a computer for later use. This can happen with an individual user or an entire service. Internet Service Providers (ISPs) often cache Web pages on their servers. America Online might cache a Web page that it subsequently serves to AOL subscribers. The initial hit from AOL is counted toward page views, because it was served by the Web-site operator. With some measurement methods, though, the requests from AOL subscribers would not count toward the total audience, because the page is actually served by AOL. Solving this problem requires technological adjustments currently being developed by audience research firms.

With Internet audience measurement, reports delivered to subscribers typically mirror those developed for traditional media options. They are, of course, provided to online subscribers who have passwords to access the data. But traditional bound reports are also produced. The demographic breaks are similar to those used by broadcast research firms, and the bottom line for advertisers is the same: who is in the audience?

Several industry organizations have developed to assist members with the sale of advertising time. The Television Bureau of Advertising (TVB) and the Radio Advertising Bureau (RAB) perform this service for broadcasters. A newer organization, the Cabletelevision Advertising Bureau, or CAB, assists cable networks and systems. And the Internet Advertising Bureau (IAB) offers its services in support of Internet advertising. Some of the industry sales information presented in this book comes from these sources.

RESEARCH QUESTIONS

Although the buying and selling of audiences happens in different places and involves people having varied motivations and levels of sophistication, there are a handful of recurring research questions that transcend these differences. Distilling these issues can simplify what is going on and help the researcher see ratings data more clearly in the context of sales and advertising. The four basic questions users ask involve audience size and composition and the cost to reach potential customers.

How many people are in the audience?   More than any other factor, audience size determines the value of media to advertisers and, in turn, to broadcasters. There are many ways to express audience size, including the most common definitions, which follow, and more technical definitions presented in the last section of this volume.

Ratings are the most frequently used descriptors of audience size. A rating is the percentage of households or people tuned to a particular channel. The simplest version of a ratings calculation is presented in Fig. 2.1, along with other standard expressions of audience size.

Two characteristics of a rating should be noted. First, the population figure on which the rating is based is the *potential audience* for the program or station.

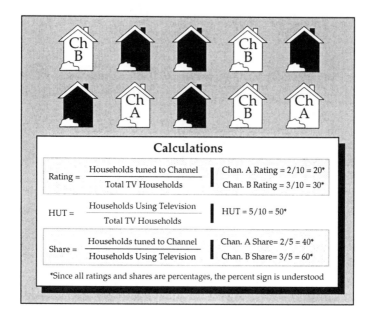

FIG. 2.1.   Simple rating and share calculations.

For local stations, this is the population in the market equipped with radios or television sets, which, for all intents and purposes, is the entire population. It does not matter whether those sets are in use or not, the population estimate is the same for all ratings calculations. In this context, the denominator of the ratings term does not vary from station to station, program to program, or time period to time period. To say a TV program had a rating of 20, then, means that 20% of the entire population in the market is tuned to the show.

Second, populations can be composed of different building blocks, or *units of analysis*. In television it is common to talk about a population of television households. One rating point, therefore, refers to one percent of the homes equipped with television in a given market. Radio and television researchers also describe populations of people, for instance a station's ratings among men or women of a certain age. As explained previously in the discussion of network dayparts, it's quite possible for a program to have a high rating among women and a low rating among men (e.g., daytime).

Another way to describe audience size is in absolute terms, the projected total number of audience members. Local radio audiences are usually counted in the hundreds of people; television audiences in the thousands at the local level and tens of thousands or millions at the network level. In some ways, absolute estimates of audience size are more interpretable. Without knowing the size of a market, for example, a local station rating of 25 indicates nothing about how many human beings were in the audience. A 25 rating in one market could describe a smaller audience than a 15 rating in a larger market. Ratings and absolute numbers are just different expressions of audience size—imperfect estimates based on the same data. In fact, much time and effort go into collecting data on which reliable estimates can be based.

In addition to determining ratings, it is frequently useful to summarize the number of people using the medium at a given time. When the unit of analysis is households, the summary is called *households using television*, or *HUT level* for short. Figure 2.1 illustrates how this measure is calculated. As indicated, HUT levels are typically expressed as a percentage of the population. As with ratings, though, it's possible to express them in absolute terms. If individuals are being counted, *persons using television*, or *PUT*, is the appropriate term. In radio, the analogous term is *persons using radio* (*PUR*).

Not everyone uses television or listens to radio at the same time, so HUT levels vary throughout the day. In fact, they change in a very predictable way, hour to hour, and week to week. Because of this, many audience analysts prefer to see a program's or station's audience expressed as a percentage of the HUT level, rather than the total population. It's as if they are saying, "Since I can't affect the size of the total audience in any given time period, just tell me how I did compared to the competition." The measure that expresses this is called an audience *share*. Figure 2.1 summarizes the audience share calculation. It is quite possible for a program to have a large share and a small rating, for instance, a popular show airing when few people have their sets on. In fact, unless everyone is using the medium at the same time, a program's share will always be larger than its rating. It should also be apparent that shares, by themselves, give no indication of the absolute audience size. As explained in chapter 10 of this volume, buyers and sellers use shares and HUTs (or PUTs) to estimate predicted ratings.

Advertisers will typically run a series of ads over a period of days or weeks. The audience for a single commercial becomes less important than the total exposure to the ad campaign. To assess the audience exposed to an advertiser's message, ratings associated with each commercial can be summed across all commercials in the campaign. This grand total is referred to as *gross ratings points*, or *GRPs*, a term used commonly in advertising and almost nowhere else.

GRPs provide a crude measure of the total audience delivered by a media campaign. In addition to summing ratings after the fact, the GRP concept signals the amount of audience advertisers wish to buy from the media. For example, the avail request described previously usually features a statement about the number of GRPs the buyer wants to accumulate in a particular campaign. GRPs, then, express the size of the campaign in audience numbers rather than dollars.

One problem with GRPs is they mask important features of audience behavior. For example, 100 GRPs could mean that 100% of an audience has seen a commercial once. It could also mean that 1% of the audience has seen the ad 100 times. Without further analysis, it is difficult to know what's happening.

How often do the same people appear in the audience?   To determine what audience behavior underlies GRPs, a researcher must know how each individual uses a medium over time. This could be, for example, a question of *audience duplication*—whether two programs with equal ratings were seen by the same or two entirely different groups of people. Fortunately, the data used to estimate gross measures of audience size, like ratings, shares, and GRPs, are also used to derive cumulative measures like audience duplication.

Advertisers are interested in how many different people see their messages and how often. These questions are addressed by measures of *reach* and *frequency*, respectively. The reach of a commercial is defined by the number of unduplicated individuals who are exposed to the ad—everyone who saw it at least once. It is often expressed as a percentage of the possible audience, like a rating. There is also a special kind of rating called a *cumulative rating*, or *cume*, that measures the unduplicated audience for a station. In either case, the statistic represents the number of different individuals who appear in the audience over a specified period of time. As noted previously, Web measurement services report a similar number, called *unique visitors*, to various Web sites.

Certain media are better at achieving large cumulative audiences than others. Prime-time network television, for example, generates considerable reach for a commercial message, since the audiences tend to be quite large. Furthermore, many people only watch TV in prime time and, therefore, are reachable only in that daypart. As a result, advertisers are often willing to pay a premium for prime-time spots. Cable networks, on the other hand, are limited by the penetration of cable systems, and so cannot hope to achieve penetration levels much in excess of 74%.

The second factor that comes into play is the frequency of exposure: how many times did people see or hear the message? Frequency of exposure is usually expressed as an average (e.g., "the average frequency was 2.8"). Of course, no one actually sees an ad 2.8 times, so it may be more useful for an advertiser to consider the full distribution on which the average is based. If the advertiser believes a person must see an ad three times before it's effective, then he or she might want to know how many people saw the ad three or more times.

As with reach, frequency varies across different media. An advertiser marketing a product to Spanish-speaking audiences could buy time on a Hispanic station having low reach but high frequency. Similarly, radio can be an effective medium for achieving a high frequency, because audiences tend to be loyal to station formats.

Reach and frequency bear a strict arithmetic relationship to GRPs: reach multiplied by average frequency equals gross rating points. Knowing any two makes it possible to calculate the third. Unfortunately, advertisers usually know only GRPs, because only ratings are easily obtained from published reports. However, a number of agencies and audience researchers have developed mathematical models for deriving reach and frequency from GRPs. These and other techniques of modeling audience behavior are discussed in the final chapter of this volume.

Who are the audience members? Because different advertisers want to reach different kinds of audiences, knowing the composition of the audience ranks just below size as the most important determinant of value. Advertisers are increasingly interested in presenting their messages to specific subsets of the mass audience. This strategy is referred to as *market segmentation*. It plays an important role in advertising and, in turn, has a major impact on the form that ratings data take.

Describing or segmenting an audience is accomplished by noting the characteristics or traits of audience members. Researchers call these characteristics *variables*. Almost any attribute can become a variable if well defined. In practice, viewer or listener attributes are usually grouped into one of four categories.

Demographic variables are the most commonly reported in ratings data. By convention, this category includes the attributes race, age, gender, income, education, marital status, and occupation. Age and gender are the most frequently reported audience characteristics, forming the basis of standard reporting categories featured in ratings books. So, for example, advertisers and broadcasters will often buy and sell "women 18 to 49," "men 25 to 54," and so forth. Most buying and selling of audiences is based on demographic variables.

Demographics are very useful segmentation variables. The categories are easy for everyone to understand and people in the industry are used to working with them. However, demographic categories tend to be over-broad. For example, there can be differences between two men of the same age that are potentially important to an advertiser. Therefore, additional methods of segmentation are used.

Geographic variables offer another common way to describe the audience. Just as people differ from one another with respect to their age and gender, so too, they differ in terms of where they live. Every TV viewer or radio listener in the country can be assigned to one particular market area. Obviously, such distinctions would be important to an advertiser whose goods or services have distinct regional appeal.

Other common geographic variables are county and state of residence (including breakouts by county size), and region of the country. Tracking a person's zip code is one popular tool of geographic segmentation. With such finely drawn areas, it is often possible to make inferences about a person's income, lifestyle, and station in life. These zip-code-based techniques of segmentation are known as *geodemographics*.

Behavioral variables draw distinctions among people on the basis of their actions. The most obvious kind of behavior to track is media use—knowing who watched a particular program makes it possible to estimate audience size. With this kind of information, audiences can be described in terms of not only age and gender but also what else they watched or listened to. Such audience breakouts, however, are only occasionally provided by the ratings service.

Other behavioral variables that weigh in an advertiser's mind relate to product purchases. Most advertisers want to reach the audience most likely to buy their products. From the advertisers' perspective, what better way to describe an audience than by purchase behaviors, by the number of heavy beer drinkers, or the amount of laundry soap it buys? One ratings company has called such segmentation variables *buyer-graphics*. This approach appeals to many advertisers.

Several research companies combine media usage data with other variables. Simmons, MRI, Scarborough, and International Demographics report on socioeconomic status and lifestyles. This is particularly useful to marketers targeting potential customers who fit narrower definitions than specific age and gender. Figure 2.2 illustrates the kinds of data generated from these studies. Data from spring 1996 show that Columbus listeners who planned to buy a new car were more likely to tune to WNCI-FM. Although this information can be valuable to advertisers, access to it comes at a price. Only organizations that pay subscription fees can use this data in their sales or buying efforts.

The fourth category of variables that deserves brief mention is *psychographics*. Definitions of this grouping vary, but basically it encompasses any attempt to draw distinctions among people on the basis of psychological attributes: values, attitudes, opinions, motivations, and preferences. Although such traits can, in principle, be valuable in describing an audience, psychographic variables are difficult to precisely define and measure.

How much does it cost to reach the audience?   Advertisers and media personnel, as well as middlemen like ad agencies and station reps, all have an interest in what it costs to reach the audience. Those on the selling side of the business try to maximize revenues, while buyers try to minimize expenses.

Although it is true that broadcasters and other forms of electronic media sell audiences, it would be an oversimplification to suggest that audience factors alone determine the cost of a commercial spot. Certainly, audience size and composition are the principle determinants, but several factors have an impact. Advertisers pay a premium, for example, to have a message placed first in a set of advertisements (called a *commercial pod*). As explained previously, advertisers who buy network time in the upfront market can get a better price. Similarly, advertisers who agree to buy large blocks of time can usually enjoy a quantity discount. But these transactions happen in a marketplace environment. The relative strengths and weaknesses of each party, their negotiating skills, and, ultimately, the laws of supply and demand all affect the final cost of time.

These factors are represented in the rates charged for commercial spots. It is common for an individual station to summarize fees in a *rate card*. A rate card,

RATINGS RANKER REPORT

* COLUMBUS, OH * MAR-APR 1996 *

ADULTS AGE 18 +

TARGET AUDIENCE: **PLAN BUY--NEW CAR/VAN/TRUCK**

REPORT PERIOD: MAR-APR 1996   RANK ORDER: CUME RATING

TOTAL AUDIENCE: 1,105,000   PERCENT IN TARGET AUDIENCE: 11.5%   NUMBER IN TARGET AUDIENCE: 126,600

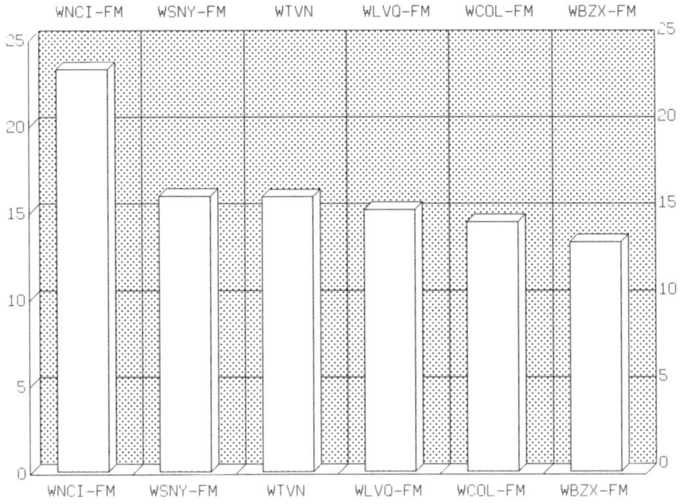

	WNCI-FM	WSNY-FM	WTVN	WLVQ-FM	WCOL-FM	WBZX-FM
PROJECTED PERSONS	29300	20100	20000	19100	18200	16700
MEDIA RATINGS	23.1	15.9	15.8	15.1	14.4	13.2

[RADIO = 7-DAY CUME]

TARGET AUDIENCE ANALYSIS BASED ON 118 RESPONDENTS OUT OF THE TOTAL SAMPLE OF 1015 ADULTS AGE 18+

FIG. 2.2.   The Media Audit. Reprinted with permission.

usually presented in the form of a table or chart, states the price of spots in different dayparts or programs. This serves as a planning guide, but the actual rates
are subject to negotiation. Although the estimated cost of a commercial spot is
important to know, from the buyer's perspective, it is largely uninterpretable

without associated audience information. The question the buyer must answer is, "What am I getting for the money?" This cannot be answered without comparing audience ratings to the rates being charged.

There are two common ways to make such comparisons. One is to calculate the *cost per thousand* (CPM) for a given spot (the "M" in this expression is the Roman numeral for 1,000). CPMs are equal to the cost of commercial time divided by the size of the commercial audience (expressed in thousands). CPMs can be produced for households, women ages 18 to 49, or whatever kind of audience is relevant to the advertiser. The calculation provides a yardstick to measure the efficiency of buying time on different stations or networks.

The second method of comparison is the *cost per point* (CPP). This is based on the cost of time divided by the number of ratings points delivered. Because ratings are not based on the same audience sizes across markets, the cost of a point will vary from market to market. A rating point in New York will be more expensive than a point in Indianapolis. CPPs are useful, however, because they are easy to relate to GRPs. If, for example, an ad campaign is to produce 200 GRPs, and the CPP is $1,000, then the campaign will cost $200,000.

This sort of arithmetic reveals the economics that drive the industry. It is also a common form of ratings analysis among buyers and sellers of time. But media companies are complex organizations whose executives can and do use audience information in a variety of ways. Similarly, those who want to study or regulate mass communication have found that the data gathered for the benefit of advertisers can offer many insights into the power and potential of the electronic media. In the chapters that follow, we discuss many of these applications. First we turn to the use of audience data in programming.

RELATED READINGS

Albarran, A. (1997). *Management of electronic media.* Belmont, CA: Wadsworth.

Lavine, J. M., & Wackman, D. B. (1988). *Managing media organizations: Effective leadership of the media.* New York: Longman.

Poltrack, D. F. (1983). *Television marketing: Network, local, cable.* New York: McGraw-Hill.

Sherman, B. L. (1995). *Telecommunications management: Broadcasting/cable and the new technologies.* New York: McGraw-Hill.

Turow, J. (1997). *Breaking up America: Advertisers and the new media world.* Chicago: University of Chicago Press.

Warner, C. (1993). *Broadcast and cable selling* (updated 2nd ed.). Belmont, CA: Wadsworth.

Zeigler, S. K., & Howard, H. (1991). *Broadcast advertising: A comprehensive working textbook* (3rd ed.). Ames, IA: Iowa State University Press.

3

Audience Research in Programming

In order to sell commercial time, the electronic media must attract the audience that gives value to that time. Broadly speaking, that is the job of a programmer. In the world of advertiser-supported media, the programmer sets the bait that lures the audience. To do this, he or she must know who comprises that audience. After sales and advertising, the most important application of audience data is in programming.

Programming involves a range of activities. A programmer must determine the source of program content. Sometimes that means playing an active role in developing new program concepts and commissioning the production of pilots. For most TV stations it means securing the rights to syndicated programs, some of which have already been produced. In this capacity the programmer must be skillful in negotiating contracts and predicting the kinds of material that will appeal to prospective audiences. Programmers are also responsible for deciding how and when material will air. Successful scheduling requires an understanding of when audiences are available and how those audiences select options offered by competing media. Finally, a programmer must be adept at program promotion. Sometimes that involves placing ads and promotional spots to alert the audience to a particular program or personality. It can also involve packaging an entire schedule to create a particular station or network image. In all such activities, ratings play an important role.

Programming functions and priorities differ from one setting to the next. Occasionally, in small stations, the entire job falls on the shoulders of one person. In larger operations, programming will involve many people. Because the media marketplace has become so competitive, the job of promoting programs and developing a certain image is increasingly assigned to specialized promotions departments.

The most significant difference in how programmers function, however, depends on medium. Television, in the early 1950s, forced radio to adapt. No longer would individual radio programs dominate the medium. Instead, radio stations began to specialize in certain kinds of music or in continuous program formats. The job of a radio programmer became one of crafting an entire program service. Furthermore, the vast supply of music from the record industry meant that stations could be less reliant on networks to define that service. Television, however, has built audiences by attracting them to individual programs. Although some cable networks now emulate radio by offering a steady diet of one type of programming (e.g., news, music, weather, financial and business information, or comedy), TV programmers generally must devote more attention to the acquisition, scheduling, and promotion of discrete units of content. Much of this work has been done by broadcast networks. However, the growth of independent TV stations, as well as a vigorous syndication market, have increased the amount of programming done by individual TV stations. To appreciate how audience research is used in programming, therefore, it is important to understand the practices of each medium.

RADIO PROGRAMMING

There are more than 10,300 commercial radio stations in the United States and another 2,000 noncommercial educational ones, each offering different—sometimes only slightly different—programming and each reaching different audiences. Most radio stations, from the smallest town to the largest markets, have a *format*. A format is an identifiable set of program presentations or style of programming. Some stations, particularly in small markets with few competitors, have wider ranging formats that include a little something for everyone. Most stations, however, zero in on a specific brand of talk or music.

Radio formats are important to the medium for two related reasons. First, radio is very competitive. In any given market, there will be many more radio stations than TV stations, daily newspapers, or almost any other local advertising medium. To avoid being lost in the shuffle, programmers have found that it helps to make their stations seem unique. This strategy is called positioning. By differentiating their station from the others, programmers hope it will stand out in the minds of listeners and induce them to tune in. Defining and promoting a format is critical in positioning a station. Second, different formats appeal to different kinds of listeners. Most advertisers want to reach particular kinds of audiences, so the ability to deliver a certain demographic is important in selling the station's time.

Radio formats run the gamut from classical to country to Top 40, and stations choose names like Smooth Jazz, Big Band, Classic Rock, and Adult Contemporary to identify their programming. Radio programmers, consultants, and analysts have fairly specific names for nearly 40 different formats. However, most of these are grouped in about 20 categories. The most common labels and the share of the U.S. audience (by region) that listens to each is described in Table 3.1.

There are different ways to program a radio station. Some stations do their own programming. They identify specific songs and how often they will play them. They may also hire prominent—and highly paid—disc jockeys who can dominate the personality of the station during certain dayparts. This customized programming is common in major markets and often accompanied by specially tailored research. These stations not only buy and analyze published ratings reports, they are also likely to use computerized access to a ratings database and engage in a variety of nonratings research projects. (Customized analyses of ratings data are discussed in chap. 8, this volume.) Typical nonratings research includes focus groups, featuring intensive discussions with small

TABLE 3.1

Radio Station Formats by Regions of the U.S.

	US	NE	MA	ENC	WNC	SA	SC	Mt	Pac
News/Talk	16%	21%	19%	19%	19%	13%	12%	15%	18%
Adult Contemporary	15	18	15	14	13	15	13	14	16
Country	11	5	4	11	17	13	18	16	8
Top 40	9	14	10	6	7	7	7	11	11
Urban	7	1	6	11	5	12	10	*	4
Album Rock	7	8	5	9	14	7	7	8	6
Oldies	6	8	6	6	6	5	5	6	5
Spanish	6	1	7	2	*	6	7	3	13
Modern Rock	4	8	5	4	6	2	3	6	4
Urban AC	4	1	6	3	2	6	4	1	1
MOR/Big Band	4	3	5	4	3	3	3	6	3
Classic Rock	4	6	4	3	3	3	5	7	3
New Age/Jazz	3	2	4	3	2	3	2	4	4
Classical	2	4	3	2	2	1	1	1	3
Religious	2	1	2	2	2	4	4	1	2
70s Oldies	1	3	*	1	*	*	*	2	1

Source: The Arbitron Company and *Billboard* format trends, fall 1996. First column is total United States, then the regions of New England, Mid-Atlantic, East North Central, West North Central, South Atlantic, South Central, Mountain, and Pacific (includes Hawaii). Columns may not total 100% due to rounding and a few miscellaneous formats (in every case less than 1%). * = less than 1%. Data are for the continuous measurement markets.

groups of listeners, and *call out research* that requires playing a short excerpt of a song over the telephone to gauge listener reactions. Organizations like Statistical Research, Inc. (SRI) also do customized research to investigate such questions as how radio audiences react to offensive materials, or whether listeners are aware of particular program services.

Many stations depend on a syndicated program service or network to define their formats. There are dozens to choose from, many targeted to a specific kind of listener. In the extreme, a station might rely on such pre-packaged material for virtually everything it broadcasts, save local advertising and announcements. But in most cases, stations air original programming during the most popular morning hours and use syndicated services, received via satellite, during the majority of the remaining hours.

Most radio stations do not worry about ratings research because the majority are located in small communities, outside the top 100 markets. Arbitron publishes audience estimates for only one third of the nation's more than 12,000 radio stations. However, stations in the top 100 markets reach 75% of the U.S. population. These measured stations account for the vast majority of the industry's revenues.

Programmers with ratings data are better equipped to know their audiences than those without ratings. They know that many popular ideas about radio use are untrue. For example, while radio audiences are largest during the 6:00–10:00 a.m. daypart, known as morning drive time, the greatest percentage of listeners in automobiles is from 4:00 p.m. to 6:00 p.m. Midday, from 10:00 a.m. to 3:00 p.m., was long considered the best time to reach women working in the home. But in most markets, just about as many men are listening to the radio as women. Furthermore, there are often just about as many car listeners during midday, as either morning or afternoon drive time. In all, the average adult spends about 20 hours per week listening to radio, nearly 3 hours per day. Contrary to popular belief, teens are not the heaviest users of radio—they listen less than any other demographic group. But teens do comprise the largest part of the audience after 7:00 p.m. These trends may vary from market to market, but the only way to know is by consulting a ratings report.

Many radio programmers go to Arbitron headquarters to study the diaries the company uses to collect ratings data. The images are available by computer and can be sorted according to any category a person chooses. A programmer or consultant hired by the station can learn whether people are remembering call letters or station slogans correctly. Often people write other comments on the diary that might be helpful.

TELEVISION PROGRAMMING

At the other end of the spectrum is the business of programming a major television network. Although they share some of the same concerns as a radio station programmer, network TV programmers are confronted with different tasks.

The most important of these differences is the programmer's involvement in the creation of new programs. In that effort, ratings data may be of some value, but as much as anything else, TV programming requires a special talent for anticipating popular trends and tastes and launching productions that cater to those tastes. Network programmers who have that talent, like Fred Silverman and the late Brandon Tartikoff, can become legends in their own right.

Most other TV programmers have less to do with creating programs. Instead, those responsible for programming stations, or even lesser networks, must find their program content elsewhere. Some stations originate material, such as news, sports, or other collaborative efforts, but most programmers work with shows that are already produced or in regular production.

The most common source of programming is the syndication market, discussed in the previous chapter. In fact, there are many different syndicated products and more are being produced every day. One obvious source is material originally aired on a broadcast network, *off-network* programming.

Off-network programs are among the most desirable of all syndicated programming from the standpoint of ratings potential. A show originally commissioned for a network has high production values, which viewers have come to expect. It also has a track record of drawing audiences, which can be reassuring for the prospective buyer. *M*A*S*H,* for instance, was enormously successful on CBS and has been equally successful in syndication. In fact, only successful network programs make it to syndication. Because these programs are often *stripped* (scheduled 5 days a week), many episodes are required. With a few exceptions, a series will be viable in syndication only after 100 episodes are available. That means it must have been on a network for 4 or 5 years, and only the most popular shows last that long. As more channels for programming develop, however, the market for syndicated programs may change considerably. Cable networks have picked up canceled network series, continuing their production as first-run cable properties. In recent years, an off-cable syndication market has emerged.

Because so many program-hungry independents and cable networks have appeared in the last decade, the demand for quality off-network product has exceeded supply. One result, aside from rising prices, is an increase in the number of programs being produced specifically for the syndication marketplace. Traditional *first-run* syndication has included both game shows and talk shows—program types that cost relatively little to produce. Inexpensive or not, shows like *Wheel of Fortune* and *The Oprah Winfrey Show* have been highly successful in the ratings. Less traditional first-run products include "newsier" shows like *Entertainment Tonight.*

There are still other sources of programming, like movie packages or regional networks, but whatever their origin, the acquisition of syndicated programming is one of the toughest challenges a TV programmer has to face. Usually it involves making a long-term contractual agreement with the distributor, or whoever holds the copyright to the material. For a popular program, that can mean a major commitment of resources.

Buying and selling syndicated programming is often informed by an extensive use of ratings data. Distributors use ratings to promote their products, demonstrating performance in different markets. These data are often prominently featured in trade magazine advertisements. Buyers use the same data to project how a show might do in their market, comparing the costs of acquisition against potential revenues. (This is discussed in greater detail in chap. 4 of this volume.)

Once programming content has been determined, television programmers at all levels have more or less the same responsibility—scheduling to achieve the greatest effect. Usually this means trying to maximize each program's audience, although some shows are knowingly scheduled against tough competition. For affiliates, the job of program scheduling is less extensive than for others, simply because their network assumes the burden for much of the broadcast day. Even affiliates, however, will devote considerable attention to programming before, during, and just after the early local news. This *early fringe* daypart, just before network prime time, is often the most lucrative for an affiliate. Audience levels are rising and the station need not share the available commercial spots with its network.

As in radio, television program production companies, network executives, and stations use a variety of nonratings research to sharpen their programming decisions. This may include the use of one or more measures of program or personality popularity. Marketing Evaluations, for example, produces a syndicated research service called TVQ that provides reports on the extent to which the public recognizes and likes different personalities and programs. These popularity scores can be used by programmers when scheduling. Knowing the appeal of particular personalities might tell them, for example, whether a talk show host would fare well against the competition in a fringe daypart. TVQ also conducts research on the popularity of programs.

Other program-related research includes theater testing, which involves showing a large group a pilot and recording their professed enjoyment with voting devices of some sort. Ultimately, however, ratings are a programmer's most important evaluative tool. As one network executive said, "Strictly from the network's point of view a good soap opera is one that has a high rating and share, a bad one is one that doesn't" (Converse, 1974).

THE INTERNET

As the World Wide Web is creating opportunities for advertisers to reach audiences, the content of Web pages is becoming increasingly important. Programming on the Web can mean anything from the simplest personal Web page to the most sophisticated corporate sites, to actual multimedia programs that viewers watch on their screens. Just like traditional electronic media, content must be planned to attract Internet audiences in the first place and to hold their attention.

There are a few major differences, though. Content on The Web can be personalized as never before possible. If users accept cookies on their computers, a programmer could theoretically serve very individualized messages—a capability Web advertisers are very interested in developing. There is also an immediate feedback mechanism with the Internet that doesn't exist in radio and television. Through email, Internet users can communicate directly with the programmer.

Although this technology is still developing, a kind of syndication market for Web programming is already emerging. Programs are produced, just as they are in the traditional media, and syndicated to Web sites. The potential exists for the creation of networks of sites coordinated by a single programmer. This kind of arrangement works for rep firms that create a portfolio of Web pages to sell to an advertiser.

The relationship between the traditional electronic media and the World Wide Web is still emerging. Broadcast networks and stations maintain Web sites offering additional services to viewers they've already reached over the air, as well as to new "viewers" who make initial contact via The Web. They may even provide advertising availabilities on these sites to enhance the value of broadcast advertising. Indeed, established media seem increasingly interested in partnering with Web sites and search engines to exploit cross-promotional opportunities. The ultimate form these connections will take remains to be seen.

However the industry evolves, programmers will need ratings-type data to track popular sites and determine the services valued by particular audiences. Studies have found, for example, that men are more likely than women to use The Web, which tells programmers something about potential audiences. No matter what the quality of content Web programmers provide for women, their female audiences will be limited by availability. Research also suggests that Internet users tend to develop patterns in their use of the technology, often seeking out the same information sources time after time. Just as cable television viewers develop a set of favorite channels that they watch repeatedly, Internet users build a set of favorite Web resources.

RESEARCH QUESTIONS

Many of the research questions a programmer tries to answer with ratings data are, at least superficially, no different from those asked by a person in sales and advertising: How many people are in the audience? Who are they? How often do the same people show up in the audience? This convergence of research questions is hardly surprising, because the purpose of programming commercial media is, with some exceptions, to attract audiences that will be sold to advertisers. The programmer's intent in asking these questions, however, is often very different. They are less likely to see the audience as an abstract commodity and more likely to view ratings as a window on what "their" audiences are doing. They need to understand not only the absolute size of a program audience, but also why they are attracting particular audiences and what can be done to improve program performance. These are some of the common concerns a programmer has when analyzing ratings data.

Did I attract the intended audience? Because the programmer's objective is drawing an audience, the obvious use of ratings is to determine whether the objective has been achieved. Consequently, it is important to be clear about the intended audience. Although any programmer would prefer a large audience to one that is smaller, the often quoted goal of "maximizing the audience" is usually an inadequate expression of a programmer's objectives. More realistically, the goal is maximizing audience size within certain constraints or parameters. The most important constraint concerns the size of the available audience, which is why programmers are alert to audience shares. Increasingly, however, it is not the programmer's intention to draw even a majority of the available audience. Success or failure is best judged against the strategy employed.

Radio programming in particular seems to lend itself to targeting. An experienced programmer can fine-tune a station's demographics with remarkable accuracy. Much of this has to do with the predictable appeal of a certain kind of music to listeners of different age and gender. Table 3.2 lists common station formats and percentages of audiences by age groups. Obviously, Big Band music offers little appeal to young people, and Top 40 fails to attract many older listeners. As discussed in chapter 10 of this volume, it is possible to depict these audience characteristics on a *demographic map* of stations, which some programmers find quite useful.

TV programmers, too, may devote their entire program service to attracting a particular demographic. This is most evident in some of the new cable networks that have emerged in the last decade. As noted in the previous chapter, many cable services, like MTV or Nickelodeon, have been programmed to draw certain age groups their owners believe will be attractive to advertisers. These services don't cater to everyone.

Even conventional TV stations offering program variety must gauge the size and composition of audiences against the strategies they employ. One common strategy is called *counterprogramming.* This occurs when a station or network programmer schedules a show having a markedly different appeal than the programs offered by its major competitors. For example, programmers for independent stations tend to broadcast light entertainment (e.g., situation comedies) when network affiliates in the market are broadcasting local news. The independents are not trying to appeal to the typical, often older, news viewer, and their ratings should be evaluated accordingly. Programmers may try counterprogramming stunts to attract viewers who are not interested in special events covered by other stations in the market. One Chicago programmer, for

TABLE 3.2

Radio Station Formats by Age & Gender

	12-17	18-24	25-34	35-44	45-54	55-64	65+	Men	Women
Top 40	29%	18%	10%	6%	4%	2%	1%	6%	8%
Urban	22	14	8	6	3	3	2	6	6
Modern Rock	11	9	7	3	1	*	*	5	2
Album Rock	7	12	13	9	4	1	*	10	4
Classic Rock	2	4	6	7	3	1	*	5	3
Adult Contemporary	8	13	17	17	18	14	8	11	19
Urban AC	2	3	4	5	4	3	1	3	4
70s Oldies	*	1	1	1	1	*	*	1	1
Oldies	3	2	3	7	13	7	3	6	6
Country	8	10	10	11	13	14	9	10	12
New Age/Jazz	*	1	2	5	5	4	2	3	3
Classical	*	*	1	1	3	5	5	2	2
MOR/Big Band	*	*	*	1	2	8	17	3	4
Spanish	5	8	8	6	5	6	5	6	7
Religious	1	1	2	2	3	3	3	2	3
News/Talk	2	4	9	14	20	30	42	21	15

Source: The Arbitron Company and *Billboard* format trends, fall 1996. Columns may not total 100% due to rounding and a few miscellaneous formats (in every case less than 1%). * = less than 1%. Data are for the continuous measurement markets. Men and women include only listeners 18+ years old.

example, broadcast a lineup of romantic dramas called "The Marriage Bowl" to compete with college football games on New Year's Day.

One device that increases the likelihood of attracting the intended audience is the promotional spot. Ratings data can be very useful in identifying programs having similar demographic profiles so that promotional announcements directed to a particular audience can be scheduled when members of that target group are watching. As we discuss more fully in chapter 10, though, most programmers are limited by budgets and time to using the gross audience measurements provided in the ratings books to approximate audience overlap. These are, at most, a rough guide.

We should also point out that the need to attract an audience is not limited to commercial media. Public broadcasters in the United States and around the world must justify their existence by serving an audience. Therefore, many public station managers use ratings as well. National Public Radio (NPR), with the Corporation for Public Broadcasting (CPB), has provided audience estimates to NPR stations since 1979. The Public Broadcasting Service (PBS), which distributes much of the programming to noncommercial stations, subscribes to national ratings for several months of each year to judge the attractiveness of its programming. And many individual stations subscribe directly to Nielsen or indirectly through research consultants who analyze these data.

Although they do not have sponsors in the traditional sense, public broadcasters care very much about reaching, even maximizing, their audiences. For one thing, many organizations that contribute money for programming are interested in who sees both their programs and the underwriting announcement—the more viewers, the happier the funding agency. Furthermore, public stations depend heavily on audience donations. Only those who are in the audience will hear the solicitation. Thus, many public TV broadcasters pay considerable attention to their cumes and ratings.

Absent funding concerns, public station programmers still might wonder, "how can I get maximum exposure for my documentary?" Documentaries and "how-to" programs often earn the same or a higher rating when repeated during weekend daytime or late night than they do during the first run in prime time. Careful ratings analysis could determine when the largest number of target viewers are available, or whether the intended audience saw the program.

How loyal is my audience?   Audience loyalty is difficult to define precisely because it means different things to different people. Generally, *channel loyalty* implies the extent to which audience members stick with, or return to, a particular station, network, program or Web site. It is something that manifests itself over time. Despite all the positive images that loyalty connotes, this quality is quite different from audience size—the attribute most valued by time buyers.

Programmers are interested in audience loyalty for a number of reasons. First, in the most general sense, it can give them a better feel for their audience and how they use programming. That knowledge can guide other scheduling decisions. Second, audience loyalty is closely related to advertising concepts like reach and frequency, so it can have an impact on how the audience is sold. Finally, loyalty can provide an important clue about how to build and maintain the current audience, often through effective use of promos.

Radio programmers use simple manipulations of ratings data to assess audience loyalty. Although the heaviest radio listening occurs in the morning when people wake up and prepare for the day, listeners turn radios on and off several times during the day. They also listen in their cars or at work. To maintain ratings levels, a radio station must get people to tune in as often as possible and to listen for as long as possible. Radio programmers employ two related measures to monitor this behavior: *time spent listening* (TSL) and *turnover.* Using a simple formula based on the average ratings and cume ratings in the radio book, one can compute TSL for any station in any daypart. Turnover is the ratio of cume audience to average audience, which is basically the reciprocal of TSL.

Careful observers can detect how radio programmers try to hold listeners: naming the songs or other items coming up, running contests, and playing a certain number of songs without commercial interruption. These tricks of the trade support quarter-hour maintenance—keeping listeners tuned in from one quarter hour to the next. The 15-minute period is important, because it is the basic unit of time used to compute and report all ratings. By tracking TSL and audience turnover, the programmer can assess audience retention.

The importance of TSL varies according to the specific format of a station. All would like to keep their listeners tuned as long as possible, but that is more likely for stations having narrower, more specialized, formats such as country, urban, Spanish, or religious. Even these may share audience if there are several similar stations in the market.

Another common measure of loyalty in radio programming is *recycling*. In addition to providing separate estimates by daypart, ratings books routinely report combined station audiences for morning and afternoon drive time, making it possible to determine how many people listened at both times. This can be a useful insight. If the number is relatively small, for example, programmers may offer similar selections, or they may do more promotion. (The precise calculations of time spent listening, turnover, and recycling are presented in chap. 11 of this volume.)

The same basic research question is relevant in TV programming. Do people who watch early evening news on a particular station return to watch late news? If the answer is no, especially if the early news is successful, the savvy programmer would promote the later newscast for the early news audience. Unfortunately, because of the way TV ratings are published, it is not possible to deduce this from information on the printed page. Customized breakouts of the ratings data will, however, answer that question and many more.

What other stations or programs does my audience use?   This is the converse of the preceding question. Most people don't listen to one and only one station. And although no two stations are programmed precisely alike or reach exactly the same audience, several stations in a large market can have very similar, or complementary, formats. Programmers know that many of their listeners hear four or five other stations in a week. Radio listeners may have favorite times for choosing different formats (e.g., news in the morning or jazz at night). It is important that a programmer be able to assess the use of other stations.

In the largest market, a station may compete among 60 or more radio signals. However, the important competition for most programmers are the other stations targeting a similar audience. These are likely to be stations with a comparable format. In general, advertisers buy only one or two stations deep to reach a specific demographic target. Knowing as precisely as possible where listeners spend the remainder of their radio time is very important.

Having basic ratings information plus a few tabulations will enable a programmer to identify all the other stations with which he or she shares listeners. Two types of information are most relevant. The first is the *exclusive cume*, the number of people listening to just one particular station during specific dayparts. Although this is actually a measure of station loyalty, when compared with the total cume, it reveals the proportion of a station's audience that has also used the competition. But this does not reveal the stations. This information is conveyed through a statistic called *cume duplication*. Cume duplication indicates the extent to which the audience for one station also tunes to each of the other stations in a market. Table 3.3 illustrates levels of audience duplication by stations of different formats.

Although many listeners usually select a favorite station, they may also try other stations with similar formats or sample something completely different. This overlap among stations suggests people have varied tastes and may choose other fare during different times of the day or week. It is clear, however, that programmers share the most listeners with competitors having similar appeal. Table 3.3 illustrates the high cume duplication between two contemporary hit (CHR) stations, and between all-news and talk stations. Although not shown in Table 3.3, this same market includes three stations that program mostly album-oriented rock. These stations overlap with each other an average of 35%. The number of stations in the market, and especially the number with similar formats, has considerable influence on overlap or cume duplication. The least overlap exists among stations that appeal to very different age categories, say various types of rock and middle-of-the-road. There is also little sharing of audience for programming of distinctly different tastes (see Table 3.3 to compare classical and rock or country and urban).

Typically, people listen to two or three stations over the course of 7 days. Only 1 in 10 persons listens exclusively to a single station during the week, as reported by station or demographic category in the exclusive cume section of the ratings book. Younger people use more stations than do older listeners, and more different stations are chosen on average in larger markets where stations are abundant. The average number of stations heard for any demographic category in any daypart can be computed by adding the cumes of all stations and dividing by the market cume reported at the bottom of the page.

For a detailed look at how home listeners tune to different stations, programmers can use a computer program such as Arbitron's Maximi$er. This program tabulates persons in the sample who heard any given station by all the categories of demographics. It provides information about which other stations listeners tune in and when they are likely to do so. It is possible to distinguish whether a cume audience includes listeners who used the station as their primary channel, or heard it only occasionally. Furthermore, Maximi$er gives demographic infor-

TABLE 3.3
Cume Duplication

Shr	Station	CHR1	CHR2	Urb	AOR	Lite	Jazz	Cou	Cls	Old	MOR	Sports	Talk	News1	News2
4.6	CHR 1	—	38	32	27	22	16	19	8	20	6	6	9	12	9
2.9	CHR 2	30	—	8	43	12	9	13	8	17	5	13	9	8	8
7.2	Urban	24	8	—	7	6	22	3	3	4	2	4	3	6	5
2.9	Alb Rock	15	30	5	—	7	5	11	2	14	2	10	7	4	6
4.5	Lite	16	11	11	9	—	19	20	12	19	14	12	12	12	15
4.8	Jazz	11	7	7	7	18	—	6	7	9	11	12	12	15	15
3.5	Country	10	9	9	11	15	5	—	5	19	9	9	13	6	9
1.7	Classical	3	3	3	1	6	10	3	—	5	12	8	6	11	8
3.4	Oldies	14	15	12	18	19	10	26	10	—	12	14	13	12	14
6.1	MOR/Talk	4	4	4	2	13	11	12	25	11	—	26	27	23	28
2.0	Sports	2	4	4	5	5	5	4	6	5	10	—	10	6	11
4.3	Talk	5	6	6	7	9	10	7	10	9	21	19	—	17	20
3.6	News 1	10	8	8	6	14	18	10	27	14	28	27	27	—	35
2.3	News 2	5	6	6	7	11	12	9	14	11	22	22	21	24	—

Source: Courtesy of The Arbitron Company. Computed using Arbitron Maximi$er, winter 1998. Figures show the Metro Cume Duplication for 14 of 33 stations in a very large market. Stations are listed here by format rather than their call letters. Formats are contemporary hit radio also called top 40 (2 stations), urban also called Black, album rock, lite or light, smooth jazz (includes some new age), country, classical, oldie rock, a so-called full service middle-of-the-road music and talk, sports talk, talk, and all-news (2 stations), news2 also does some play-by-play sports. The share of audience for each station is also given in the column at the far left. Read each column down, so that for all listeners who hear the CHR1 station anytime during the week, 30% also listen to CHR2; 24% hear the Urban station. Note, for example, that those who tune in either of the all-news stations also listened to the other news station more than they hear any other format. While the classical station, shown above, has very little overlap with other formats, it does share half of its audience with another station in this market that also programs classical music.

mation about all reported listeners with the zip codes in which they live. The zip code data indicate holes in a signal area or places to do more advertising—billboards, for example. Computer analysis helps a programmer customize a presentation to an advertiser, showing precisely what type of listener can be offered based on demographics and other lifestyle and consumption variables.

This same kind of information is also valuable to television stations. The average TV viewer undoubtedly watches more channels than the average radio listener uses stations. Programmers can use promos for the station more effectively by knowing when different kinds of viewers are watching. Sometimes that will mean paying attention to the geodemographics of the audience, as an advertiser would. But it is especially important to know when people who normally watch a competitor's program are watching your station. That can be the perfect opportunity to entice those viewers with promotional messages.

How will structural factors like scheduling affect program audience formation? One of the recurring questions confronting a television programmer is how to schedule a particular program. Scheduling factors often are considered when a program is acquired. Some programs sold in barter syndication are required to be broadcast at a particular time. As explained in chapter 2, syndicators also sell time to advertisers, and only certain scheduling arrangements allow them to deliver a desired audience. In any event, how and when a program is scheduled will have a considerable impact on who sees it.

Programmers rely on a number of different "theories" for scheduling guidance. There are nearly as many of these theories as there are programmers. Some have been, or could be, systematically investigated through analyses of ratings data. Among the more familiar programming tactics are the following

A *lead-in strategy* is the most common and most thoroughly researched. This theory stipulates that the program that precedes, or leads into, another show will have an important impact on the second show's audience. If the first program has a high rating, the second show will benefit; a low rating for the first program will handicap the second. This relationship exists because the same viewers tend to stay tuned, allowing the second show to inherit the audience. In fact, this feature of audience behavior is sometimes called an *inheritance effect* (see Webster & Phalen, 1997).

Another strategy that depends on inheritance effects is *hammocking*. As the title suggests, hammocking is a technique for improving the ratings of a relatively weak, or untried, show by "slinging" it between two strong programs. In principle, the second show enjoys the lead-in of the first, with an additional inducement for viewers to stay tuned for the third program. NBC used this strategy effectively during the 1990s with its Thursday night lineup. By scheduling new programs in the 90 minutes between *Friends* and *ER*, the network programmers were able to build audiences for programs like *Suddenly Susan*, which was later moved (along with its new audience) to another time period.

Block programming is yet another technique for delivering audiences from one program to the next. In block programming, several shows of the same general type are scheduled in sequence. If viewers like one program of a type, they might stay tuned to watch a second, third, or fourth such offering. Public broadcasting stations have used this strategy to build weekend audiences by scheduling a block of how-to programs. This block has often earned some of the highest ratings for stations. A variation on block programming is to gradually change program type as the composition of the available audience changes. For example, a station programmer might begin in mid-afternoon when school lets out by targeting young children with cartoons. As more adults enter the audience, programming gradually shifts to shows that appeal to grownups, thereby cultivating a more suitable lead-in to local news.

All of these strategies attempt to exploit or fine-tune *audience flow* across programs. Incidentally, many of these programming principles were recognized soon after the first ratings were compiled in the early 1930s. Then, as now, analyses of ratings data allow the programmer to investigate the success or failure of the strategies by tracking audience members over time. Conceptually, the necessary analytical techniques are the same as those used to study the loyalty, or "disloyalty," of a station's audience. We discuss both the theory and practice of such cumulative analyses in the final section of this volume.

When will a program's costs exceed its benefits?   Programming decisions must ultimately be based on the financial resources of the media. Although some new stations or networks can be expected to operate at a loss during start-up, the eventual cost of programming must not exceed the revenues it generates. This hard economic reality enters into a programmer's thinking when new content is acquired or when existing material must be canceled. Because ratings have a significant impact on determining the revenues a program can earn, they are important tools in sorting the costs and benefits of a programming decision.

When station managers assess the feasibility of a new TV program, either a syndicated program or a locally produced show, it is typical to start with the ratings for the program currently in that time period and then, based on current ratings and station rates, calculate potential revenue in that time period. This can be a bit involved, because many factors affect program revenues—uncertainty about the size and composition of the new program's audience; size of the commercial inventory in the program; if bartered, whether some avails are gone, and so forth. Still, the station may not completely sell out what inventory it does have. Station management must also anticipate commissions for agencies and sales reps coming out of program revenues. And there are larger marketplace issues, like the strength of the economy and changes in competing media. Making these projections is a tricky business (as explained more fully in chap. 4 of this volume).

When a programmer is not evaluating programs to acquire, he or she may have to worry about possible program cancellations. Much of the reporting about television ratings concerns network decisions to cancel specific programs that are well liked by small, often vocal, segments of the audience. Ordinarily, a program will be canceled when its revenue-generating potential is exceeded by costs of acquisition or production. The cost of 1 hour of prime-time programming has risen steadily over the years. Today, an hour of prime-time drama can easily cost more than $1 million to produce. On the other hand, the cancellation threshold has fallen over the years. In the mid-1970s, network executives routinely canceled programs when their ratings fell to the high teens. By the mid-1990s programs with ratings in the low teens could remain in the schedule (see Atkin & Litman, 1986; Hwang, 1998). This has happened because the cost of commercial time has increased, as has the size of the television viewing population. Even so, a prime-time network program with a rating below 12 or 13 is unlikely to survive.

The job of programming has probably never been more challenging. Intense competition among electronic media has complicated the task of building and maintaining an audience. TV programmers, in particular, must contend with more stations, more networks, new modes of delivery like the Internet and DBS, and equipment such as VCRs and remote controls that allow viewers to flip, zip, and zap their way through programming at the touch of a button. In all of these challenges, the analysis of ratings data offers programmers a useful tool for understanding the audience and its use of media.

RELATED READINGS

Carroll, R. L., & Davis, D. M. (1993). *Electronic media programming: Strategies and decision making.* New York: McGraw-Hill.

Eastman, S. T., & Ferguson, D. A. (1997). *Broadcast/cable programming: Strategies and practices* (5th ed.). Belmont, CA: Wadsworth.

Ettema, J. S., & Whitney, C. D. (Eds.). (1982). *Individuals in mass media organizations: Creativity and constraint.* Beverly Hills: Sage.

Fletcher, J. E. (Ed.). (1981). *Handbook of radio and TV broadcasting: Research procedures in audience, program and revenues.* New York: Van Nostrand Reinhold.

Fletcher, J. E. (1987). *Music and program research.* Washington: National Association of Broadcasters.

Gitlin, T. (1983). *Inside prime time.* New York: Pantheon Books.

MacFarland, D. T. (1997). *Future radio programming strategies: Cultivating listenership in the digital age.* (2nd ed.). Mahwah, NJ: Lawrence Erlbaum Associates.

Newcomb, H., & Alley, R. S. (1983). *The producer's medium.* New York: Oxford University Press.

4

Audience Research
in Financial Analysis

Although the most obvious uses of audience data are in sales and programming, this information is also helpful to financial managers and economists who use it to analyze media markets. In effect, media analysts cannot estimate future revenues without estimating future audiences.

It should be apparent by now that audiences are a valuable commodity. They are a critical component in a media organization's ability to make money. And audiences frequently determine whether a particular media operator succeeds or fails. As the principal index of the audience commodity, ratings are often used in day-to-day financial planning, as well as in more theoretical studies of industry economics. In these applications, audience information is employed to answer different questions from the ones posed by advertisers or programmers.

The people most immediately concerned with the financial implications of ratings data are media owners and managers. Advertiser-supported media companies exist to make a profit, and in order to do that they try to minimize expenses while maximizing revenues. Besides programming-related costs, expenses include salaries, servicing a firm's debt, and a host of mundane budget items. One way to improve profits is to reduce those expenses. But there is a limit as to how much cost cutting can be done. The only other way to improve profitability is to increase revenues.

For commercial media, increasing revenues generally implies increasing the income from advertising sales. Broadcast stations generate virtually all revenues from time sales. In the case of radio, the majority of this income is generated from local advertisers. Television stations, especially in large markets, often

51

get roughly equal amounts of revenue from local and national spot markets. Networks also depend heavily on advertising revenues, although cable networks typically derive additional income through direct payments from cable systems. And program syndicators can realize substantial revenues from selling barter time to national advertisers.

The financial analysis of media markets concerns people who work for media companies as well as those not directly involved in buying and selling audiences. Media organizations have separate finance departments to analyze the planning, monitoring, and evaluating of business decisions. Wall Street analysts project the financial health of media firms in order to evaluate investments. Analysts for trade organizations, such as the National Association of Broadcasters (NAB) and the National Cable Television Association (NCTA), conduct financial evaluations to assess the economic health of their industries and to lobby on behalf of their clients. Economists from industry and academe study the characteristics of economic transactions in media markets. And policymakers at organizations like the FCC examine the impact of their policies on the marketplace.

The goal of this chapter is not to explain financial management in detail, which is done elsewhere (e.g., Sherman, 1995; Albarran, 1997), but rather to consider applied questions characteristic of corporate financial managers to show the critical importance of audience ratings in financial planning. Although specific processes and procedures vary across firms, and even within departments at a given company, this discussion focuses on factors that remain constant across organizations. The analytical concepts are more important than the formats of particular analyses.

Within media organizations, financial analysis cuts across all functional areas. For example, the sales department projects advertising revenue and sets prices for advertising time, while the programming department analyzes the costs and income potential of programs. Both groups must collaborate, because decisions made in one department affect the other. However, each contributes different expertise and a different set of priorities. A finance department will collect information from all areas to generate analyses and projections. If the organization is part of a group—which occurs increasingly with consolidation in the radio and television industries—a corporate finance department is also involved in the process.

The audience data essential to financial analysts are the quantitative reports from services like Nielsen, Arbitron, and SRI. The reason is straightforward—ratings provide an index to revenues. Although the correlation is imperfect (see chap. 2, this volume), ratings represent an excellent predictor of advertising income. In fact, although financial people use audience data in different ways, they must understand ratings as well as programmers and sales managers do.

Dozens of questions arise related to finance and ratings data. The broad questions that follow illustrate the use of these data in assessing the ongoing economic activity of a firm, planning expenditures, estimating the value of media firms, and specifying the relationship between audiences and revenues.

RESEARCH QUESTIONS

How effectively does the organization compete for market revenues?
Monitoring financial performance requires ongoing analysis of sales effort and market conditions. This involves comparing earned revenues with the potential revenues in the marketplace. Because revenues are determined by audience size and composition, a station's share of market revenue should reflect its share of audience. A statistic called the *power ratio* (also called the *conversion ratio*) expresses this relationship. The calculation is very simple:

$$\text{POWER RATIO} = \frac{\text{SHARE OF MARKET REVENUE}}{\text{SHARE OF AUDIENCE}}$$

This calculation produces the percent of revenue a station earns for each audience share point. Share is readily available to Nielsen and Arbitron subscribers. The revenue part of the equation is more problematic.

While a media firm's analysts know their own sales figures, they would not ordinarily have access to data from competitors. Some organizations, such as Competitive Media Reports, do routinely collect this. But these data are subject to a great deal of error, because such services usually rely on self-reports of prices based on the word of buyers and salespeople. Both groups have an incentive to give false information. Sellers would want to inflate prices so their clients wouldn't think that they overpaid, and buyers would want to deflate prices so they wouldn't appear to have made bad deals. Consequently, such data have serious limitations in terms of estimating market revenues.

This problem has been addressed in some media markets by independent auditing firms that conduct confidential market share analyses. These firms collect sales data directly from media clients and report those figures in monthly, quarterly, or yearly statements available exclusively to participating clients. Subscribers usually learn only the overall market revenue and their own share of that revenue, although in some markets they have access to competitors' data as well.

Table 4.1 displays the kind of information typically appearing in a broadcast market share report. In the sample city's local market, radio advertising revenue in December was $4,577,000. Of that, $351,000 went to the hypothetical radio station WCPA—a figure representing 7.7% of the market's radio advertising during the month. The next highest share of revenue was 8.0%, and the next lowest was 7.2% (note that stations garnering those shares are not identified). WCPA can calculate its power ratio using this information. If Arbitron shows an audience share of 7%, for example, then WCPA's power ratio is 1:1. This means the station earns 1.1% of total advertising revenue for every 1% of audi-

TABLE 4.1

Radio Revenue Report

Revenue category	Sample city Revenue (In $ thousands)			WCPA Revenue (In $ thousands)			WCPA Revenue Share		Rank		Nearest shares Dec. 98		Dec. 97	
	Dec. 98	Dec. 97	chg.	Dec. 98	Dec. 97	chg.	Dec. 98	Dec. 97	1998	1997	above	below	above	below
Local	4,577	4,351	5%	351	264	33%	7.7%	6.1%	6	6	8.0%	7.2%	6.1%	5.9%
National	601	600	0%	53	39	36%	8.8%	6.5%	6	7	10.1%	8.8%	6.8%	4.2%
Network	58	45	29%	—	—	—	—	—	8	6	5.2%	—	6.7%	—
Total Cash Sales	5,236	4,996	5%	404	303	33%	7.7%	6.1%	6	6	8.1%	7.6%	6.6%	5.7%
Trade	460	380	21%	31	50	38%	6.7%	13.2%	8	3	8.0%	5.4%	14.7%	12.6%
Total Sales	5,696	5,376	6%	435	353	23%	7.6%	6.6%	6	7	7.8%	7.5%	7.3%	5.8%

Note. Adapted from sample report provided in *The Hungerford Radio Revenue Report: Users Guide*, by Hungerford, Aldrin, Nichols, & Carter, 1998, Grand Rapids, MI. Used with permission.

ence share. Generally the Arbitron shares are adjusted to reflect share of audience only among those stations that report revenue figures. The value of this system is that it equips media analysts to evaluate their sales effort without compromising proprietary information.

The power ratio can be calculated on the basis of any demographic. If a radio station format were designed to appeal to men 18–49, then the sales representatives would want to know the station's share against that group. The same holds for television sales. As noted in chapter 2, the buying of advertising time on television is usually done on persons demographic ratings, so a household conversion ratio would be of limited use. The statistic can be calculated on any daypart for which information is provided by the auditing firm. However, the conversion ratio by itself conveys very little information. Analysts also consider trends in the daypart to learn whether the share of revenue is increasing or decreasing and determine whether this is a result of audience share differences or changes in overall sales revenue. It must also be compared to historical data on the performance of particular formats in a market, because different formats can be expected to garner different shares of sales revenue.

What is the value of a programming investment?   After its investment in personnel, a broadcast station's largest cost item is generally programming. Each program purchase is evaluated according to its potential to generate station revenue. Analysts must determine how much money the programs will earn for the station and how much revenue will be lost by displacing other programs from the schedule. This may involve fairly straightforward analysis of costs and revenues, or it could involve complex analysis of properties, such as sports rights.

Several factors determine the balance of costs and benefits in a program purchase decision. These include the seller's license fee, the amount of time available for local sales, the likely price program spots will command in the advertising marketplace, the opportunity cost of purchasing the program, and the revenue the program is likely to generate over the life of a contract. Because programs are often purchased 3 or 4 years before stations can air them, analysts need to generate planning estimates for 3–5 years in the future. The information needed to conduct this analysis requires input from several departments in the organization.

When a program property becomes available, financial decisionmakers assemble a *pre-buy analysis*. Although the format differs across organizations, the information needed is essentially the same. One of the most important elements in the revenue projection is the estimated audience the program will attract. Predicting that audience is both science and art, involving historical data as well as experienced judgment. The historical data are in the form of ratings.

For an off-network syndicated television program, for example, analysts are interested in how a program performed in its original run. The national ratings indicate popularity and audience composition. However, a program could do poorly nationally but be fairly popular in a station's home market. There are several reasons for this. The show might have a distinct cultural appeal in certain parts of the country, or it might simply have been carried on stronger stations in some markets than in others. The difference could also be attributable to different demographic profiles of potential audiences across DMAs. Whatever the reasons, the local market ratings have to be taken into account when analysts project ratings for a particular market.

Analysts would also be interested in the performance of programs in previous syndication runs, because some syndicated programs are sold for two or more cycles. If a program were in its second cycle, the ratings it earned in the first cycle would be of major importance. Analysts could compare how the program did in its original network run with how it performed in syndication (using some of the syndication ratings sources described in chap. 8 of this volume). They could use this information to predict how it might do a third time around.

Ratings for programs similar in content to the one being evaluated also offer insight. This is especially important with first-run syndication, where there are no track records to consult. By assuming that the program will attract audiences similar to others of its type, ratings can be projected based on those audiences. The savvy user of audience data will, of course, consider not only program content but also the scheduling patterns.

A predicted rating also depends on time slot. Competition varies by daypart, by season, and by day of week. Time periods also have different levels of available audience, so the ratings vary considerably across dayparts (see chap. 9, this volume). Programmers take all of this into consideration when they decide on a schedule, and financial analysts factor the information into their calculations of future revenue.

Large media organizations may have the resources in-house to make these kinds of predictions, but most firms rely on information supplied by services such as rep firms. Programmers at rep firms at times participate in program purchase decisions, helping programmers and general managers evaluate and negotiate deals. More often, they serve a consulting role, providing ratings information to their clients. They share not only ratings data, but also the experience gained in various markets, which can be very valuable to financial planners.

Revenue projections take into consideration the number of spots available for sale in a given program. This depends on the program length and on commitments to other uses for those spots. A barter program, for example, will have less time available for local sale than a syndicated program purchased with cash. Stations might also reserve a number of spots to use for promotional announcements, making this inventory unavailable to the sales staff. All of this affects the number of units sold to advertisers, and thus the revenue that is generated.

Just as researchers use historical ratings information and experience to project the likely audience for a program, salespeople use historical data and first-hand knowledge of market conditions to estimate a cost per point that the program will command. The program's schedule will have a significant effect on the prices that the advertising sales staff can charge. Even if a program is projected to earn a very high rating, it cannot be sold at a prime-time cost per point if scheduled in late fringe.

Table 4.2 illustrates a sample pre-buy analysis for a fictitious program called *Family Time*. Due to space constraints, the table covers only the first 3 years of a 6-year analysis, but it reveals many of the factors previously discussed. The first columns describe the season and likely scheduling patterns. Programmers determined that *Family Time* should start in early fringe, probably maintaining that time slot for the first few years. Subsequent columns report the estimates that affect quarterly revenue projections.

Working with other departments at the station, financial analysts estimate the program's ratings, the price it will likely command in the advertising marketplace, and the sell-out percentage (how much of the available advertising time will be sold). In this case the analysts project the program to earn a 6.0 household rating in the first year when airing at 5:30 p.m. In the second and fourth years of the contract, the rating drops to 5.0, and by the end of the year 2002, the program is projected to earn a 4.0. This drop in projected ratings is based on the assumption that some of the available audience has already seen the series, and that competing stations might have more recent or otherwise more attractive programming. Although the data are not shown in Table 4.2, programmers plan to move *Family Time* to the early afternoon toward the end of the contract, which brings the estimated audience down to a 3.0.

The cost per point (CPP) varies by quarter, and the cost per spot (also called *average unit rate*) varies according to the estimated rating and the CPP. These figures represent the program's value to salespeople in the marketplace. Sellers offered this program on a cash-plus-barter basis, requesting 1 minute of barter time for the first 2 years of the contract. Note that station personnel are selling 11 avails through the 3rd quarter of 2001 when they regain the one minute of barter time given to the syndicator as part of the original contract. Analysts estimate that 95% of the available spots will be sold during the first 2 years of the program's run, dropping to 90% in year 3. The last column, net revenue, is calculated by combining the advertising cost and sell-out information with the number of times the program is aired.

This analysis is completed, quarter by quarter, for the life of the contract. Financial analysts projected that *Family Time* would generate close to $7.1 million in revenue, while costing the station only about $1.6 million in license fees. This means the program would produce a profit of $5.5 million over its 6-year contract—attractive, but highly unrealistic. Most programs are likely to show a much smaller profit margin.

The revenue a program generates is only part of the financial calculation. Analysts also need to consider alternative uses of airtime and whether these al-

TABLE 4.2
Hypothetical Pre-Buy Analysis: KZZZ Family Time

Qtr	Year*	Time period	HH Rtg	CPP ($)	Average Unit Rate ($)	Avails**	SO %	Air'gs	Net Rev. ($000)
3rd/4th	1999	MF 5:30pm	6.0	110.00	660	11	95%	85	586.2
1st	2000	MF 5:30pm	6.0	80.00	480	11	95%	65	326.0
2nd	2000	MF 5:30pm	6.0	120.00	720	11	95%	65	489.1
3rd	2000	MF 5:30pm	6.0	90.00	540	11	95%	65	366.8
4th	2000	MF 5:30pm	5.0	114.40	572	11	95%	65	388.5
1st	2001	MF 5:30pm	5.0	83.20	416	11	95%	65	282.6
2nd	2001	MF 5:30pm	5.0	124.80	624	11	95%	65	423.9
3rd	2001	MF 5:30pm	5.0	93.60	468	11	95%	65	317.9
4th	2001	MF 5:30pm	5.0	119.00	595	11	95%	65	417.7
1st	2002	MF 5:00pm	5.0	86.50	433	12	90%	65	303.6
2nd	2002	MF 5:00pm	5.0	129.80	649	12	90%	65	455.6
3rd	2002	MF 5:00pm	5.0	97.30	487	12	90%	65	341.5
4th	2002	MF 5:00pm	4.0	123.80	495	12	90%	65	347.6
1st	2003	MF 5:00pm	4.0	90.00	360	12	90%	65	252.7

*First 3 years of contract, primary run.
**Avails = Gross avails—barter—promos (one spot is reserved for promotional announcements in this program.)
Estimating a 4% annual growth rate.

ternatives would be more profitable for the station. Perhaps a different program scheduled in the same time slot would sell at a higher cost per point. Or a program with more local avails would be more profitable than an all-barter program. The question in each instance is whether the benefits of acquiring a property justify lost revenue from other options. Another way of phrasing this is that financial planners must consider the *opportunity cost* of scheduling one program instead of another. This consideration affects all levels of the analysis.

Another factor impacting costs and benefits of a program acquisition is its affect on the rest of the schedule. High-profile programs, such as *Oprah Winfrey* or major sporting events, might attract new viewers and create promotional opportunities to build audiences for other parts of the schedule. They could provide large lead-in audiences to locally produced programs, such as the news. Or the schedule might benefit from a *halo effect* that draws viewers to the channel. Higher ratings for these other programs would translate into higher revenues overall.

There is no standard threshold that determines whether a program is acquired after the pre-buy analysis. Different types of programs have vastly different profit margins. In the off-network syndication market, for example, a blockbuster program often earns less for the station in direct advertiser revenue because much of the advertising time is allocated to national barter. But, for the image reasons previously listed, the program could be an excellent asset. Other shows might be projected to attract comparatively small audiences but with the sale of all local availabilities would generate higher profits. Usually, financial managers and programmers will seek a mix of both kinds of shows.

Sports-rights deals require a more complex analysis than other programs or series. They also require, in the opinion of some industry professionals, more instinct. Deal structures vary widely, from a team purchasing a station's 3-hour block and selling the time themselves to deals that share production costs and permit the media organization to sell the time. Arrangements such as revenue sharing are not uncommon. This means the same questions are asked about ratings predictions and opportunity costs, but there are additional considerations specific to the sports property. One complicating factor is that the times and lengths of games fluctuate from week to week. The regular schedule will be interrupted in inconsistent ways, which could drive regular viewers from the channel. It also means that advertisers in these regular programs might be bumped if a game goes late, which has repercussions on the way the time is sold. However, although the analysis differs based on the proposed terms of the deal, the basic question remains the same: "What can I earn with one option compared to another?" As explained previously, the likely audience that each option will attract is a key factor in assessing whether the balance of revenue lost or gained is in the organization's favor.

Group ownership affects financial planning at media organizations. When a station becomes part of a group, the corporate culture of the new owner, as well as its long-term image goals, are likely to affect decision making at the station level. Stations that once functioned on their own might be subject to corporate approval for program purchases. For example, a station might determine, based on a pre-buy analysis, that a sports programming opportunity is not in the best interests of the local sales effort. But this decision would not serve a group owner who wanted to create a national image as a sports broadcaster. The national goals would have to figure into the cost–benefit calculation made by the individual station.

Consolidation of businesses could also mean consolidation of financial expertise. As corporate financial analysts gain experience across many different markets, they can incorporate that knowledge into pre-buy analyses for individual group-owned outlets. Ordinarily a smaller organization unaffiliated with a media group would not have access to this kind of expertise on a regular basis. In any case, group ownership means that program acquisition decisions are no longer done in isolation. Financial analysts at the newly acquired company might be accountable to financial managers at the corporate office. The group owner may even require approval before a purchase is made, which effectively removes decision making from the local level in some instances.

Financial analysis helps program directors or general managers negotiate deals. It offers some indication of reasonable prices for a program and how high they should be willing to go to purchase it, or whether they should give it serious consideration at all. Analysis also helps executives negotiate specific terms of a deal, such as the amount of barter time given to the syndicator. Because the value that local television stations attach to a spot could be very different from the value that syndicators assess, stations might want to keep more time for local advertising sales. Of course, this example is hypothetical. While buyers in most markets do not have the option to negotiate the amount of barter time, some in smaller markets can still do this.

Though all departments have to cooperate in financial analysis, there is frequently tension among them stemming from differing agendas and priorities. A program director wants to build an audience over the course of a day, while a sales account executive wants inventory to sell potential clients. Some programs won't fit the program director's strategies. Occasionally a programmer will decide to preempt regular programming to cover an important news event. This creates problems for the sales staff. If regular programs are continually preempted, advertisers need make-good spots to compensate for lost audiences. The finance managers are likely to be aware of these priorities, but must remain focused on bottom-line considerations that benefit the company as a whole.

These same principles regarding the acquisition of syndicated programs apply to program production and distribution decisions. Before producing a 1-hour first-run syndication program, for example, a production company would study audience information for similar 1-hour shows. Producers would estimate the clearance they would be able to achieve and likely audience shares they would garner. The supply of similar programming would also be a consideration, because supply and demand affect prices in both the program and advertising markets. This analysis also takes place with the introduction or change of locally produced programs. A station news director might want to add a half hour of local news. Financial analysts would look at other markets or similar stations to determine whether it would be profitable to expand news operations. They would have to consider makeup of the audience for the new schedule and whether the benefits justify the lost viewership that could occur due to the change.

To check the accuracy of the planning process, financial analysts may conduct a post-buy analysis after a program runs (similar to the one described previously in chap. 2 for advertising post-buys). Basically, the planning procedure is repeated after the "real" data are collected, and the results are compared with predictions made before the investment. If any significant discrepancies are found, further analysis is needed to identify whether the error was due to faulty audience projections, unforeseen changes in viewing patterns or market conditions, or lower-than-expected advertising rates.

What is the value of a media property?   Many media companies are publicly traded, meaning that individual or institutional investors can buy shares in the company from a stock exchange. Just as investors would study the prospects of any potential acquisition, a thorough financial analysis is critical in decisions involving media concerns. This is likely to include an inspection of a company's ratings performance—past, present, and future. Even if shares in a media company are not traded on exchanges, investors can buy properties directly. Stations are brokered much like houses. Here again, investors must determine whether the property in question will generate sufficient revenues to justify the acquisition. Projecting audience ratings is critical to those judgments.

Financial analysts also recognize that although audiences are an important determinant of media revenues, there may be some discrepancy between a media property's share of the audience and its share of market revenues. They must consider other factors, which can have practical implications for evaluating the desirability of acquisitions. Table 4.3 illustrates how a financial analyst might evaluate the long-term revenue potential of a television station. The top row represents net revenue for all stations in the market. This number is likely to be a function of the overall market economy, especially the annual volume of retail sales. It is estimated by looking at historical trends in the market and making careful judgments about the economic outlook for especially important sectors. The second row represents the station's current and estimated share of the television audience. Here again, the analyst would consider recent trends and the chances that the station's overall ratings performance will improve or decline. There are many factors that affect a station's ability to attract an audience (as discussed in chap. 9, this volume). In this example, the analyst estimated that the station would eventually be able to attract and hold 25% of the audience.

TABLE 4.3
Station Revenues Based on Audience Share Projections

Factors	1998	1999	2000	Maturity
Net market revenue	$70 million	$74 million	$80 million	X
Station audience share	21%	22%	23%	25%
Over/undersell factor	0.80	0.83	0.86	0.90
Station revenue share	16.80%	18.30%	19.80%	22.50%
Station revenue	$11.76 million	$13.54 million	$15.84 million	X(.225)

But this does not guarantee the station can expect to capture 25% of market revenues. In fact, this station has regularly commanded a smaller portion of market revenues than its share of the audience. In other words, it undersells its audience share. That factor is recognized in the third row across the table. The analyst believed that the undersell factor could be improved but, to be conservative, projected that revenue share would always fall short of audience share.

Once these factors have been estimated, it is possible to make a reasonable projection of station revenues. When these revenue estimates are compared with projected operating expenses, the analyst can determine whether this property would have sufficient cash flow to cover its debt and provide the owners with an acceptable return on their investments.

What determines the value of an audience?   Although the station's salespeople and financial analysts are very good at reading market signals, they may not be as concerned with quantifying abstract determinants of economic value. Under a system of advertiser-supported media, audiences are a commodity, bought and sold like other commodities. They are also perishable, and their supply is unpredictable—which hardly distinguishes them from other goods in a marketplace. As with other commodities, analysts have tried to figure out what determines their value, at least as it is reflected in prices. Knowing the determinants of a commodity's price is certainly of practical value to those who do the buying and selling, but it can also illuminate the operation of media industries.

The economic value of an audience is largely determined by supply and demand. Corporations and other organizations demand advertising time and the media supply it. Generally speaking, when the U.S. economy is strong, and corporate profits are high, demand increases and advertising expenditures rise. Whereas such macroeconomic variables establish an overall framework for prices, a number of factors operate within that framework to determine the value of specific audiences.

On the demand side, some companies cannot curtail their advertising expenditures as easily as others. For instance, the makers of many nondurable goods, like soft drinks, cosmetics, and fast foods, fear significant losses in market share if they stop advertising. Consequently, they may continue to advertise heavily, even if times are hard. Local merchants, on the other hand, often cut advertising budgets to reduce expenses. For these reasons, during an economic downturn, local advertising markets may soften more readily than national markets, depressing the price of local audiences.

As previously noted, different advertisers demand different sorts of audiences, and this interest in market segmentation has had a marked effect on ratings. Audiences are routinely categorized by their demographic and geographic attributes. Increasingly, they are segmented by psychographics and product-purchasing behavior. Not all audience segments, however, are as easily supplied as others. Some people spend more time in the audience and are therefore more readily available to advertisers. Others constitute a tiny part of the population (e.g., executives earning more than $500,000) and are, therefore, rare. This tends to make them a more valuable commodity.

These aspects of supply and demand come into play when determining the value of an audience, represented ultimately in cost calculations (e.g., CPMs) for the electronic media. Advertisers sometimes make trade-offs between print and electronic media based on the relative cost of audiences. Table 4.4 summarizes recent CPMs for the major advertiser-supported media. Although such contrasts can be an apples–oranges comparison, the price of competing media is another factor that determines the market value of a television or radio audience. This is especially true in local advertising where newspapers can provide stiff competition for the electronic media.

What contribution do ratings make to revenues?   The preceding discussion runs the risk of suggesting that audiences have some inherent value that translates directly into revenues. A number of factors account for the fact there is no lockstep relationship between audience size and revenues. These may be of considerable importance to both economic and financial analysts.

The first thing to remember is that electronic media audiences are, themselves, invisible. The only index of this commodity is ratings data—an estimate of who is probably out there. It is the ratings points that are bought and sold. If media personnel are limited to estimates of audience size and shape, the estimates effectively become the commodity. Although ratings companies are under considerable pressure to produce accurate audience measurements, certain biases and limitations do exist. Some may be inherent in the research methods these companies use; others are more the result of how the ratings business has responded to marketplace demands. In any event, the media buyers and sellers must operate within the constraints imposed by ratings, which may hinder selling certain audiences. In effect, the ratings data themselves can distort the link between audience size and audience revenues.

For example, as noted, cable has gradually eroded the broadcast television audience. The cable industry, however, has had some difficulty marketing that audience, because historically the ratings business has been geared to estimating broadcast audiences. With the introduction of the peoplemeter, and the expansion of passive meters into additional local markets, Nielsen is now in a better position to provide cable ratings. The shifts in share of revenue illustrate how that change has affected the placement of advertising. Table 4.5 shows how advertising expenditures have changed over the years. While radio's share of revenue has remained fairly steady since the early 1980s, cable has claimed an increasing share at the expense of broadcast television.

The second thing to remember is that audiences are made available to advertisers in the form of spot announcements, which are limited in number. A broadcaster could exhaust the inventory of available spots before meeting the demand for audiences. If demand is high early in the buying season, and broadcasters sell out, then even those advertisers who would pay a premium to reach

TABLE 4.4

Cost-per-1000 Projections for Four Media

1998		Ad unit	Cost-per-1000	
			Men	Women
TV				
	Network prime time	:30	$19.00	$15.20
	Cable prime time	:30	9.25	8.80
	Network daytime	:30	—	5.35
	National spot early evening	:30	13.90	11.35
	Network late fringe	:30	19.25	16.85
Radio				
	Network	:30	5.80	4.50
	Spot	:30	7.75	6.75
Magazines*				
	Mass dual audience	P4C	7.20	5.00
Newspapers**				
	Dailies	1/3 P B&W	19.70	19.25

Note. From TV Dimensions '98, © Media Dynamics, Inc., New York, NY.
*Assumes through-the-book readership levels and negotiated off-card rates.
**Top 50 markets.

TABLE 4.5
Share of Total TV/Radio Advertising Revenue*

Year	Radio	Television	Cable
1950	73%	27%	0%
1960	29%	71%	0%
1970	26%	74%	0%
1980	24%	75%	1%
1985	23%	74%	3%
1990	23%	70%	7%
1995	23%	66%	11%
1996	23%	65%	12%
1997	23%	63%	14%

*Based on revenue estimates provided by RAB, TVB, and CAB.
Percentages represent share of total for the 3-media advertising revenues only.

the intended audiences will be unable to purchase spots. The result is that some audience revenues go unrealized.

The amount of advertising time the electronic media have to sell is affected by several factors. Certain dayparts have more commercials than other dayparts. Prime time, for instance, has fewer spot announcements than late night or daytime television. The type of station also affects the amount of commercial inventory. Network affiliates have less time to sell to local advertisers than independents, because network programming reduces the size of their inventories. Inventories can be increased by adding commercial time to a program or reducing the duration of spots (e.g., from 30 to 15 seconds), but like cost cutting, there is a practical limit to how much can be done without being counterproductive. Indeed, broadcasters sometimes argue about how much commercial time can be sold within each hour before listeners might be driven away to another station. Programmers frequently try to lure listeners to a new, or revised, format by presenting very few commercials or guaranteeing x commercial-free minutes.

Even if ratings data were completely accurate and inventories more flexible, audiences are not the only factor in determining revenues. A sales force must take audience data into the marketplace and persuade advertisers to buy the commodity. Selling is a very human, and often imperfect, process. Some sales managers are more aggressive than others in their approach to time buyers. Some salespeople are more effective in dealing with clients than others. In addition, no two advertisers are alike. Some, for example, may purchase heavy schedules early in the season and routinely receive quantity discounts. The

TABLE 4.6
Determinants of Economic Value*

Potential Determinants	References
Size of market or audience	Besen (1976)
	Fisher et al. (1980)
	Fournier & Martin (1983)
	Fratrik (1989)
	Levin (1980)
	Takada & Henry (1993)
	Wirth & Bloch (1985)
	Webster & Phalen (1997)
Audience demographic composition	Fisher et al. (1980)
	Fournier & Martin (1983)
	Fratrik (1989)
	Webster & Phalen (1997)
Audience location (ADI/TSA)	Fisher et al. (1980)
	Fratrik (1989)
	Poltrack (1983)
Certainty of audience delivery	Fournier & Martin (1983)
	Webster & Phalen (1997)
Daypart	Fisher et al. (1980)
	Poltrack (1983)
Overall strength of market economy	Poltrack (1983)
	Vogel (1986)
	Webster & Phalen (1997)
Number of stations in the market	Besen (1976)
	Fournier & Martin (1983)
	Fratrik (1989)
	Levin (1980)
	Poltrack (1983)
Number & circulation of newspapers	Poltrack (1983)
Market power or concentration	Fournier & Martin (1983)
	Wirth & Bloch (1985)
Ratio of national spot to local revenue	Poltrack (1983)
Level of cable penetration	Fratrik (1989)
	Wirth & Block (1985)
	Webster & Phalen (1997)

continued on next page

Determinants of Economic Value* (continued)

Potential Determinants	References
VHF versus UHF	Besen (1976)
	Fisher et al. (1980)
	Fratrik (1989)
	Levin (1980)
Network affiliation or ownership	Besen (1976)
	Fisher et al. (1980)
	Fournier & Martin (1983)
	Takada & Henry (1993)
Total levels of media use in market	Poltrack (1983)
Season of the year	Poltrack (1983)
Size of sales transaction	Fournier & Martin (1983)

*Note. References do not necessarily find the same relationship between determinants and measures of economic value. Dependent variables are not uniform among these studies.

result is that two audiences that seem to be identical may sell for different amounts of money.

Economists have devoted a good deal of attention to the relationship between audience ratings and audience revenues. For readers who are interested in learning more about this relationship, Table 4.6 lists research in the area. In addition to the factors already described, there are other, less benign, explanations for a discrepancy between an audience's size and its market value. If, for instance, there are relatively few competitors in a market, they may be tempted to collude and set prices above competitive levels. Although we know of no cases of such collusion, the potential exists. What is clear, however, is that demand affects price. Advertiser demand for TV has been, and will probably remain, high. This has meant higher rates (proportional to the audience delivered) in markets with fewer stations. In less concentrated markets, the cost of audiences tends to be lower, but studies of this sort have been inconclusive.

RELATED READINGS

Albarran, A. (1997). *Management of electronic media*. Belmont, CA: Wadsworth.
Alexander, A., Owers, J., & Carveth, R. (1998). *Media economics: Theory and practice* (2nd ed.). Mahwah, NJ: Lawrence Erlbaum Associates.
McKnight, L. W., & Bailey, J. P. (Eds.). (1997). *Internet economics*. Boston: MIT Press.

Noam, E. M. (Ed.). (1985). *Video media competition: Regulation, economics, and technology.* New York: Columbia University Press.

Owen, B. M., & Wildman, S. S. (1992). *Video economics.* Cambridge, MA: Harvard University Press.

Sherman, B. L. (1995). *Telecommunications management: Broadcasting/cable and the new technologies.* (2nd ed.) New York: McGraw-Hill.

Turow, J. (1984). *Media industries.* New York: Longman.

Vogel, H. L. (1998). *Entertainment industry economics: A guide for financial analysis* (4th ed.). Cambridge: Cambridge University Press.

5

Audience Research
in Social Policy

The electronic media play a central role in our society's economic and social
life. They contribute to the smooth functioning of markets by facilitating the
exchange of goods and services. They open or foreclose the *marketplace of ideas*,
so essential to democracies. They may even shape our perceptions of reality, as
many people have persuasively argued. Given the powers commonly attributed
to the media, it should come as no surprise that they are scrutinized by social scientists from a wide variety of disciplines.

From the very beginning of radio broadcasting in the 1920s, proponents and
critics of the medium wondered how it might affect American society. By the
early 1930s, a high-powered government committee on social trends appointed
by President Hoover listed more that 150 specific effects attributable to radio,
from homogenizing regional cultures to encouraging morning exercise
(Ogburn, 1933). The newly formed networks had also begun assessments of the
radio audience, and academics—especially from psychology, sociology, marketing, and education—became interested in the study of broadcasting as well.

There were already a number of studies in psychology comparing the effects
of visual versus aural media. A comparison between radio and print advertising
was almost inevitable. One of the first studies of memory from "ear and eye" was
conducted by Frank Stanton (1935), a pioneer in communications research,
who would later become the president of CBS. The interest of psychologists
broadened considerably and quickly. Stimulated by the use of media for political purposes, especially in the United States and Germany, they began to examine the use of radio by Franklin Roosevelt, various religious and political

69

demagogues, and the manipulation of motion pictures by Adolf Hitler. In 1935, Hadley Cantril and Gordon Allport, of Harvard University, published *The Psychology of Radio,* reporting many of their early findings.

By then, Stanton had earned his doctorate from Ohio State, with a dissertation that focused on methods for studying radio listening behavior. He and Cantril sought, and eventually secured, a grant from the Rockefeller Foundation to study the methodologies of measuring radio. As luck would have it, Stanton had become director of research at CBS, and so was unable to head the project. Instead, they asked Paul Lazarsfeld to be the director, with Stanton and Cantril serving as co-directors. Thus began the Princeton Radio Research Project, which, after 2 years, moved to Columbia University as the Bureau of Applied Social Research.

Many collaborative research efforts fell under the auspices of the Bureau, as well as a string of studies regarded as the beginning of communication research in the United States. Virtually all of this research was tied to the measurement of radio listening. The exciting new field of radio, and especially the need to measure its audience, was largely responsible for establishing Lazarsfeld as one of the founders of the scientific study of communications. Indeed, the emergence of ratings research, at least in those early days prior to World War II, was intertwined with the development of the new field of mass communications, and, in a broader sense, with the growth of all social/behavioral research. Audiences to the electronic media were becoming recognized as appropriate subjects for communication research.

Today, audience data play an important, if little appreciated, role in social scientific inquiry and the study of communications. Such data influence the work of policymakers, social advocacy groups, and academics, and they are used to justify policy positions in contentious debates about mass media and society.

Most of the individuals and organizations involved in the process of communication policymaking are intent on securing a special advantage for themselves or handicapping their opponents. Others have a genuine commitment to the public interest. No matter their intent, most have found some occasion to use audience data to support their case.

This regular, if sometimes manipulative, use of audience information has a number of explanations. Most significant, audience ratings go to the heart of the media's power. Why is it that electronic media have any economic value? Because they have an audience. Why is it that news and entertainment programs are capable of any social impact? Because they have an audience. Why do political campaign announcements influence the outcome of elections? Because they have an audience. And although ratings alone cannot reveal the effects of media on society, they can frequently index the potential. Ratings are the most consistent and verifiable evidence of audience exposure to the mass media. These factors, in addition to the wide and continuous availability of ratings data, have made ratings an attractive tool in crafting communications law and social policy.

Among the people and institutions most involved in making communications policy, those most likely to use audience data are the federal government, industry, and the public. These interested parties and the dynamic interactions among them determine the course of public policy.

Government.   By the mid-1920s, it had become apparent that broadcasting would not operate as an unregulated marketplace. The number of people who wanted to broadcast exceeded available frequencies. To solve the problem, the U.S. Congress created the Federal Radio Commission (FRC), replaced in 1934 by the Federal Communications Commission (FCC). The commission was charged to license stations, and, more generally, to uphold service in the public interest. Although prevailing philosophies of what best serves the public interest have changed over the years, three interrelated objectives have endured. First, the commission tried to limit certain undesirable social effects that could be attributed to broadcasting. Children have often been the special targets of their concern. Second, the commission attempted to promote diversity in media content, for example by structuring markets in a way that makes them more responsive to audience demand. And third, like many other regulatory agencies, the FCC tried to ensure the economic health of the industry it regulates.

The last of these is surely the subject of the most argument. Many broadcasters would point out that the FCC hindered "free, over-the-air" TV by allowing—indeed, openly promoting—rapid growth of cable in the early days. Although it is true that the commission has tended to promote competition in the electronic media, it has historically stopped short of instituting policies that would debilitate licensees economically. This concern is evident in the Commission's early approach to questions of audience diversion (reviewed later in this chapter). More recently, it is apparent in the FCC's efforts to award broadcasters additional spectrums to develop digital broadcasting.

Still, the FCC is not free to implement whatever policies it chooses. Other federal institutions are often involved. The president, the courts, and especially the Congress can and do make their wills known. In 1996, Congress passed what many call the most sweeping communications legislation since the original Communications Act of 1934. The Telecommunications Act of 1996 affected many areas of the business, from ownership to content. Legislators required the FCC to review long-standing rules and revise anything that had become outdated.

Other independent agencies, like the Federal Trade Commission or the Copyright Arbitration Royalty Panel (CARP), also deal with communications policy. And some offices of the executive branch, like the Department of Commerce or the Department of Health and Human Services, may enter the picture. In the early 1970s, the Surgeon General oversaw a massive study of the impact of violence on television. Studies such as these can often be used to influence legislators to vote for particular bills. But, although the government ultimately sets communications law, other interests weigh heavily in the policymaking process.

Industry. The organizations with the most direct interest in communications policy are the media themselves. Sometimes individual companies, like the broadcast networks, represent themselves in Washington. Usually, however, trade associations represent industries. For broadcasters, the most important of these is the National Association of Broadcasters (NAB). The NAB serves the interests of commercial broadcasters by lobbying Congress and the FCC, testifying before congressional committees, filing briefs in relevant judicial proceedings, and participating in rulemakings and inquiries at government agencies. In many of these activities, the NAB submits research that bears on the issue at hand. In fact, the NAB has a special department of research and planning that frequently performs policy studies using ratings data. The National Cable Television Association (NCTA) represents the cable industry. The NCTA engages in the same activities as the NAB and likewise maintains a department of research and policy analysis. The other trade associations most likely to use ratings data include the Motion Picture Association of America (MPAA) and the Association of Local Television Stations (ALTV).

The Public. Although government and industry have a major influence on the formation of public policy, they don't completely control it. The public itself enters the process in a number of ways—most directly, of course, by electing government representatives. Occasionally, one of these government officials will take the lead on a matter of communications policy, inviting citizens to either support or reject that position. More highly organized public participation comes in the form of public interest groups. Some of these, like Action for Children's Television (ACT), were formed specifically to affect communications policy. ACT in particular was successful at drawing the attention of Congress and the FCC to matters of children's television. Since its closing in the mid-1990s, some groups have tried to replace ACT, but none has been successful. Other organizations, like the Parent/Teacher Association (PTA) or the American Medical Association (AMA), do not make communications law and regulation their central focus, but nonetheless, express occasional interest in social control of media.

The academic community also contributes to policymaking. Professors in disciplines having an interest in broadcasting and other electronic media have been attracted to policy questions related to the media's social and economic impact. The academic community can affect policy in several ways. Most notably, researchers publish reports relevant to questions of public policy. Because they are often viewed as experts, and relatively objective, their work may carry special influence with the government. Academic researchers may also work as consultants for other participants in the policymaking process, and exercise direct influence in a less public, and usually less objective, manner. Finally, of course, they can indirectly affect policy through their students. Many people who are involved in determining communications policy today would credit certain professors with influencing their views on matters of law, regulation, and social responsibility.

RESEARCH QUESTIONS

Not all, or even most, questions of communications policy can be illuminated by analyses of ratings data, but there is a surprisingly broad range of applications for audience information. Very few bodies of social scientific data can be interpreted, or "read," in so many different ways. The use of ratings data in policymaking can be organized as responses to one of three broad questions, which correspond to the three long-term concerns of the FCC:

1. Limiting the undesirable effects of media.
2. Promoting more diverse and responsive programming.
3. Tending to the economic condition of its client industries.

What do the media do to people?   Limiting undesirable effects requires first identifying what those effects might be. Researchers have been asking this effects question in one form or another since the earliest days of mass communication. Even before radio was established, a number of sociologists and educators were concerned about the impact of newspaper reports on children. In the early 1930s, sociologists tried to determine the impact of movies on young people. Later in the decade, psychologists studied the effects of wartime propaganda, while marketing researchers measured how press coverage could influence voter behavior. More recently, these examinations have explored television's role in promoting violence, sexual or racial stereotypes, and distorted perceptions of social reality.

Central to these and other effects questions is the cause–effect relationship: "Does exposure to the media (cause), make other things happen (effect)?" This is an extremely difficult question for social scientists. An important starting place, however, is knowledge of what people listen to or watch, because any direct media effect by definition must begin with audience exposure to media messages.

Although a media encounter may not determine a particular outcome (again, the effect), hearing or seeing a message does define a potential. The greater the exposure, the greater the potential for effects. Advertisers have long realized this fact, and so have paid dearly for access to audiences. The value of this potential is also obvious in the recurring debate over free airtime for political candidates. The opportunity to reach the electronic-media audience is perceived by many as a right candidates should enjoy. They assume that citizens' voting behavior will be influenced by exposure to campaign messages. Conversely, if no one is exposed to a message, its direct impact is not felt.

Academics, too, have recognized that exposure is the wellspring of media effects (e.g., Bryant & Zillmann, 1994). One of the most outspoken has been George Gerbner, a proponent of *cultivation analysis*. Gerbner has argued that television content is so uniform and people so unselective that researchers need only consider the amount viewed to determine the medium's social impact. Usually, these arguments are buttressed with references to ratings information.

According to the 1998 Nielsen Report on Television, the TV set in a typical home is in use for about 7 hours each day. Actual viewing by persons older than 2 years averages more than 4 hours each day. Some argue that with that much viewing, there can be little selectivity. And the more people watch, the less selective they tend to be. Most regular and heavy viewers watch more of everything (Gerbner et al., 1986). According to Gerbner, then, TV's power to cultivate mistaken notions of what is real can be revealed in simple comparisons of heavy and light viewers.

Other researchers are less convinced that audience selectivity is a fiction. Studies of *selective exposure* are important to the history of media research (see chap. 9, this volume). Although varied in origin, these studies assume that audience members are capable of discernment, which they demonstrate in their consumption of media content. Depending on the content chosen, different media effects may follow. In the Surgeon General's report on TV violence, for example, Israel and Robinson (1972) used viewing diaries to assess how much violence various segments of the population consumed. The operating assumption was that those who watched more violence-laden programming would be more likely to show its ill effects. So, whether one considers specific content or, as Gerbner would argue, TV viewing in general, exposure sets the stage for subsequent media effects.

Government regulators have also used audience information to gauge the media's potential to create undesirable social effects. The FCC, for instance, has a congressional mandate to control indecent language in broadcasting. Although the commission might tolerate excesses if only adults heard them, the presence of children in the broadcast audience has created a problem. Some policymakers consider this problem so serious that they have tried to channel offensive language away from time periods when children are likely to be in the audience. To identify those time periods, the commission's staff used ratings data. Hence, the detrimental effects that might result from exposure to indecent content are limited by the size of the child audience.

The FCC has also expressed special concern about the audience for local news and public affairs programming. The commission has historically encouraged localism in broadcasting, an effort motivated, at least in part, by a desire to keep people informed about issues of public importance. The growth of cable television has been seen as a threat to localism because of its ability to divert audiences from local broadcasts. In a 1979 report on the relationship between cable and broadcasting, the FCC elaborated:

> Television may have an important effect in shaping the attitudes and values of citizens, in making the electorate more informed and responsible, and in contributing to greater understanding and respect among different racial and ethnic groups .... Historically, the FCC has encouraged particular types of programming—local news, public affairs, instructional programs—on these grounds. To the extent that a change in broadcast-cable policy would dramatically change the amount by which these programs are not only broadcast but also viewed, these issues could be an important component of a policy debate. (p. 639)

In a line of reasoning analogous to its indecency rules, then, the FCC expressed concern that undesirable social consequences might flow from people not watching certain content. Here again, the first index of effects is audience size, an index that is readily available in ratings data.

What do people want?   Another important goal of communications policy has been to provide the public with diverse media content. This objective is very much in keeping with First Amendment ideals and the benefits thought to result from a free marketplace of ideas. But how does one accomplish this objective? Although policymakers have different opinions on the subject, the most popular solution has been to structure media industries so a large number of firms compete for audience attention. In such an environment, competitors will supposedly respond to audience likes and dislikes as expressed in their program choices. Under this system, ratings serve as a feedback mechanism. Arthur Nielsen, Jr. (1988) has described the link between ratings and preferences as follows: "Since what the broadcaster has to sell is an audience to advertisers, it follows that in order to attract viewers, the broadcaster must cater to the public tastes and preferences. Ratings reveal these preferences" (p. 62.).

Many commentators find the industry's argument that they "only give the people what they want" to be self-serving and deceptive, because most media programmers respond to advertisers' demands, not audience members. Because some audiences are less valuable to advertisers than others, these viewers may be underserved. In addition, the use of advertiser-supported media by audience members is not an expression of how much they like a particular program, but only an indication that they elected to use it (factors that complicate the link between preference and choice are discussed in chap. 9). Nevertheless, a considerable number of theorists, in both psychology and economics, view people's choices as a function of their preferences, and this provides more than adequate justification for the use of ratings in policymaking.

The most relevant theories have been developed in the study of *welfare economics*, a branch of the discipline concerned with how citizens can maximize the overall well-being of society. Like other economists, welfare economists assume people are rational and will attempt to satisfy their preferences for goods and services—at least insofar as their pocketbooks allow. Economists refer to this notion as the "theory of revealed preference." They postulate that deducing preferences from behavior may be superior to direct questioning about a person's likes and dislikes. Because a media system under advertiser support imposes no direct costs on viewers (i.e., they do not pay a per-program fee), their preferences are freely expressed in program choices. These concepts and their consequences for how public policy might maximize viewer satisfaction are fully discussed in Owen and Wildman (1992).

Welfare economists, therefore, have used ratings data to address questions of communications policy. One category of FCC rules that has received scrutiny is the commission's position on media ownership. To increase diversity in programming, the commission has sought to restrict certain classes of media from owning local television stations (e.g., local newspapers and radio). The idea is that different owners will contribute different viewpoints to the marketplace of ideas. Unfortunately, existing media may be more adept than newcomers at offering local programming that appeals to viewer preferences. Parkman (1982) has, consequently, argued the following:

> If these classes of owners produce more popular programming than other classes of owners, the reduction in popular programming should be taken into consideration as [a] cost of the diversification policy. To determine if certain news gathering organizations are more successful than others in attracting viewers, we can look at the end result that these organizations produce as judged by the viewers, i.e., the ratings. (pp. 289–290)

After analyzing the ratings of local television news programs, Parkman concluded that the commission's policy imposed, "costs on individual viewers by forcing them to choose programs considered by them as less desirable" (p. 295).

The FCC itself has relied on ratings as a kind of revealed preference. The most notable example has been the commission's designation of stations as *significantly viewed*. This concept was introduced into FCC rules in the early 1970s to determine the popularity of a signal in a given geographical area. It has affected many areas of regulation, such as must-carry, syndicated exclusivity, effective competition, and compulsory copyright. Although the definition has changed, a station was deemed significantly viewed in a market if it achieved a weekly 2% share of audience and 5% weekly circulation in noncable homes. Even though these determinations might be made on the basis of a very small number of diaries in any given county, they were treated by regulators as reliable. Thus the ratings (subject to the errors described in chap. 7, this volume), have been used to justify and enforce public policies that affect the operation of media firms.

What economic implications will various policies have? A number of government laws and regulations affect the financial condition of the media and related industries. Because these policies have an impact on the bread and butter—or in some cases the Mercedes and BMWs—of those businesses, they attract the attention of many participants in the policymaking process. Even the FCC, which in recent years has favored increased competition in the media, must remain alert to the economic consequences of various policies. If broadcasters are driven out of business by an ill-conceived government policy, the result might compromise the commission's mandate to serve the public interest.

Financial statements that describe the media's revenues, expenses, and profitability are one obvious source of information on the economic condition of the industry. But for a number of reasons, these data are not always used. For one thing, the commission stopped collecting financial statements from broadcasters many years ago, so they are not readily available. For another, economic injury to the industry might be too far advanced by the time it surfaces on company ledgers. One common alternative to a dollars-and-cents measure of economic impact is to use audience ratings. Because ratings measure the commodity that media sell, policies that adversely affect a station's audience are often seen to damage its economic interests. Despite the fact that ratings and revenues are not perfectly correlated, evidence of lost audiences is often, in effect, evidence of lost revenues, and vice versa.

A succession of studies using ratings information attempted to demonstrate audience diversion or erosion from established media. Such analyses have been a frequent feature in skirmishes between broadcasters and the cable industry. Almost from the beginning, broadcast interests used claims of economic injury to encourage policies that would restrict cable's growth. Allowing cable to enter a market, it was argued, would so erode a station's audience as to threaten its survival. In 1970, Rolla Park, of the Rand Corporation, assessed this threat through an analysis of local market ratings data. This study helped shape the FCC's rules on cable television issued in 1972. The commission again considered the economic relationship between cable and broadcasting in an inquiry in the late 1970s. Again, Park (1979) and a number of interested parties, assessed the state of audience diversion through sophisticated analyses of audience ratings information. The commission referred extensively to these studies in its final report.

The FCC also encountered claims of audience diversion in the context of its rules on *syndicated exclusivity*. These rules, first adopted in the early 1970s, were intended to insure that broadcasters who bought exclusive rights to syndicated programming would not have that privilege undermined by a cable system that imported a distant signal containing the same program. The import, it was assumed, would divert the audience that rightly belonged to the local station. In subsequent debates over the rule, the parties at interest (e.g., NAB, NCTA, INTV) submitted analyses of ratings data purporting to show that audience losses did or did not occur in the absence of the rule. This rule was dropped for some time, but when the FCC reimposed it they reasoned: "The ability to limit diversion means broadcasters will be able to attract larger audiences, making them more attractive to advertisers, thereby enabling them to obtain more and better programming for their viewers" ("Whys and Wherefores," 1988, p. 58).

A more recent example of the use of ratings data in policy research concerns television ownership restrictions. The Telecommunications Act of 1996 granted owners of UHF stations special consideration with regard to total audience reach. As stipulated in the Act, the combined audience reach of all stations owned by one person or entity cannot exceed 35% of the U.S. audience. However, because UHF stations have traditionally operated at a disadvantage vis-à-vis VHF stations, lawmakers discounted their reach figures. Only 50% of the coverage of UHF stations counts toward the calculation of U.S. audience. Thus a group owner of all UHF stations might have potential coverage of more than 50% of all TV households, but under the FCC rules that would count as only 25%. When this arrangement was challenged, the NAB prepared a report showing that UHF stations consistently drew smaller audiences because they operate on the UHF band. After accounting for other factors that could reduce ratings, the NAB found that channel assignment was correlated with lower ratings. For example, UHF stations affiliated with Fox earned an average of 1 rating point lower than their VHF counterparts, and NBC affiliates demonstrated a difference of 3.6 rating points between UHF and VHF stations (Everett, 1998).

Interpretations of ratings data have also influenced the distribution of fees derived from the *compulsory license*. Cable systems pay these fees for the right to carry broadcast signals, creating an annual pool of nearly $200 million. The Copyright Arbitration Royalty Panel (CARP) is responsible for allocating that money among claimants. Those with a claim are copyright holders, including program suppliers, commercial broadcasters, public broadcasters, and Canadian broadcasters. It is logical that audience shares would figure in the computation of awards. After all, the economic value of a program or program service rests largely on its ability to attract an audience.

The uses of audience information in legal or regulatory proceedings are considerable. Despite these and many other applications of the data, it appears that social scientists have only scratched the surface of analytical possibilities. Generally, these uses of ratings have dealt with gross measures of audience size—not surprisingly, given that such estimates are the most readily available. Indeed, that is what the ratings are. Using ratings to track individuals over time, engaging in cumulative analyses, would seem a logical next step for social scientific inquiry.

Consider, for example, the effects question. Although the number of people who are exposed to a message suggests something about its potential effect, so too does the regularity of exposure. Advertisers have recognized this concept in their attention to frequency—the average number of times audience members see or hear a message. Effects researchers might similarly ask how often people see or hear a particular kind of programming: Do all children see the same amount of violence on television, or do some consume especially heavy doses? Is there a segment of the child audience that seems to be violence junkies? If so, who are those children? Do they come from poor or affluent families? Do they watch alone or with others? The answers to such questions, which can be gleaned from audience data, might contribute much to understanding the impact of televised violence. Similar questions could be asked about the audience for news and information.

Studies of audience duplication might reveal more about people's preferences for programming as well: Does a particular program have a small-but-loyal following, or is it just small? As noted in chapter 3, programmers and marketing researchers recognize a certain feature of audience duplication called channel loyalty. Religious, Spanish-language, and music-video services are among the kinds of programming that seem to attract small-but-loyal audiences. Does this intensity suggest something about how the audience values a service beyond the number who use it at a particular point in time?

The economic value of an audience transcends its size and composition. Advertisers may specify reach and frequency objectives in their media plans. Those who seek a high frequency of exposure might pay a premium for a small-but-loyal audience. In a similar vein, channel loyalty and inheritance effects undoubtedly contribute to the audience of a syndicated program. If a station adds value to the program by delivering an audience predisposed to watch, then perhaps the station should enjoy a greater share of credit for a program's success.

Even media critics distrustful of social science might learn through inventive uses of ratings data how audience members encounter media. For instance, analysts of popular culture have become increasingly interested in how people read, or make sense of, television programming. One insight from this line of research is that viewers experience the medium not as discrete programs but as strips of textual material called *flow texts*. It might be illuminating to explore the emergence of flow texts through analogous studies of audience flow.

All of these analyses, and many more, could be realized through the application of commercial audience data. Unfortunately, the effective use of such data in the social sciences and related disciplines has been uneven. In part, this is because proprietary syndicated research is too expensive for strictly academic analyses (for more on buying data, see chap. 8, this volume). Some academics, however, may fail to exploit available data, simply because they do not recognize the possibilities for analysis. We hope the remainder of this book helps remedy the latter problem. Subsequent chapters acquaint the reader with audience measurement services, the data they collect, the products they offer, and the theory and techniques of ratings analysis.

RELATED READINGS

Besen, S. M., Krattenmaker, T. G., Metzger, A. R., & Woodbury, J. R. (1984). *Misregulating television: Network dominance and the FCC.* Chicago: University of Chicago Press.

Bryant, J., & Zillmann, D. (Eds.). (1994). *Media effects: Advances in theory and research.* Mahwah, NJ: Lawrence Erlbaum Associates.

LeDuc, D. R. (1987). *Beyond broadcasting: Patterns in policy and law.* New York: Longman.

Levin, H. J. (1980). *Fact and fancy in television regulation.* New York: Russell Sage.

Lowery, S., & DeFleur, M. L. (1994). *Milestones in mass communication research* (3rd ed.). New York: Addison-Wesley.

Owen, B., & Wildman, S. (1992). *Video economics.* Cambridge, MA: Harvard University Press.

Rowland, W. D. (1983). *The politics of TV violence: Policy uses of communication research.* Beverly Hills: Sage.

II

Research Data

6

The Audience
Measurement Business

Since the beginning of radio, the broadcaster has been interested in how the owner of a receiver reacts to the programs presented over the air. Some of the questions to which the broadcaster, whether he is an educator or advertiser, is anxious to secure the answers are as follows:

1. When does the listener use his receiver?
2. For how long a period does he use it?
3. To what station or stations does he listen?
4. Who listens (sex, age, economic and educational level)?
5. What does he do while the receiver is in operation?
6. What does he do as a result of the program?
7. What are his program preferences?

—*Frank N. Stanton* (1935)

Frank Stanton, who later became president of CBS, wrote those words in his doctoral dissertation. Little has changed since that time. The electronic media have undergone great transformations, but the basic research question—a need to know the audience—has been one of the most enduring features of the industry. In this chapter, we trace the evolution of the audience measurement business. Our purpose is not to offer a comprehensive history of audience measurement. Rather, our interest in the growth of ratings is motivated by a desire to better understand the industry's present condition, and perhaps to anticipate its future.

Even the first broadcaster wanted to know who was listening. After more than 5 years of research, experimentation, and building on the work of others, Reginald A. Fessenden broadcast the sound of human voices on Christmas Eve in 1906. He played the violin, sang, recited poetry, and played a phonograph record. Then the electrical engineer promised to be back on the air again for New Year's Eve and asked anyone who had heard the broadcast to write him. Apparently, he got a number of letters from radio operators, many of them on ships at sea, who were astonished to hear more than Morse code on their headphones. Other early station operators asked for letters from listeners as well. Dr. Frank Conrad, who in 1920 developed KDKA in Pittsburgh for Westinghouse, played specific records requested by his correspondents.

A need to know the audience, however, quickly became more than just a curiosity about unseen listeners. By the early 1920s, AT&T executives had demonstrated that charging clients a toll to make announcements over its station was an effective way to fund the medium. It was a short step from the concept of toll broadcasting to the notion of selling commercials to advertisers.

By 1928, broadcasting was sufficiently advanced to provide listeners with consistent and quality reception. Many had developed the habit of listening to radio, and broadcasters, in cooperation with advertisers, were developing program formats "suitable for sponsorship" (Spaulding, 1963). Despite public controversy over whether radio should be used for advertising, the Great Depression, beginning in 1929, caused radio station owners to turn increasingly to advertisers for support.

For radio to be a successful advertising medium, time buyers had to know who was in the audience. Newspapers were already providing authenticated figures on distribution through the Audit Bureau of Circulation. Theater and movie audiences could be measured by ticket sales. Phonograph popularity could be measured by sales and later jukebox plays. But broadcasters and their advertisers were left with irregular, and frequently inadequate, assessments of audience size and composition.

Many radio advertisers, for example, offered coupons or prizes in an attempt to measure response. In 1933, about two thirds of NBC's advertisers offered incentives listeners could send for—mostly novelty items, information booklets, or a chance to win a contest. Sometimes responses were overwhelming. In answer to a single announcement on a children's program, WLW in Cincinnati got more than 20,000 letters. The program's sponsor, Hires Root Beer, used these responses to select specific stations on which to advertise in the future. But soliciting listener response had risks. The makers of Ovaltine, a drink for children, and the sponsors of Little Orphan Annie, asked fans to send in labels in order to free Annie from kidnappers. As you might imagine, this provoked an uproar from parents.

Early station operators used equally primitive techniques to estimate audience size. Some counted fan mail, others simply reported the population, or number of receivers sold, in their markets. These unreliable methods invited exaggeration. The networks were more deliberate. NBC commissioned a study in 1927 to determine not only the size of its audience, but the hours and days of listening. Analysts sought information on the economic status of listeners, fore-shadowing the use of demographics, now so much a part of audience research. CBS conducted an on-the-air mail survey in 1930, offering a free map to all who would write the station to which they were listening. Reviewers compared the response to the population of each county and developed the first CBS coverage maps. But none of these attempts offered the kind of regular, independent mea-surement of the audience that the medium would need to sustain itself.

THE DEVELOPMENT OF AUDIENCE MEASUREMENT

The history of ratings research provides an account of the broadcasting busi-ness. It is a story of individual researchers and entrepreneurs, of struggles for in-dustry acceptance, and the evolution of research methods. Every major ratings research company rose to prominence by perfecting and promoting its research-ers' approach. Most major changes in the structure and services of the industry have also been tied to research methods. For this reason, we have chosen to or-ganize our discussion of the industry's history around the methods these firms have used.

Telephones

From 1930 to 1935 the revenues and profits of the network companies nearly doubled, at a time when the country and other businesses were in deep eco-nomic depression. American families had no money to spend on other diver-sions, but they found radio entertaining. The audience grew rapidly. An important stimulant to that growth, however, was the emergence of a system for providing audience estimates that advertisers could believe. The first such sys-tem depended on another technological marvel—the telephone.

Then, as now, advertisers were the driving force behind ratings research, and it was advertisers who helped create the first regular ratings company. In 1927, a baking powder company hired the Crossley Business Research Company to sur-vey the effectiveness of its radio advertising. Two years later Crossley analysts conducted a similar survey for Eastman Kodak using telephone interviews to ask people if they had heard a specific program. Although the telephone was an unconventional tool for conducting survey research, it seemed well suited for measuring something as far-flung and rapidly changing as the radio audience.

Archibald Crossley, the research company president, and a well-known pub-lic opinion pollster, suggested to the Association of National Advertisers (ANA) that a new industry association might use the telephone to measure ra-dio listening. His report, entitled "The Advertiser Looks at Radio," was widely distributed and ANA members quickly agreed to a monthly fee for regular and continuous listening surveys. The American Association of Advertising Agencies (AAAA) also agreed on the need for regular audience measurements.

This new service, officially called the Cooperative Analysis of Broadcasting, or CAB, began in March 1930. More often than not, however, its reports were referred to in the trade press as the Crossley ratings. Even the popular press began to note the rise or fall of a specific program or personality in the ratings. Initially, only advertisers paid CAB for its service, but soon advertising agencies began to subscribe. The network analysts had access to the reports as well, using them for selling and making programming decisions, but they could not make "official" use of them. Significantly, it was not until 1937 when NBC and CBS were allowed to become subscribers, thus sharing the cost.

Crossley revised his methods and expanded the information provided a number of times in the early years. By the 1935–1936 season, surveys were being conducted in the 33 cities that had stations carrying CBS and the two NBC networks. Calls were placed four times during the day and respondents were asked to recall the radio listening during the previous 3–6 hours. Hence, Crossley's method was known as *telephone recall*. Monthly, and later biweekly, reports were provided giving audience estimates for all national network programs. Further, 3 times each year there were more explicit summaries providing detailed reports on station audiences hour by hour, with breakdowns for geographic and financial categories.

There were, however, problems with the CAB methods. One problem was measuring radio listeners who lacked telephones. Oddly enough, this was less a problem in the early years of the service because the first families to purchase radios were high-income households likely to have telephones. But the growth of radio homes quickly outpaced those with telephones. By the end of the 1930s, CAB researchers had to alter their sampling procedures to include more low-income homes to compensate.

The most serious limitation to the CAB method was the requirement that listeners recall (remember) what they had heard. Users of another technique that featured a simultaneous or coincidental telephone survey challenged Crossely's early dominance of the ratings business. George Gallup measured audience size by conducting personal interviews and asking what stations respondents listened to as early as 1929, while at Drake University in Iowa. Soon thereafter, he went to work for Young and Rubicam, a major advertising agency, where he did a *telephone coincidental* on a nationwide basis. There were other pioneers of the telephone coincidental, like Pauline Arnold, Percival White, and John Karol, who became director of research for CBS.

In 1933, Pauline Arnold specifically compared the telephone recall and coincidental methods, as summarized in Lumley (1934):

> The results showed that some programs, which were listened to by many listeners, were reported the next day by only a few. In general, dramatic programs were better remembered than musical programs. However, the rank correlation between the percentage of listeners hearing 25 (half-hour) programs and the percentage reporting

having heard them was about 0.78. This is a measure of the adequacy of the Crossley survey as compared with the simultaneous telephone survey. (pp. 29–30)

The telephone coincidental provided a methodological advantage that opened the door for CAB's first ratings competitor. This happened when Claude Hooper and Montgomery Clark quit the market research organization of Daniel Starch in 1934 to start Clark–Hooper. Dr. George Gallup assisted them in arranging for their first survey. Hooper later wrote, "Even the coincidental method which we have developed into radio's basic source of audience size measurement was originally presented to us by Dr. George Gallup" (Chappell & Hooper, 1944, p. vii). In the fall of that year, Clark–Hooper launched a syndicated ratings service in 16 cities.

Ironically, Clark–Hooper was first supported by a group of magazine publishers unhappy that radio was claiming a larger share of advertiser dollars. The group believed Crossley's recall technique overstated the radio audience. Although it was expected then that coincidental ratings would capture certain unremembered listening, the publishers hoped Clark–Hooper would show that many people were not at home, and many others at home were not listening to the radio. In fact, the first Clark–Hooper results did show lower listening levels than those of CAB.

In 1938, Clark–Hooper split, the former taking the company's print research business. With great faith in the future of radio, Hooper stayed in business for himself. His research method was simple. Those answering the phone were asked:

- Were you listening to the radio just now?
- To what program were you listening?
- Over what station is that program coming?
- What advertiser puts on that program?

Then they were asked the number of men, women, and children listening when the telephone rang.

Hooperatings, as his audience estimates came to be called, were lower than CAB's for some programs but higher for others. Hooper argued, people were better able to remember programs that ran longer, were more popular, and had been on the air for a longer period of time. Respondents were also much more likely to recall variety programs, and most likely to forget having listened to news (Chappell & Hooper, 1944). The industry began to regard C. E. Hooper's coincidentals as more accurate than CAB's recall techniques.

But methodological superiority was not enough. As a creature of the ANA and AAAA, CAB was entrenched with the advertising industry. Hooper decided to pursue the broadcast media themselves, arguing that, because CAB was set up to serve the buyer of radio time, his objective would be establishing a service that would furnish audience measurements to both the buyer and the seller of radio time. If CAB saw fit to ignore networks and stations, Hooper would enlist them as clients and provide the audience research they needed. This strategy was perceptive, for today, it is media organizations that account for the majority of ratings service revenues.

Hooper also promoted the popular acceptance of Hooperatings. Each month he released information on the highest rated evening programs, not only to the trade press, but to popular columnists as well. In this way, C. E. Hooper, Inc. became the industry's most visible and talked-about supplier of audience information. Radio comedians even began to joke about their, or the competition's, Hooperatings.

In addition to promoting popular consciousness about program ratings, Hooper was also responsible for establishing many of the traditions and practices of contemporary ratings. He instituted the "pocketpiece" format for ratings reports, now the hallmark of the national Nielsen ratings, as well as concepts like "available audience" and "sets in use." He also instituted audience shares, which he called "percent of listeners," and the composition of the audience in terms of age and gender. Thus, by the end of the 1930s the pattern of commercial audience research for broadcasting was set.

Hooper and his company were efficient and aggressive. He researched methods to improve accuracy and added new services, especially to help the networks and stations. He was also relentlessly critical of the CAB recall method. As a part of this battle, in 1941, Hooper hired Columbia University psychology professor Matthew Chappell to study recall and memory. Two years later they wrote a book trumpeting the advantage of telephone coincidental.

Hooper's aggressiveness paid off, and, just after World War II, he bought out CAB, on the verge of collapse. C. E. Hooper was the unquestioned leader in ratings research. But as Hooper reached his zenith, broadcasting began to change. The number of radio stations expanded rapidly, and the new medium of television altered the way people used leisure time. A new methodology and company were ascendant as well. Although he continued to offer local measurement of radio and television, in 1950, Hooper sold his national ratings service to A. C. Nielsen.

Personal Interviews

In-person, formal interviews were often used in early radio surveys, especially by academics with a sociology or marketing background. This method is no longer a mainstay of the ratings industry, although personal interviews in the home and focus groups are used to obtain other types of audience information. These methods are used, for example, in evaluations of local news programming and tests of radio formats and program pilots. Knowing something about the method, therefore, is relevant both to current practice and an understanding of how audience measurement shapes the industry it serves.

Most of the early Daniel Starch studies for NBC were personal interviews, beginning with the first in spring 1928. And even though the first ratings services had come into existence, in the 1930s, CBS commissioned Starch to do a series of reports. CBS argued that this provided more accurate information, because Hooper's methodology missed all non-telephone homes—which biased results against viewers in the smaller communities. Because CBS had fewer and, often, less powerful affiliated stations than NBC, the network's management felt they could only benefit from this type of audience research (CBS, 1937).

In the late 1930s, while Crossley and Hooper differed over telephone data collection, and Nielsen perfected his metering device, the personal interview was still the most accepted method of collecting sociopsychological behavior information. Dr. Sydney Roslow in particular, who had a doctorate in psychology, became intrigued with the technique while interviewing visitors at the New York World's Fair. With the encouragement of Paul Lazarsfeld, Roslow adapted these techniques to radio listening. In the fall of 1941, he began providing audience estimates, called "The Pulse of New York," based on a personal interview *roster-recall* method he developed. Respondents were contacted and given a list of programs, or roster, to aid in their recall of listening for the past few hours. Because Hooper, and later Nielsen, concentrated on network ratings, Roslow's local service expanded rapidly—especially with the proliferation of stations after the war. By the early 1960s, Pulse was publishing reports in 250 radio markets around the country and was the dominant source for local radio measurement.

The roster-recall method had significant advantages over Roslow's competitors. It could include out-of-home listening (e.g., automobile and work), and measure radio use during hours not covered by the telephone coincidental—Hooper was limited to calls from 8 a.m. to 10:30 p.m. Furthermore, roster recall provided more demographic detail and information on minority and foreign-language stations popular with those unlikely to have phones.

The easy availability of local radio ratings offering information on listeners hard to reach with other methods had a significant impact on the shape of local radio. Roslow's emphasis on measuring audiences in the metro area, versus Nielsen's nationwide measurement of network programs, contributed to the rise of Top 40 and popular music format stations. Local advertisers were interested only in the number of listeners in their marketing area. These rock music stations usually had lower transmission power but very high shares within their smaller coverage area. Thus, "The Pulse of New York" was a boon to the growth of rock formats when more local stations were going on the air and more network programs and personalities were transferring to TV or drifting into oblivion.

In the 1970s, yet another ratings company, featuring another method, took control of local radio ratings. The American Research Bureau, or ARB (described in the sections that follow), took its success with television diary techniques to radio. A subsidiary of a large computer company, ARB had superior computing power, which facilitated the timely production of market reports. Rock and ethnic stations that favored the interview method were not as aggressive in selling to advertising agencies, which increasingly came to accept the diary technique promoted by news and easy-listening stations. In 1978, Pulse went out of business.

Meters

The advantage of making a permanent, continuous record of what people were actually listening to, as it happened, was obvious from the beginning of radio. But technical obstacles precluded this development until the 1930s. Recording systems were uncommon until the late 1940s, but when these meters finally arrived, they had a profound and lasting impact on the ratings business.

While a student at Columbia University in 1929, Claude Robinson—later a partner with George Gallup in public opinion research—patented a device to "provide for scientifically measuring the broadcast listener response by making a comparative record of … receiving sets … tuned over a selected period of time" (Beville, 1988, p. 17). RCA, parent of NBC, bought the patent, but nothing more is known of the device. Despite the advantages of a meter, none had been perfected, leading Lumley (1934) to report:

> Although the possibilities of measurement using a mechanical or electrical recording device would be unlimited, little development has taken place as yet in this field. Reports have been circulated concerning devices to record the times at which the set is tuned in together with a station identification mark. None of these devices has been used more than experimentally. Stanton, however, has perfected an instrument which will record each time at which a radio set is turned on. (pp. 179–180)

The reference was to Lumley's student Frank N. Stanton. For his dissertation—which began with the paragraph that opens this chapter—Stanton built and tested 10 recorders "designed to record set operation for [a] period as long as six weeks" (Lumley, 1934, p. 180). On wax-coated tape, one stylus marked 15-minute intervals while another marked when the set was switched on. The device did not record station tuning. It was used instead to compare listening as recorded on questionnaires. Stanton found that respondents tended to underestimate time spent with the set on (a bias that holds true today).

In 1930 and 1931, Robert Elder of the Massachusetts Institute of Technology conducted studies of radio's advertising effectiveness that were published by CBS. In 1933–1934, he and Louis F. Woodruff, an electrical engineer, designed and tested a device to record radio tuning. The device scratched a record on paper by causing a stylus to oscillate as the radio tuner was moved across the dial. Elder called his device an *Audimeter* and sought a patent. Elder discovered RCA's (Robinson) patent and was granted permission to proceed. The first field test used about 100 of the recorders in the Boston area. In 1936, Arthur C. Nielsen heard a speech by Elder describing the device and apparently began negotiating to buy the rights to the technique immediately.

An electrical engineering graduate of the University of Wisconsin, Nielsen had opened a business to test the efficiency of industrial equipment. He began in 1923 during a period of great expansion for inventing, manufacturing, and the rapid deployment of new assembly-line techniques. The business survived but did not prosper. In 1933, a pharmaceutical client suggested to a Nielsen employee that what they really needed was information on the distribution and turnover of their products. Nielsen responded with a consumer survey based on a panel of stores to check inventory in stock. A food index was added, and the company expanded and prospered. The A. C. Nielsen Company was on its way to becoming the largest marketing research firm in the world. But it was the acquisition of the Elder–Woodruff audimeter that ultimately imprinted the Nielsen name in Americans' consciousness.

With his profits and engineering background, Nielsen redesigned the device. Field tests in 1938 in Chicago and North Carolina compared city and rural listening. Despite war shortages, by 1942 the company launched the Nielsen Radio Index (NRI), based on 800 homes equipped with the device. Nielsen technicians had to visit each home periodically to change the paper tape, which slowed data collection. However, the company also provided information about product purchases, based on an inventory of each household's "pantry." Having already established a good reputation with advertisers, Nielsen began to overtake the dominant ratings supplier, C. E. Hooper.

During the 1950s, Nielsen continued to expand his ratings business and perfect the technology of audience measurement. In 1950—the same year he acquired Hooper's national ratings service—he initiated the Nielsen Television Index (NTI), the company's first attempt to measure that fledgling medium. By the middle of the decade, he launched the Nielsen Station Index (NSI) to provide local ratings in radio and television. His engineers perfected a new version of the audimeter that recorded tuner activity on a 16mm film cartridge. More important, the cartridge could be mailed directly to Nielsen sample households and mailed back to Nielsen headquarters, thereby speeding the rate of data collection. Nielsen had also begun to use diaries for gathering audience demographics. To improve their accuracy, he introduced a special device called a recordimeter, which monitored hours of set usage and flashed a light to remind people to complete their diaries.

The 1960s were more tumultuous for Nielsen and all ratings companies. In an atmosphere charged by quiz show scandals on television, reports of corruption and payola in the music industry, and growing social unrest, the U.S. Congress launched a far-reaching investigation of the ratings business. Recognizing the tremendous impact ratings had on broadcasters, and concerned about reports of shoddy research, Oren Harris, chairman of the House Committee on Interstate and Foreign Commerce, orchestrated a lengthy study of industry practices. In 1966, the Harris Committee issued its report. Although it stopped short of recommending legislation to regulate audience measurement, the investigation had a sobering effect on the ratings business—still evident in the scrupulous detail with which methods and the reliability of ratings are reported, and by the existence of the Media Rating Council (until 1982 the Broadcast Rating Council; from 1982 to 1998 the Electronic Media Rating Council).

As the premier ratings company, Nielsen was particularly visible in the congressional hearings, especially its radio index. In response, Mr. Nielsen personally developed a new radio index that would be above criticism. But potential customers resisted the increased costs associated with data collection. An angry Nielsen withdrew from national radio measurement altogether in 1964. In fact, a year earlier Nielsen had discontinued local radio measurement, leaving Pulse unchallenged.

A new company, Statistical Research, Inc. (SRI), filled the void left by Nielsen's exit. SRI was formed in 1969 by Gerald Glasser, a statistics professor at New York University, and Gale Metzger, former director of research for the Nielsen Media division. Three years later, the company took over operation of a collaborative industry research effort called Radio's All Dimension Audience Research (RADAR®), for which Glasser had been a consultant. Since then, SRI has provided bi-annual reports on radio network audiences and, as discussed in a later section, was able to mount a credible threat to Nielsen with its SMART system.

The need to measure Internet audiences has introduced new types of metering to electronic media analysis. Firms like Nielsen and Arbitron have traditionally used survey research techniques and special meters to measure mass media consumption. Newer companies interested in computer usage have simply taken advantage of existing desktop machines. Usage is tracked with software products that consumers download onto their computers. It is this system of tracking that is currently the mainstay of the Internet ratings business. Audience measurement firms like Media Metrix collect data through computer programs that monitor the online activities of those who agree to be part of their samples.

Diaries

Radio-set builders and listeners in the 1920s had little interest in programs. Instead, they sought to hear as many different and distant stations as possible. They kept elaborate logs of the signals they heard, when they heard them, and noted things like station call letters, city of origin, slogans, and program titles. Despite this early practice and the occasional use of diaries by radio ratings firms, the diary method did not take hold in commercial audience research until the rise of television.

The first systematic research on diaries was done by Garnet Garrison, a professor at the University of Michigan. In 1937, he began to "experiment developing a radio research technique for measurement of listening habits which would be inexpensive and yet fairly reliable" (Garrison, 1939, p. 204). Garrison, aware of other methods for capturing audience data—telephone survey, either coincidental or unaided recall, personal interviews, mail analysis or surveys, and "the youngster automatic recording"—borrowed something from each. It could be sent and retrieved by mail, included a program roster, and was thought to be objective. Garrison's table was arranged in a grid from 6 a.m. to midnight divided into 15-minute segments. He asked respondents to list station, programs, and the number of listeners. He concluded that: "With careful attention to correct sampling, distribution of listening tables, and tabulation of the raw data, the technique of 'listening tables' should assist materially in obtaining at small cost quite detailed information about radio listening" (p. 205).

CBS researchers experimented with diaries in the 1940s but apparently thought the data applicable only to programming rather than sales. It was used to track such things as audience composition, listening to lead-in or lead-out programs, and charting audience flow and turnover. In the late 1940s, Hooper added diaries to his telephone sample in areas that could not be reached practically by telephone. This mixture of diary and coincidental was unsatisfactory. Indeed, one reason for Hooper's slippage against Nielsen was that the telephone method was basically confined to large metro areas where TV first began to siphon the radio audience. Hence, Hooper tended to understate radio listenership.

It wasn't until the late 1940s that diaries were introduced as the principal method of a syndicated research service. As director of research for the NBC-owned station in Washington, DC, James Seiler had proposed using diaries to measure radio for several years. The station finally agreed to try a survey for its new TV station. NBC helped pay for several tests, but Seiler set up his own company to begin a regular ratings service.

He called the company American Research Bureau (ARB), and in Washington, just after the war, the name sounded official, even patriotic. Seiler issued his first local market report in 1949. Based on a week-long diary, spanning May 11–18, Ed Sullivan's *Toast of the Town* Sunday variety program earned a 66.4 rating. *Wrestling*, on the ABC affiliate at a different time, got a 37.5, and *Meet the Press* on NBC got a 2.5.

By fall, the company was also measuring local TV in Baltimore, Philadelphia, and New York. Chicago and Cleveland were added the next year. The company grew slowly while television and the diary research methodology gained acceptance. Diaries were placed in TV homes identified by random phone calls. From the beginning, Seiler was careful to list the number of diaries placed, and those "recovered and usable." Further, "breakdowns of numbers of men, women, and children per set for specific programs [could] be furnished by extra tabulation" (American Research Bureau, 1947, p. 1).

Another research company had begun diary-based ratings in Los Angeles in 1947, using the name Tele-Que. The two companies merged in 1951, adding reports for Los Angeles, San Diego, and San Francisco and bringing to ARB several young, bright researchers, among them Roger Cooper and R. R. "Rip" Ridgeway, who would help lead the company's growth.

Through the 1950s, ARB emerged as the prime contender to Nielsen's local TV audience measurement, especially after 1955, when it took over Hooper's local TV ratings business. The company expanded and by 1961 was measuring virtually every TV market twice a year, and larger markets more often. Network and station programmers responded by scheduling attractive programming during these sweeps periods. Local radio reports, also compiled from diaries, appeared in 1965, which eventually put Pulse out of business and, for many years, left ARB the undisputed provider of local radio ratings.

ARB also attempted to one-up Nielsen by developing a meter whose contents could be tapped by a telephone call. In 1957, ARB used phone lines in 300 New York City households and began to provide day-after ratings with an instantaneous meter. Advertisers and media executives approved, because it meant Nielsen might face effective competition. Unfortunately for ARB, Arthur Nielsen and his engineers had patented almost every conceivable way of metering a set. ARB's new owner, a firm named CEIR, was forced to pay Nielsen a fee for the rights to the device. Nevertheless, this spurred Nielsen to quickly wire a New York sample with meters, and later, in 1973, to introduce a Storage Instantaneous Audimeter (SIA) as the data-collection device for its full national sample.

By 1967, ARB was acquired by the computer company, Control Data Corporation. Smarting from its run-in with Nielsen, ARB used the new owner's expertise to develop a metering technology that would not infringe on Nielsen patents. In 1973 the company changed its name to Arbitron. After the turbulent 1960s, what sounded patriotic after World War II now evoked a "big brother" image. A name change, it was thought, might improve response among suspicious respondents. The diary, however, remained the backbone of Arbitron's ratings research business. In November of 1993, Arbitron left the television audience measurement business to focus exclusively on local radio, continuing a dynamic history spawned six decades ago (see Table 6.1).

THE AUDIENCE MEASUREMENT BUSINESS TODAY

Although a number of companies conduct research on audiences, a few firms dominate the ratings business. Nielsen, Arbitron, and Statistical Research, Inc. (SRI) are the dominant players in traditional television and radio markets, and Media Metrix, Inc., which includes the resources of RelevantKnowledge, competes with the newer Nielsen-NetRatings venture in the Internet ratings business. Nielsen Media Research, formerly a part of the larger A. C. Nielsen Company, became an independent, publicly traded company in July 1998. The

TABLE 6.1

Ratings Research Companies and Methodologies

Person/Company	Methodology	Notes
Archibald Crossley Cooperative Analysis of Broadcasting (CAB)	Same-day telephone recall	Founded in 1930 Supported by the Association of National Advertisers Measured national network programs
Claude Hooper and Montgomery Clark Clark–Hooper; later Hooper, Inc.	Telephone coincidental	Founded in 1934 First supported by magazine publishers Produced Hooperatings Bought out CAB after WWII
Sydney Roslow The Pulse of New York	Interviews—roster–recall	Founded in 1941 Measured local radio stations Went out of business in 1978
Arthur C. Nielsen A. C. Nielsen Company, later Nielsen Media Research	Audimeter (later added diary collection)	Launched "radio index" in 1942 Acquired Hooper's national business in 1950 Ended radio measurement in 1964 to focus on TV
James Seiler American ResearchBureau, later Arbitron	Diary	First survey in 1949 Merged with Tele-Que in 1951 Took over Hooper's local business in 1955 Left television business in 1993 to focus on local radio
Tom Birch Birch Radio	Telephone recall	Provided competitive service to Arbitron until 1992
Gale Metzger and Gerald Glasser Statistical Research, Inc.	Telephone recall (for RADAR®)	Founded RADAR® in 1969 Measures network radio listening
	Meter (for SMART)	Uses wireless technology to record actual program viewing

continued on next page

TABLE 6.1 (continued)
Ratings Research Companies and Methodologies

Kurt Hanson Strategic Media Research AccuTrack	Telephone recall	Qualitative information to complement Arbitron Built on concept of "core listeners"
Media Metrix	Software to record Internet usage	Parent company developed PC Meter in 1995
RelevantKnowledge	Software to record Internet usage	Founded in 1996. Merged with Media Metrix in 1998

firm measures national and local television audiences and has expanded to include Internet and other new media. VNU, a Dutch company, agreed to purchase Nielsen in 1999. Arbitron, now owned by Ceridian, continues to provide research for local radio stations, and SRI measures network radio listenership. In recent years, SRI has developed a metering technology that could lead to direct competition with Nielsen in the national television market. These firms supply the currency for the sale of advertising time in the traditional mass media: ratings.

Small audience research firms come and go. Some carve out niches that are unfilled by large firms. Like the companies described previously, their creation and growth are attributable to entrepreneurs. However, these firms usually complement rather than substitute for the established research companies. For example, AccuTrack, an initiative of Kurt Hanson's Strategic Media Research, looks at the "awareness, attitudes and behavior" of radio listeners, which is intended to supplement rather than replace data supplied by Arbitron. This service doesn't measure quarter hour radio listening at all. Researchers work from the premise that the nature of the station is what's important about radio. The service is marketed to stations rather than advertisers and presented as a tool for programmers and general managers more than for salespeople.

One research firm did mount a challenge to Arbitron's dominance in radio measurement. As a radio programmer, Tom Birch conducted research that helped him develop a popular format. Several stations asked him to do call-out research for them. From this, Birch started to measure radio use, and in 1980, he was providing a service based on telephone interviews to 18 markets, and soon expanded to more than 250. But the industry's verbal support for a competitor to Arbitron did not translate into monetary support. Birch's parent company, VNU, discontinued the local radio service in early 1992, and Birch sold his qualitative Scarborough service to his competitor, Arbitron.

It is interesting to note that SRI, AccuTrack, and Birch Radio returned to the method pioneered by Archibald Crossley—the telephone recall. These modern companies employed computers and long-distance calling from centralized facilities. Furthermore, the universal penetration of the telephone has minimized many of the problems of sample bias inherent in early applications of the method. While some limitations still exist, the comparative advantages of this technique (discussed in the following chapter) make such services viable even today.

Although Nielsen remains the sole supplier of national TV network ratings, for a time in the 1980s, the firm was challenged by a serious contender for a share of the market. Audits of Great Britain (AGB) had long supplied England and other countries in Europe and Asia with ratings research. With a new measurement technology called the peoplemeter, AGB hoped to establish itself in the U.S. market (see chap. 7, this volume). Peoplemeters expanded the capabilities of traditional household meters by allowing viewers to enter information about who was watching television. AGB personnel worked hard for industry funding, including money from advertisers and the media. Within a couple of years they had sufficient support to wire the Boston market with peoplemeters and begin a field test of the system. Nielsen developers responded by announcing plans to test and implement its national peoplemeter service. In 1987, Nielsen began basing its NTI services on a sample of households equipped with peoplemeters. AGB held on for a time, but with equivocal support from the industry, especially the broadcast networks, its position was untenable. In 1988, it ceased U.S. operations.

The introduction of peoplemeters reveals a good deal about the ratings business in America. On one hand, AGB received genuine encouragement from the industry, especially advertisers. This was not unlike the support Arbitron got when it tried to best Nielsen with an instantaneous meter in the late 1950s. Almost everyone, except Nielsen, is inclined to believe that competition would lead to improved services and lower costs to clients. In fact, the AGB threat undoubtedly accelerated the implementation of the Nielsen peoplemeter, although the company had been experimenting with that technology for years.

On the other hand, the introduction of peoplemeters was accompanied by complaints from ratings users, ranging from biases in the data, to too much data being served up too fast, to data that was not provided in a useful or usual format. Despite a desire for innovation, an inertia grips the people who use the data. Constancy in the supply of ratings data—knowing what is coming from one month to the next, or being able to make comparisons one year to the next—does have its value. Therefore, changes in the production of ratings must grow up around the supply of assured data, and most changes must be reconciled with historical industry practices.

The introduction of peoplemeters is revealing for another reason. Ratings research is imperfect. Occasionally, biases will operate to the advantage of some and disadvantage of others. Because the peoplemeter system does a better job of measuring small, demographically targeted audiences, advertiser-supported cable networks are likely to be beneficiaries. This is one reason why the broadcast networks were cool to the technology. If peoplemeter data allow cable to compete more effectively with the major networks for advertiser dollars, it might ultimately have an impact on the kinds of programming appearing on television. The point is, not only does industry demand shape the nature of ratings data, but the availability of certain kinds of data can shape the industry too—just as the Pulse data benefited the development of local radio.

Improvements in research technology are on the horizon, and again the threat of competition forced Nielsen to sharpen its methods of measuring audiences. The challenge came from SRI, which developed a technology to enhance peoplemeter measurement. The System for Measuring and Reporting Television (SMART) employs wireless technology that records electronic codes embedded in programs. These universal program codes enable precise tracking of individual programs. Unlike the Nielsen system, SMART does not require that television-set tuners be wired to meters, nor does it depend on an extensive matching of channels tuned to program guides for a determination of which programs were viewed. One impetus for this change was the growth of new technologies, like Direct Broadcast Satellite. Alternative delivery systems require nontraditional audience research methodologies. Unfortunately, SRI had to discontinue its implementation of SMART in 1999 due to a lack of funding.

Nielsen designers developed a technology to compete directly with SMART, called the *Active/Passive (A/P) Meter.* Using a method that Nielsen calls AMOL 2, the A/P meter resembles SRI's technology. The meter reads the video and audio signatures and records actual program viewing. Although the process seems straightforward, it is more complex than it sounds. When a program is not coded, computers compare a sample of video and audio signals to a library of signatures to determine which program is being viewed—a feat that comes at a price. The users of this research, particularly the networks and stations that bear the lion's share of the cost, must evaluate whether the increased accuracy is worth the corresponding increase in price.

Although television has taken center stage in the development of measurement technology, radio researchers are also seeking better methods of tracking listenership. At Arbitron a personal meter has been in development for some time. This meter would travel with the respondent and record listenership by picking up audio signals throughout the day. This technology diminishes the reliance on memory for radio measurement. Nevertheless, there are many hurdles to be overcome before this technology is viable in the marketplace.

Developments like new measurement technologies and computer systems to manipulate data are not one-sided benefits to the media industries. More data is not always a good thing. Many prospective buyers are ill equipped to evaluate the increasing flow of ratings information. One area in which ad agencies and stations have been willing to cut expenses is in hiring personnel to deal with media research. In the long run, this combination could threaten the integrity and reliability of the audience measurement industry. As Gale Metzger (1984) warned, there are "… too many naive buyers who will take any kind of information and use it because it is there; too many suppliers who will provide data without the first concern for quality, because they are salable" (p. 47).

As the new millennium approaches, audience research companies face many challenges, including the growth of the Internet and convergence of personal-computer applications with television viewing. Audience measurement technologies will have to keep pace. The first companies to take on Internet audience measurement were firms with an expertise in estimating computer usage rather than mass-media consumption. It remains to be seen whether research on Internet audiences will continue to develop along these lines or will favor the more traditional methods of mass-media research.

Assuming that methods continue to improve in accuracy, and that measurement technologies keep abreast of changing audiences, ratings data are likely to remain a powerful presence for many years. These numbers have been a central feature of the broadcast industry and the public's perception of that industry for more than half a century. Networks, stations, advertising agencies, syndicators, and virtually every other related business prosper or suffer by them. One need only glance at the trade press to realize how pervasive ratings data are. In fact, the general public now receives rather detailed ratings reports in publications like *USA Today*, *The New York Times*, *Wall Street Journal*, and other daily newspapers. As the electronic media become more competitive, as advertisers seek increasingly targeted markets, and as the methods of research and analysis become more sophisticated, it seems certain that ratings will continue to influence the shape and psyche of American media.

RELATED READINGS

Beville, H. M. (1988). *Audience ratings: Radio, television, cable* (rev. ed.). Hillsdale, NJ: Lawrence Erlbaum Associates.

Buzzard, K. S. (1990). *Chains of gold: Marketing the ratings and rating the markets.* Metuchen, NJ: Scarecrow Press.

Chappell, M. N., & Hooper, C. E. (1944). *Radio audience measurement.* New York: Stephen Daye.

Ettema, J. S., & Whitney, D. C. (Eds.). (1994). *Audiencemaking: How the media create the audience.* Thousand Oaks, CA: Sage.

Lumley, F. H. (1934). *Measurement in radio.* Columbus, OH: The Ohio State University.

7

Audience
Research Methods

Audience data inform a great many decisions. Billions of dollars are spent on the media in accordance with the ratings. Perhaps it is even fair to say that millions of lives are affected by the programming and policy decisions that hinge on this information. Yet no method for producing audience data is without bias or limitations. It is therefore important to know the source of the data and to understand how research techniques affect the final product.

Although the practice of commercial audience research has obviously changed over the years, certain issues have endured—especially questions about methods. Matters of audience sampling and measurement remain as important today as when Archibald Crossley launched the CAB. They will undoubtedly define future debates about the quality of ratings data as well, whether for traditional broadcast and cable audience research or for new media like the World Wide Web.

This chapter describes the methods used by audience measurement companies and, in particular, the ratings services. We do not intend to review every technical detail. For those who want a timely and detailed description of methodology, the ratings firms will provide the necessary documents. It is our intention to ground readers in the methods these companies use so they can assess the strengths and weaknesses of the numbers and understand the jargon of ratings reports. We begin with a discussion of sampling and then turn to issues of measurement methods used in most commercial audience research (as outlined in chap. 1, this volume).

SAMPLING

When researchers collect information about electronic media audiences, they are interested in an entire population of radio listeners, Internet users, or television viewers. But with a population of 98 million television households, it would be logistically impossible to survey all users of a given medium, so research companies estimate audiences from a subset of the population called a *sample*. Virtually all survey research, from marketing studies to public opinion polls, depends on sampling. Indeed, sampling is used in many scientific endeavors. As Arthur Nielsen, Sr. was fond of saying, "If you don't believe in sampling, the next time you have a blood test, ask them to take it all out."

In any survey, the quality of the sample has a tremendous impact on accuracy. All samples can be divided into one of two classes: probability and nonprobability. They differ in how they identify who will be included. *Probability* samples, sometimes called *random samples*, are formed by a process of random selection that allows every member of the population to have an equal, or known, likelihood of selection. Although probability samples are expensive and time-consuming to construct, researchers generally have more confidence in them. *Nonprobability* samples, in which membership is determined by happenstance or convenience, are more likely to produce biased results.

Researchers for all of the ratings companies described in this volume try to achieve, or at least approximate, the virtues of probability sampling. Their technical documents are laced with the language of probability samples. To acquire the needed working vocabulary, therefore, one must be familiar with the principles of probability sampling, which follow. (This discussion does not assume a background in quantitative methods. Readers who are familiar with sampling may wish to proceed to the section on measurement.)

The Language of Sampling

A sampling researcher begins by defining the population of interest, which requires a decision about what to study—called *elements* or *units of analysis,* in the parlance of researchers. The researcher must decide which of those elements constitutes the relevant population. In ratings research, units of analysis are either people or households. Because the use of radio is thought to be a rather individualistic, one-on-one experience, radio ratings have long used people as the unit of analysis. For television, it is more appropriate to speak of households, although the buying and selling of advertising time is done on the basis of individual populations of people defined by demographics (e.g., women 18–34 years old).

Researchers must define the *population* (or *universe*) so they can tell who belongs to it. For example, to create national television ratings, all households in the United States with 1 or more sets might be appropriate. Local markets are more problematic due to confusion about who lives, say, in Washington, DC, as opposed to Baltimore. As a practical matter, Nielsen analysts define markets, called *Designated Market Areas (DMAs)*, by using counties as building blocks. They do this by determining which stations people in a particular county listen to and assigning counties accordingly.

After the population is defined, the next step is to obtain a complete list of all the elements included in it. That list is called a *sampling frame*. It is from the sampling frame that specific elements will be identified for inclusion in the sample. For example, if we have a list of all the television households in Baltimore (assume 1 million for convenience), and randomly picked one home, we would know that it had a one-in-a-million chance of selection, just like every other home in the population. Hence, we would have met the basic requirement of probability sampling. All we would have to do, then, is repeat the process until we have a sample of the desired size.

This procedure produces a *simple random sample*. Despite its conceptual elegance, this sampling technique is seldom used in audience measurement, because the real world is less cooperative than this approach assumes. It is virtually impossible to compile a list of every television home in the United States and then sample randomly from it. Researchers instead employ more efficient and powerful sampling designs.

Sample Designs

Systematic Random Sampling.   One variation on simple random sampling is called *systematic random sampling*. This approach also requires a sampling frame, usually purchased by ratings firms from companies whose business it is to maintain and sell such lists. These frames are typically lists of telephone households. Homes with unlisted numbers can be included through the use of randomly generated numbers. Frames that have been amended in this way are called *expanded* or *total* sampling frames.

Once an appropriate frame is available, systematic sampling becomes straightforward. Because the sampling frame lists the entire population, that analyst knows how large it is. The required sample size is determined by mathematical formulas that take into account the desired level of statistical significance. Dividing population size by sample size determines how often to pull a name or number from the list. For example, suppose the analysts wants a sample of 1,000 from a population of 10,000 individuals. Selecting every 10th name starting at the beginning of the list would create a sample of the desired size. That *nth* interval is called the *sampling interval*. The only further stipulation for systematic sampling—an important one—is that the starting point must be random. In that way, everyone has an equal chance of selection, which fulfills the requirement imposed by probability sampling.

Systematic sampling, as the ratings companies implement it, is imperfect. For one thing, an absolutely complete list of the population is almost impossible to obtain. People living in temporary or group housing may be hard to track down. In many markets, a substantial portion of households lack a telephone. If lists are limited to homes with telephones, some people will be underrepresented in the final ratings report. Conversely, households with more than one telephone number may have a greater probability of selection than other homes. Any of these factors can introduce biases into samples.

Multistage Cluster Sampling.   Fortunately, not all probability samples require a complete list of every element in the population. One sampling procedure that avoids that problem is called *multistage cluster sampling*. Cluster sampling repeats 2 processes: listing the elements and sampling. Each 2-step cycle constitutes a stage. Although systematic random sampling is a 1-stage process, multistage cluster sampling, as the name implies, goes through several stages.

A ratings company might use multistage sampling to identify a national sample, since coming up with a list of every household in the nation would be quite a chore. However, it is possible to list every county. The research company could then draw a random sample of counties. In fact, this is essentially what Nielsen does to begin the process of creating a national sample of U.S. households. After that, block groups within those selected counties are listed and randomly sampled. Then, specific city blocks within selected groups are listed and randomly sampled. Finally, with a manageable number of city blocks identified, researchers might be placed in the field, with specific instructions, to find individual households for participation in the sample.

Because these clusters are listed and sampled at each stage by geographic area, this type of sampling is sometimes called a *multistage area probability sample*. Despite the laborious nature of such sampling techniques, compared to the alternatives, they offer important advantages. Specifically, no sampling frame listing every household is required, and researchers in the field can contact households even if they do not have a telephone.

However, a multistage sample is more likely to be biased than a single-stage sample, because a certain amount of error accompanies each round of sampling in the selection process—the more stages, the more possibility of error. Suppose that while sampling counties as described earlier, areas from the northwestern United States were overrepresented. That could happen by chance, and it would be a problem carried through subsequent stages. Now suppose that bias is compounded in the next stage by the selection of block groups from a disproportionate number of affluent areas, again within the realm of chance. Even when random selection is strictly observed, a certain amount of sampling error creeps in. (This is explained more fully in this chapter under Sources of Error.)

Stratified Sampling.   Using a third kind of sampling procedure called *stratified sampling* can minimize some types of error. This is one of the most powerful sampling techniques available. Stratified sampling requires the researcher to group the population under study into homogeneous subsets, called *strata*. Suppose a sampling frame indicates the gender of everyone in the population. Analysts could then group the population into males and females and randomly sample the appropriate number from each strata. Combining these subsamples into one large group would create a probability sample having exactly the right proportions of men and women. Without stratification, that factor would be left to chance. This step improves the representativeness of the sample. That added precision could be important when studying things related to gender, like watching sports on TV, or purchasing products like cosmetics and tires.

Stratified sampling requires that the researcher have relevant information about the elements in the sampling frame (e.g., the gender of everyone in the population). In single-stage sampling, that is sometimes not possible. In multi-stage sampling, there is often an abundance of information because researchers tend to know more about the large clusters defined at the start. Consider, again, the process that began by sampling counties. An analyst could not only list all U.S. counties, but also group them by the state or region of the country, the size of their populations, and so forth. Other groupings, such as the concentration of people with certain demographic characteristics, could be used at subsequent stages. Combining stratification with multistage cluster sampling, then, increases the representativeness of the final sample. That is what most ratings services do.

Cross-Sectional Surveys.   The sample design issues discussed thus far have all dealt with how the elements in the sample are identified. Another aspect of design deals with how long the researcher studies the population or sample. *Cross-sectional surveys* occur at a point in time, in effect taking a snapshot of the population. Much of what is reported in a ratings book could be labeled cross-sectional. Such studies may use any of the sampling techniques just described. They are alike insofar as they reveal what the population looks like now, not how it has changed over time. But information about such changes can be quite important. Suppose, for instance, the ratings book indicates a station has an average rating of 10. Is that cause for celebration or dismay? The answer depends on whether that represents an increase or decrease in audience size, and true cross-sectional studies will not determine that.

Longitudinal Studies.   Information about changes over time can be derived from *longitudinal studies*. In ratings research, there are two kinds of longitudinal designs in common use: *trend studies* and *panel studies*. In a trend study, a series of cross-sectional surveys, based on independent samples, is conducted on a population over a period of time. The definition of the population remains the same throughout the study, but individuals may move in and out of the group. In the context of ratings research, trend studies can be created simply by considering a number of market reports done in succession. Tracing a station's performance across a year's ratings books constitutes a trend study. People may have moved to or from the market during that time, but the definition of the market (i.e., the counties assigned to it) is unchanged. Most market reports provide trend information from past reports.

Panel studies draw a sample from a population and continue to study it over time. The best example of a panel study involves the metering of people's homes. This way of gathering ratings information (described later in this chapter), may keep a household in the sample for years.

The way individuals are targeted for inclusion in a sample affects the end result of audience research. Techniques like random-digit dialing can bias a sample by systematically eliminating nontelephone households from the frame. Sometimes it is difficult to develop a sampling frame that includes the entire population. In the case of Internet users, for example, there is no handy list of everyone who accesses The Web. For one thing, the universe changes daily. Some measurement companies have tried to circumvent this problem by asking potential respondents to sign up online. But this creates other problems by making the sample nonrandom. The cost of various methods of recruitment must be balanced with the limitations these methods impose. The consumer of audience research data should understand how respondents were solicited to assess how this might affect the end result.

Sources of Error

One of the principal concerns of both users and producers of audience research is error in the data. The concept of error is not just a matter of mistakes. Rather, it addresses the extent to which ratings information based on samples fails to disclose what is actually happening in the population. Error is the difference between what the ratings estimate to be true and what is true. A sophisticated user understands the source of error and how audience research companies deal with it.

There are four sources of error in ratings data: *sampling error, nonresponse error, response error,* and *processing error.* The first two involve sampling and are dealt with first. The last two involve measurement and the production process, respectively, and will be covered in the sections that follow.

Sampling Error.   This is the most abstract of the different kinds of error. It is a statistical concept common to all survey research, one recognizing that as long as we try to estimate what is true for a population by studying less than the entire population, we risk missing the mark. Even very large, perfectly executed random samples can misrepresent the populations from which they are drawn. This is inherent in the process of sampling. Fortunately, if we employ random samples, we can, at least, use the laws of probability to make statements about the amount of sampling error we are likely to encounter. In other words, the laws of probability will tell us how likely we are to get accurate results.

The best way to explain sampling error, and a host of terms that accompany the concept, is to work our way through a hypothetical study. Suppose the Super Bowl were played yesterday and ratings analysts wanted to estimate what percent of households watched the game (i.e., the game's rating). Suppose also that exactly 50% of U.S. homes were tuned to the game. (Of course, ordinarily no one would know that, but we need to assume this knowledge to make our point.) The true population value is represented in the top half of Fig. 7.1.

To estimate the game's rating, the analysts draw a random sample of 100 households from a list of all the television households in the country. Given a complete sampling frame (unlikely, but convenient), every home has had an equal chance of being selected. Next, researchers call each home and ask if the occupants watched the game. Because they all have telephones, perfect memories, and are completely truthful (again, convenient), the team can assume they have accurately recorded what happened in the sample homes. After a few quick calculations, it appears that only 46% of those interviewed saw the game. This result is also plotted in the top half of Fig. 7.1.

Clearly, there is a problem. The best guess of how many homes saw the game is 4 percentage points lower than what was, in fact, true. In the world of media buying, 4 rating points can mean a lot of money. It should, nevertheless, be intuitively obvious that even with convenient assumptions and strict adherence to sampling procedures, such a disparity is entirely possible. In fact, it would have

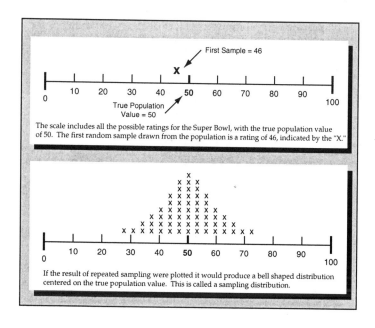

FIG. 7.1.   A sampling distribution.

been surprising to hit the nail on the head the first time. That 4-point difference does not mean anything was done wrong, it is just sampling error.

Given the luxury of a hypothetical case, assume the analysts repeat the sampling process. This time, 52% of the sample say they watched the game. This is better but still in error, and still a plausible kind of occurrence. Finally, suppose they draw 1,000 samples like the first two. Plotting the results of the sample produces a graph that would look like the lower half of Fig. 7.1.

The shape of this figure reveals a lot, and is worth considering for a moment. It is a special kind of frequency distribution that a statistician calls a *sampling distribution*. The hypothetical case forms a symmetrical, bell-shaped curve indicating that more of the sample estimates hit the true population value (i.e., 50%) than any other single value. It also indicates that although most of the estimates clustered close to 50%, a few were far off. In essence this means that when using probability sampling, reality tends to anchor the estimates and keep most of them fairly close to what is true. It also means that, sooner or later, the analyst is bound to hit one that's way off the mark.

Equally important, this sampling distribution will take on a known size and shape. The most frequently used measure of that size and shape is called the *standard error* (SE). In essence, this is the average "wrong guess" analysts are likely to make in predicting ratings. For those familiar with introductory statistics, this resembles a standard deviation. It is best conceptualized as a unit along

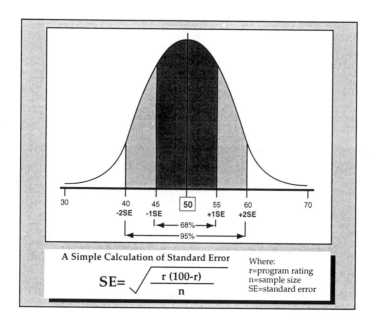

FIG. 7.2.   Relationship of standard error to sampling distribution.

the baseline of the distribution. Figure 7.2 gives the simplest formula for calculating standard error with ratings data.

What is remarkable about standard error (and what you will have to accept on faith unless you want to delve more deeply into calculus) is that when it is laid out against its parent sampling distribution, it will bracket a precise number of samples. Specifically, +/– 1 SE will always encompass 68% of the samples in the distribution; +/– 2 SE (technically, that should be 1.96), encompasses 95% of all samples. In this example, the SE works out to be approximately 5 ratings points, which means 68% of the hypothetical samples will have produced results between 45% and 55% (i.e., 50% +/– 5 percentage points). That relationship between SE and the sampling distribution is depicted in Fig. 7.2.

None of this would interest anyone other than a mathematician were it not for the fact that such reasoning provides a way to make statements about the accuracy of audience data. Remember the first sample found 46% watching the Super Bowl. Ordinarily, that would be the single best guess about what was true for the population. Recognizing the possibility of sampling error, however, analysts would want to know the odds of the true population value being something different than the estimate. Those odds could be stated using the estimated rating (i.e., 46) to calculate SE and placing a bracket around the estimate, just like the one in Fig. 7.2. Because the analysts know that 95% of all sample means would fall between +/– 2 SE, they also know that 95% of all sample means will fall between +/– 10 points in this example. The resulting statement would sound like this: "We estimate that the Super Bowl had a rating of 46, and we are 95% confident that the true rating falls between 36 and 56."

The range of values given in that statement (i.e., 36 to 56) is called the *confidence interval*. Confidence intervals are often set at +/– 2 SE and will therefore have a high probability of encompassing the true population value. When someone qualifies the results of a survey by saying something like, "These results are subject to a sampling error of plus or minus 3%," they are reporting the confidence interval. What is equally important, but less often heard, is how much confidence should be placed in that range of values. To say "we are 95% confident" is to express a *confidence level*. At the 95% level, analysts know that 95 times out of 100 the range reported will include the population value. Of course, that means that 5% of the time they will be wrong, because it is always possible the sample was one of those that was not representative. But at least the analysts can state the odds and be satisfied that an erroneous estimate is a remote possibility.

Such esoteric concepts take on practical significance, because they go to the heart of ratings accuracy. For example, reporting that a program has a rating of 15, +/– 10, leaves a lot of room for error. Even fairly small margins of error (e.g., SE = 1), can be important if the estimates they surround are themselves small (e.g., a rating of 3). That is one reason why ratings services will routinely report *relative standard error* (SE as a percentage of the estimate) rather than the absolute level of error. In any event, it becomes critically important to reduce sampling error to an acceptable level. Three factors affect the size of that error: complexity of the population, sample size, and sample design. One is beyond the control of researchers, two are not.

The source of sampling error beyond control relates to the population itself—some populations are just more complicated than others. A researcher refers to these complexities as variability or heterogeneity in the population. To take an extreme case, if everyone in the population were exactly alike (i.e., perfect homogeneity), then a sample of one person would suffice. Unfortunately, media audiences are not homogeneous, and to make matters worse, they are getting more heterogeneous all the time. Think about how television has changed over the years. Once, people could watch the three networks, maybe an independent or public station, and that was it. Now most homes have cable or VCRs, and more station choices. All other things being equal, that makes it more difficult to estimate who is watching what.

The two factors researchers can control are related to the sample itself. *Sample size* is the most obvious and important of these. Larger samples reduce the magnitude of sampling error. Common sense teaches researchers to have more confidence in results based on a sample of 1,000 than a sample of 100. What is counterintuitive is that sample size and error do not have a one-to-one relationship. Doubling sample size does not cut the SE in half. Instead, the analyst must quadruple the sample to reduce the SE by half. Consider the calculation of SE in Fig. 7.2. Reducing the SE to 2.5 from 5 requires an increase in sample size to 400 from 100. Note also that the size of the population under study has no direct impact on the error calculations. All other things being equal, small populations require samples just a big as large populations.

These aspects of sampling theory are more than curiosities. They have a substantial impact on the conduct and economics of the ratings business. Although it is always possible to improve ratings accuracy by increasing sample size, one quickly reaches a point of diminishing returns. This is nicely demonstrated in research conducted by CONTAM, an industry group formed in response to a congressional hearing of the 1960s. That study collected viewing records from more than 50,000 households around the country. From that pool, 8 sets of 100 samples were drawn. Samples in the first set had 25 households each. Sample sizes for the following sets were: 50; 100; 250; 500; 1,000; 1,500; and 2,500. The results are shown in Fig. 7.3.

At the smallest sample sizes, individual estimates of the *Flintstones* audience varied widely around the actual rating of 26. Increasing sample sizes from these low levels produced dramatic improvements in the consistency and accuracy of sample estimates, as evidenced in tighter clustering. Going from 100 to 1,000 markedly reduced sampling error and only required adding 900 households. Conversely, going from 1,000 to 2,500 resulted in a modest improvement, yet it required an increase of 1,500 households. Such relationships mean the suppliers of syndicated research and their clients have to strike a balance between the cost and accuracy of audience data.

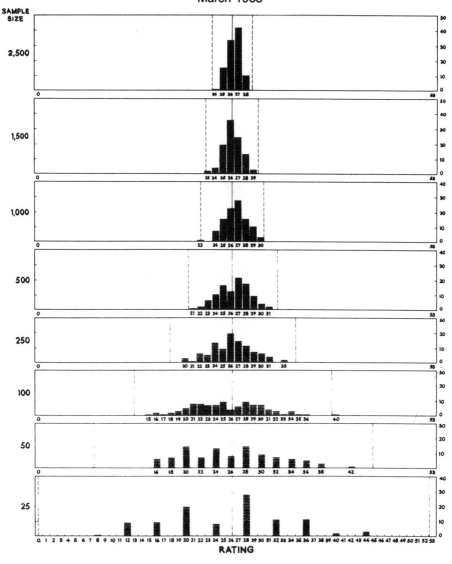

FIG. 7.3.   Effect of sample size on sampling error (from Beville, 1988).

In practice, several other factors determine the sample sizes that a research provider uses. As suggested earlier, more complex populations require larger samples to achieve a certain level of sampling error. Radio requires bigger samples than television, because there have been more radio stations to fragment the audience. Similarly, studying relatively small segments of the audience (e.g., men 18–21) requires larger overall samples. And even though larger populations do not, theoretically, need bigger samples, because of their relative complexity and the volume of media dollars available, larger markets are studied with larger samples.

The only other factor the researcher can employ to reduce sampling error is to improve the design of the sample. For reasons already discussed, certain kinds of probability samples, like stratified samples, are more accurate than others. This strategy is commonly used, but there is a limit to what can be achieved. It is also important to note that when these more complex sample designs are used, the calculation of SE becomes more involved than Fig. 7.2 indicates. We address those revised computations later.

Nonresponse Error.   This is the second major source of error encountered in the context of sampling. Not everyone analysts might wish to study will cooperate or respond. Although the discussion of sampling error assumed everyone in the sample supplied the desired information, in the real world that does not happen. To the extent that those who do not respond are different from those who do, there is a possibility that samples may be biased. Many of the procedures that the ratings services use represent attempts to correct nonresponse error

The magnitude of nonresponse error varies from one ratings report to the next. The best way to get a sense of it is to look at the response rates reported by the ratings service. All ratings company analysts identify an original sample of people or households they wish to use in the preparation of ratings estimates. This ideal sample is usually called the *initially designated sample*. Some members of the designated sample, however, will refuse to cooperate; others will agree to be in the sample, but then fail to provide complete information. In short, many will not respond as hoped.

Only those who do respond can be used to tabulate the data. The latter group constitutes what is called the *in-tab sample*. The *response rate* is simply the percent of people from the initially designated sample who actually gave the ratings company useful information. Different techniques for gathering ratings data are associated with different response rates. Telephone surveys, for example, tend to have relatively high response rates. The most common measurement techniques, like placing diaries or meters, will often produce response rates of 50% or less. Furthermore, different measurement techniques work better with some kinds of people than others. The nonresponse errors associated with measurement are discussed in the next section.

Because nonresponse error can bias ratings, research companies employ one of two general strategies to minimize or control it. First, they take action before the fact to improve the representativeness of the in-tab sample. Second, they adjust the sample after data have been collected. Usually both strategies are employed. Either way, the analyst must know what the population looks like to judge the representativeness of the in-tab sample and to gauge the adjustments to be made.

Population or universe estimates, therefore, are essential in correcting for nonresponse error. Determining what the population looks like (i.e., age and gender breakdowns, etc.) is usually done with U.S. Census information. Although the Census is updated every 10 years, parts are revised, based on sampling, more frequently. Ratings companies often buy current universe estimates from other research companies. Market Statistics, Inc. is one such company that has supplied both Arbitron and Nielsen. Occasionally, certain attributes of the population that have not been measured by the Census Bureau, like cable penetration, must be estimated. To do this, it may be necessary to conduct a special *enumeration study* that establishes important universe estimates.

Once the targets are defined, corrections for nonresponse error can be made. Before-the-fact remedies include special recruitment techniques and buffer samples. The optimal solution is to entice cooperation from as many of those in the originally designated sample as possible. This requires a deep understanding of the reasons for nonresponse plus effective counteractive measures. Ratings services, for example, often provide sample members with monetary incentives. Different types of incentives will work better or worse with different types of people. Following up on initial contacts or making sure that interviewers and research materials use the respondent's primary language will also improve response rates. Managers at the major ratings companies are aware of these alternatives, and on the basis of experience, know where they are likely to encounter nonresponse problems. They sometimes use special recruitment techniques to improve, for example, minority representation in the sample.

If improved recruitment fails, additional sampling can increase underrepresented groups. *Buffer samples* are randomly generated lists of additional households held in reserve. If, as sampling progresses, it becomes apparent that responses in one county are lagging behind expectations, the appropriate buffer sample can be employed to increase the size of the sample drawn from that area. Field workers might use a similar procedure if they encounter an uncooperative household. They would probably have instructions to sample a second household in the same neighborhood, perhaps even matching the key attributes of the original household.

Once data are collected, another technique can be used to adjust for nonresponders. *Sample weighting,* sometimes called *sample balancing,* is a statistical procedure that gives the responses of certain kinds of people more influence in the ratings estimates than their numbers in the sample would suggest. Basically, the ratings companies compare the in-tab sample and the universe estimates (usually on geographic, ethnic, age, and gender breakdowns), and determine where they have too many of one kind of person and not enough of another. Suppose, for example, that 18- to 24-year-old men accounted for 6% of the population, but only 3% of the in-tab sample. One remedy would be to count the responses of each young man in the in-tab twice. Conversely, the responses of overrepresented groups would count less than once. The way to determine the appropriate weight for any particular group is to divide their proportion in the population by their proportion in the sample (e.g., 6% / 3% = 2).

Buffer samples or weighted samples are inadequate solutions to nonresponse. Although these procedures can make in-tab samples look like the universe, they do not eliminate nonresponse error. The people who are drawn through buffer samples or whose responses count more than once might still be systematically different from those who did not cooperate. That's why some people question the use of these techniques. Failing to make these adjustments, though, also distorts results. For example, a programmer at a radio station that catered to 18- to 24-year-old men would be unhappy that they tend to be underrepresented in most in-tab samples, and would probably welcome the kind of weighting just described, flaws and all. Today, the accepted industry practice is to weight samples. (We return to this topic when we discuss the process of producing the ratings.)

Because of nonresponse error—and certain techniques used to correct for such error—the ratings services actually use imperfect probability samples. That fact, in combination with the use of complex sample designs, means that calculations of standard error are more involved than the earlier discussion indicated. Without going into detail, suffice it to say that error is affected by the weights in the sample, whether analysts are dealing with households or persons, and whether they are estimating the audience at a point in time or the average audience over a number of time periods. Furthermore, actual in-tab sample sizes are not used in calculating error. Rather, the ratings services derive *effective sample sizes* for purposes of calculating SE. These take into account the fact that their samples are not simple random samples. Effective sample sizes may be smaller than, equal to, or larger than actual sample sizes. No matter the method for calculating SE, however, the use and interpretation of that number is as described earlier.

MEASUREMENT

While sampling methodology is essential to audience research, methods of measurement are just as important. It is one thing to create a sample by identifying who should be studied, and another to measure audience activity by recording what they see on television or hear on radio.

Technically, *measurement* is defined as a process of assigning numbers to objects according to rules of assignment. The objects the audience research analysts are usually measuring are people, although households can also be the unit of analysis. The numbers simply quantify the characteristics or behaviors under study, which simplifies managing relevant information and summarizing sample attributes. For example, if a person saw the CBS *Evening News* last night, an analyst might assign him or her a "1." Those who did not see the news might be assigned a "0." Reporting the percentage of 1s could produce a rating for the CBS news. The numbering scheme actually used is more complicated than that, but in essence, that is what happens.

Researchers who specialize in measurement are concerned with the accuracy of the numbering scheme they use. After all, anyone can assign numbers to things, but capturing something meaningful with those numbers is more difficult. Researchers express their concerns about the accuracy of a measurement technique with two concepts: *reliability* and *validity*. Reliability is the extent to which a procedure will repeatedly produce consistent results. If the object of measurement does not change, an accurate measuring device should assign the same number time after time. So, the measure is said to be reliable. Just because a measurement procedure is reliable, however, does not mean it is accurate. It must also be valid.

Validity is the extent to which a measure actually quantifies the characteristic under examination. For instance, to measure a person's program preferences, an analyst might record which shows he or she watches most frequently. This approach might produce a very consistent, or reliable, pattern. However, it does not necessarily follow that the program a person sees most often is his or her favorite. Scheduling, rather than preference, might produce such results. Therefore, measuring preferences by using a person's program choices could be reliable but not particularly valid.

What Is Being Measured?

One of the first questions involved in assessing measurement techniques is, "What are you trying to measure?" Confusion on this point has led to many misunderstandings about ratings data. At first glance, the answer seems simple enough. Ratings measure exposure to the electronic media. But even that definition leaves much unsaid. Two factors need to be considered: (a) What do we mean by "media"? and (b) what constitutes exposure?

Defining the media side of the equation raises a number of possibilities. It might be, for example, that there is no interest in the audience for specific program content. As noted in chapter 5, some effects researchers are concerned only with how much television people watch overall. But knowing the amount of exposure to a medium, though useful in some applications, is not particularly relevant to advertisers. Radio station audiences and, to a certain extent, cable network audiences, are reported this way. Here the medium may be no more precisely defined than attendance during a broad daypart or an average quarter hour.

In television ratings, exposure is usually tied to a specific program, although questions concerning definition can still be raised. How much of a program must people see before they are included in that program's audience? If a few minutes are enough, then the total audience for the show will probably be larger than the audience at any moment. Some measurement techniques (discussed in the following section) are too insensitive to make such minute-to-minute determinations, but, for other approaches, this consideration is important.

Advertisers are most interested in who sees their commercials. To them, the most relevant way to define the media is not program content but commercial content. Such "commercial ratings" are not routinely produced by the major ratings services, but newer measurement technologies raise the possibility that audiences for brief commercial messages could be quantified. SRI's SMART, for example, could provide viewing data for 10-second intervals.

The other aspect of this question is the meaning of exposure. *Exposure* is usually defined as viewer choice of a particular station or program—the only thing relevant is who is present when the set is in use. In fact, some measurement techniques are incapable of recording who is in the room. Once it has been determined that audience members have tuned to a particular station, further questions about the quality of exposure are left unanswered.

It is well documented, however, that media use is often accompanied by other activities. People may read, talk, eat, play games, or do the dishes while the set is in use. During a large portion of the time that people are in the audience, they are paying little attention. This leads researchers to argue that defining exposure as a matter of choice overstates people's real exposure to the media. An alternative would be to stipulate that "exposure" requires that a person is paying attention to the media, or perhaps even understanding what is seen or heard. However, measuring a person's level of attention or perception is extremely difficult to do in an efficient, valid way.

Another shortcoming critics of the ratings services have raised from time to time is that operational definitions of exposure reveal nothing about the quality of the experience in an affective sense. Do people like what they see, or find it informative and enlightening? *Qualitative ratings* such as these have been produced on an irregular basis, not as a substitute for existing services, but rather as a supplement. In the early 1980s, the Corporation for Public Broadcasting, in collaboration with Arbitron, conducted field tests of such a system. Another effort was initiated by an independent Boston-based company named Television Audience Assessment, which tried selling qualitative ratings information. That effort failed, and at present, there does not seem to be enough demand for this particular type of qualitative information to sustain its continuous production, though it is more common in some European countries.

The question of how to define exposure is a key concern with the measurement of Internet audiences. Some argue that the presence of a banner advertisement on a Web page served to a user is sufficient "exposure" to warrant counting. Others contend that exposure can only be truly recorded when a viewer clicks on the message to receive more information. It remains to be seen how the industry will ultimately define it.

Obviously, these questions of definition help determine what the data really are and how they are to be interpreted. If different ratings companies used vastly different definitions of exposure to media, their cost structures and research products might be quite different as well. The significance of these issues has not been lost on the affected industries. In 1954, the Advertising Research Foundation (ARF), released a set of recommendations on many of these concerns. In addition to advocating the use of probability samples, ARF recommended that tuning behavior be the accepted definition of exposure. That standard has been the most widely accepted and has effectively guided the development of the measurement techniques used today.

Measurement Techniques

Ratings services use several techniques to measure people's exposure to electronic media, and each has advantages and disadvantages. The biases inherent in these techniques contribute to the third kind of error mentioned earlier, response error. *Response error* includes inaccuracies contained in the responses generated by the measurement procedure. To illustrate these biases, we consider each major approach to audience measurement in general terms. (To avoid getting bogged down in details, we may gloss over differences in how each ratings company operationalizes a particular scheme of measurement. Here again, the reader wishing more information should see each company's description of methodology.)

Diaries. Diaries are the most widely used of all measurement techniques. Although they are no longer employed to estimate national network audiences, huge numbers of diaries are used to determine local radio and television audiences. In one television ratings sweep alone, Nielsen will gather diaries from 100,000 respondents to produce audience estimates in all the markets around the country.

A diary is a paper booklet containing a record of media use for a 1-week period. To produce television ratings, one diary is kept for each TV set in the household. Figure 7.4 illustrates the first page from a Nielsen television diary. It begins on Thursday at 6:00 a.m. and thereafter divides the day into quarter-hour segments ending a 2:00 a.m. Each of the remaining days of the week is similarly divided. During each quarter hour a set is in use, the diary keeper is expected to note the relevant call letters, channel number, and program title, as

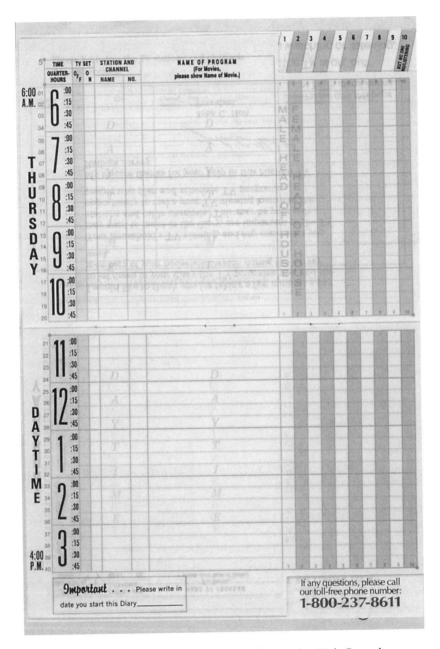

FIG. 7.4. Sample of a Nielsen television diary. Source: Nielsen Media Research.

well as which family members and/or visitors are watching. The diary also includes additional questions about household composition and the channels received in the home. One major limitation to this method is that the viewing is tied to a set rather than to a person, so out-of home viewing may be significantly understated.

Radio audiences are also measured with diaries, but these diaries are supposed to accompany people rather than sets. That way, an individual can record listening that occurs outside the home. Figure 7.5 shows the first page of an Arbitron radio diary. It begins on Thursday, and divides the day into broader dayparts than the rigid quarter-hour increments of the TV diary. Because a radio diary is a personal record, the diary keeper does not note whether other people were listening. The location of listening, however, is recorded.

Diary placement and retrieval techniques vary, but the usual practice goes something like this. The ratings company representatives call members of the originally designated sample on the telephone to secure the respondent's cooperation, and collect some initial information. Those who are to be excluded (e.g., people living in group quarters), or those who will receive special treatment (e.g., Spanish-speaking households) are identified at this stage. Follow-up letters may be sent to households that have agreed to cooperate. Diaries are then either mailed or delivered to the home in person by field personnel. Incidentally, although respondents are asked to cooperate, diaries are often distributed to those who say they are not interested in cooperating. And the response rate is just about as high for those who initially say they are unwilling as for those who agree.

Often a monetary incentive of $1 or so is provided as a gesture of goodwill, but goodwill is more likely to be used in certain markets that have traditionally had lower response rates. During the week, another letter or phone call may encourage the diary keeper to note his or her media use. Diaries are designed to be sealed and placed directly in the mail, which is typically how the diary is returned to the ratings company at the end of the week. Occasionally, a second monetary reward follows the return of the diary. In some special cases, homes are called and the diary information is collected via telephone.

Diaries have significant advantages that account for their popularity. They offer a relatively inexpensive method of data collection. Considering the wealth of information that a properly completed diary contains, none of the techniques discussed here is as cost effective. Most important, diaries report which people were actually in the audience. In fact, until 1987, diaries were used in conjunction with expensive metering techniques to determine the demographic composition of the national television audience. Even if the newer peoplemeters become the standard in large media markets, it seems likely that diaries will continue to be used locally.

Nevertheless, there are problems associated with diaries, problems of both nonresponse and response error. We have already discussed nonresponse error in the context of sampling. It should be noted, however, that diaries are particu-

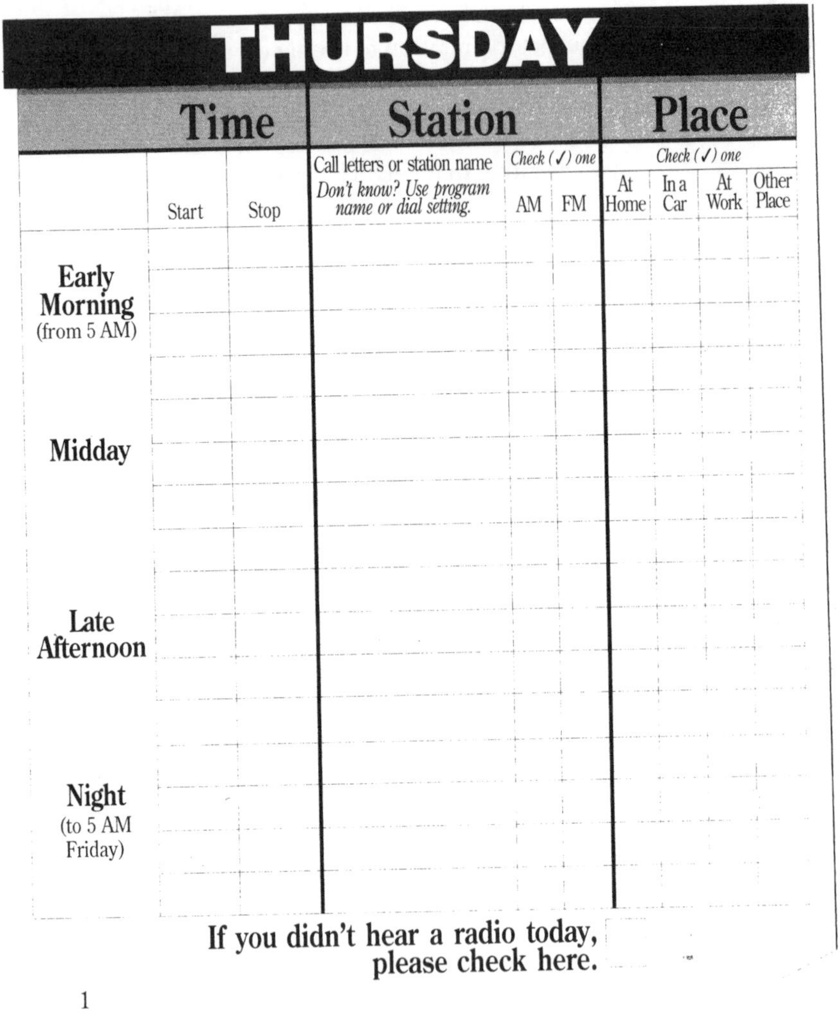

THURSDAY

Time			Station			Place			
			Call letters or station name	Check (✓) one		Check (✓) one			
	Start	Stop	Don't know? Use program name or dial setting.	AM	FM	At Home	In a Car	At Work	Other Place
Early Morning (from 5 AM)									
Midday									
Late Afternoon									
Night (to 5 AM Friday)									

If you didn't hear a radio today, please check here.

1

FIG. 7.5. Sample of an Arbitron radio diary. Courtesy of the Arbitron Company.

larly troublesome in this regard. Response rates on the order of 40% are common, and in some markets will drop below that. Obviously, diarykeepers must be literate, but methodological research undertaken by industry personnel suggests those who fill out and return diaries are systematically different in other ways. Younger people, especially younger males, are less responsive to the diary technique. Blacks, too, are less likely to complete and return a diary. There is also evidence that those who return a television diary are heavier users of the medium than nonrespondents.

A number of response errors are also typical of diary data. There is anecdotal evidence that indicates diarykeepers frequently do not note their media use as it occurs but try to recollect it at the end of the day or the week. To the extent that entries are delayed, errors of memory are more likely. Similarly, it appears that diarykeepers are more diligent in the first few days of the measurement period than the last. This *diary fatigue* may artificially depress viewing or listening levels on Tuesdays and Wednesdays. Viewing during late night, viewing of short duration, viewing of less well-known programming, and viewing of secondary sets (e.g., in bedrooms, etc.) is typically underreported. Children's use of the television is also likely to go unreported if they watch at times when an adult diarykeeper is not present.

These are significant, if fairly benign, sources of response error. There is less evidence on the extent to which people deliberately distort reports of their viewing or listening behavior. Most Americans seem to have a sense of what ratings data are and how they can affect programming decisions. Again, anecdotal evidence suggests that people view participation in a ratings sample as an opportunity to vote for deserving programs, whether they are actually in the audience or not. While diary data may be more susceptible to such distortions than other methods, instances of deliberate deception, although real, are probably limited in scope.

A more serious problem with diary-based measurement techniques has emerged in recent years, because the television viewing environment has become increasingly complex. Most homes now subscribe to cable and/or have a VCR attached to a TV set. In addition, remote control devices have become commonplace, as have small highly portable sets. These technological changes make the job of keeping an accurate diary more burdensome than ever. A viewer who has flipped through 20 channels to find something of interest may not know the channel to which he or she is tuned. Even if viewers record the channel indicated by the set, they may be in error because cable systems often change channel designations of an over-the-air station. These changes are difficult to track, although Nielsen gives each home a list of cable systems and channel numbers to improve the accuracy of diary entries. For reasons such as these, it is generally acknowledged that diaries underreport the audience for most cable networks and independent television stations. Other measurement techniques, however, can be used to compensate for these shortcomings.

Household Meters. The best known metering device is Nielsen's Audimeter, an important alternative to diary-based audience measurements. The original Audimeter recorded radio listening and required Nielsen field representatives to go to homes equipped with these devices to retrieve their contents. Later, the record of radio or TV tuning, recorded on motion picture film, was mailed back to the Nielsen office in Chicago. Today, meters are more sophisticated and used only to record TV usage and channel tuning.

Modern meters are essentially small computers attached to all of the television sets in a home. They perform a number of functions, the most important of which is monitoring set activity. The meter records when the set is on and the channel to which it is tuned. This information is typically stored in a separate unit hidden in some unobtrusive location. The data it contains in memory are retrieved through a telephone line and downloaded to Nielsen's computers.

For years, that was the scope of metering activity, and as such, it had enormous advantages over diary measurement. It eliminated much of the human error inherent in diarykeeping. Viewing was recorded as it occurred. Even exposure of brief duration could be accurately recorded. Members of the sample did not have to be literate. In fact, they did not have to do anything at all, so no fatigue factor entered the picture. Because information was electronically recorded, it could also be collected and processed much more rapidly than paper-and-pencil diaries. Reports on yesterday's program audiences, called the *overnights*, could be delivered.

There were only two major shortcomings to this sort of metering. First, it was expensive to manufacture, install, and maintain the hardware necessary to make such a system work. That is still true today. As a practical matter, this means that metered measurement is viable only in relatively large media markets (i.e., nationally or in large urban areas). Second, household meters could provide no information on who was watching, save for what could be inferred from general household characteristics. The need to provide "people information," so essential to advertisers, has caused dramatic changes in how meters now function, at least at the national level.

Peoplemeters. Meters capable of generating individual-level data had been under development in the United States and abroad for some time, but in fall 1987, Nielsen began using them to generate national network ratings. Peoplemeters do everything conventional household meters do and more. Every member of the sample household is assigned a number that corresponds to a button on the metering device. When a person begins viewing, he or she is expected to press a pre-assigned button on the meter. The button is again pressed when the person leaves the room. When the channel is changed, a light on the meter flashes until viewers reaffirm their presence. All systems have handheld units, about the size of a TV remote control, that allow people to enter selections from remote locations in the room.

As with conventional meters, data are retrieved via telephone lines. At that point, all the button-pushing and set-tuning activity can be combined with data stored in a central computer to create people ratings. The introduction of peoplemeters triggered a storm of controversy about the method of measurement, and the samples on which it was based. As a relative newcomer, the merits and biases of this measurement technique are in somewhat greater doubt than more established techniques. Nevertheless, a number of generalizations and concerns seem warranted. These can, again, be categorized as issues of nonresponse and response error.

As is the case with diaries, a great many people who are sampled refuse to accept a peoplemeter. Both Nielsen and AGB, while in operation, experienced initial acceptance rates on the order of 50% to 60%. One potential deterrent to cooperation from families is the actual installation of the equipment, which requires wiring the set in the home. As always, the question is, "Are those who participate systematically different from those who do not?" For example, although peoplemeters do not impose a formal literacy requirement, some have speculated that there is a kind of technological literacy required of respondents. The broadcast network executives, who have seen their audience shares decline with the introduction of peoplemeters, have also criticized peoplemeter samples for overrepresenting those who subscribe to cable services. Moreover, lapses in button pushing and hardware failures reduce the effective in-tab samples on a day-to-day basis.

A number of response errors are associated with peoplemeters as well. Most notably, the meters are believed to underrepresent viewing by children. Youngsters, it seems, are not terribly conscientious button-pushers. More generally, there is concern about button-pushing fatigue. How, for example, does one interpret instances in which the set is on but no one is reported watching? Conventional meters once remained in households for 5 years. Doubts about the long-term diligence of peoplemetered homes, as well as pressure from the television networks, have caused Nielsen to rotate these households after only 2 years. Even so, some critics still believe current metering methods are flawed.

Many of these problems could be solved if, like the old meters, peoplemeters required no effort on the part of respondents. The ideal device would be unobtrusive yet capable of detecting specific individuals within the room. These devices, called *passive peoplemeters*, have been under development for some time, but none has overcome the problems inherent in the technology. Three technologies hold promise, though. Infrared sensors will detect heat sources, like human beings, in the room. The problem has been discriminating between different individuals, or for that matter, between dogs and children. As an alternative, sonic sensing devices could detect movement in the room. Here again, discrimination is a problem: how to distinguish between a moving person and a curtain blowing in the breeze.

The most promising technology for creating a passive meter is a computerized image-recognition system. One system, being developed by Nielsen, translates a person's image into a set of distinguishing features stored in a computerized memory. The system scans a pre-defined visual field and compares the objects encountered with memory to identify family members or visitors. Pictures of viewers, per se, are not stored or reported, only the incidence of recognized images.

Advancements in metering technology have created new possibilities for measuring audience behavior. For example, new meters can monitor VCR use, an important attribute, because 4 out of 5 American households own a VCR. The system introduced by AGB worked by fingerprinting a tape while recording. An electronic code, laid down on an unused portion of the video signal, noted the date and channel being recorded by the VCR. The fingerprint also imposed a running clock on the tape. When the tape was replayed, the meter could determine when the program originally aired, and which sections of the show were played in fast-forward. The latter information is of special importance to advertisers, because many people zip or zap commercials during replay.

Internet Measurement Software. *Internet measurement software* is a data collection methodology used by organizations like Media Metrix to monitor on-line computer usage. Respondents download software that records Web and other Internet activity, and the data are returned to a central location for processing. The system generates an overwhelming amount of information, which is condensed into monthly reports for subscribers.

The obvious disadvantage to this methodology is that users might be reluctant to allow software to run resident on their computers. Privacy is a significant concern when every action is monitored with such precision. It is very likely that people who allow this technology into their home will differ from people who do not want it installed. And even if they don't differ in terms of demographic profile, the presence of this monitoring technology might influence their choices when they use the Internet. Another problem is that a great deal of Internet usage occurs in the workplace. If employers are reluctant to allow this software to run on their equipment, then the respondent base will be biased in favor of home use.

Interviews. *Interviews* are one of the oldest formal methods of data collection used by ratings services. As described in chapter 6, phone interviews formed the mainstay of the ratings industry at its inception. Still used today, they are the standard against which other methods of measurement are judged. Data collection over the telephone takes one of two forms: recall or coincidental.

Telephone recall requires respondents to remember what they have seen or heard over some period of time. Two factors affect the quality of recalled information. One is how far back a person is required to remember—the more removed from the present, the more it is subject to memory error. Second is the salience of the behavior in question. Important or regular occurrences are better remembered than trivial or sporadic events. Because most people's radio listening tends to be regular and involve only one or two stations, it is believed that the medium's use can be accurately studied with telephone recall techniques.

SRI researchers base their RADAR® reports on a random sample of respondents who are asked to report recent radio listening. Interviewers ask questions that identify listening at specific times within specific dayparts. If a respondent does not know a station's call letters, other identifying information, like a station's frequency or slogan, can be used. SRI interviewers contact a person once each day for a week, asking about radio use from the time of the previous contact to the present. It is important for the research analyst to keep in mind that there are several possible variations within this recall technique. For example, Birch Radio used telephone recall, but the approach was to interview respondents only once, asking about the prior day's listening. The two methods, although following a similar overall design, will yield very different kinds of listening data.

Telephone recall techniques have some advantages compared to the major alternative, radio diaries. First, telephone interviewing achieves higher levels of cooperation. RADAR® has reported response rates as high as 55% to 65%. Although people without telephones are, by definition, excluded, overall higher response rates reduce the likelihood of nonresponse error. Second, because respondents are verbally questioned, there is no literacy bias in the method. If a Hispanic household is sampled, a Spanish-speaking interviewer can be employed. Third, because the research firm takes the initiative by calling respondents each day, there is no end-of-the-week diary fatigue. Fourth, telephone techniques are well suited to gathering data from younger listeners who tend to be poor diary keepers.

Like all other methods of data collection, however, telephone recall has limitations. If people are only questioned about their previous day's listening, week-long patterns of audience accumulation can only be inferred from mathematical models (see chap. 11, this volume). The use of interviewers can also introduce error. Although interviewers are usually trained and monitored in centralized telephone centers, they can make inappropriate comments or other errors that bias results. Finally, the entire method is no better than a respondent's memory. Even though people are only expected to recall yesterday's listening, there is no guarantee that they can accurately do so.

As C. E. Hooper argued in the 1940s, *telephone coincidentals* offer a way to overcome problems of memory. These surveys work very much like telephone recall techniques, except that the questioners ask respondents to report what they are seeing or listening to at the moment of the call. Because respondents can verify exactly who is using what media at the time, errors of memory and reporting fatigue are eliminated. For these reasons, telephone coincidentals are widely regarded as the standard against which other methods of measurement should be evaluated. Most new measurement techniques, therefore, are obliged to offer a comparison of their results with a concurrently executed telephone coincidental.

Despite this acknowledged superiority, no major ratings company routinely conducts telephone coincidental research. There are two problems with

TABLE 7.1

Summary of Major Methods of Audience Measurement

	Advantages	Disadvantages
Telephone recall	Immediacy of data collection Personal contact with respondent Generally higher response rates than other methods	Memory problems Deliberate misrepresentation Limited times when researcher can call the home Biased sample—some homes don't have phones Costly method
Telephone coincidental	Less chance for deliberate misrepresentation No memory problems Immediacy of data collection Personal contact with respondent Generally higher response rates than other methods	Limited times when researcher can call the home Biased sample—some homes don't have phones Costly method
Diaries	Less costly than other research methods Potential to collect detailed information including demographics Non-intrusive, completed at respondents' convenience	Time lag to collect and process the data Memory problems Deliberate misrepresentation Literacy requirement Error prone in complex media environments Lower response rates
Household (passive) meters	Fast turnaround Accuracy—only records when set is on No literacy requirement Requires no effort on the part of respondent Higher response rates than other methods	Cost—expensive to make, install & maintain Household level data tells nothing about individual people Installation requirements may deter participants and consequently bias the sample May require matching program log information to meter data for program specific information Low turnover of sample means same households could be surveyed for up to 5 years

continued on next page

	Advantages	Disadvantages
Peoplemeters	Accuracy—only records when set is on Fast turnaround Records actual program viewing with electronic codes No literacy requirement Continuous measurement allows for analysis of short time periods Demographic data available	Cost—expensive to make, install & maintain Requires active participation on the part of respondents (high burnout) Button-pushing, especially by children, may be unreliable Intrusiveness of technology may deter participation and bias the sample Low turnover of sample means same people can be measured for up to 2 years
PC Meter	Option to run software resident on the computer so respondent does not have to deal with technology Provides continuous record of Internet (or Web) activity	Sample bias due to privacy concerns Awareness of metering may alter respondents' behavior Expensive system to design and maintain

coincidentals that militate against their regular use. First, a coincidental inter-view captures only a glimpse of a person's media use. It sacrifices quantity for quality. As a result, to describe audiences hour to hour, day to day, and week to week, huge numbers of people would have to be called around the clock, a very expensive proposition. Second, as with all telephone interviews, there are prac-tical limitations on where and when calls can be made. Much radio listening oc-curs in cars lacking cellular phones, and much television viewing occurs late at night, when it would be inappropriate to call. These behaviors cannot be cap-tured with strictly coincidental techniques. For these, and other reasons, the coincidental telephone method is no longer used for any regular rating service.

These methods of audience measurement in the electronic media are sum-marized in Table 7.1. Obviously, this discussion does not exhaust the possibili-ties for data collection. Data could be collected by monitoring television-set use on specially designed cable systems or scanning the airwaves with radar-like de-vices that determine how nearby sets are tuned. Some researchers have sug-gested replacing conventional diaries with pager-like portable meters. Because major U.S. producers of audience research are not currently using these meth-ods, we do not delve into their advantages and drawbacks here.

RELATED READINGS

Anderson, J. A. (1987). *Communication research: Issues and methods*. New York: McGraw-Hill.

Babbie, E. (1995). *The practice of social research* (7th ed.). Belmont, CA: Wadsworth.

Beville, H. M. (1988). *Audience ratings: Radio, television, cable* (rev. ed.). Hillsdale, NJ: Lawrence Erlbaum Associates.

Churchill, G. A. (1995). *Marketing research: Methodological foundations* (6th ed.). Fort Worth, TX: Dryden Press.

Fletcher, A. D., & Bower, T. A. (1988). *Fundamentals of advertising research* (3rd ed.). Belmont, CA: Wadsworth.

Wimmer, R. D., & Dominick, J. R. (1997). *Mass media research: An introduction* (5th ed.). Belmont, CA: Wadsworth.

8

Ratings Research Products

Often I read articles that make it clear to me the writer doesn't understand the most basic differences between national ratings, overnight meter ratings and full sweeps ratings.
　　　—Moira Farrell, SVP, Research, King World (*Electronic Media*, 3/9/98 p. 9)

When it comes to audience research, the old cliché that you can't believe everything you hear applies with a vengeance. Some users of ratings data don't acknowledge that audience information is produced and analyzed in ways that affect its meaning. Whether this is the fault of a journalist who doesn't know the subtleties of audience measurement, or a researcher who spins the data to deliberately misstate a case, the user of ratings information needs to know the source of an estimate to interpret it correctly. Basic questions about which population is being measured, sample characteristics, and collection methodologies must be asked before data can be thoroughly understood.

Up to this point we have concentrated on the evolution of audience measurement firms, and how they collect data. However, like any commercial enterprise, research companies must produce goods or services that can be sold in the marketplace. This means converting a sea of data into manageable information that clients can use for decision making. The result is an array of ratings reports and services. In this chapter, we consider some of the products the ratings companies offer for sale.

The enormous databases that research firms compile equip them to create more reports than can possibly be reviewed in one short chapter. Moreover, the number of products is on the rise, as ratings data are combined with other sources of information and as computers facilitate new ways to manipulate, merge, and present the data. Both the data and the formats in which they are presented evolve constantly. In light of this, our description provides only selected examples of the better known and more widely used reports and services. By concentrating on these, we can acquaint the reader with the most common report formats and demonstrate how some of the research concepts introduced in the previous chapter emerge in the context of an actual ratings report. We leave it to our readers to explore for themselves the many variations on a theme that the ratings services offer.

The most influential consumers of audience research are those who buy and sell time. Although other users of ratings data are certainly important, this group is critical in terms of product development. For that reason, it makes sense to organize ratings products by the advertising markets they are intended to serve. As described in chapter 2, the local market is comprised of broadcast stations and cable systems; the national market includes networks and syndicators. We deal with the Internet separately, since this nontraditional technology is not limited by geographic definitions of market used by broadcasting and cable. Before discussing the individual research products in each of these markets, we consider the general effects of production procedures on the content of audience research reports.

FROM DATA TO SALABLE COMMODITY

As discussed in the previous chapter, issues of sampling and measurement are well known to survey researchers, and there are large bodies of academic literature offering research and theory on these topics. There are well-established criteria by which to judge the work of the ratings services. But sampling and measurement alone do not make a ratings book. The data collected by these methods must undergo a production process, just as other raw materials are turned into products. Standards of what is or is not appropriate are harder to define. Yet, no discussion of ratings methods would be complete without mention of the production process. Every research company does things differently, but the basic process involves three activities: editing the data, adding new information, and making projections.

Editing

Audience measurement companies are flooded with data that must be digested and turned into useful products. Diaries are among the most difficult data sources to process. Hundreds of thousands of handwritten diaries arrive at Arbitron and Nielsen each measurement period. They must be checked for accuracy, logical inconsistencies, and omissions. They must also be converted into computer form. The process of getting clean, accurate, complete data ready to be processed is called *editing.* It can be a laborious activity and, despite serious efforts at quality control, it is here that *processing error* is most likely to be introduced.

Diary editing involves a number of activities performed by people and machines. First, it must be determined that a returned diary is usable. It might, for example, have been filled out in the wrong week, mailed too late to be useful, or simply be incomplete. It must be logical and consistent. When transferring entries into computer data, operators use aids in the computer program that allow them to check station call letters in each market, as well as program titles, station slogans, and other information. Suppose that a television diary reports someone watched a program, but it lists the wrong channel number or call letters. Strict editing procedures will usually prescribe a way to resolve these discrepancies.

What if information is just plain missing? Rather than discard an otherwise usable diary, research companies will often fill in the blanks through a process called *ascription*. These procedures typically use computer routines to determine the answer with the highest probability of correctly filling that blank. For example, if Nielsen receives a diary with the age of the male head of household (e.g., 31), but not the age of the female head of household, it consults age and gender tables, and "guesses" her age would be 3 years lower than her husband's (i.e., 28). Analogous ascription techniques are used to determine the identity of stations heard or the duration of media use if such data are missing. While these practices strike some as questionable or improper, ascription is typically based on systematic methodological research and is a standard procedure in virtually all survey work.

Editing can also involve questions of definition. Take, for instance, data recorded by a meter. If a person watches less than half a program, should they nonetheless be included in the program's total audience? The standard practice in television viewing has been to credit one quarter hour of viewing to a program if at least 5 minutes of use has taken place. Under that definition, of course, a person might show up in more than one program audience in a given quarter hour. Similarly, RADAR® credits a listener to a commercial on a radio network if he or she heard the radio for at least 3 minutes in a quarter-hour period and identifies the station on which the commercial was broadcast some time during that quarter hour.

Often there is no clear right or wrong answer to such questions. It is more a matter of what the industry will agree to accept. As media and measurement technologies change, new questions arise, and new solutions must be negotiated by the parties at interest. If a household watches one program but tapes a second one on the VCR, should that household be credited to the second program's audience? At present, the answer is yes. The ratings services treat that household as if it had viewed the program at the time it aired. If a household is viewing a picture within a picture, then viewing is credited to whichever channel is being heard. Obviously, there are other ways to credit the audience for the taped programs and multiple pictures. The resolution of these questions is sometimes arbitrary. If, however, some party feels disadvantaged by a particular editing procedure, it may become the subject of a political struggle within the industry.

Programs, Schedules, and Other Information

Despite the vast amounts of information collected by diaries, meters, and telephone calls, these data alone are insufficient to produce audience ratings. Other information must be added to make a complete, usable product. The most important addition to data on people's set-tuning behavior is information about the programming on those sets. At the local level, the accuracy of diary entries is checked against station schedules. Furthermore, even the most sophisticated passive household meter is incapable of determining what program was on which channel at what time. These data must be collected and added to the ratings database.

Because radio listening is generally credited to stations rather than to specific programs, the problem is comparatively simple. Arbitron mails radio stations a "Station Information Packet," in which stations verify their call letters and report their network affiliations, broadcast schedules, and current slogans, catch phrases, and station identifications (e.g., 96 Rock, News Radio 88, All News 67, Continuous Country, Z 104, and 98 FM). There are frequent arguments and occasional lawsuits over who is entitled to phrases such as "More Music" or "Music Radio." If two stations in nearby markets broadcast at 102.7 and 103.1, there may be confusion if both use "one-oh-three" in their phrase. It is useful for station personnel or consultants to look at diaries in order to identify uncredited listeners. As we noted in chapter 3, they also find it useful to read specific comments written by listeners.

Television viewing, on the other hand, must be associated with very specific programs, so more detailed information is needed. Ratings companies obtain this by having stations complete program title logs. These require the station to report the programs airing in every quarter hour, of every broadcast day, for every day of the week, across all survey weeks. Handling program schedules like these would be problem enough, but the growth of television technologies has expanded the problem. For example, there are about 10,000 cable systems in the United States. A majority of these have more than 30 channels of programming, including dozens of cable networks, access channels, and local stations—the latter sometimes from several different TV market areas. Different cable systems can, and do, carry these services on different channels. Even local TV stations may be reassigned to a new channel number. In any television market area, there may be several such cable systems—frequently using different channel assignments. Imagine that situation repeated in various markets around the country. This is what confronts a TV ratings service.

The job of figuring out what is on TV would be easier if each program contained a signature that a machine could simply read. As discussed in chapter 6, this is precisely what SRI and Nielsen are attempting to do. The broadcast networks have cooperated with Nielsen for several years by imposing a special electronic code in the video portion of their broadcast signal. This system, called the *Automated Measurement of Lineups (AMOL)* allows detection devices in each market to determine when affiliates are broadcasting a network program. Unfortunately, not all programs (e.g., local productions, some network reruns, and some syndication) contain such an electronic code, so more traditional techniques must still be employed.

In addition to programming information, other data enter into the production of ratings reports. For example, stations occasionally have technical difficulties that affect audience ratings. These are reported in the ratings books. Stations may also engage in extraordinary activities to boost ratings during a sweeps period. The ratings services scrutinize any special station activities that might bias or distort the ratings to protect the integrity of the entire process. Depending on the transgression, the ratings companies will either note the offending station's crime in the ratings book or drop the station's ratings from the book altogether.

Projections

The research services use sample information to project what is true for the entire population and publish their estimates of audience size and composition. Suppose a sample of 1,000 individuals were selected to study a population of 1 million. In effect each member of the sample would represent 1,000 people in the population. If 50 people in our sample watched a local news show, researchers could project the show's actual audience to be 50,000. That is essentially what the ratings services do. They determine the number of people represented by one in-tab diary and assign that diary an appropriate number. If people are the unit of analysis, the number is called *persons per diary value (PPDV)*. If households are the unit of analysis, the number is labeled *households per diary value (HPDV)*.

This illustration works well for perfect probability samples, in which all members of the population are proportionately represented. As shown, however, that is never the case. Because of nonresponse error, some people will be overrepresented and others underrepresented. Remember also that the most common remedy for this problem is to weight the responses of some sample members more heavily than others. In the illustration just given, suppose 18- to 24-year-old males were underrepresented in the in-tab sample. They constitute 4% of the sample but are believed to be 8% of the population. Males in this group would receive a weight of 2.0 (i.e., 8%/4% = 2.0). Therefore, to project total audience size for this group, each young man should have a PPDV of 2,000 (i.e., 1,000 × 2.0), instead of 1,000. Conversely, overrepresented groups should have PPDVs of less than 1,000.

In practice, the weights assigned to different groups are rarely so extreme as the illustration just given. Usually they come closer to 1.0. Furthermore, ratings services weight a single respondent on a number of variables besides age and gender to determine PPDVs. Although this method of audience projection is not without biases, it is generally accepted as the best practical remedy for nonresponse errors.

Could similar, statistical solutions correct for some of the measurement errors we reviewed in the preceding section? It is clear, for example, that certain kinds of response errors are associated with certain kinds of measurement. Some work in this area has been done, but there is less consensus on how such statistical corrections should be applied to published audience estimates.

The best illustration of this problem occurs in reconciling meter- and diary-based estimates of television audiences. In metered markets, Nielsen integrates the diary data with the information collected through the household meter to make a single best guess of audience size and composition. Because metered data are assumed to more accurately measure set usage, they are used to fix audience size; whereas diary data (which often show smaller audiences) are extrapolated to determine the likeliest demographic breakdown. A ratings analyst should know the consequences of these methodological issues when using the services of research companies.

LOCAL RATINGS

Television

The types of ratings data available to a TV station differ according to market size. Ratings research in larger markets is based on bigger samples, usually offers different measurement options and more services, and is much more expensive. It is no coincidence that larger markets also tend to be richer in terms of the dollars spent on media. For these reasons, it is important to expand on the earlier discussion of local markets.

Each DMA comprises counties in which the preponderance of total viewing can be attributed to local or home-market stations. That is, counties are assigned to markets on the basis of which stations the people in those counties actually view. Figure 8.1 shows a U.S. map divided by DMA. Notice that DMAs vary substantially in terms of their geographic extension. More important to media buyers and sellers, though, these markets differ in terms of population (see Appendix A for a ranking of DMAs by the number of television households in each). Of course, shifts in the U.S. population cause changes in how markets are ranked. But because market areas are ultimately defined by viewing behavior, changes in programming, transmitters, cable penetration, and so on, can also alter market size and composition.

Every year Nielsen analysts reconsider how markets should be constituted, and changes do occur. Sometimes counties bordering adjacent markets will be

NSI Designated Market Areas 1997–98
Metered Measurement in 38 Markets

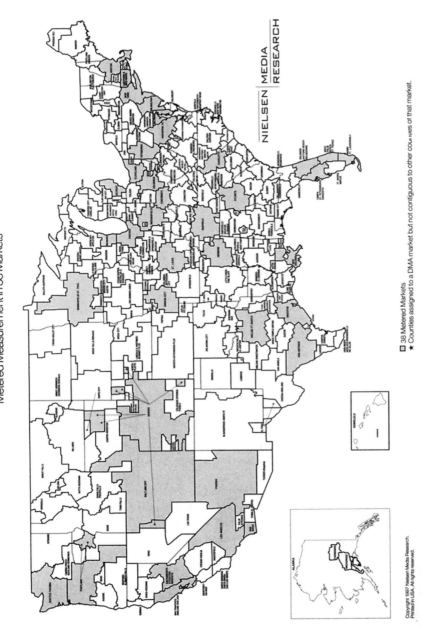

NIELSEN | MEDIA | RESEARCH

□ 38 Metered Markets
★ Counties assigned to a DMA market but not contiguous to other counties of that market.

Copyright 1997 Nielsen Media Research.
Printed in USA. All rights reserved.

FIG. 8.1.   Nielsen television markets.   Source: Nielsen Media Research.

133

moved from one to the other. Such changes are no small matter. For instance, national spot buys are sometimes made in the top 20 or top 50 markets. If the loss of a county causes a market to drop below an important breakpoint, it can have a detrimental impact on every station in the market. However, the new market configuration could also have a differential impact on local stations. Due to factors like geography and transmitter location, some stations cover certain areas of the market better than others. If the reassigned county is one in which a particular station has a clear technical advantage, it could alter the relative standing of stations in the ratings.

The standard local ratings report in television is called a *Viewers in Profile (VIP)*. Figures 8.2 and 8.3, from the Denver ratings book, are typical of the first pages of any local market report. These pages contain a good deal of information about the market.

The first thing to notice on the DMA map is that the television market is divided into several non-overlapping areas. The heavily shaded areas plus the white areas comprise the entire DMA. This particular DMA includes counties from 3 states: Colorado, Wyoming, and Nebraska. The reason for this is that Denver stations account for a large share of viewing in those counties through carriage on local cable systems. The area that appears white on this map is what Nielsen calls the *metro area*. This is the core retail area of the market, which generally corresponds to the Metropolitan Statistical Areas (MSAs) used by the federal government.

Figure 8.3 contains several tables from the VIP offering detailed information about the Denver DMA, including market characteristics and sample size. VIP Table 1, for example, indicates there are 1,185,410 television households in the DMA, and 849,100 television households in the metro area. VIP Table 2 shows the market is 10% Hispanic and that cable penetration is 62% (much lower than the national average). VIP Table 3 notes that the market is measured with meters and diaries and that the in-tab sample sizes are 366 and 1100, respectively. The upper right-hand corner of the page lists the measurement dates: October 31–November 27, 1996. And the list of television stations in VIP Table 4 provides some idea of the competition in the marketplace.

Nielsen measures DMAs at regular intervals throughout the broadcast year. All DMAs are measured at least 4 times, during November, February, May, and July. These measurement periods are called ratings *sweeps*. Some larger markets, like Chicago, are measured as many as 10 times each year.

During a ratings sweep, Nielsen places and retrieves television diaries in households throughout the market. Because the standard diary only records one week's worth of viewing, diary data collected in a sweep is based on four independent samples drawn in consecutive weeks. These data are combined to provide a single monthly estimate of audience size and composition.

A ratings sweep is more than just a random occasion for collecting data. The dates of each sweep are known well in advance, so local stations can and do

MARKET TYPE

DMA TV Ratings Estimates

MAP LEGEND

● City Location

— State Line

METRO AREA

DENVER

LOCAL DMA

DENVER

See Table 5 for NSI Area County Lists

THE NSI® TECHNIQUE

FIG. 8.2.   Nielsen *Viewers in Profile*, Denver DMA. Source: Nielsen Media Research.

TABLE 1 - UNIVERSE ESTIMATES - JAN. 1997

AREA	TOTAL HOUSEHOLDS	TV HOUSEHOLDS	A	B	C	D
			TV HOUSEHOLDS BY COUNTY SIZE †			
METRO	863,900	849,100				
DMA	1,210,000	1,185,410	849,100	139,350	196,960
%		100	72	12	17
NSI	1,832,200	1,792,790	1,029,040	338,200	425,550
%		100	57	19	24

TOTAL HOUSEHOLDS are estimated by Market Statistics (MS), used by special permission of that organization. They are the base against which television ownership percentages have been applied.

TELEVISION OWNERSHIP PERCENTS are Nielsen estimates based on combining historical projections from the 1960 and 1970 Censuses with estimates from the NSI telephone interviews from a number of all market measurement periods.

HOUSEHOLDS ARE OCCUPIED HOUSING UNITS. The household universe estimates shown in Table 1 are estimates of year-round households, i.e., housing units occupied year round. Seasonal housing units which are occupied only during certain seasons of the year are not included in the Household Universe Estimates. Thus, the number of households during the survey period may differ from the estimate in Table 1.

† See NSI Reference Supplement for definition of county size.   LT Less than 1%.

TABLE 2 - PENETRATION ESTIMATES

AREA	BLACK %	HISPANIC %	MULTI-SET %	CABLE TV %	VCR %
			PERCENT OF TV HOUSEHOLDS		
METRO	6	11		59	
DMA	4	10	71	62	85
DENVER	12	19	NA	NA	NA

Multi-set estimates are based on the metered sample. Multi-set, Cable TV and VCR estimates are based on the latest available data. Black and Hispanic estimates are as of January 1, 1997. See NSI Reference Supplement for detail.

TABLE 3 - SAMPLE SIZES: HOUSEHOLDS

AREA	METER SAMPLE IN-TAB AVG.	DIARY SAMPLE(1) INITIALLY DESIGNATED HOUSEHOLDS LISTED	UNLISTED	TOTAL	IN-TAB DIARY HOUSEHOLDS LISTED	UNLISTED	TOTAL
METRO	262 (EST'D)	1169	543	1712	458	167	625
DMA(INCL.METRO)	366 (2)	2143	847	2990	837	263	1100
NON-DMA		4123	1253	5376	1741	433	2174(3)
NSI(INCL. DMA)	366	6266	2100	8366	2578	696	3274

(1) The Non-DMA (Diary) sample is combined with the DMA meter sample for compiling Station Total households; the entire diary sample is used for Audience Composition data.
(2) Yields an approximate equivalent simple random sample size of 714.
(2) + (3) NSI Area Station Total households herein are based on these in-tab samples and yield an approximate equivalent simple random sample size of 1173.
Equivalent simple random sample size is a term sometimes used for the statistical equivalent of the sample size for computing sampling errors or statistical tolerances.
For sample selection procedures in Total Telephone Frame markets, see NSI Reference Supplement.

TABLE 4 - TELEVISION STATIONS

CITY OF ORIGIN	STATION	CHANNEL	AFFILIATION
BROOMFIELD	*KBDI	12	PBS
DENVER	*KCEC	50	UNI
DENVER	*KCNC	4	CBS
DENVER	*KDVR+	31	FOX
FORT COLLINS	*KFCT	22	SATELLITE OF KDVR
DENVER	*KMGH	7	ABC
DENVER	*KRMA	6	PBS
DENVER	KRMT (L)	41	IND
DENVER	*KTVD	20	UPN
BOULDER	KTVJ (L)	14	IND
DENVER	*KUBD (L)	59	IND
DENVER	*KUSA	9	NBC
DENVER	*KWGN	2	WB
CASTLE ROCK	KWHD (L)	53	IND
ATLANTA	*WTBS (D)	17	TBS
CABLE	AEN (D)		
CABLE	CNN (D)		
CABLE	DSC (D)		
CABLE	ESP (D)		
CABLE	FAM (D)		
CABLE	FSRM (D)		
CABLE	MTV (D)		
CABLE	NIK (D)		
CABLE	TNT (D)		
CABLE	USA (D)		

(L) THIS LOCAL STATION IS REPORTABLE IN THE DAYPART SECTION ONLY
(D) THIS OUTSIDE STATION IS REPORTABLE IN THE DAYPART SECTION ONLY

IN ADDITION TO THE REPORTABLE STATIONS SHOWN ABOVE, THE FOLLOWING STATIONS ORIGINATE IN OR ARE ASSIGNED FOR REPORTING PURPOSES TO THIS MARKET BUT DID NOT MEET THE MINIMUM REPORTING STANDARDS (SEE REPORTING STANDARDS, INSIDE BACK COVER)

GLENWOOD SPRNGS	*KREG	3	CBS
STEAMBOAT SPGS	KSBS	24	TEL

NOTE: KREG IS A TOTAL SATELLITE OF KREX, GRAND JUNCTION.

STATION KSBS-TV CHANGED THEIR AFFILIATION FROM FOX TO TELEMUNDO EFFECTIVE WITH THE MAY 1996 MEASUREMENT.

TABLE 5 - TV HOUSEHOLDS AND IN-TAB DIARY HOUSEHOLDS BY SAMPLING AREA

ADJ DMA CNTY	COUNTY & STATE		MRS TERRI- TORY†	EST. TV HHLDS JAN. 1997	CABLE TV HHLDS % NOV 1996	IN-TAB DIARY SIZE†	DIARY HHLDS
	MD ADAMS	CO WC		111,180	60	B	78
	D ALAMOSA	CO WC		5,000	65	D	47
	MD ARAPAHOE	CO WC		185,930	65	B	121
	ARCHULETA	CO WC		2,470	61	D	3
#3	BACA	CO WC		1,650	56	D	2
	MD BOULDER	CO WC		101,290	62	B	74
	D CHAFFEE	CO WC		6,570	61	D	6
	D CLEAR CREEK	CO WC		3,850	62	D	2
	CONEJOS	CO WC		2,740	50	D	5
	D COSTILLA	CO WC		1,140	56	D	22
	D DELTA	CO WC		10,360	61	D	11
	MD DENVER	CO WC		223,730	54	B	161
	D DOLORES	CO WC		640	27		1
	MD DOUGLAS	CO WC		36,090	49	B	39
	D EAGLE	CO WC		10,920	94	D	12
#3	D ELBERT	CO WC		5,430	8	D	4
#3	EL PASO	CO WC		179,940	67	B	303
	D GARFIELD	CO WC		13,880	73	D	25
	D GILPIN	CO WC		13,810	67	D	12
	D GRAND	CO WC		1,340	64	D	1
	D GUNNISON	CO WC		3,610	99	D	1
	D HINSDALE	CO WC		4,410	98	D	6
	D HUERFANO	CO WC		200	90	D	
	D JACKSON	CO WC		2,640	70	D	1
	MD JEFFERSON	CO WC		590	49	D	
	D KIT CARSON	CO WC		190,880	59	B	152
	D LAKE	CO WC		2,820	57	D	4
	D LA PLATA	CO WC		2,490	77	D	3
#3	D LARIMER	CO WC		14,340	53	D	32
	D LAS ANIMAS	CO WC		85,040	68	B	94
	D LINCOLN	CO WC		5,480	74	D	7
#2	D LOGAN	CO WC		1,750	68	D	1
	D MESA	CO WC		6,900	68	C	4
	D MINERAL	CO WC		42,810	68	C	209
	D MOFFAT	CO WC		190	79	D	
#2	MONTEZUMA	CO WC		4,390	72	D	4
	D MONTROSE	CO WC		7,510	38	D	19
	D MORGAN	CO WC		11,470	53	D	66
	D OURAY	CO WC		9,110	65	D	7
	D PARK	CO WC		980	41	D	3
	D PHILLIPS	CO WC		3,920	52	D	5
	D PITKIN	CO WC		1,670	98	D	3
	D PROWERS	CO WC		6,030	98	D	8
#3	D PUEBLO	CO WC		5,330	80	D	5
	D RIO BLANCO	CO WC		50,030	67	C	171
	D RIO GRANDE	CO WC		2,570	54	D	2
	D ROUTT	CO WC		4,210	59	D	11
	D SAGUACHE	CO WC		6,660	81	D	4
	D SAN JUAN	CO WC		1,860	64	D	26
	D SAN MIGUEL	CO WC		790	95	D	
	D SEDGWICK	CO WC		2,010	99	D	3
	D SUMMIT	CO WC		1,060	60	D	1
#3	D TELLER	CO WC		7,130	97	D	8
	D WASHINGTON	CO WC		6,770	49	D	8
	D WELD	CO WC		1,770	45	D	2
	D YUMA	CO WC		54,310	54	C	43
	BEAVERHEAD	MT WC		3,510	47	D	6
	DAWSON	MT WC		290	66	D	23
	FALLON	MT WC		3,530	73	D	162
	GALLATIN	MT WC		1,140	62	D	17
	RICHLAND	MT WC		22,890	54	D	149
	ROOSEVELT	MT WC		3,840	57	D	14
	ROSEBUD	MT WC		3,610	52	D	8
	SILVER BOW	MT WC		3,470	57	D	6
	D YELLOWSTONE	MT WC		14,270	67	D	89
	D BLAINE	NE WC		49,730	62	C	174
	D BOX BUTTE	NE WC		290	31	D	
	D CHEYENNE	NE WC		4,860	77	D	5
	D DAWES	NE WC		3,870	73	D	4
	D DEUEL	NE WC		3,450	73	D	6
	D GARDEN	NE WC		890	56	D	10
	D KEITH	NE WC		840	52	D	5
	D KIMBALL	NE WC		3,510	66	D	43
#1	SCOTTS BLUFF	NE WC		1,600	99	D	1
	SHERIDAN	NE WC		14,700	69	D	84
	D EUREKA	NV WC		2,660	59	D	7
	HUMBOLDT	NV P		670	44	D	
	LANDER	NV P		5,680	50	D	19
	MCKINLEY	NM SW		2,030	65	D	8
	WILLIAMS	ND WC		16,320	66	D	17
	TODD	SD WC		7,720	69	D	31
	D ALBANY	WY WC		2,420	35	D	
	BIG HORN	WY WC		11,930	73	D	12
	D CAMPBELL	WY WC		4,190	53	D	17
	D CARBON	WY WC		10,440	75	D	8
	CONVERSE	WY WC		5,650	79	D	3
	FREMONT	WY WC		4,460	64	D	27
#1	D GOSHEN	WY WC		5,380	50	D	34
	D JOHNSON	WY WC		4,820	55	D	5
#1	D LARAMIE	WY WC		2,440	61	D	5
	NATRONA	WY WC		30,570	78	C	131
	NIOBRARA	WY WC		1,090	78	D	106
	PARK	WY WC		54		D	4
	D PLATTE	WY WC		9,660	59	D	48
	SHERIDAN	WY WC		3,300	59	D	6
	SUBLETTE	WY WC		10,090	78	D	32
	WASHAKIE	WY WC		2,170	56	D	5
				3,280	77	D	20

METRO TOTAL			849,100	59		625
DMA TOTAL			1,185,410	62		1,100
NSI AREA TOTAL	**		1,792,790	63		3,274

#1 = CHEYENNE-SCOTTSBLUFF-STRLNG   #2 = GRAND JUNCTION-MONTROSE
#3 = COLORADO SPRINGS-PUEBLO
NOTE: VIEWING IN ADJACENT DMA's IS NOT LIMITED TO NSI AREA COUNTIES IN TABLE 5. THE ABOVE LIST OF COUNTIES DOES NOT NECESSARILY REPRESENT ENTIRE AREA FOR WHICH VIEWING OCCURS TO STATIONS IN THIS MARKET SEE INSIDE BACK COVER FOR FURTHER STATION TOTAL AREA DESCRIPTION.

Initially, approximately 82% of the predesignated Denver DMA basic meter sample households are recruited and installed. For a typical report period, approximately 56% of the installed meter sample are predesignated households.

Audience estimates are computed separately for each week. Reported multi-week averages are the average of the appropriate individual week audience estimates. Some of the above counties may have been combined for projecting individual week audience estimates. Viewing among the households in the in-tab sample for all counties that are combined are projected to the Total TV Households for the combined counties. These county groupings are available upon request.
M = Metro County; D = Designated Market Area County (for definition see Section II).
** The DMA meter sample currently approximates 411 television households in which meter equipment is installed. This figure includes households replaced during the survey period) provided records meeting Nielsen accuracy standards during one or more days of this survey interval, including 366 households on the average individual day.

† See NSI Reference Supplement for explanation of MRS Territory and County Size.

FIG. 8.3.   Nielsen *Viewers in Profile*, Denver DMA. Source: Nielsen Media Research.

adapt their programming to attract the largest audiences possible. This may manifest itself in the local television news airing particularly sensational stories. Even the networks, which are continuously measured, try to help their affiliates by running blockbuster movies and heavily promoted mini-series. Sometimes, though, a station will cross the hazy line between reasonable promotional efforts and illegal practices known as hyping or *hypoing*. These unfair practices artificially inflate the ratings, leading to a misrepresentation of average audiences to the stations. Indeed, such abuses were one of the concerns motivating the congressional investigations in the 1960s.

Hypoing can involve a number of activities designed to distort or bias ratings results. For example, a station might try to enhance its ratings by directly addressing diarykeepers in its programming, by conducting a survey to learn the identity of actual diarykeepers, or by conducting particularly heavy-handed contests and promotions. If the ratings companies learn of such "special station activities," they may take several actions, from placing a special notice in the rating book to deleting the station's audience estimates altogether. The Denver VIP discussed earlier, for example, contains the following warning:

> Nielsen Media Research has been advised that the following station(s), network program(s), and/or syndicated program(s) conducted a contest, on-air announcement, research survey, or other activity in this market during all or part of the November 1996 measurement period which, in the judgment of Nielsen Media Research, may have affected viewing.

The page lists 2 stations and 3 programs in violation of hypoing rules.

Problems with hypoing during sweeps months have prompted many industry participants to call for continuous measurement of local markets. This would, in the opinion of many, eliminate the incentive for stations to schedule all their best programming at predictable times of the year. And because continuous measurement would give advertisers detailed trend data, it would reduce the ability of stations to strategically inflate ratings levels. The major drawback to this, of course, is cost. Clients pay for Nielsen's service, and many doubt the benefits of measuring markets 365 days a year would outweigh the costs.

Assuming that data collection goes according to plan, Nielsen analysts will have about 100,000 diaries to process at the end of a nationwide sweep. Sample sizes vary widely from market to market. The largest markets could have household samples of 1,900; the smallest markets just over 200 households in-tab. Response rates also vary from market to market, but average around 45%. In any particular market, information on sample placement and response is contained in the local market report.

Local television ratings in the VIP are reported in various ways. Market reports provide audience estimates by daypart, or more discrete time periods. They provide audience trend information for different demographic groups, and they describe audiences for specific television programs. Figure 8.4 depicts

138

DENVER, CO

TUESDAY 8:00PM - 9:00PM

METRO HH		STATION PROGRAM	DMA HOUSEHOLD				MULTI-WEEK AVG		SHARE TREND			DMA RATINGS																													TNS	CHILD
			RATINGS WEEKS									PERSONS												WOMEN							MEN								
RTG	SHR		1	2	3	4	RSHTIRG	MAY '96	FEB '96	NOV '95	2 +	18-24	12-24	12-34	18-34	18-49	21-49	25-54	35-54	35-50	50+	18+	12-24	18-34	18-49	25-49	25-54	WKG	18+	18-34	21-49	25-49	25-54	12-17	2-11	6-11
1	2		3	4	5	6	7	8	11	12	13	15	16	17	18	19	20	21	22	23	24	25	26	27	28	29	31	32	34	35	36	37	38	39	40	41	42	43
3 1	3 1	R.S.E. THRESHOLDS 25+% (1 S.E.) 4 WK AVG 50+%	3 1	3 1	3 1	2 LT					2 LT	2 LT	6 2	4 1	3 1	3 1	2 1	2 LT	2 LT	2 1	2 1	9 2	7 2	3 1	3 1	3 1	3 1	2 1	8 2	4 1	4 1	4 1	3 1	10 3	9 2	12 3
		8:00PM																																			
1	1	KBDI AVG. ALL WKS	<<	<<	1	1	1	1	2	2																												
<<		ELECTN-COVERGE	<<			<<																																
1	1	CHANCER		<<	1	1	<<																															
1	1	KCEC AVG. ALL WKS	<<	1	<<	<<	<<	NR	NR	NR				1								1	1															
<<		TU Y YO-UNI	<<			<<																																
1	1	CANVRL-PSN UNI		1	<<	<<	<<								1																							
9	16	KCNC AVG. ALL WKS	8	11	9	8	9	14	12	12	14	5	1	4	4	4	5	5	4	7	6	10	8	1	6	5	5	6	5	8	5	3	3	4	4	3	2	2
9	14	CAM96-EL8P-CBS	8				9	12				4	1	3	3	3	5	5	4	6	6	7	7	1	5	5	5	5	5	5	3	3	3	4	4			
10	15	CBS TUE MOV		11	9	8	9	14				6		5	4	4	5	5	4	7	6	10	7	1	5	5	5	6	5	8	5	3	3	4	4			
9	14	KDVR+ FOX TU NITE MV	8	6	11	10	9	14	9X	10	7	9	2	7	7	6	7	6	6	6	6	6	9	2	7	7	7	7	6	8	12	9	10	8	8	4	3	3
14	22	KMGH AVG. ALL WKS	14	14	12	14	13	19	22	23	27	9	5	8	8	8	9	10	11	11	9	8	8	2	8	8	9	10	9	8	9	7	7	7	7	8	7	10
9	14	96VOTE-10.00PM		8			8	13				6	3	5	6	5	6	6	7	8	6	5	6	2	5	5	5	5	5	6	5	5	5	5	5			
15	24	HOME IMPRV-ABC		14	12	14	13	21				4	5	7	7	7	9	10	11	11	9	9	11		10	10	11	11	11	8	8	8	7	8	8			
4	6	KRMA AVG. ALL WKS	3	3	3		3	5	4		3	6	1	2	4	3	3	3	3	4	4	2	1	1	1	1	1	1	1	3	2	2	2	3	3			
4	7	KRMA NEWS SPCL					3	5				1			1	1	1	1	1	1			1	1	1	1	1	1	1	3	2	2	2	3	3			
4	7	GREAT WAR-PTV					3	5				1	2		1	2	1	2	1	1	2		1		1	1	1	1		3	2	2	2	1	1			
4	7	NTL GEO ON ASG			3		3	5				1		1		1	1	3	1	3	2									2	1	1	1	1	1			
4	5	AMR-WHEELS-PTV				3	3	5				1	1	1	3	2	2	1	1	5	2									2	1	1	1	1	1			
2	4	KTVD AVG. ALL WKS	2	2	2	3	2	3	3	5	2	1	1	2	3	2	2	1	2	2	1	1	2	1	2	2	2	2	2	3	1	1	1	1	1	2		
3	4	MOESHA SP-UPN				2	3					1	3	2	1								4							1	1	1	1			4		
2	4	BURNING ZN-UPN				2	4					1	1	2	1	1	1	1	1	1	1				1	1	1	1		1	1	1	1					
18	24	KUSA AVG. ALL WKS	13	16	13	16	15	23	20	24	21	9	11	5	8	9	11	11	13	12	14	6	10	10	8	13	13	14	12	10	8	10	10	11	11	6	2	3
15	23	DECSN96 2-NBC	13				13	21				9	10		9	9	10	12	12	14	14	6	9	9		12	13	14	13	11	9	10	11	11	11			
16	25	FRASIER-NBC		16	13	16	15	24				10	12		8	10	12	12	13	12	13	7	11	11		13	16	16	13	10	9	10	10	11	11			
5	8	KWGN AVG. ALL WKS	7	4	5		5	8	13	7	11	3	2	5	2	2	2	2	2	2	1	1	1	1	2	1	1	1	1	3	3	3	2	4	3	2		
6	10	CINEMA 2	7	4			5	8				3	3		2	2	2	2	2	2	1	1	1	1		1	1	1	1	3	2	2	3	4	3			
4	7	NUGGETS BKBL			5	4	6	7				2	2		2	2	2	2	2	2			1	1		1	1	1	1		3	3	3	4	3			
64		HUT/PUT/TOTALS*	62	66	64	63	64		62	65	64	44	50	35	39	43	46	46	54	50	62	51	35	42	45	46	46	50	49	43	45	46	46	46	30	22	26
		8:30PM																																			
1	1	KBDI AVG. ALL WKS	<<	<<	1	1	<<	1	2	2																												
<<		ELECTN-COVERGE	<<			<<																																
1	1	CHANCER		<<	1	1	1																															
1	1	KCEC AVG. ALL WKS	<<	1	<<	<<	<<	NR	NR	NR				1								1	1															
<<		TU Y YO-UNI	<<			<<																																
1	1	CANVRL-PSN UNI		1	<<	<<	<<								1								1	1															
11	17	KCNC AVG. ALL WKS	9	12	11	9	10	18	14	14	15	6	1	5	6	6	7	8	8	9	7	12	9	1	7	7	7	8	6	8	4	4	4	5	5	3	4	
9	14	CAM96-EL8P-CBS	9				9	12				6	1	3	4	4	6	6	5	9	7	11	8	1	6	7	7	7	6	6	4	4	6	7	7			
12	18	CBS TUE MOV		12	11	9	11	17				7		5	8	6	7	8	9	9	7	12	9		7	7	7	8	7	8	4	4	4	5	5			
11	17	KDVR+ FOX TU NITE MV	9	7	14	11	10	18	10X	12	7	8	1	6	7	6	8	7	6	8	5	6	10	2	6	7	7	7	7	8	14	10	10	8	8	4	3	3
11	16	KMGH AVG. ALL WKS	10	12	10	10	10	16	20	19	24	9	4	8	9	8	9	7	9	10	7	8	8	4	8	9	8	9	8	7	7	7	7	7	7	4	3	5
11	16	96VOTE-10.30PM	10				10	15				6		5	7	6	7	5	7	9	6	9	6		6	6	5	6	6	6	6	6	6	6	6			
12	18	SPIN CITY-ABC		12	10	10	11	16				7	4	5	9	8	9	7	9	10	7	8	9		10	10	10	11	9	7	8	8	8	7	7			
4	6	KRMA AVG. ALL WKS	5	4	2	3	4	6	4		5	7	2	3	5	4	4	4	5	6	4	9	7		6	10	10	10	10	4	4	2	2	3	3	5	4	6
4	7	KRMA NEWS SPCL					4	5				2		2	2	2	2	2	2	1		9	7		6	10	10	10	10	4				3	3			
4	7	GREAT WAR-PTV		4			3	5				3		3		3	3	1	1	1			1							5				4	4			
4	7	NTL GEO ON ASG			3		3	5				1		1	1	1	1	2	2	2	3				2	2	3	3		2	1	1	1	1	1			
4	6	AMR-WHEELS-PTV				3	3	5				2			1	2	1	1	1	2	2	2	3		1	1	1	1		2	2	2	2	2	2			
3	5	FILLER				3	3	5				2		1		1	1	1	1	2	2	1			1					1								
2	4	KTVD AVG. ALL WKS	1	2	2	3	2	3	4	6	2	1		1	1	1	1	1	1	2	1	1	1		2	2	2	2	1		1	1	1	1	1			
2	3	SPARK SP-UPN	1			3	2					1			1	1	1	1	1	2	1	1	2		3	1	1	2	2	1								
2	3	BURNING ZN-UPN			2		2					1			1	1	1	1	1	1	1				1	1	1	1		1	1	1	1					
13	21	KUSA AVG. ALL WKS	12	15	12	13	13	20	18	22	20	9	8	2	7	9	9	9	11	11	12	6	8	8	7	11	10	10	9	7	7	8	9	10	9	4	2	3
12	18	DECSN96 2-NBC	12				12	18				8	6		7	7	8	9	10	11	11	5	7	7		11	10	11	10	8	7	8	9	9	9			
14	22	CAROLN-CTY-NBC		15	12	13	13	21				9	11		6	8	9	9	11	11	12	6	9	9		11	11	12	11	7	6	9	9	10	9			
6	10	KWGN AVG. ALL WKS	7	4	5		5	8	12	8	12	4	3	6	3	3	3	3	3	3	2	1	1	1	3	1	1	1	1	3	3	3	2	3	3	5	1	2
6	10	CINEMA 2	7	4			5	8				4	4		2	3	3	3	3	3	2	1	1	1		1	1	1	1	3	2	2	3	3	3			
4	7	NUGGETS BKBL			5	4	6	8				3	3		2	3	3	3	3	3			1	1		1	1	1	1		3	3	4	5	7			
64		HUT/PUT/TOTALS*	66	66	65	62	64		63	64	65	44	51	34	41	45	46	47	47	53	49	61	52	35	48	48	49	48	49	49	42	44	46	46	46	29	22	25

FIG. 8.4. Nielsen *Viewers in Profile*, Denver DMA. Source: Nielsen Media Research.

the "Time Period Estimates" section of the Viewers in Profile, again from the Denver DMA.

The column headings describe the contents of the numbers directly below. On the left-hand side of the page is information on specific stations and the programs they broadcast. It is organized by day of the week, and within that, by half-hour (and sometimes by quarter-hour) time periods. This particular page reports viewing on Tuesday from 8:00 p.m. to 9:00 p.m. At the bottom of each half-hour time period is a line of numbers labeled "HUT/PUT/TOTALS," which gives the audience viewing levels by half hour. This gives an indication of the number of people who were available to watch a given program (see chap. 10, this volume).

After the program title, the first four columns give audience estimates for each of the four weeks that comprise a sweep. This can be useful, because sometimes program changes during a sweep mask an "average" rating. For example, several stations ran programs related to the presidential election during the first week of this measurement period. Ratings for specials like these could vary significantly from other programs in those same time slots.

The remaining columns report average program ratings and shares. For ease of reference, the columns are numbered below their titles. Columns 7 and 8, for example, contain rating and share information for television households (TVHH) in the DMA. During the 8:00–8:30 p.m. time period, station KMGH aired *Home Improvement* and achieved a 13 rating and a 21 share. The next page in this ratings book (not shown) contains projected audience estimates, reported in thousands, for the same programs.

Note also that at the top of the page, below the column headings, are two rows of numbers labeled "R.S.E. Thresholds," which stands for "Relative Standard Error." R.S.E. reminds users that the numbers reported are merely estimates based on samples and are therefore subject to sampling error. More specifically, each column indicates the point at which one standard error will constitute either 25% or 50% of an estimate. Column estimates based on smaller samples sizes (e.g., women 12–24 versus women 18+) are subject to more error, hence thresholds are relatively high. In the example shown, 1 standard error would be within 25% of the estimate only if the rating among women 12–24 were at least a 9.

Nielsen distributes ratings data through a variety of computer programs for buyers and research analysts. Usually, market reports are stored on computer disks and read by using a desktop computer. Not only can one read the book this way, but more important, the audience estimates contained within can be more easily manipulated. This is, essentially, an electronic version of the market report. As computer and audience measurement technology change, these programs are revised and re-issued. The ratings services provide brochures describing them in detail. Independent vendors also sell software for analyzing market reports. The exact capabilities of each package differ, but they can typically locate the relative strengths and weaknesses of each station in the market by ranking various criteria; identify a package of avails to match an advertiser's request; help manage audience inventories; and project audiences based on historical data. (These specific analytical techniques are discussed in the final chapter of this volume.)

Many large markets, like Denver, are metered markets, which means Nielsen uses passive household meters in combination with diaries to generate the ratings. There are more than 40 metered markets accounting for about 60% of all U.S. television households, and Nielsen continues to add more each year. Usually there are between 300 and 500 meters installed in a given DMA, depending on the size and makeup of the market. There has been some discussion about replacing passive household meters in local markets with peoplemeters. Should that happen, it would presumably eliminate diarykeeping in those markets, although the overlapping NSI areas of metered and nonmetered markets would become problematic.

The availability of metered data affects both ratings and how ratings are used. First, as described in the previous chapter, meter-based data are employed to adjust the audience estimates derived from diary data. Second, because data collection is fast, meters enable delivery of overnight ratings. Although these are only household level data in local markets, they allow programmers to respond quickly to audience trends. As was the case with local market reports, Nielsen sells PC-based software to manipulate electronically delivered overnight data. Figure 8.5 shows a sample of overnight data from the Chicago market. Each column of numbers represents ratings for a different station, so it is very easy to compare the competition by time period.

Radio

The local radio ratings business is also dominated by one research provider, Arbitron. This firm measures approximately 268 radio markets twice yearly using diary methodology. Ratings are based on a 12-week survey period rather than the 4-week standard used in local television measurement. At present, 93 radio markets have continuous measurement, with 4 books issued yearly. Radio listenership is estimated for Metro Survey Areas, which generally correspond to governmentally designated metropolitan areas. In addition, Arbitron routinely reports Total Survey Area (TSA) estimates for the larger geographic area in which radio listening may occur. In the top 100 radio markets, Arbitron reports DMA audiences in the fall and spring, matching its own county designations to Nielsen's television market assignments. The regular Arbitron books contain information for only commercial stations. However, data for public stations is accessible through software products.

Although the 7-day personal diary is the standard way to collect data on radio audiences, other methods are used. Telephone surveys, for example, seem to favor formats that cater to young listeners. The best single explanation for such differences appears to be response rates. Nonresponse among diary keepers is acute in younger age groups. These listeners tend to favor formats like rock and urban contemporary. The bias this creates is the nonresponse error referred to earlier. The underrepresentation of younger listeners can be alleviated by weighting the data in favor of younger listeners who do return a diary. Unfortunately, those who respond may have different format preferences than their peers who do not respond, and weighting the data by demographic categories cannot compensate for that difference. It is helpful for ratings users to know which groups are under or overrepresented. This information is generally provided in the form of unweighted in-tabs for each demographic compared to population estimates.

Arbitron reports feature a large section called "Listener Estimates" that includes audience trend information separated into 20 demographic subsets. Individual station audiences are reported across several dayparts within each category. Figure 8.6 illustrates one such page for the spring 1997 Arbitron Radio Market Report for Tulsa.

Each page of the report gives information on 5 dayparts, noted in the column headings across the top. This page includes station audience estimates among men 18–49 years old for weekday dayparts. Beneath each daypart heading are 4 estimates: (a) projected audience size in an average quarter hour (AQH); (b) cumulative audience in that same daypart; (c) AQH audience expressed as a rating; and (d) AQH audience expressed as a share. The first two numbers are always reported in hundreds (with the last two zeros understood). Every listener in an AQH will be included in the associated cume audience. Therefore, in any given daypart, the cume will always be equal to or greater than the AQH audience.

The left-hand side of the table lists stations reported in the book. Usually these are stations assigned to the home market, but if stations assigned to neighboring markets have significant audiences, they will appear below a dotted line on the same page. Such stations are usually powerful stations from a big city that reach into smaller towns and markets. For each station, listener estimates are provided for the current survey period along with an estimate for the previous 4 books (markets measured only twice yearly will show a 2-book average).

Other data is routinely reported in the Radio Market Report, including AQH and cume audience composition, time spent listening, cume duplication, exclusive cumes, and, because much listening occurs outside the home, "location of listening" estimates. Arbitron can also include selected qualitative information in the regular radio book in about 100 markets where its qualitative services Scarborough or RetailDirect are available.

Although Arbitron's service is primarily for the local metro market, the company also issues a "County Coverage" report on audiences, county by county. In addition, the service repackages market-level data to create products that provide national radio listening information. These reports estimate audiences for network and syndicated programming. They provide some basis

NIELSEN STATION INDEX METERED DAILY AUDIENCE ESTIMATES
ENTIRE CONTENTS OF THIS REPORT COPYRIGHT A.C. NIELSEN CO. 1998

CHICAGO DMA   ***** PRELIMINARY REPORT *****
PROGRAM AVERAGES/   PROGRAM NAMES AS OF 16:21 ON 08/05/98
QUARTER HOUR RATINGS   WEDNESDAY 8/05/98   461 REPORTING HOUSEHOLDS

TIME	HUT	WTTW (RTG SH)	WBBM (RTG SH)	WFLD (RTG SH)	WGBO (RTG SH)	WGN (RTG SH)	WLS (RTG SH)	RTQ
2.00P	32.5	1.5 5 BAKE-JULIA-PTV	2.2 7 MARTHA STEWART	1.5 5 BTL MX MTH-FOX	0.7 2		4.3 13 GENRL HOSPITAL	7.
	31.5	_1.4_4_32.0	_2.1_7_32.0	_1.4_4_32.0	0.7 2		5.2 17	6.
2.30P	31.7	0.9 3 DESSERT CIRCUS	1.7 5 GAYLE KING	2.0 6 LIFE-L MF-FOX	0.7 2		5.4 17	6.
	32.5	_1.0_3_32.1	_1.6_5_32.1		0.7 2		5.6 17	7.
3.00P	31.9	0.9 3 IL ADVENTURE	2.4 7 REAL TV	2.4 7 CRTN CB MF-FOX	0.7 2		5.9 18 INSIDE EDITION	7.
	33.8	_.6_2_32.8	_2.3_7_32.8	_2.4_7_32.1	0.4 1 CRISTINA UNI		5.6 17	7.
3.30P	35.8	0.4 1 WISHBONE-PTV	2.2 6 REAL TV B	2.2 6	0.7 2		4.6 13 JEOPARDY	8.
	36.9	_.7_2_36.3	_3.4_9_36.3	_1.7_5_34.6 SPIDRMN MF-FOX	0.4 1		5.6 15	9.
4.00P	38.2	1.1 3 ARTHUR-PTV	2.8 8 HARD COPY	4.3 11 SPIDRMN MF-FOX	0.2 1		5.6 15 ABC7 NWS-400P	9.
	38.8	_3.2_8_38.5	_4.6_12_38.5	_2.2_6_38.5 PWR-PL-MTH-FOX	_.4_1_34.6	4.9_14_33.9 10TH INNING	5.9 15	10.
4.30P	40.3	3.7 9 ARTHUR-PTV B	5.0 13 NWS2CHICAGO430P	5.6 14 PWR-PL-MTH-FOX	0.4 1 PRIM IM MF UNI	4.8 12 10TH INNING		10.
	41.6	_4.4_11_40.9	_5.4_13_40.9	_1.6_4_40.9 HOME IMPROV MF	0.4 1	2.8 7 HOWIE MANDEL	2.0 5	9.
5.00P	39.0	3.9 10 BARNEY&FRIENDS	5.9 15 NWS2CHICAGO-5P	5.2 12 HOME IMPROV MF	0.4 1	2.0 5 HANGN-MR.COOPR	2.2 6 ABC7 NWS-500P	8.
	41.9	_2.8_7_40.4	_5.4_13_40.4	_4.9_12_40.4	0.9 3 NOTICIAS 66	_2.4_6_40.9	_8.0_20_40.4	8.
5.30P	44.0	3.0 7 NITE BSNSS RPT	5.4 12 CBS EVE NWS	5.4 12 SIMPSONS	1.1 3 _1.0_2_40.4 NOTICRO UNIVSN	2.2 6 FULL HOUSE	4.6 10 ABC-WORLD NWS	8.
	45.1	_1.6_4_44.5	_5.0_11_44.5	_6.4_14_44.5	1.3 3	_2.3_6_40.4	5.2 12	8.
6.00P	48.6	2.2 5 NEWSHOUR-LEHR	4.8 10 NWS2CHICAGO-6P	4.8 10 HOME IMPROV MF	1.5 3 _1.4_3_44.5 MI PEQUENA-UNI	4.9_11_44.5 MAD ABOUT YOU	2.4 5 ABC7 NWS-600P	11.
	48.6		_4.5_9_48.6	_7.7_16_48.6	2.6 5	2.6 5	2.6 5	10.
6.30P	50.3	2.2 5	4.6 9 ENT TONIGHT 30	4.3 9 SEINFELD	2.8 6	2.5_5_48.6 LIVING SINGLE	2.2 4 WHEEL-FORTNE	11.
	52.1	_2.3_5_49.9	_4.9_10_51.2	_7.0_14_51.2	2.2 4 _2.6_5_49.9 VIVO-ELENA-UNI	2.3 4 _2.3_4_51.2	2.4 5 _10.9_23_48.6	13.
7.00P	50.1	2.4 5 CHICAGO TONITE	4.1 8 NANNY-CBS	3.9 7 FOX WED NTE MV	2.4 5	2.4 5 WAYANS-8P-WB	1.3 9 DHARMA&GRG-ABC	8.
	52.3	_2.4_5_51.2	_4.0_8_51.2	(BLANKMAN)	1.7 3 _4.5_9_51.2	_4.5_9_51.2	4.8 9 _8.4_17_51.2	

142

FIG. 8.5. — Nielsen Station Index Metered Daily Audience, Copyright © A. C. Nielsen Co., 1998

Time / HUT column:

Time	HUT
7.30P	54.4 / 54.2
8.00P	56.4 / 58.8
8.30P	61.6 / 62.3
9.00P	63.8 / 65.1
9.30P	64.2 / 64.2
10.00P	60.1 / 59.2
10.30P	53.6 / 49.2
11.00P	44.5 / 40.8
11.30P	37.3 / 34.7
12.00M	33.4 / 30.2
12.30A	29.7 / 26.2
1.00A	24.9 / 23.4
1.30A	22.3 / 21.3

Programs by station (program name with rating_rank_share where shown):

Independent station
- GOOD-BEAUTIFUL
- LENA HORNE (IN HER-VOICE) — 4.5_8_58.7
- CHICAGO TONITE — 3.2_5_63.4
- AS THE GOES BY — .9_2_56.4
- CHUCK CLOSE — 1.5_3_46.8
- (PORTRT-PRGRS)
- CHARLIE ROSE — 1.0_3_36.5
- NWS2CH-10PM R
- CHICAGO TONITE — 1.1_4_28.7
- HARD COPY R — .7_3_26.9
- THIS OLD HOUSE — .4_2_24.1
- PAID PROGRAM 2 — 1.0_4_22.8
- PAID PROGRAM 2 — .4_2_21.8

CBS
- STYL&SUBST-CBS
- CNTRYFST98-CBS — 4.4_8_54.3
- NWS2CHICGO-10P — 4.5_7_62.0
- D LETTERMAN-CBS — 5.7_10_59.6
- TOM SNYDER-CBS — 2.5_5_47.0
- CHARLIE ROSE — 1.5_4_33.9
- NWS2CH-10PM R
- HARD COPY R — .7_3_26.9
- PAID PROGRAM

FOX
- FOX NWS CHICAGO — 3.4_6_56.2
- FRASIER — 4.7_7_64.3
- SIMPSONS — 4.8_8_59.6
- JRRY SPRINGR R — 5.9_11_51.4
- MAGIC HOUR — 4.9_13_39.3
- PAID PROGRAM — 2.6_9_29.8
- — 1.6_7_22.9

UNI (Univision)
- PUEBL-GRND-UNI — 1.7_3_52.7
- LENTE LC W UNI — 1.6_3_59.7
- FUERA-SERI UNI — 1.4_2_64.4
- NOTICIAS 66 — 1.6_2_64.2
- NOTC UNI LATE — 1.2_2_59.6
- AL-NCHE-WD-UNI — 1.1_2_51.4
- CLUB-M-F R-UNI — <_.2_1_36.8
- CRISTINA R UNI — .4_1_27.9
- — .2_1_22.9

WB
- JAMIE FOXX-WB
- WAYANS BROS-WB — 4.4_8_54.3
- S. HARVEY-WB — 4.9_9_57.6
- WGN NEWS — 1.6_3_59.7
- MURPHY BROWN — 6.4_10_64.3
- MAD ABOUT YOU — 2.8_5_59.6
- CHEERS — 3.5_7_51.4
- MARRIED-CHLDRN — 3.9_9_42.6
- CHEERS — 4.0_11_36.0
- HONEYMOONERS — 3.3_11_31.8
- SUSAN POWTR — 2.1_9_27.9
- UNFRGTTBL 60'S — 1.1_5_24.1
- — 1.2_6_21.8

ABC
- 2GUYS-PZZA-ABC
- DREW CAREY-ABC — 7.1_13_54.3
- WHO'S LINE-ABC — 9.8_17_57.6
- PRMTM LIVE-ABC — 9.0_15_61.9
- ABC7 NWS-10P — 10.3_16_64.3
- ABC-NITELINE — 15.3_26_59.6
- OPRH WINFREY R — 10.3_20_51.4
- POLIT INCT-ABC — 6.1_16_39.3
- AMERCN JOURNAL — 4.8_15_31.8
- ABC7 NWS-RPT — 3.3_12_27.9
- ABC-NWS NOW — 2.6_11_23.5

Legend:

R = REPEAT	S = SPECIAL	P = PREMIER
A (SPLS&ROSTI)	B (SPLSA&ESPST)	C (SNDRS&ESPST)
D (SNDRS&ROSTI)		

143

Target Listener Trends

Men 18-49

	Monday-Sunday 6AM-MID				Monday-Friday 6AM-10AM				Monday-Friday 10AM-3PM				Monday-Friday 3PM-7PM				Monday-Friday 7PM-MID			
	AQH (00)	Cume (00)	AQH Rtg	AQH Shr	AQH (00)	Cume (00)	AQH Rtg	AQH Shr	AQH (00)	Cume (00)	AQH Rtg	AQH Shr	AQH (00)	Cume (00)	AQH Rtg	AQH Shr	AQH (00)	Cume (00)	AQH Rtg	AQH Shr
KAKC-AM																				
SP '97	2	68	.1	.6	3	21	.2	.6	4	33	.2	.8	1	22	.1	.2	1	19	.1	.7
WI '97	2	90	.1	.6	4	40	.2	.9	5	35	.3	1.0	1	17	.1	.2	1	23	.1	.7
FA '96	2	59	.1	.7	4	33	.2	.9	1	14	.1	.2	3	30	.2	.8	2	24	.1	1.6
SU '96	2	59	.1	.6	2	14	.1	.4	4	39	.2	.9	5	25	.3	1.2		10		
4-Book	2	69	.1	.6	3	27	.2	.7	4	30	.2	.7	3	24	.2	.6	1	19	.1	.8
SP '96	3	71	.2	.9	2	25	.1	.4	3	25	.2	.6	8	48	.4	1.8	3	29	.2	1.9
KBEZ-FM																				
SP '97	7	189	.4	2.1	9	65	.5	1.8	12	83	.7	2.4	8	57	.4	1.8	3	44	.2	2.2
WI '97	13	239	.7	4.1	16	85	.9	3.5	23	111	1.3	4.8	17	109	.9	4.1	8	76	.4	5.8
FA '96	8	153	.4	2.6	11	75	.6	2.5	13	60	.7	2.8	12	104	.7	3.1	2	55	.1	1.6
SU '96	13	202	.7	4.0	16	127	.9	3.5	19	113	1.0	4.0	17	118	.9	4.2	8	82	.4	4.4
4-Book	10	196	.6	3.2	13	88	.7	2.8	17	92	.9	3.5	14	97	.7	3.3	5	64	.3	3.5
SP '96	16	217	.9	4.7	17	98	.9	3.3	27	89	1.5	5.4	21	127	1.1	4.8	9	58	.5	5.7
KCFM-FM																				
SP '97	2	51	.1	.6	1	17			1	21	.1	.2	3	26	.2	.7	1	25	.1	.7
WI '97	2	65	.1	.6	1	15	.1	.2	1	14	.1	.2	4	26	.2	1.0	1	21	.1	.7
FA '96	1	71	.1	.3	1	29	.1	.2	2	31	.1	.4	2	40	.1	.5	1	10	.1	.8
SU '96	9	118	.5	2.8	11	70	.6	2.4	12	59	.7	2.6	11	74	.6	2.7	5	63	.3	2.8
4-Book	4	76	.2	1.1	3	33	.2	.7	4	31	.3	.9	5	42	.3	1.2	2	30	.2	1.3
SP '96	9	182	.5	2.6	8	91	.4	1.6	16	95	.9	3.2	11	114	.6	2.5	5	66	.3	3.1
KCFO-AM																				
SP '97	1	44	.1	.3	3	32	.2	.6	2	26	.1	.4	1	11	.1	.2		11		
WI '97	2	74	.1	.6	4	47	.2	.9	3	38	.2	.6	1	24	.1	.2		10		
FA '96	1	21	.1	.3	2	16	.1	.4	1	11	.1	.2		5			1	21	.1	.8
SU '96	1	34	.1	.3	2	14	.1	.4	4	24	.2	.9		10			1	5	.1	.6
4-Book	1	43	.1	.4	3	27	.2	.6	3	25	.2	.5	1	13	.1	.1	1	12	.1	.4
SP '96	2	46	.1	.6	4	41	.2	.8	2	30	.1	.4	4	24	.2	.9	1	23	.1	1.3
KQSY-FM																				
SP '97	2	22	.1	.6		6			3	12	.2	.6	3	7	.2	.7	2	11	.1	1.5
WI '97	3	43	.2	.9	4	43	.2	.9	4	32	.2	.8	2	14	.1	.5	2	10	.1	1.5
FA '96		17				5								6				5		
SU '96		6				6														
4-Book	1	22	.1	.4	1	15	.1	.2	2	11	.1	.4	1	7	.1	.3	1	7	.1	.8
SP '96																				
KCKI-FM																				
SP '97	9	163	.5	2.7	15	117	.8	3.1	13	83	.7	2.5	11	93	.6	2.5	4	39	.2	2.9
WI '97	5	126	.3	1.6	8	55	.4	1.8	3	42	.2	.6	6	77	.3	1.4	4	45	.2	2.9
FA '96	13	254	.7	4.2	18	108	1.0	4.0	23	117	1.3	5.0	15	130	.8	3.8	4	53	.2	3.2
SU '96	9	189	.5	2.8	9	88	.5	2.0	12	96	.7	2.6	14	130	.8	3.4	9	65	.5	5.0
4-Book	9	183	.5	2.8	13	92	.7	2.7	13	85	.7	2.7	12	108	.6	2.8	5	51	.3	3.5
SP '96	14	203	.8	4.1	17	115	.9	3.3	19	95	1.0	3.8	15	124	.8	3.5	9	63	.5	5.7
KEMX-FM																				
SP '97	1	17	.1	.3	1	11	.1	.2	1	17	.1	.2	1	12	.1	.2	1	12	.1	.7
WI '97		14				4				5				4				4		
FA '96																				
SU '96																				
4-Book		8		.1		4		.1		6		.1		4		.1		4		.2
SP '96	1	12	.1	.3		6				6										
KGTO-AM																				
SP '97	*												*				**	**	**	**
WI '97	1	14	.1	.3					1	10	.1	.2	1	10	.1	.2	**	**	**	**
FA '96	2	18	.1	.7	4	18	.2	.9	3	18	.2	.6					**	**	**	**
SU '96		20			1	10	.1	.2					1	10	.1	.2	1	10	.1	.6
4-Book	1	13	.1	.3	1	7	.1	.3	1	7	.1	.2	1	5	.1	.1	**	**	**	**
SP '96		6				6								6						

** Station(s) not reported this survey.   * Listener estimates adjusted for reported broadcast schedule.   + Station(s) changed call letters - see Page 13.   4-Book: Avg. of current and previous 3 surveys.   2-Book: Avg. of most recent 2 surveys.

ARBITRON

86

FIG. 8.6.   Arbitron Radio Market Report, Tulsa. Courtesy of the Arbitron Company.

Top Five Format Preferences

Black listener format preferences change by age and differ from those of the general radio audience.

Monday-Sunday 6A-Mid

Persons 12+

Rank	Black	General Audience
1	Urban	News/Talk
2	News/Talk	Adult Cont.
3	Religious	Country
4	Top 40	Urban
5	Adult Alt.	Top 40

Persons 12-24

Rank	Black	General Audience
1	Urban	Top 40
2	Top 40	Urban
3	Adult Cont.	Album Rock
4	Religious	Country
5	News/Talk	Adult Cont.

Persons 18-34

Rank	Black	General Audience
1	Urban	Adult Cont.
2	Top 40	Album Rock
3	Adult Cont.	Top 40
4	Adult Alt.	Urban
5	News/Talk	Country

Persons 25-54

Rank	Black	General Audience
1	Urban	Adult Cont.
2	News/Talk	News/Talk
3	Religious	Country
4	Adult Alt.	Urban
5	Adult Cont.	Album Rock

Persons 35-64

Rank	Black	General Audience
1	Urban	News/Talk
2	News/Talk	Adult Cont.
3	Religious	Country
4	Adult Alt.	Oldies
5	Adult Cont.	Urban

Source: Black National Database, Fall 1995

FIG. 8.7.   Source: Courtesy of the Arbitron Company.

for assessing overall listening trends, or comparing the performance of certain types of stations.

Arbitron uses its national database to generate special reports on individual listener groups. One example is the Black Radio Today report issued in 1996. Using data from fall 1995, Arbitron analysts compared general audience listenership to trends among Blacks. The information in this report includes comparisons of format preferences by age. Figure 8.7 illustrates some of the differences found in the study.

This figure shows differences between Black audiences and general audience trends and, within the Black audience, differences by age groups. Similarly, a special report on Hispanic radio published in 1998 found, among other things, that Spanish-language programming claims a 47% share of listening among Hispanic Americans aged 18–34, but the corresponding share for Hispanic-American teenagers was only 28%.

Just like television market data, the information contained in radio market reports is now available on computer. Arbitron markets software called *Maximi$er* to radio stations and another called *Media Professional* to advertisers and ad agencies. The firm's acquisition of Tapscan further extended its software product capabilities.

NATIONAL RATINGS

Network

Network television ratings are the most visible of all ratings products. For most Americans, the name Nielsen is synonymous with ratings. That identification occurs for good reason—Nielsen has been the dominant supplier of national audience ratings for many years. Nielsens are often held to account for the cancellation or renewal of network television programs—an explanation that belies the complexity of programming decisions. The service that provides network ratings is called the *Nielsen Television Index (NTI)*.

As noted in chapter 6, Nielsen used meter–diary methodology for its national television service until 1987, when it switched to the peoplemeter. There are approximately 5,000 households in the national sample, and each household provides data for approximately 2 years. With an average of 2.6 people in each home, this sample includes roughly 13,000 individuals. At any point in time, however, the number of respondents providing useful data will be lower. Before looking at the reports Nielsen publishes, it is worth reflecting on the enormous amount of data this system generates. Thousands of people watching various combinations of broadcast television, VCRs, and cable, being monitored minute by minute over a period of years, creates a vast flow of raw material to be refined into reports and services.

The best known, and longest continuously produced, television network ratings report is NTI's National TV Ratings, better known as the *pocketpiece*.

Named for its small vest pocket size, the pocketpiece is issued weekly and provides a variety of commonly used audience estimates.

Figure 8.8 shows two facing pages of a pocketpiece report. NTI displays the TVHH ratings for prime-time network programs in a way that highlights the scheduling characteristics of those programs. The pages shown depict ratings for a Sunday night in November. The banner indicates the time periods, in quarter hours, and the HUT level associated with each time period. Notice the HUT level was highest between 8:45 and 9:00 p.m. During that time, Nielsen estimated that 69.5% of TVHH had a set in use. Because network programs run at different times in different time zones, Nielsen adjusts its audience estimates to Eastern Time.

The left-hand side displays the various networks, or station categories, households are likely to be watching. The upper page lists the four major broadcast networks—ABC, CBS, NBC, and Fox—the lower page displays estimates for WB and UPN, plus independents, cable networks, and public television. Notice that no specific program audience information is presented for this latter class of program services.

On this particular Sunday, the network prime-time schedule began with ABC's *Wonderful World of Disney*, CBS's *60 Minutes*, and NBC's *Dateline NBC*. Audience information appears below each program title by quarter hour, half hour, and complete program. The first number is the rating—the average audience for the program. To the right is the projected number of households watching in an average minute. For example, *Touched by an Angel*'s rating of 17.2 translates into 16,810,000 households in an average minute. Beneath the rating is the Total Audience, or cume. *Touched by an Angel*'s cume of 21.4 indicates more than one fifth of all TVHH tuned in to some part of this program. Below the Total Audience estimates is the share, in this case an average of 25% during the hour. The last row of numbers under the program title is the average audience rating for each quarter hour. Note that at 8:15 and 8:45 Nielsen provides (in the second row of numbers) estimates of rating and share by half hour.

This arrangement provides a clear sense of the competition among network and non-network services. It also suggests something about audience flow from one quarter hour to the next, although bona fide analyses of audience flow require access to different data.

These tables do not disclose demographic composition of program audiences. The pocketpiece reports that information in a different section of the book. Nielsen arranges network program audience estimates alphabetically by time period, reporting estimated viewers per 1,000 viewing households. In these sections individual program audiences are divided into age and gender combinations, including categories for "working women" and "LOH W/CH <3" (lady of house with child less than 3). Precise demographic categories vary by daypart. Nielsen also reports the contribution of VCRs to the audience. Rarely does a VCR audience account for more than 1 rating point.

NATIONAL *NielsenTV* AUDIENCE ESTIMATES — EVE. SUN. NOV. 16, 1997

TIME	7:00	7:15	7:30	7:45	8:00	8:15	8:30	8:45	9:00	9:15	9:30	9:45	10:00	10:15	10:30	10:45	11:00	11:15
HUT	61.8	63.1	63.8	64.7	66.3	67.7	68.6	69.5	68.4	68.2	67.4	66.6	63.1	60.5	58.1	55.8	49.0	43.5

ABC TV

Programs: WONDERFUL WORLD OF DISNEY — OLIVER TWIST (7:00–9:00) → ABC SUNDAY NIGHT MOVIE — MEDUSA'S CHILD, PART 1 (9:00–11:00)

Metric	7:00	7:30	8:00	8:30	9:00	9:30	10:00	10:30	11:00
HHLD AUDIENCE % & (000)	7.8 (7,610)				7.2 (7,040)				
74% AVG. AUD. 1/2 HR %	14.1	8.0*	7.9*	7.4*	13.1	6.7*	6.9*	7.5*	7.7*
SHARE AUDIENCE %	12	12*	12*	11*	11	10*	10*	12*	13*
AVG. AUD. BY 1/4 HR %	7.5	7.8 / 8.1 / 8.0	8.0 / 7.8	8.0 / 7.7	6.7 / 6.7	7.1	7.3 / 7.6	7.5	7.8

CBS TV

Programs: 60 MINUTES (7:00–8:00) → TOUCHED BY AN ANGEL (8:00–9:00) → CBS SUNDAY MOVIE — BELLA MAFIA, PT. 1 OF 2 (9:00–11:00)

Metric	7:00	7:30	8:00	8:30	9:00	9:30	10:00	10:30	11:00
HHLD AUDIENCE % & (000)	17.2 (16,810)				14.8 (14,550)				
74% AVG. AUD. 1/2 HR %	21.4	16.3*	17.6	18.0*	21.2	15.5*	14.8*	14.6*	14.4*
SHARE AUDIENCE %	25	24*		26*	23	23*	22*	24*	25*
AVG. AUD. BY 1/4 HR %	16.0	16.6	17.6	18.4	15.8	15.2 / 15.0	14.6 / 14.9	14.4 / 14.5	14.4

NBC TV

Programs: DATELINE NBC-SUN (7:00–7:34)(PAE) → DATELINE NBC-SU (7:34–8:00)(B)(PAE) → JENNY (SPECIAL) → NBC SUNDAY NIGHT MOVIE — BATMAN FOREVER

Metric	7:00	7:34	8:00	8:30	9:00 → (movie)				
HHLD AUDIENCE % & (000)	13.9 (13,620)		5.9 (5,780)	5.0 (4,930)	5.0 (4,890)	8.3 (8,150)			
74% AVG. AUD. 1/2 HR %	20.5	12.6*	8.5	6.6	6.7	18.4	8.5*	8.7*	9.3*
SHARE AUDIENCE %	22	20*	9	7	7	13	13*	15*	15*
AVG. AUD. BY 1/4 HR %	11.7	13.5 / 15.0	6.1	5.1 / 5.0	5.1 / 4.9	6.0	8.5 / 8.7	8.7 / 9.4	9.1 / 8.8

FOX TV

Programs: WORLD'S FUNNIEST! (1) → SIMPSONS (PAE) → KING OF THE HILL → X-FILES

Metric	7:00 (World's Funniest)	8:00 (Simpsons)	8:30 (King of the Hill)	9:00 (X-Files)	9:30	10:00
HHLD AUDIENCE % & (000)	9.4 (9,200)	11.6 (11,340)	12.5 (12,220)	13.0 (12,730)		
74% AVG. AUD. 1/2 HR %	17.4	13.6	14.5	15.9	13.0*	13.0*
SHARE AUDIENCE %	15	17	18	19	19*	19*
AVG. AUD. BY 1/4 HR %	9.1 / 9.7	11.2 / 11.9	12.3 / 12.6	13.0	13.0 / 12.9	13.0

WB TV

	NICK FRENO: LIC. TEACH-WB	PARENT 'HOOD. THE - WB	JAMIE FOXX SHOW. THE - WB	TOM SHOW. THE - WB	UNHAPPILY EVER AFTER - WB	ALRIGHT ALREADY - WB
HHLD AUDIENCE% & (000)	2.7 2,650	3.0 2,970	3.1 3,050	2.5 2,460	2.7 2,690	2.1 2,060
T/4%. AVG. AUD. 1/2 HR %	3.6	3.8	3.7	3.1	3.3	2.6
SHARE AUDIENCE %	.4	.5	.5	.4	.4	.3
AVG. AUD. BY 1/4 HR %	2.7	2.9	3.0	2.7	2.7	2.1

UPN TV

HHLD AUDIENCE% & (000)						
T/4%. AVG. AUD. 1/2 HR %						
SHARE AUDIENCE %						
AVG. AUD. BY 1/4 HR %						

INDEPENDENTS (Inc. superstations except TBS)	AA% 6.2	7.2	7.3	6.7	6.9	6.1	13.8 (+F)	10.0 (+F)	7.4 (+F)
	SHR% 10	11	11	10	10	9	22	18	16
PBS	AA% 1.6	1.6	3.0	3.3	2.4	2.3	1.7	1.7	0.9
	SHR% .3	.2	.4	.5	.3	.3	.3	.3	.2
CABLE ORIG. (Including TBS)	AA% 21.2	23.8	23.9	23.6	23.7	23.9	22.0 (+F)	20.2 (+F)	16.4 (+F)
	SHR% 34	37	36	34	35	36	36	36	35
PAY SERVICES	AA% 2.5	2.6	3.2	3.1	3.5	3.0	2.9	2.9	2.8
	SHR% .4	.4	.5	.5	.5	.4	.5	.5	.6

U.S. TV Households: 98,000,000
(1) FOX NFL SUNDAY-NATIONAL VARIOUS TEAMS AND TIMES.FOX.(MULTI SEGMENT)(PAE)

For explanation of symbols. See page B.

For SPANISH LANGUAGE TELEVISION audience estimates, see the Nielsen Hispanic Television Index (NHTI) TV Audience Report.

A-17

FIG. 8.8. Nielsen PocketPiece. Source: Nielsen Media Research.

With the introduction of the peoplemeter, Nielsen was able to provide demographic information within 24 hours of a broadcast. Consequently, NTI overnights contain a potentially overwhelming amount of data. Clients manage this data by selecting the demographic information they want to receive regularly. Figure 8.9 shows an example of overnight ratings from the peoplemeter sample for Tuesday, July 21, 1998: networks on the left-hand side, demographics across the top. Each row contains data on the number of stations carrying the program, the program length (DUR, for duration), coverage, days of broadcast, and corresponding rating/share information.

Nielsen offers a host of other published reports, among them cable network ratings, provided through the *Nielsen Homevideo Index (NHI)* division. Other divisions offer reports on viewing in Hispanic households and viewing of specific sporting events.

Television, of course, is not the only advertiser-supported medium providing network service to the public. Radio networks still attract millions of advertiser dollars and, although they cannot rival the amounts spent on television, these networks need audience research. As noted in chapter 6, shortly after Nielsen ended its radio network measurement, a research effort called RADAR® filled the void. Today, Statistical Research Inc. (SRI) publishes the RADAR® report, the standard network radio ratings service.

RADAR® ratings are based on telephone interviews conducted with a sample of 12,000 respondents. SRI analysts determine which households to call through random digit dialing (RDD). Within each home, SRI randomly selects one individual age 12 or older, and interviews him or her once a day for one week. Interviewing proceeds during 48 weeks each year. Response rates are generally about 45%.

RADAR® reports are issued in three volumes, available electronically through a software package called PC 2001. Until summer 1998, reports were issued in the spring and fall. Now they are issued quarterly, with one fourth of the 12,000-person sample updated in each report. The first volume, called *National Radio Listening*, contains general information about audience composition and listening habits during different dayparts and quarter hours, without regard to specific networks. Analysts estimate the size of the audience in an average quarter hour (AQH), as well as 1-day, 5-day, and 7-day cumes. These summaries are subdivided by standard age–gender groupings as well as other demographic (e.g., income and education), geographic, and behavioral variables. The data also include a summary of listening by location (home vs. out-of-home).

Volumes 2 and 3 are entitled *Network Audiences to All Commercials* and *Network Audiences to Commercials Within Programs*, respectively. Basically, these are estimates for the 20 or so network subscribers. RADAR® analysts combine program and commercial clearance data obtained from the networks with station listening information obtained from respondents. However, because some

PRIME - ALL DEMOS   NIELSEN TELEVISION INDEX

DATA FOR TUESDAY   07/21/98

OVERNIGHT TOTAL PROGRAM

DAYPART: PRIME PRELIMINARY

NET TIME STN	DUR CVG	PROGRAM NAME EPISODE TITLE	(MTWRFSS)	HH AA%	HH SHR	Women 25-54 AA%/AVPVH	Women 18-49 AA%/AVPVH	Adult 18-34 AA%/AVPVH	Child 2-11 AA%/AVPVH	TTeen 12-17 AA%/AVPVH	Adult 18-49 AA%/AVPVH	Adult 25-54 AA%/AVPVH	Women 25+ AA%/AVPVH
ABC													
8:00P 220	30 99	HOME IMPROVEMENT	(T (R))	6.2	12	4.2 410	4.0 412	3.3 334	1.6 107	3.2 116	3.8 768	3.9 743	4.3 629
8:30P 219	30 99	SOUL MAN	(T (R))	5.4	10	3.8 418	3.5 409	2.2 257	1.4 106	2.4 101	3.0 701	3.2 708	4.0 675
9:00P 221	30 99	SPIN CITY	(T (RP))	5.2	9	3.6 417	3.4 420	2.7 320	1.4 106	2.7 116	3.1 745	3.3 758	3.6 631
9:30P 220	30 99	SPIN CITY SPEC-7/21	(T (RS))	6.0	10	4.0 404	3.8 398	3.2 337	1.2 79	3.4 127	3.7 775	4.0 784	4.0 610
10:00P 220	30 99	NYPD BLUE	(T (R))	5.6	10	3.8 408	3.1 359	1.9 216	0.6^ 45^	1.7 70	2.8 643	3.5 740	4.1 66ể
CBS													
8:00P 213	60 99	JAG	(T (R))	6.5	13	3.7 342	3.0 297	1.7 165	1.0 63	1.2 41^	2.4 461	3.1 559	5.5 770
9:00P 213	120 99	CBS TUESDAY MOVIE SCARLETT, PT.3 OF 4	(T (R))	5.2	9	3.3 386	3.1 381	1.7 213	0.5^ 42^	1.3^ 58^	2.0 486	2.2 506	4.9 857
NBC													
8:00P 220	30 98	MAD ABOUT YOU	(T (R))	4.8	10	3.7 469	3.8 507	2.8 363	0.9 74	1.2^ 58^	2.8 736	2.8 701	3.8 716
8:30P 220	30 99	NEWSRADIO	(T (R))	4.8	9	3.8 479	3.9 519	3.8 499	0.5^ 43^	0.6^ 29^	3.4 905	3.4 832	3.3 65ể
9:00P 221	30 99	FRASIER	(T (R))	7.6	14	5.8 462	5.3 449	5.2 433	1.0 53	1.5 45	4.9 821	5.2 816	5.5 66ể
9:30P 218	30 99	3RD ROCK FROM SUN TUE9:30	(T (R))	6.6	11	5.6 511	5.1 488	4.2 398	0.9 57	2.3 80	4.5 853	4.8 861	4.3 ?65
10:00P 219	60 99	DATELINE NBC-TUE	(T)	10.7	20	8.3 465	7.2 429	5.1 297	1.2 46	2.9 61	5.9 694	6.7 736	7.0 758
FOX													
8:00P 198	120 98	FOX TUESDAY NIGHT MOVIE THE BEVERLY HILLBILLIES	(T (R))	5.2	10	3.3 383	3.2 395	2.9 349	2.5 190	4.4 191	3.0 731	3.1 716	3.0 535
UPN													
8:45P 198	1 98	SOUNDS OF THE GAME-TUE (1)	(T)	5.1	10	3.3 382	3.2 396	3.0 364	2.5 196	4.2 183	2.9 723	3.0 698	3.0 535

FIG. 8.9.   Nielsen Television Index, national overnights.

151

stations extract network commercials from network programs and air them separately, audience estimates are reported in two volumes. Volume 2 reports the audience for network commercials, whether aired with the program or not. Volume 3 estimates do not include commercials outside the program. Needless to say, audience estimates in Volume 2 are greater than or equal to those reported in Volume 3.

SRI also publishes specialized studies for a variety of media clients. The firm is often contracted to do the telephone coincidentals against which other measurement techniques are evaluated.

In 1996, Arbitron tried to compete with SRI in the national radio research business by issuing its own proposal to four major radio networks. While aspects of the Arbitron proposal were attractive, such as large sample size and greater frequency of measurement, a short-term renewal of the SRI contract eventually led to improved service on the part of SRI and a longer commitment from stations. For a short time, the two companies discussed the possibility of a joint service, but talks collapsed due to fundamental differences in approach. Many in the industry credited this threat of competition with prompting SRI to offer better software to handle RADAR® data. Whether Arbitron can successfully launch a viable national service remains to be seen.

Syndication

Nielsen measures audiences for syndicated programming by drawing on its NTI peoplemeter sample and its NSI diary samples. This information is marketed by the *Nielsen Syndication Service (NSS)*. Because syndication carries national advertising, the industry needs audience estimates that are comparable to broadcast and network ratings. These estimates are based on the peoplemeter sample and are published as pocketpieces and other standard reports similar to the audience information available for networks. The syndicated pocketpiece resembles the network version and is used in the same way by salespeople and media buyers. Additionally, NSS publishes the *Report on Syndicated Programs (ROSP)* after each of the 4 major sweeps. This report provides program ratings market by market, by extracting the ratings performance of every syndicated program from local data. This information is organized by program so users can see the program's average performance across all markets, as well as in each market that carried the show. This is useful for programmers at local stations and for the syndicators themselves who need to prove success in order to sell the program to more stations.

Figure 8.10 is a page from the Nielsen February 1998 ROSP. It is the first of several pages in the report that describe the audience for *This Old House*, a popular how-to program. The upper right-hand corner of the page lists information on the program's coverage, distributor, and so forth. This program aired on 130 stations that, taken together, reach 79% of all TVHH in the United States. The upper third of the table summarizes how *This Old House* did across all of those

THIS OLD HOUSE
30 MIN.

REPORT ON SYNDICATED PROGRAMS
NSI AVERAGE WEEK ESTIMATES
FEB 1998

MARKETS REPORTING 127
STATIONS REPORTING 130
TOTAL TV HH'S IN DMA'S 77,626,990
DMA % OF U.S. 79
EPISODES AVAILABLE N/A
DIST: WARNER BROS. DOMESTIC TV DIST.
TYPE: UNCLASSIFIED

SUMMARY BY DAYPARTS

DMA HOUSEHOLD SHARES BY MARKET RANK

DAYPART	1-25		26-50		51-100		101+	
	NO.OF DMA'S	% SHARE	NO.OF DMA'S	% SHARE	NO.OF DMA'S	% SHARE	NO.OF DMA'S	% SHARE
DAYTIME (M-F)†								
EARLY FRINGE (M-F)								
PRIME ACCESS (M-SAT)								
PRIME (S-S)						1		6

DAYPART	1-25		26-50		51-100		101+	
	NO.OF DMA'S	% SHARE	NO.OF DMA'S	% SHARE	NO.OF DMA'S	% SHARE	NO.OF DMA'S	% SHARE
POST PRIME (S-S)	1	7	1		3	2	3	4
WEEKEND DAYTIME(S&S)	19	6	22	7	36	5	39	5
WEEKEND PRE-PRIME(S&S)	1	7	1	6	2	8	5	7
AVG. ALL TELECASTS	20	6	23	7	37	5	47	6

TOTAL HOUSEHOLDS AND PERSONS

DAYPART	NO. OF MKT's	NO. OF DMA's	% U.S. TV	DMA HH AVG. QH RTG	SHR	TOTAL HHLDS (000)	WOMEN 18+ (000)	V/CVH	18-49 (000)	V/CVH	25-54 (000)	V/CVH	MEN 18+ (000)	V/CVH	18-49 (000)	V/CVH	TEENS 12-17 (000)	V/CVH	CHILDREN 2-11 (000)	V/CVH
DAYTIME (M-F)†																				
EARLY FRINGE (M-F)																				
PRIME ACCESS (M-SAT)	1	1		2	6	5	3	64	2	36	2	36	2	54	1	30				
PRIME (S-S)																				
POST PRIME (S-S)	8	8	3	‹‹		13	3	27	2	14			3	20	3	20				
WEEKEND DAYTIME(S&S)	116	116	76	1	7	1157	657	57	295	25	379	33	567	49	319	28	29	3	31	3
WEEKEND PRE-PRIME(S&S)	9	9	4	2	7	104	54	52	19	18	23	22	59	57	22	21	3	3	1	1
TOTAL DAY	127	127				1207	681		309		395		588		312		31		31	
AVG. ALL TELECASTS			1	6		10	5	53	2	23	3	29	5	51	3	26				

LINE 1	REPORTABLE STATIONS	FOUR WEEK AVERAGE TIME PERIOD AUDIENCES			PROGRAM AUDIENCE SECTION (SYNDICATED PROGRAM ONLY)			COMPETING FOUR WEEK AVERAGE TIME PERIOD AUDIENCES		
MARKET	T.Z. ON AIR	(THIS PROGRAM vs. PRECEDING HALF HOUR)								
LINE 2	TOTAL DAY									
STATION CH. NET. DMA SHARE		DESIGNATED MARKET AREA	DMA		STATION TOTALS					
LINE 3 START NO. OF			% VS	(000)				CORRESPONDING TIME PERIOD-3 HIGHEST COMPETING STATIONS	DMA %	
DAY TIME T/CS.										

This table continues with station-by-station data:

LEAD-IN-PROGRAM	DMA % RTG	SHR	PERSONS SHARE % ‡ WOMEN 18+	18-49	25-54	MEN 18+	18-49	TEENS 12-17	CHD 2-11	HH RTG	SHR	DMA % VS V/100VH	(000) V/100VH	TOTAL HHLD	TOTAL ADULTS	WOMEN 18+	18-49	25-54	MEN 18+	18-49	TEENS 12-17	CHILD 2-11	STATION PROGRAM	HH RTG	SHR
ALBANY-SCH-TROY EA 6														13	14	15	16	17	18	19	20	21		22	23
WXXA CH.23 F 6%																									
FRI 1.30A 4T/C	‹‹			5	9					‹‹		(000)			1			1	1			WRGB # VRS /PD PRG	1	17
COPS	‹‹	2	3	8	14							V/CVH		245				245	245			WNYT FRI NIGHT-NBC	1	16
SUN 11.00A 4T/C	1	4	3	5	3	7	8	4	4	1	4	(000)	5	6	2	2	1	4	2			WTEN+# PAID PROGRAM	1	
FOX23 IN FOCUS	‹‹											V/CVH		122	38	23		75	47		25	WTEN+ THIS WEEK-ABC	3	15
																						WRGB MARTHA STWT WK	3	14
MARKET AVG.									1	4	(000)	3	3	1	1	2	1			WMHT # KRATTS CRT-PTV	‹‹	
ALBANY, GA EA 4												V/CVH		128	44	36	22	84	58		23			
WGVP CH.44 I %																								
SUN 9.00A 4T/C	‹‹			3	5	5				‹‹		(000)										WALB 1ST MTHDST CHR	2	8
REMODLNG TODAY	‹‹			3	5							V/CVH										WABW # ARTHUR-PTV	1	5
ALBUQ-SANTA FE MT 7																						WFXL FOX NWS SUNDAY	‹‹	
KOB + CH. 4 N 14%																								
SAT 4.00P 4T/C	1	6	4	2	4	6	5	8		1	6	(000)	8	8	3	1	2	5	3			KASY+# PAID PROGRAM	2	8
#SPORTS-SAT-NBC	1	6	2	1	1	9	5	5	12			V/CVH		98	38	11	19	61	35			KROE+# ADVENTURE RIO	2	8
SUN 6.30A 4T/C	1	13	12		6	15	8	7	56	1	13	(000)	4	4	2			2	1			KASA # HONEY I-KIDS	1	5
ALL NWS CHANNL	1	20	15	18	28	21	22	21	99	53		V/CVH		106	46			60	14			KOAT+ ACT7-MRN NM SU	2	33
																						KASA ADVNTR-O TWIST	‹‹	
MARKET AVG.									1	7	(000)	6	6	3		1	4	2			KLUZ CLUB-TG SU UNI	‹‹	
ANCHORAGE YU 6										1	7	V/CVH		101	40		16	61	28					
KIMO CH.13 A 8%																								
SUN 3.00P 4T/C	1	4	5	2	2	5				1	4	(000)	1	2	1			1				KTUU # SUN AFT MOVIE	4	18
ANCHORG-TEMPLE	1	2	2		2		6					V/CVH		142	70			71				KTBY PENSACOLA-GOLD	2	9
ANNISTON CE 4																						KTVA # DUE SOUTH	2	9
WJSU CH.40 A 15%																								
SUN 6.00A 4T/C	1	7	11	21	18					1	7	(000)	1	1	1			1				WBRC GOSPEL-JUBILEE	2	23
												V/CVH		87	87							WVTM MCDOUGALL	1	11
AUSTIN CE 7																						WPXH NAVY NEWS	‹‹	
KTBC CH. 7 F 13%																								
SAT 7.00A 4T/C	1	8	7	6	11	14	29	28		1	8	(000)	3	4	1	1	1	2	2			KXAN+ FIRSTCAST SAT	3	15
BETTER-GARDENS	‹‹	16	16	23	6							V/CVH		105	41	15	36	65	62			KVUE DISNY-DLMT-ABC	1	12
																						KEYE # CBS NW SA MORN	1	5
BAKERSFIELD PA 6																								
KUVI CH.45 I 5%																								
SAT 7.00A 4T/C	‹‹	5	11	11	3	5	5			‹‹		(000)	1	1	1			1				KGET SATURDAY TODAY	5	28
REBECCA GARDEN	‹‹											V/CVH		163	105	105	105					KABE CHAVO-SA-UNI	1	7
																						KERO DISNY-DLMT-ABC	1	5
BALTIMORE EA 7																								
WMAR CH. 2 A 11%																								
SAT 11.30A 4T/C	1.	4	3	4	6	7	3	6		1	4	(000)	16	16	6	4	4	10	6	3		WBFF SILVR SURF-FOX	3	11
BILL NYE-GUY	1	5	5	7	9	7	9	10			6	V/CVH		97	37	23	23	60	39	16		WBAL # NBA INSD STUFF	3	10
																						WMPB+# J WILSON-COOKN	3	8

FIG. 8.10.   Nielsen ROSP. Source: Nielsen Media Research.

markets. Most stations ran it in the Weekend Daytime daypart, but a few aired it during Weekend Pre-prime, Prime Access, and Post Prime. Averaged across dayparts, the program earned a 1 rating and a 6 share.

Each market that carried the program is listed alphabetically, with the corresponding ratings information. This section provides more than simple audience estimates for the program. As noted in previous chapters, audience size is affected by competition and the ratings of the lead-in program. The ROSP provides information about both in every market that carried the program. Figure 8.10 shows *This Old House* aired on Saturday at 4 p.m., with a lead-in from NBC sports. It was also scheduled on Sunday at 6:30 a.m., after news programming. If station personnel are trying to evaluate the performance of a program in their market, they can look for an appropriate comparison by finding similar market situations. Nielsen produces a similar report for public television called the *Report on Public Television Programs* (ROPP).

The Internet

For any new media technology to attract the sustained attention of advertisers, a system of audience measurement must be in place. This is as true today of the World Wide Web as it was of radio and television broadcasting 50 years ago. Companies that generate audience research data for the Web provide data monthly to online subscribers. These numbers convey similar information to that available in television and radio ratings reports. Subscribers can learn the number of visitors to a Web site, how long they spent on a particular page, and the demographic profile of audiences for specific types of content. Media Metrix publishes reach estimates by location, giving subscribers information about home and work usage. In November 1998, for example, AOL Web sites achieved a reach of 49.2% at home, and 36.3% at work. Yahoo Sites were accessed by more people from work, with a reach of 49.6%.

Audience data affect the rates that advertisers pay for Internet availabilities, but the determination is still qualitative in nature, because the standards for audience measurement and reporting remain under development. Differences in methodologies can lead to vastly different audience estimates from competing research firms, and it is difficult to predict which sampling and measurement methods will be universally adopted by Internet research providers. For details about the methods and products offered by the principal Internet measurement firms, Media Metrix and NetRatings, visit their Web sites listed in Table 1.1 of this volume.

CUSTOMIZED RATINGS REPORTS

The products reviewed previously have been the standard offerings of the major ratings companies. Usually, they appear as published reports, although increasingly, such reports are delivered in a form computers can read. In either case, they are reports designed to answer the common research questions developed in chapters 2 and 3. But while standard reports are useful, some questions can only be addressed by a creative analysis of ratings data. Often, these questions are so specialized they do not justify the publication of a standardized report. Nevertheless, if paying customers want something not found in a ratings book, ratings firms have ways to accommodate them. Clients can request any number of customized reports, from analyses of specific socioeconomic groups to reach and frequency estimates to studies of audience flow. These *custom reports* are priced individually and conform to the client's specifications. Depending on the data requested, these studies can cost anywhere from a few hundred to several thousand dollars.

Customized reports are derived from one of three methods, distinguished by the source of the data. First, ratings company analysts can devise special studies based on individual client requests. Second, the data collected in the usual way can be combined with data available from other sources. Third, ratings companies can gather more data than they would otherwise collect.

The first option for creating a customized analysis is the most common. Standardized reports only scratch the surface of the analytical possibilities offered by a ratings database (see chap. 11, this volume). Suppose a programmer is interested in knowing whether the audience for a syndicated game show stays tuned and watches the local news that follows it. No ratings book published in the United States contains the answer. Even if the game show and news have the same rating, an analyst cannot tell whether the same people watched both programs. But diaries track audience members from one time period to the next, so analysis of individual diaries would yield the desired information. The ratings services vary in the degree to which they offer subscribers direct access to respondent level data. Arbitron sells this data as part of its subscription packages; Nielsen does not.

The array of customized services gets more confusing when new sources of data are introduced into the mix. Recall that advertisers are most often interested in what audience members are likely to buy. For this reason there is considerable pressure on the ratings companies to introduce product-usage data into the ratings database. Although the single-source technology described earlier may be the most powerful tool for producing these data, those systems have never passed the testing stage. More typically, product usage data, along with information on lifestyles, home ownership, and so forth are added to ratings data after the fact.

This is done by matching audience behavior in a small geographic area, usually a zip code, to other information about that area. Zip codes tend to be relatively homogeneous in composition. Some areas are known to be affluent, others poor. Some neighborhoods have large owner-occupied homes, others have a lot of rental units. This information, along with product purchase information is used by services like Claritas and Scarborough to identify certain "clusters" or categories based on similarities. By assuming that a diarykeeper living in a particular kind of area is like others in that area, it is possible to associate ratings data with other variables not in the original database.

The last kind of customized research available from the ratings services involves collecting additional data at the behest of the client. Of course, if the price is right, a ratings company might be persuaded to gather almost any kind of audience data, but two methods of new data collection are worth mentioning here. First, even though it is not their standard method of data collection, both Arbitron and Nielsen will conduct telephone coincidentals. This gives a client the option of getting a ratings report from a major supplier, especially when there is no ratings sweep in progress. Second, it is possible to arrange for diarykeepers to be interviewed after their diaries have been collected. By asking questions of a diarykeeper and matching responses with the diary record, new insights into the behavior of the audience may emerge. In either case, because new data must be gathered for a single client, these services are costly.

Although customized ratings reports can provide analysts with many insights otherwise not available, the users of these reports should exercise caution in the interpretation of the numbers they contain. Ratings companies are in business to make a profit, and finding new ways to exploit or resell existing databases represents a golden opportunity. Remember also that customized reports by their nature are not subject to the same ongoing scrutiny of a syndicated report. Ratings companies may very well give a buyer the kind of report asked for, even if it does not make good sense as a piece of research. We have seen, for example, customized market areas constructed from a handpicked group of counties with too few diaries in-tab to offer reliable audience estimates. In evaluating any ratings report, but especially a customized product, the user must be sure he or she understands the research design upon which the data are based.

BUYING RATINGS DATA

The fees charged for syndicated research products vary greatly. A television station in a small market might spend as little as $12,000 a year for basic ratings reports. An affiliate in a major market might spend close to $1 million on ratings and related services. A broadcast network will spend more. A number of factors affect the cost of ratings data, and prices may well be subject to negotiation—especially if a station is owned by a powerful group that accounts for a large share of a research firm's subscription revenues.

One determinant of price is market size. Stations in small markets can expect to pay less for ratings than stations in big markets. In part, this is a reflection of the cost of data collection. Within a given market, there may also be differences in the cost of ratings to different clients. Agencies typically pay less than stations. In fact, in local market research, broadcasters account for about 90% of ratings service revenues. Different stations may also pay different amounts depending on whether they are independents or affiliates, UHF stations, or VHF stations. Generally, stations with smaller audiences receive a discount. Although we have never seen any analysis of this, it is likely that the price stations pay for basic ratings data varies more or less in tandem with the advertising rates they charge based on those same audience estimates. The length of the contract a client signs can also affect prices. Those who sign long-term contracts should get a discount. A station's subscription to a ratings service will usually run from 3 to 5 or even 7 years. Stations making longer commitments can lock in a lower yearly increase for the service. In metered markets, however, longer commitments may be required in advance to induce the ratings company to establish the service.

Academic users can also get special pricing consideration. Nielsen offers packages of both NTI and NSI data designed for educational institutions, and Arbitron provides miscellaneous reports to academics upon request. It has also established an archive of its ratings at the University of Georgia. Unfortunately, Nielsen has no public archive of its data, although individual Nielsen offices may maintain informal collections.

Generalizing about the cost of customized ratings reports is even more difficult. Despite the analytical possibilities offered by such research, these still account for only a modest portion of ratings service revenues. To learn more about them, or the specific cost of any ratings product, you must deal with the rating services directly.

Occasionally, a ratings company and one of its clients will have serious differences. A station might be suspected of inappropriate practices during a sweep, or a ratings company might be suspected of mishandling some aspect of the research process. Sometimes a good deal of money can ride in the balance. Although going to court is always a possibility, the parties may find it advisable to opt for a less costly solution. If normal channels of communication fail, the Media Rating Council (MRC) can invoke mediation procedures that involve representatives from the appropriate industries and trade associations.

RELATED READINGS

Arbitron. A *guide to understanding and using radio audience estimates* (annual). New York: Author.

Beville, H. M. (1988). *Audience ratings: Radio, television, cable* (rev. ed.). Hillsdale, NJ: Lawrence Erlbaum Associates.

Fletcher, A. D., & Bower, T. A. (1988). *Fundamentals of advertising research* (3rd ed.). Belmont, CA: Wadsworth.

Nielsen Station Index. *Your guide to reports & services* (annual). New York: Nielsen Media Research.

Poltrack, D. F. (1983). *Television marketing: Network, local, and cable*. New York: McGraw-Hill.

III

Analytical Techniques

9

Understanding
Audience Behavior

Audience research comes in many forms having a wide variety of applications. At first glance, this abundance may be overwhelming. How does one make sense of all those numbers? What is a high rating, or what is a low one? What is an unusual or important feature of audience behavior, and what is routine? This chapter offers a framework for evaluating and analyzing the information contained in audience data, with an emphasis on broad concepts and theories. This approach is intended to give readers a sense of perspective on the audience—to help them see the forest instead of an endless succession of trees.

The information collected by the research firms is conceptually straightforward. At their core, databases simply record people's reported exposure to media. Databases reveal nothing about the effects of that exposure or motivations for listening or viewing. Any useful framework for analyzing these data, then, requires understanding the complexities of how people use media. If researchers know what determines exposure to media and can predict patterns of use likely to emerge under given circumstances, then they have a way of interpreting the numbers that confront them.

The chapter contains four sections. First, we take a closer look at just what a ratings analyst is trying to assess—exposure to media. We categorize and discuss the principal measurements of audience behavior. Second, we review the most common theories for explaining people's choice of media offerings. These rely heavily on individual preferences to explain what the audience is doing. Third, we introduce factors that seem critical to understanding audience formation. Finally, we present a model of audience behavior that reflects all of these considerations and offers a more complete way to understand exposure to media. This is the key to interpreting audience information.

EXPOSURE TO MEDIA

As noted previously, most commercial audience research is simply a record of what kinds of people are exposed to what kinds of media. The practice in the television and radio industries has been to define exposure as program choice, or tuning behavior, rather than as attention or involvement. By studying a properly drawn sample of individuals and accurately measuring each one, researchers can have considerable confidence in their ability to describe exposure to media, using various definitions of exposure. Of course, research firms encounter myriad problems in sampling, measurement, and data processing. These exact a toll on accuracy. But even experienced users who are aware of data error tend to take numbers at face value in their day-to-day work. For the most part, that is our approach. When substantial methodological problems or biases suggest a qualified interpretation of the data, it is noted; but otherwise, we treat audience ratings as valid measures of exposure.

We have already encountered ways to measure or somehow quantify media audiences—some are reported by ratings services, others are calculated by ratings users. It is useful, at this point, to draw a broad distinction between these various measurements and indices. One type is called *gross measures* and the other *cumulative measures*, depending on whether the behavior of individuals is tracked over time. If an audience statistic does not depend on tracking, it is a gross measure. If it does, it is cumulative. This temporal quality in the data defines a fundamental distinction that is carried through the rest of this volume.

Gross Measures of the Audience

Gross measures of exposure include estimates of audience size and composition made at a single point in time. The best examples are audience ratings and market shares, although summaries like the circulation of print media or total sales (e.g., movie ticket or record sales) are also gross measures of the audience. Even the number of hits on a Web site would seem to qualify. In effect, the gross measures are snapshots of the population that give no clear sense of the number of repeat customers involved.

Electronic media take these snapshots with the greatest rapidity. Ratings services estimate how many people listened to a station in an average quarter hour or watched a program in an average minute. As projections of total audience size, HUT and PUT levels belong in this category as well. Gross measures of exposure can also include secondary calculations derived from other measurements. Gross rating points (GRPs)—a summation of individual ratings over a schedule—are such calculations. Simple cost calculations, like cost per point (CPP) and cost per thousand (CPM), can also be thought of as gross measures.

Gross measures are the most common audience summaries, and comprise most of the numbers reported in syndicated research reports. As a result, they are the best known and most widely used of audience measurements. Useful as they are, however, they fail to capture information about how individual audience members behave over time. That kind of behavior is expressed in cumulative measures.

Cumulative Measures of the Audience

The most familiar example of the second group of audience measurements is a station's cumulative audience, or *cume*. To report a weekly cume audience, a ratings company must sort each person's media use for a week and summarize how many used the station at least once. Analogous summaries are *reach* and *unduplicated audience*. A closely related cumulative measure increasingly familiar to advertisers is *frequency*—how often an individual sees a particular advertising message over time. Studies of program audience duplication, likewise, depend on tracking individual media users over time.

With the exception of the various cume ratings, cumulative measures are less commonly reported by syndicated research services than are gross measurements. Customized studies of audience duplication, however, may be useful in a variety of applications. For example, a programmer studying audience flow, or an advertiser tracking the reach and frequency of a media plan, is concerned with how the audience is behaving over time. Indeed (as suggested in chap. 5) this sort of tracking can be illuminating for social scientists interested in any number of questions. Table 9.1 lists the most common gross and cumulative measures of media exposure.

TABLE 9.1
Common Measures of Exposure to Media

Gross Measures	Cumulative Measures
Audience Ratings	Cume Ratings
Market Shares	Reach
Circulation	Frequency
Web-site Hits	Audience Duplication
Sales	Inheritance Effects
Attendance	Channel Loyalty
Rentals	Repeat Viewing

Comparing Gross and Cumulative Measurements

To get a clearer picture of the difference between gross and cumulative measures, and to begin to appreciate the analytical possibilities offered by such data, consider Fig. 9.1. The large box in the upper left-hand corner represents a simplified ratings database. The data are from a hypothetical sample of 10 households, numbered 1 through 10, down the left-hand column. The media use of each household is measured at 10 points in time, from Time 1 to Time 10 across the top of the page. Both types of measures can be generated for such a database.

In practice a sample would include hundreds or thousands of units of analysis, which could be individual people or households, as indicated in the figure. There would also be many more points in time. For example, a standard television diary divides each of 7 days into 80 quarter hours. Each person is measured across 560 (i.e., 7 × 80) points in time, rather than the 10 illustrated in this example. Now try to imagine how many points in time could be identified in peoplemeter data that track viewing moment to moment over a period of years.

Figure 9.1 portrays household television viewing, but radio listening or Web-site visits could be conceptualized in the same way. This illustration assumes a 3-station market, which means that each household can be doing one of four things at each point in time. It can be tuned to Channel A, Channel B, Channel C, or nothing at all. These behaviors are indicated by the appropriate letters, or a blackened box, respectively.

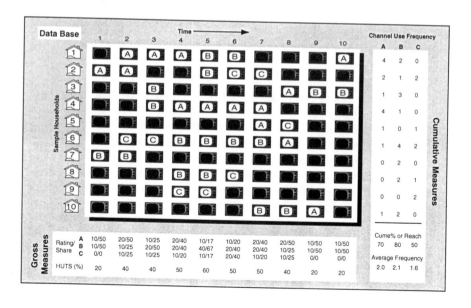

FIG. 9.1. Gross vs. cumulative measures in ratings data.

The most commonly reported gross measures of exposure are shown in the box directly under the database. Each column of data is like Fig. 2.1 (see p. 28), and is treated in the same way. Hence, Channel A has a rating of 20 and a share of 40 at Time 4. All one needs to do is look down the appropriate column. Unlike the calculation of a cume, whatever happened before or after that time period is irrelevant to the calculation of a rating.

The box on the right-hand side of the page includes common cumulative measures. To calculate these, an analyst must first examine each household's viewing behavior across time. That means moving across each row in the database: The first household watched Channel A 4 times, Channel B 2 times, but never watched Channel C. Each channel's column of cumulative viewing indicates its reach, or cume. Each channel's cumulative audience is expressed as a percentage of the sample who viewed it at least once over the 10 points in time. Therefore, the first household would be included in the cume of A and B, but not C. Furthermore, the analyst can report mean frequency of viewing among those who viewed a channel by computing the average of numbers in the column. This is essentially what an advertiser does when calculating reach and frequency, with the relevant points in time being determined by when a commercial message runs.

Studies of program audience duplication can also be executed from this database. An analyst might be interested in how well Station A retains an audience from one show to the next. This can be determined by seeing how many people who watched Station A at one point continued to watch the program that aired after it. The analyst could also compare any pair of program audiences to assess repeat viewing, audience loyalty, and so on. Each case requires tracking individual households across at least two points in time, which would be a cumulative measure of exposure.

Depending on the question, ratings analysts would interpret gross measures, cumulative measures, or numbers derived from these two ways of defining exposure. A large number of analytical techniques can be organized in this way. In fact, these techniques are likely to maintain their usefulness even as the new technologies develop. Whether audiences are reached through the Internet, DBS, or traditional over-the-air broadcasting, the concepts of gross and cumulative measurements convey important information to programmers and advertisers. Exploiting those analytical techniques to their fullest, however, depends on a better understanding of the factors that shape audiences from moment to moment.

COMMON THEORIES OF MEDIA CHOICE

The question most often asked by students of audience behavior is, "why do people choose specific media content?" The answer most commonly provided is, "they choose what they like." This reasoning is typical of industry practice, communications policy, and most academic theories of choice. It suggests equivalence between program preferences and program choices. This section reviews four of the most popular theories of choice: working theories used by industry practitioners, economic models of program choice, selective-exposure theory; and uses and gratifications research. All are based heavily, if not exclusively, on the idea of preferences. They provide a background against which our framework can be better understood.

Working Theories of Program Choice

Working theories are the principles and assumptions used by media professionals while conducting their jobs. These "rules of thumb" may or may not have been subjected to systematic investigation. They may or may not correspond to academic theories of choice. But they certainly deserve attention. Programmers and media planners base these working theories on a day-to-day familiarity with how the audience responds to the media environment.

The people who craft media content monitor trends in popular culture in anticipation of audience behavior. Often, interest centers on what types of content people will like: in television—soap operas, cop shows, game shows, and situation comedies; in radio—station formats, like contemporary hits, country, new age, or all news. These are the familiar industry categories, but we can also define program types in other ways. For example, content could be grouped as entertainment or information, adult or children's, and so on.

It is widely assumed that media consumers will consistently prefer content of a type. Anecdotal evidence supports such reasoning within media industries. Popular movies become television series of the same sort. Hit TV programs are imitated on the assumption that there is an audience out there who likes that kind of material. In television, as one pundit put it, nothing succeeds like excess. Market researchers have conducted formal studies to identify the content characteristics that seem to polarize people's likes and dislikes. What they have generally discovered is that common sense industry categories come as close to a viewer-defined typology as anything. In simple terms, the people who like one soap opera do, in fact, tend to like other soap operas, and so on. Similar preferences for rap music, country-western, opera, and most other types of music are also common (MacFarland, 1997).

An interesting facet of program preferences has emerged from this type of research: dislikes are more clearly related to program type than likes. In other words, what people like may be eclectic, but their dislikes are more readily categorized. A simple test involves listing the five TV shows one likes most, and the five one likes least. For some people, it is hard to express dislikes in anything other than program types. If program choice is as much a matter of avoidance as anything else, this could be an important insight.

Another significant feature of program type preferences is the linkage found between certain types of content and audience demographics. In television, it is well established that news and information draw an older audience. Similarly, men tend to watch more sports than women do, children are drawn to animation, and popular programs among African Americans feature Black characters. The same linkages exist in other forms of media. Women are the usual readers of romance novels. Young men prefer action-adventure films. Internet use also relates to age and gender. None of these associations is intended to suggest a lock-step connection between preferences and demographics, only correlations. But working professionals should certainly be aware of their existence.

As important as preferences are in determining people's choice of media materials, programmers know well that other factors enter the picture. Recall from chapter 3 the importance of audience flow. Radio and television programs appear in a carefully crafted lineup. A program scheduled immediately after a popular show will enjoy a significant advantage in building an audience. Programming strategies such as lead-in effects and block programming depend on this reasoning.

It is also important to consider when the audience is likely to be using the medium in question. Conventional wisdom and some formal theories of audience behavior suggest that other factors than programming determine who is in the audience. In 1971, the late Paul Klein, then a researcher at NBC, offered a tongue-in cheek description of the television audience. Struck by the amazing predictability of audience size, Klein suggested that people turn the set on out of habit, without much advance thought about what they will watch. After the set is on, they simply choose the *least objectionable program (LOP)* from available offerings. In effect, Klein suggested that audience behavior is a two-stage process in which a decision to use media precedes the selection of specific content. The tendency to turn on a set without regard to programming is often taken as evidence of a *passive audience*, although this seems a needlessly value-laden label. The conceptual alternative, a thoroughly *active audience*, appears to be unrealistic. Such an audience would turn on a set whenever favorite programs were aired, and turn off a set when they were not. It is known, however, that daily routines (e.g., work, sleep, etc.) effectively constrain when sets are turned on. It is also known that many people will watch or listen to programming that they are not thrilled with, rather than turning off their sets.

Of course, this is a broad generalization about audience behavior. It is not intended to rule out the possibility that people can be persuaded to turn their sets on by media content. Major events, like the Super Bowl or dramatic news stories, undoubtedly attract people to the media who would not otherwise be there. Promotion and advertising may also get the attention of potential viewers who then remember to tune in. It is also likely that levels of activity vary by medium. Print and the Internet may be intrinsically more engaging although they require more effort on the part of media consumers. Moreover, levels of activity can vary over time. The same person might be choosy at one time and a "couch potato" the next. Overall, though, a two-stage process, including the role of habit, appears to explain audience behavior rather well.

Economic Models of Program Choice

Economic theory presents a more formal model for explaining program choice. Though it is more abstract, it shares many of the elements embedded in working theories. Peter Steiner (1952) is credited with groundbreaking work in this field. He, and those who have extended his work (e.g., Owen & Wildman, 1992), take the approach that a person's choice of programming is analogous to his or her choice of conventional consumer products. Hence, older theories of product competition have served as models for economic theories of program choice.

These theories stem from two important assumptions. The first is that program types can be defined in terms of audience preferences. Stipulating that a program typology must be "defined in terms of audience preferences," as the economists do, forces us to consider exactly which categories of content are systematically related to audience likes and dislikes. In theory, such a typology must mean that people who like one program of a type will like all other programs of that type. Conversely, people who dislike a program must dislike all others of that type. As we have shown, there is reason to believe that such program types exist.

The second assumption is that advertiser-supported programs are a "free good" to the audience member. This deserves further consideration. In the process of stating the assumption, those who invoke it often acknowledge, then ignore, both the opportunity cost of audience time and the potential increased costs of advertised products. If programs are likened to consumer products, the free-good assumption carries an important implication: If programs are free, it seems logical to explain audience choice as preference. The assumption that preference causes choice is consistent with other economic theories and resembles the psychologist's expectation of attitude–behavior consistency.

Economic models of program choice differ in how they resolve the active–passive question. Steiner (1952) assumed a thoroughly active audience in which audience size was determined by the availability of preferred program types. According to Steiner's model, when a favorite program type wasn't on, neither was your set. Subsequent models, however, have relaxed that stringent assumption and adopted a 2-stage process that allows for second and third choices, much like that proposed by Klein.

With these assumptions in place, it is possible to predict the distribution of audiences across channels. For example, if it is assumed there is a large audience for some particular type of programming, then two or more competing channels or stations will split that audience by offering programming of that type. This will continue until that program-type audience has been divided into small enough segments that it makes sense for the next competitor to counterprogram with different types of shows. Consequently, when there are only a few competitors, similar programs tend to be offered across channels. According to this body of theory, as the number of competitors increases, program services become more differentiated. This leads to a phenomenon known as *audience fragmentation*, as the audience is divided among competing program providers.

Selective-Exposure Theory

Selective-exposure theory offers another way to explain people's use of media content. It has been developed by social psychologists interested in understanding media effects. In its earliest form, selective-exposure theory assumed that people had certain attitudes, beliefs, or convictions they were loath to change. These predispositions led people to seek communications consistent with their beliefs and avoid material that challenged them. Simply put, people were thought to "see what they wanted to see," and "hear what they wanted to hear."

This commonsense notion gained credibility in the 1950s and 1960s with the introduction and testing of formal psychological theories, like cognitive dissonance. Early studies indicated people selected media materials to support their existing belief systems or cognitions. Hence, selective exposure to news and information appeared to be an important principle in understanding an individual's choice of programming.

By the 1970s, however, more exacting studies cast doubt on the lockstep nature of selective exposure to information. Although research in this area languished, recent, broader variations of selective-exposure theory have been introduced. For example, experimental studies have shown that people's choices of entertainment vary with their moods and emotions. Excited or overstimulated people are inclined to select relaxing program fare, whereas people who are bored are likely to choose stimulating content. Emotional states, in addition to more dispassionate cognitions, all seem to influence program preferences. This particular type of research in selective exposure is being pursued under the general heading of "mood management theory" (Zillmann, 1988).

Uses and Gratifications Theory

Gratificationist theory provides a closely related, if somewhat more comprehensive, perspective on audience behavior. Studies of "uses and gratifications," as they are often called, are also the work of social psychologists. This approach emerged in the early 1970s, partly as a reaction against the field's apparent obsession with media effects research. Gratificationists argued that researchers should ask not only "what media do to people," but also "what people do with the media." Katz, Blumler, and Gurevitch (1974) spelled out the research agenda of this approach, stating that gratificationists

> [a]re concerned with (1) the social and psychological origins of (2) needs, which generate (3) expectations of (4) mass media or other sources, which lead to (5) differential patterns of media exposure (or engagement in other activities), resulting in (6) need gratifications and (7) other consequences, perhaps mostly unintended ones. (p. 20)

Since the early 1970s, gratificationist research and theory have attracted considerable attention. Of central importance is the gratificationist's approach to explaining patterns of media exposure. Under this perspective, those patterns are determined by each person's expectations of how well different media or program content will gratify their needs. Such needs might be short-lived, like those associated with mood states, or they may be constant. In any event, it seems likely that the gratifications being sought translate into preferences for the media and their content.

Gratificationist theory, therefore, has much in common with economic models of program choice and theories of selective exposure. All cast individual preferences, however they have emerged, as the central mechanism for explaining exposure. Grandiose theories aside, this view of audience behavior also has a great intuitive appeal. Why does the audience for a hard-rock radio station tend to be young men? Because that is the kind of music they like. Why do males watch more televised sports than females? Because they like it more.

However, the power of preferences to determine exposure to media is not absolute. Audience formation is ultimately determined by factors that fall outside these bodies of theory, such as those explained by the working theories reviewed above. But some of this is as much industry lore as a systematic body of knowledge. Economic theory attempts to integrate industry structure and program choice but gives very little understanding of nuances like audience flow. Selective-exposure and gratificationist theory are concerned primarily with an individual's choices, but reveal little of the larger forces shaping a media audience. Understanding how media audiences form and change over time requires consideration of a number of other factors.

TOWARD A COMPREHENSIVE UNDERSTANDING OF AUDIENCE BEHAVIOR

If exposure to media constitutes an interface between audience and media content, it is possible to identify many things that affect how that interface takes shape. In this section we consider both sides of the equation: *audience factors* and *media factors*. Each has a substantial effect on patterns of exposure. Within each category, we have made a further distinction between structural and individual determinants. Although the latter distinction is sometimes elusive, it is intended to highlight differences in the levels of analysis, and reflect traditional divisions in research and theory on media exposure. *Structural determinants* are factors common to, or characteristic of, populations—macrolevel variables typically conceptualized as common to markets or masses of people. *Individual determinants* are descriptive of a person or household—microlevel variables that vary from person to person. Together these factors offer a thorough analytical framework for identifying the causes of exposure to the media.

Audience Factors

Structural Features of the Audience. The first structural feature of the audience that shapes exposure to media is the size and location of potential audiences. Sometimes, potential audience is easy to determine, for instance the number of people living within reach of a broadcast signal. But the potential audience can also be more illusive. For example, through universal postal service any newspaper can technically reach a national audience; yet as a practical matter most papers have a distinctly local character. Other forms of media, like films, CDs, and Web pages may have a truly global potential. Obviously, no medium can have an audience larger than the size of the relevant market population. The population, in effect, sets a ceiling on the audience for any program service. The larger the potential, the more media organizations are willing to invest to win a piece of the pie.

In broadcasting, ratings services typically divide the country into more than 200 local market areas (see Appendix A, this volume). Clearly, the potential audience for a station in one market can be vastly larger than the audience in another. This does not guarantee that large-market stations will have larger audiences, especially because large markets tend to have more media outlets. Nevertheless, it sets the stage for bigger audiences and bigger audience revenues.

But potential audiences are not just a matter of the sheer number of people living within reach of a medium. The composition of the population can have an impact on long-term patterns of exposure as well. As the demographic makeup of potential audiences changes, it is reasonable to expect that patterns of media exposure will change as well. According to census data, for example, there have been shifts in the relative size of white-collar and blue-collar populations, the age of the population, and notably in the level of education throughout the population. Occupation, age, and education are often associated with the choice of certain types of programming. A farsighted media operator will take population shifts into account, most of which are predictable, when planning the future.

The rise in Spanish-language programming can be viewed, in part, as a result of newly emerging potential audiences. In 1970, Latinos or Hispanics accounted for 4.5% of the U.S. population. By 1990 that figure had doubled. By some estimates, it will double again by 2025, with even higher concentrations in some U.S. markets. Rapid growth rates also characterize the U.S. Asian population. Such changes in ethnic or linguistic populations provide new markets for advertisers and the media and may explain corresponding changes in media use.

The second structural attribute of audiences, and one of the most powerful determinants of exposure to the electronic media, is audience availability. Although potential audience specifies a physical limit on audience size, daily routines set a practical limit on how many people are likely to be using either radio or television at a point in time. It is widely believed that the number of people using a medium has little, if anything, to do with programming and almost everything to do with who is available. Most practitioners take the size of the available audience as a given, just as they would the size of the population itself. In practice, the available audience is usually defined as the number of people using a medium at a given time.

The size of the available audience, like other forms of mass behavior, is predictable. Three patterns are apparent: seasonal, daily, and hourly. Seasonal patterns of media use are more evident in television than in radio. Nationwide, television use is heaviest in January and February; Nielsen reports the average household has a set in use for almost 7.5 hours a day at this time of year. During the summer months, household usage drops to about 6.5 hours. This shift seems to occur because viewers have more daylight in the summer and pursue outdoor activities. Seasonal changes mean lower HUT levels in summer and higher HUT levels in winter. But household level data can mask important differences within demographic groups. When school is out, daytime viewing among children and teenagers soars. The same vacation time phenomenon appears to account for seasonal differences in movie theater attendance.

Audience size also varies by day of the week. Nationally, prime-time television audiences are higher on weeknights and Sunday, and lower on Fridays and Saturdays. The late-night audience (e.g., midnight) on Friday and Saturday, however, is larger than it is during late night the rest of the week. This too reflects a change in social activities on weekends. Radio audiences also look different on weekdays than on weekends. The early-morning audience is smaller on Saturday and Sunday, with a peak later during midday.

The most dramatic shifts in audience availability, however, occur on an hourly basis. It is here the patterns of daily life are most evident. Figure 9.2, based on RADAR® data, depicts the size of the radio audience at various times during the day, Monday through Friday. It also indicates where listening occurs: at home, in an auto, or elsewhere. Notice the size of the audience increases rapidly from 5:00 a.m. to 7:30 a.m. Much of that listening occurs in cars as people commute to work, hence the name "drive time." During this time period, a radio station can typically capture its largest audiences, so it may devote considerable resources to programming. Other stations, of course, are doing the same thing, and competition for the drive-time audience can be intense. Throughout the rest of the day the audience gradually shrinks, with much listening in the workplace. At about 2:30 p.m. the audience picks up again, creating what is called the afternoon drive-time, which is longer than morning drive, as listeners are often picking up children at school, shopping, and running errands. Thereafter, it trails off as people return home and television begins to command their attention.

Figure 9.3 represents the size of the television audience hour by hour. In some ways, it is the mirror image of the radio audience. The early-morning audience is small, and throughout the day it grows. At about 5:00 p.m., when people arrive home from work, sets go on and HUT levels rise sharply. The audience size peaks between 9:00 p.m. and 10:00 p.m., which marks the height of prime time—a peak that is slightly depressed in summer. As noted in chapter 1, it is during prime time that broadcast networks charge a premium for commercial time. It is also during this time period that networks air the most expensive programming. The competition is stiff, but the rewards for winning a healthy share of this large audience can be substantial.

Thus far, our approach to explaining exposure has had almost nothing to say about people's preferences, or the appeals of different kinds of programming. Remember, however, that audience behavior emerges in a two-stage process. Turning on a set may have little to do with specific content, but once a decision to use the media has been made, people's likes and dislikes, as well as other factors, do play a role. These factors are the microlevel determinants of audience behavior.

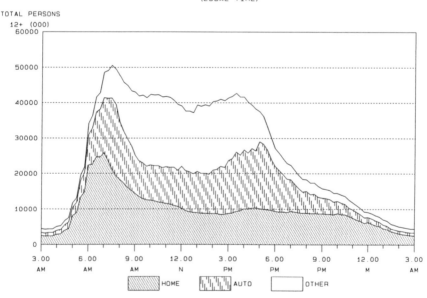

FIG. 9.2.   Hourly variation in radio audience size, RADAR® 57, Spring 1988.
Copyright © Statistical Research, Inc.

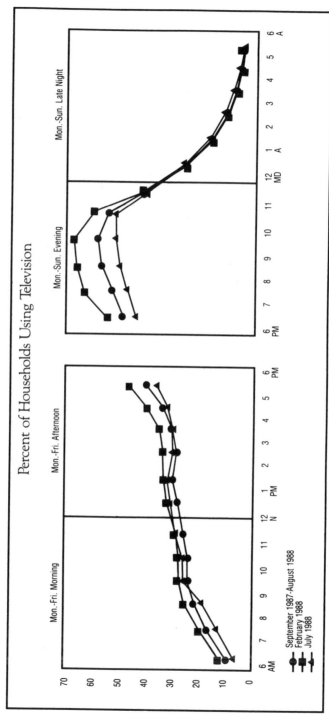

FIG. 9.3.   Hourly variation in television audience size (reprinted with permission of Nielsen *Media Research*).

Individual Audience Characteristics. The most important individual-level determinants of exposure to programming are people's *preferences.* Much of a programmer's skill in building an audience depends on an ability to judge what people will or will not like. As noted previously, this strategy for explaining audience behavior also guides academics from a variety of disciplines, including marketing, economics, and social psychology. While program preferences are an important determinant of choice, researchers need to improve their understanding of how they operate in the real world of media use.

Most research and theory on the relationship between preference and choice focuses on the individual and assumes that personal preferences can be freely exercised in the selection of programming. Economic models of program choice, selective-exposure theory, and gratificationist theories all rely on this assumption. It is often justified on the basis of laboratory experiments that evaluate how individuals choose media content when they are alone. However, much media use is done not in isolation, but in the company of others. This is especially true of television viewing.

The second individual level audience factor, then, is *group viewing.* This is a rather common phenomenon, even today when most households have more than one set. In the typical group configuration, much of the family is viewing together, followed by husband and wife together. What little research there is on the dynamics of group viewing suggests that negotiation among competing preferences is common. Different family members exercise more or less influence at different times of the day. For example, programmers make much of the fact that children are often in control of the television set in the late afternoon when they return from school. Exposure to television programming, then, results not only from who is available and what they like, but who is actually selecting the programs. People get their first choices some of the time but can be outvoted at other times. Even if overruled, however, they often stay with the group. Ask any parent of a young child whether he or she is watching more *Sesame Street* since the child's arrival. Ask children if they see more of the evening news than they would like. In effect, some exposure to media is enforced, in spite of preferences. Group viewing, or, for that matter, group music listening or group movie attendance, can constrain the relationship between preference and choice. More solitary forms of media use (e.g., reading or Internet) may offer a cleaner linkage between these factors.

The last audience factor affecting the relationship between preference and choice is *awareness.* Awareness means knowledge of the media content that is available. Much theorizing about the audience presupposes perfect awareness on the part of audience members. In other words, media selections are assumed to occur with a full knowledge of the content options. Although that assumption might be workable on an abstract level, or in very simple media environments, it does not work well in the media-rich environments confronting most audience members.

If, as is sometimes the case, people select programming without a full understanding of their options, the interpretation of program choice as an expression of preference is oversimplified if not evaluated along with other factors. How often have you missed a show you might have enjoyed because you unthinkingly watched something else? Have you ever "discovered" a favorite program or station that had been on the air for some time? The same issues of awareness exist for the bewildering number of print media and Web sites. As more services compete for audience attention, these breakdowns between preference and choice are likely to be increasingly common. Analysts who seek to explain why someone chose a particular offering without assessing the broad awareness of the full range of choices risks a mistaken conclusion.

The role that audience preferences play in determining audience behavior is more complex than many researchers assume. For example, a low audience rating might indicate that people do not like a particular station or program, it might also indicate that the desired audience was unavailable to tune in or that they simply did not know what was on. Any interpretation of media use should consider all of these factors, as summarized in Table 9.2. But audience factors are only half the picture. The structures of the media themselves have an impact on patterns of exposure.

Media Factors

As with audience factors, media factors can be grouped as structural or individual. The structural attributes of the media complement the structural features of the audience. They include market conditions and how available content is organized. Individual-level media factors vary in tandem with individual audience attributes, defining differences in the media environment from household to household.

TABLE 9.2
Audience Factors Affecting Exposure

Structural	Individual
Potential Audiences	Preferences
Local versus National versus Global	Program Type Preferences
Demographic Factors	Tastes
Ethnic or Linguistic Populations	Gratifications Sought
Available Audiences	Group versus Solitary Media Use
Seasonal Variation	Awareness of Options
Weekly Variation	
Hourly Variation	

Structural Features of the Media. The first structural characteristic of the electronic media is *coverage*, the extent to which people are physically able to receive a particular channel or medium of programming. In the United States, the universal availability of radio and television is usually taken for granted. In other countries, especially in developing nations, universal coverage is not the rule. Even in the United States, newer forms of media are not available to all households. Table 9.3 summarizes the growth of U.S. electronic media.

Obviously, a medium's coverage of the population has a powerful impact on its ability to attract audiences. Early television audiences were small because few people had receivers. Similarly, cable television's audiences are shaped, in the first instance, by the fact that about three fourths of U.S. households subscribe to that medium. Barring some major change in the technology or regulation of cable services, its coverage will always be more limited than the broadcast networks. The same is true of audiences reached through the Internet. While the number of households with personal computers continues to climb, most households still do not have access to the Internet. Coverage of this medium is likely to remain well below 100%, which greatly limits its poten-

TABLE 9.3

Growth of Electronic Media in the United States

		Percent of Households with:					
Year	U.S. Households	Radio	Television	Cable	VCRs	Computers	Internet Online
1930	30,000,000	46					
1940	35,000,000	81					
1950	43,000,000	95	9				
1960	53,000,000	96	87				
1970	61,000,000	98	95	6			
1980	78,000,000	98	98	19	1		
1990	94,000,000	99	98	55	67	23	1.6
1991	94,000,000	99	98	58	71	25	2.0
1992	96,000,000	99	98	59	73	28	2.6
1993	96,000,000	99	98	60	76	30	3.3
1994	97,000,000	99	98	61	77	32	4.7
1995	98,000,000	99	98	62	80	35	7.5
1996	99,000,000	99	98	64	80	38	13.6
1997	100,000,000	99	98	64	80	44	23.0

Sources: Adapted from Lichty and Topping (1975); Veronis, Suhler, and Associates (1998); Webster and Phalen (1997); U.S. Bureau of Census.

tial to reach large audiences. Moreover, the pricing of connect time may alter the "free good" character associated with electronic media.

Even when media organizations offer "free" content to a truly national audience, local outlets may affect coverage by refusing to carry certain programs. For example, with the exception of the TV stations owned and operated by the networks (O & Os), affiliates are self-interested independent businesses. This means that an affiliate may not carry (or clear) network programming if it believes some other programming strategy will be more profitable. This could involve an entire series, or it could be a simple preemption for a program having more interest to the local community, or one likely to obtain higher revenues. These variations in *network clearance* mean that some programs don't reach the entire population. The same is true of syndicated program clearances. Once again, this puts a cap on the possible audience size.

For any medium, a number of other structural factors affect audience behavior. The first consideration is the sheer number of options that confront the audience. For most forms of media, that number has increased dramatically in recent years. In the world of 1950s television, for example, the average household could receive roughly four channels. Today, with the inclusion of cable television, the average household receives more than 40 channels. For those with access to the Internet, the number of available Web sites seems limitless.

TABLE 9.4
Television Viewing in Cable and Noncable Homes

Programming Source	Household Category			
	Total TV Households	Noncable Households	All Cable Households	Pay Cable Households
Broadcast Network Affiliates				
ABC	14.0%	17.7%	12.7%	12.0%
CBS	13.4%	18.5%	11.7%	10.5%
NBC	15.4%	19.6%	13.6%	12.8%
FOX	8.7%	12.7%	7.6%	7.3%
Total	51.5%	68.5%	45.6%	42.6%
Cable Programming				
Basic	36.0%		45.9%	45.8%
Pay	7.0%		8.2%	13.1%
Total	43.0%		54.1%	58.9%
Independents	11.7%	18.5%	9.2%	9.3%
Public	3.3%	5.4%	2.5%	2.3%

Source: Cable Advertising Bureau, as published in CAB's *1998 Cable TV Facts.*

Presenting the audience an array of services, most of which are in competition for a limited amount of audience time and attention, has a number of important consequences for exposure to media messages. More competitive markets inevitably means smaller ratings and shares for each of the competitors. To gain a sense of how different levels of competition affect audience size, compare the viewing of households with and without cable illustrated in Table 9.4.

The left-hand column summarizes viewing shares in all television households. On average, network affiliates account for nearly 52% of the viewing, while cable services claim a 43% share. The remaining 15% go to independents and public stations. The second column provides the same information for noncable homes. By definition, these homes are restricted to watching only those signals they can receive over the air, including affiliates, independents, and public TV stations. Under such circumstances, network affiliates command 69% of all the television viewing done in the home. The third column is a summary of viewing in all cable homes. Here, cable sources account for 54% of all television viewing, and affiliate share of audience drops to 46%. The final column represents the viewing of homes having at least one pay cable service, like HBO. Combined with basic cable use, these services account for about 59% of all viewing, and leave the affiliates with a 43% share. Certainly, no one cable service is likely to match the audience of a broadcast network, but they fragment the audience and in combination take a considerable toll, just as economic theory would predict.

All these aspects of program or network coverage complicate the number of options from which the audience member must choose. In the aggregate, they are powerful determinants of audience size. But the structural attributes of the media go beyond channel or program availability. In radio and television, programs are offered as a series of forced choices. It is quite possible to encounter situations in which two desirable programs are on opposite one another and the viewer has to choose between them. Had they been scheduled at different times, the viewer could have watched both. Consequently, *program scheduling*, within and across channels, is widely believed to be an important factor in shaping the size, composition, and duplication of audiences.

As explained previously, programmers use their knowledge of audience flow to encourage people to watch their programs rather than those of the competition. Indeed, patterns of audience duplication, such as inheritance effects, channel loyalty, and repeat viewing, are well documented and seem to derive from structural factors (Goodhardt et al., 1987; Webster & Phalen, 1997). Although the ability to tape and replay programming can, in principle, break this rigid structure, in practice relatively little taping is done.

There appear to be structural biases built into the Internet as well. Search engines may have protocols favoring some Web sites over others. Within Web pages, there are various links that encourage certain patterns of audience duplication and discourage others. This competitive scheduling is another reason why a person's preferences may not be the best guide to actual patterns of exposure. But even these factors do not entirely exhaust explanations of variability among audience members. There are a few microlevel media factors that we should review to complete the picture.

Individual Media Environments.   Factors like network coverage and program scheduling are beyond the control of an audience member. But certain aspects of the media environment are within the individual's control. In fact, this is truer today than it has ever been. As new technologies and programming alternatives enter the marketplace, people have greater latitude in shaping a media environment to suit their purposes. These decisions affect exposure to media and are closely related to the microlevel audience factors reviewed earlier.

One of the first considerations is the kind of technologies owned by individuals. Although radio and television have been in virtually all U.S. households for decades, the characteristics of these receivers have changed. Color television, once a novelty, is in 99% of U.S. television households. Nearly three fourths of homes have multiple sets. The location and capability of these receivers are all within the control of individual viewers and can affect the quality of the media environment within the home.

In the 1980s, for example, the widespread introduction of remote-control devices (RCDs) signaled major changes in exposure patterns. Because remotes made channel changing easy, they struck fear in the hearts of advertisers and programmers alike. From the advertiser's perspective, viewers might be more likely to switch channels when an advertisement appeared. This practice, called *zapping*, could obviously reduce exposure to commercial messages. From the programmer's perspective, audiences lost during commercial breaks or a lull in a program, could be difficult to regain. This inclination to change channels at the drop of a hat has been dubbed *grazing*. It now seems that many of the initial concerns regarding RCDs were overblown. Nonetheless, such phenomena are worth watching.

Videocassette recorders (VCRs) are another technology that alters one's media environment. Virtually nonexistent at the beginning of the 1980s, VCRs have surpassed cable penetration and are in 84% of all households. Many analysts have likened their adoption curve to that of color television. If so, VCR penetration could become universal.

VCR usage falls into two categories: *time-shifting*, and *library use*. As the label suggests, time-shifting involves taping a program for replay at a more convenient time. The lag time between taping and replay varies with how often a program is broadcast (e.g., stripped shows are replayed faster than weekly offerings). It is also predictable—researchers have likened the rate of replay to a radioactive decay curve. The most-taped programs are those broadcast by the major networks, although many programs recorded for time-shifting are never watched.

Library use also involves off-the-air taping, but with the intention of adding the tape to a personal collection. Increasingly, people will buy or rent tapes for home viewing. Virtually all VCR owners report using their machines to show rented cassettes, usually major motion pictures that were successful in theatrical release. As this market grows, however, more programming made specifically for home viewing is likely to be produced.

Despite these important changes, the total amount of time people spend watching taped programming is tiny compared to the total amount of television consumed. For example, the time-shift audience for a prime-time network program rarely accounts for more than 1 rating point. That could change, so the impact of VCRs on exposure should be carefully monitored.

More recent technological changes will also help shape the media environment in individual homes. People with receivers capable of reproducing HDTV signals are likely to choose programs produced in that format. Digital television and sets capable of Internet access will create further differences among households, and the lines between radio, television, cable, and computers may dissolve. The speed at which these developments take shape remains to be seen, but the rate of adoption will certainly vary with household characteristics, further complicating understandings of audience behavior.

Subscriptions are another type of personal decision. People have long subscribed to different newspapers, magazines, and book clubs. More recently, consumers are subscribing to Internet service providers, direct broadcast satellites (DBS), and video stores. This obviously fragments patterns of exposure.

Perhaps the most widely studied form of electronic media subscription is cable television. Although cable's organization and availability are appropriately regarded as a structural variable, the decision to subscribe is ultimately made by each household. This self-selection into the cable universe is one reason that comparisons of cable and noncable households must be made with caution.

Just why people subscribe to cable varies. Cable subscribers have higher incomes than nonsubscribers, and cable households tend to have more people living in them. This is especially true of families that buy a pay cable service. With more children, or more money to spend, subscription to cable makes sense. Gratificationists have pointed out that cable subscribers express a need for greater variety and control over their viewing environment. Others subscribe just to improve the quality of over-the-air reception.

Researchers have also observed that cable subscribers differ in their viewing styles. Confronted with a large number of channel choices, cable subscribers develop a *channel repertoire*, or set of frequently viewed channels. This repertoire is a subset of all available channels—the more channels, the larger is the repertoire. But there is not a one-to-one correspondence. As the number of channels increases, the proportion used decreases. The net result is that each cable viewer constructs an array of channels from which to choose on a day-to-day basis. This may effectively cancel out viewing on some channels, even if they can be received on the set. Many TV remote-control devices now allow users to create a menu of preferred choices. The newest radio tuners even allow the listener to indicate a format preference, which the tuner then seeks. The same phenomenon is likely to develop with the Internet, as users create bookmarks or other shortcuts to favorite Web sites. Table 9.5 summarizes the media factors affecting patterns of exposure.

AN INTEGRATED MODEL OF AUDIENCE BEHAVIOR

Now that we have introduced the range of factors influencing audience behavior, we can try to forge an overall framework for examining media exposure. Using a comprehensive model of audience behavior, the job of summarizing, evaluating, and anticipating the data contained in the ratings will be more manageable.

Audience researchers have devoted much time and effort to understanding people's use of electronic media. Ad agencies and programmers have engaged in pragmatic studies of audience formation, economists have developed abstract theories of program choice, and social psychologists have performed a succession of experiments and surveys to reveal the origins of audience behavior. Despite this progress, there remains a tendency for each group to work in isolation. Collaborations among theorists and practitioners or even across academic disciplines are, regrettably, rare.

At the risk of oversimplifying matters, two distinct approaches to understanding the audience can be identified. The first emphasizes the importance of the individual factors, which is typical of work in psychology, communication

TABLE 9.5

Media Factors Affecting Exposure

Structural	Individual
Coverage	Technologies Owned
Household Penetration	Radio & TV Sets
Signal Carriage	VCRs
Clearance	Computers
Content Options	Subscriptions
Number of Choices	Print Media
Program Schedules	Cable
Linked Web Sites	DBS
	Internet Service
	Repertoires
	Channel Repertoires
	Bookmarking

studies, marketing, and economics. It has enormous intuitive appeal and is likely to characterize most commonsense explanations of the audience. Because audiences are simply collections of individuals, understanding behavior at the individual level helps explain patterns of mass behavior. To conceptualize audience behavior at the individual level, researchers try to explain what distinguishes one person from another. Preferences are usually invoked to explain behavior. But this focus misses trends that become clear at different levels of analysis. For instance, it is doubtful that any one television viewer chooses to create an "inheritance effect," yet night after night the audience manifests this form of behavior.

The second perspective emphasizes structural factors as key determinants of mass behavior. This approach is more typical in sociology, human ecology, and at least some forms of marketing and advertising research. It downplays individual needs and wants and concentrates on things like total audience size, coverage areas, and program schedules to understand behavior. Although this work can successfully produce statistical explanations of aggregate data, it often rings hollow, prompting questions like "What does this mean in human terms—what does it tell us about ourselves?" Such explanations are usually possible, but not always apparent.

It is important to recognize that neither approach is right or wrong. They are simply different ways to know the audience. It is also important to note that neither approach stands alone. Models of audience behavior are sometimes advanced as mutually exclusive alternatives, but there is much to be gained by trying to integrate them. Specifically, analyses of individual behavior might be enhanced by a more deliberate consideration of the structural factors suggested here. Researchers know through observation that these variables are highly correlated with audience behavior, and weaving them into microlevel studies might increase the latter's power and generalizability. Conversely, research in mass behavior might be more explicit about its relationship to theoretical concepts central in the individual approach. This could improve its popular acceptance and utility. It is in this spirit that we propose the following model.

The Model

The model presented in Fig. 9.4 is intended to organize thinking about audience behavior as commonly defined in audience research. Although the model suggests broad relationships, it does not provide testable hypotheses. It certainly falls short of being a mathematical model and serves instead as a springboard for discussing several such models in chapter 11. We should also point out that this model focuses primarily on short-term features of audience behavior.

The central component to be explained is exposure to media. As argued in chapter 1, audience analysts are interested in mass behavior, which can be categorized as gross or cumulative. Two broad categories are shown as the causes of exposure: audience factors and media factors. The shape of the boxes indicates

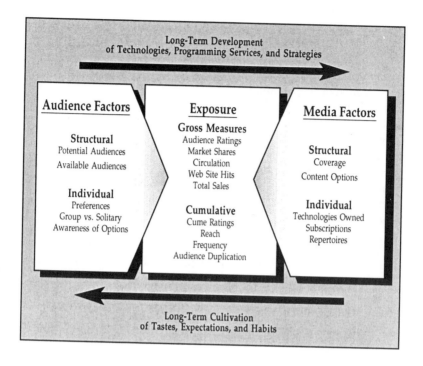

FIG. 9.4.   A model of audience behavior.

the direction of influence. For example, the model suggests that audience factors help determine ratings, not vice versa. There are also cause–effect relationships among factors within each box. For instance, audience preferences probably contribute to patterns of availability, and cable subscription helps shape cable network coverage. We have opted to omit the arrows suggesting these interrelationships for simplicity.

To use the model, an analyst would identify the audience behavior he or she wished to explain. Is the researcher concerned with the size of an audience at a single point in time (i.e., a gross measure), or with how audience members behave across time (i.e., a cumulative measure)? To begin the process of evaluating, explaining, or predicting that behavior, the analyst considers structural determinants first. We recommend this approach for three reasons. First, they begin at the mass level of analysis, like the measures of exposure being analyzed. Second, they are knowable from program schedules, network coverage, and audience research reports. Individual factors, like audience awareness and the use of remote-control devices, are harder to pin down. Third, we know from experience that structural explanations work well with most forms of audience data. If they fail to provide a satisfying answer, attention should be directed to the individual-level factors on either side of the model.

A Sample Scenario. While working through an example to get a better sense of the model, keep in mind it is not designed to provide quick answers to difficult audience research questions, but rather to guide the analyst in considering all the relevant factors. Consider, for instance, the ratings of a local television news program. Why do some stations have high ratings and others have low ratings? What factors will shape a station's audience size in the future? Advertisers, as well as local station managers and programmers, would probably have an interest in this analysis. Imagine that you work for a station and want to assess its situation.

Remember that a rating is a gross measure of audience size. Local news ratings, in particular, have an important impact on station profitability. To explain the size of a station's news audience, we should first consider structural factors. If audience size is to be expressed as an absolute number, we would need to know the size of the potential audience defined by the population in the market. At the same time, we would want to consider the nature of the station's coverage area. Is it a VHF or a UHF station? If UHF, you are probably already at a disadvantage. Is there anything about the station's signal or local geography that would restrict its ability to reach the entire potential audience?

Next, we would want to know the size of the audience when the news is broadcast. An analysis of share data might overlook this, but since we are interested in ratings, the bigger the available audience, the better the chances of achieving a large rating. We might pay special attention to audience segments more likely to be local news viewers, usually older adults. Next, we would consider a variety of program scheduling factors.

The first scheduling consideration would involve assessing the competition. How many competitors are there? As they increase in number, your ratings are likely to decrease. Do other stations enjoy advantages in covering the market? To what extent has cable television penetrated the market? How many households have access to the Internet, and what do the usage patterns look like? What are your principal competitors likely to program opposite the news? Will you confront only news programs, or will the competition counterprogram? Counterprogramming is more likely if you are a network affiliate with independents in the market. If the available audience contains a large segment unlikely to watch the news (e.g., children and young adults), that could damage your ratings. Consider the programming on before and after the news. A highly rated lead-in is likely to help your ratings, especially if it attracts an audience of news viewers. If you are an affiliate, pay close attention to the strength of your network's news program. Research has shown a strong link between local and network news ratings.

Usually, these structural factors explain most of the variations in local news ratings. A station can control some things, like lead-in programming. Other things, like the number of competitors, are beyond control. Because a single ratings point might make a substantial difference in a station's profitability, however, consideration of individual factors may be warranted, especially if these are things a station can manipulate.

Among the most likely candidates for consideration are viewer preferences and awareness. Are there certain on-air personalities or program formats that are more or less appealing to viewers? Every year, consultants to stations, called "news doctors," charge large fees to make such determinations. Are there certain news stories that will better suit the needs and interests of local viewers? In markets not measured continuously, stations often schedule sensationalist special reports to coincide with the ratings sweeps. A riveting investigative report is unlikely to boost a program's ratings, however, unless additional viewers are made aware of it. So stations must simultaneously engage in extraordinary promotion and advertising. Of course, all the stations in a market are probably doing the same thing. Therefore, although catering to audience preferences is very important in principle, in practice, it may not make a huge ratings difference. Even so, a small edge can be crucial to profitability.

The analysis of radio audience behavior resembles that in television, except exposure is typically defined in terms of stations and dayparts rather than programs. Listeners occasionally tune to specific programs, but more often they select a station rather than a discrete radio show. The key determinants of radio audience size and flow are still structural, but individual factors take on added salience. Radio stations usually operate in competitive markets and specialize in one kind of programming. The choice of stations is more likely to be the decision of a single individual than a group. Radio listeners are also likely to select a station by searching through a limited repertoire. They may leave the radio tuned to a favorite station all the time or they may select a station by pressing a preset button instead of consulting a program guide. For all these reasons, people's preferences and awareness of a station's offerings weigh more heavily in the analysis of radio audience behavior.

There is more to learn about the behavior of Internet audiences. In a media environment where there are fewer structural constraints, it seems reasonable to expect that notions of selective exposure and related theories may gain new adherents. Web users are typically characterized as individuals actively seeking information, so a theory that posits an active audience seems to offer an appealing interpretation of behavior. Even the term "user" implies a more actively engaged individual than does the more passive term "viewer."

Finally, consider the long-term nature of exposure to media. One danger of characterizing audience behavior as the result of nicely drawn arrows and boxes is that things are made to seem simpler than they are. For instance, the model defines exposure as the result, not the cause, of other factors. Over a period of months or weeks, ratings can have a substantial effect on the structure of the media. Programs are canceled, new shows developed, schedules altered, and clearances changed, often on the basis of audience behavior. Such relationships have been the subject of a number of interesting investigations. Similarly, the model, as we have presented it, suggests a high degree of independence between audience and media factors. In the short term, that seems to be a workable assumption. Over time, however, it could distort the picture of audience behavior.

To address these issues, we have specified some long-term relationships between audience and media factors. For example, the growth of potential audiences and patterns of availability clearly affect the development of media services and programming strategies. Conversely, the structure and content of the media undoubtedly cultivate certain tastes, expectations, and habits on the part of the audience. These are important relationships, but not central to our purpose. Bearing such limitations in mind, we hope the model can provide a useful framework for evaluating ratings data and exploiting the analytical techniques discussed in the remaining chapters. We also hope that it dispels the myth that preference translates easily into choice.

RELATED READINGS

Barwise, P., & Ehrenberg, A. (1988). *Television and its audience*. London: Sage.

Bower, R. T. (1985). *The changing television audience in America*. New York: Columbia University Press.

Comstock, G., & Scharrer, E. (1999). *Television: What's on, who's watching, and what it means*. San Diego, CA: Academic Press.

Goodhardt, G. J., Ehrenberg, A. S. C., & Collins, M. A. (1987). *The television audience: Patterns of viewing* (2nd ed.). Aldershot, UK: Gower.

Heeter, C., & Greenberg, B. S. (1988). *Cable-viewing*. Norwood, NJ: Ablex.

MacFarland, D. T. (1997). *Future radio programming strategies: Cultivating listenership in the digital age*. Mahwah, NJ: Lawrence Erlbaum Associates.

McPhee, W. N. (1963). *Formal theories of mass behavior*. New York: The Free Press.

McQuail, D. (1997). *Audience analysis*. Thousand Oaks, CA: Sage.

Neumann, W. R. (1991). *The future of the mass audience*. Cambridge: Cambridge University Press.

Owen, B. M., & Wildman, S. W. (1992). *Television economics*. Cambridge: Harvard University Press.

Rosengren, K. E., Wenner, L. A., & Palmgreen, P. (Eds.). (1985). *Media gratifications research: Current perspectives*. Beverly Hills: Sage.

Steiner, G. A. (1963). *The people look at television*. New York: Alfred A. Knopf.

Webster, J. G., & Phalen, P. F. (1997). *The mass audience: Rediscovering the dominant model*. Mahwah, NJ: Lawrence Erlbaum Associates.

Zillmann, D., & Bryant, J. (Eds.). (1985). *Selective exposure to communication*. Hillsdale, NJ: Lawrence Erlbaum Associates.

10

Audience Ratings:
Analysis of Gross Measures

The preceding chapters outline the many uses of audience research, how audience data are collected and reported, and a general framework for understanding audience behavior. It should be clear that many questions can be asked and answered using audience research techniques. However, for many people who deal with electronic media, audience research means nothing more or less than ratings research. Although not everyone in the business holds that view, it is true that no other form of audience research so dominates the industry. For that reason, we have focused more consciously on systems for generating audience ratings. The final two chapters examine specific analytical techniques used with ratings.

Although ratings are straightforward audience research, they can be analyzed in many ways. The practice of ratings analysis may be constrained more by the skill and imagination of analysts than limitations inherent in the data. Describing common analytical techniques, as we do in chapters 10 and 11, risks discouraging inventive ways of looking at data. That is certainly not our intent. Anyone with an understanding of audiences and a basic knowledge of quantitative research methods has the tools to analyze ratings data.

There are, however, advantages to becoming familiar with common techniques of ratings analysis. First, the techniques have been tested; their strengths and limitations are well known. Second, there is real value in standard analytical techniques. If everyone calculated the cost of reaching the audience in a different way, comparisons would be difficult or impossible to make, which would limit the utility of the analysis. In the same vein, standardization can help generate a systematic body of knowledge about audiences and their role in the operation of the electronic media. If one study can be directly related to the next, progress, or dead ends, can be more readily identified.

Consistent with the distinction made in chapter 9, we have organized analytical techniques into two chapters—one dealing with gross measures, the next with cumulative measures. This distinction is not always easy to make, for analyses of one sort are often coupled with the other. There can be strict mathematical relationships between gross and cumulative measures. Nonetheless, this scheme of organization will help the reader manage a potentially bewildering assortment of ways to manipulate the data.

Each chapter progresses from the least complicated techniques to the most complicated. Although some of the language is complex and arcane, the majority of analytical techniques described here involve simple arithmetic. In discussions of multivariate statistics, we try to limit technical jargon.

GROSS MEASURES

Gross measures are snapshots of the audience, taken at a point in time. Included in this category are the measures themselves (e.g., ratings and shares), any subsequent manipulations of those measures (e.g., totaling GRPs), or analyses of the measures using additional data (e.g., calculating CPPs). Excluded from this category are audience measurements that require tracking individual audience members over time.

Basic definitions of terms like rating and share ignore nuances an analyst should know. In fact, it is important to recognize these measures as a kind of first-order data analysis. Ratings, shares, and gross audience projections are products of mathematical operations applied to the database.

Projected audiences are the most basic gross measurements of the audience. In this context, projection suggests extracting from the sample an estimate of what is happening in the population. It should not be confused with predicting future audiences. These projections are estimates of absolute audience size, intended to answer the question "How many people watched or listened?" Audience projections can be made for specific programs, specific stations, or for all those using a medium at some point. Projections can be made for households, persons, or subsets of the audience (e.g., how many men 18 to 49 watched the news). Most numbers reported in a ratings book are simply estimates of absolute audience size.

The straightforward method of projection is to multiply the proportion of the sample using a program, station, or medium by the size of the population. To determine how many households watched program Z, for example, an analyst would look at the sample, note that 20% watched Z, and multiply that by the estimated number of TV households in the market, say 100,000. The projected number of TVHH watching program Z would be 20,000. That proportion is a rating. Hence, projected audiences can be derived by the following equation:

PROJECTED AUDIENCE = RATING (%) × POPULATION

Nielsen uses this approach with its metered samples, nationwide and in large markets. Nielsen analysts assume the in-tab sample, without further adjustments, adequately represents the population. Many local market samples, however, do not meet that assumption. Recall, for example, that in-tab diary samples tend to overrepresent some groups and underrepresent others. In such instances, it is common to weight the responses of underrepresented groups more heavily than others. The specific variables used for weighting, and the way these weights are combined, vary across markets. The result, however derived, is that the weighted responses of households or individuals, commonly expressed as households per diary value (HPDV) or persons per diary value (PPDV), are combined to project audience size. Unlike the simple procedure previously described, here projected audiences must be determined before ratings. If sample weighting or balancing is used, audience projections are used to calculate a rating, not vice versa.

As explained in chapter 8, audience projections for radio reveal how many hundreds of people listened to a station in an average quarter hour. The total number of people listening to radio without regard to stations is called persons using radio (PUR). In television, audiences are typically associated with specific programs in specific quarter hours. Depending on the unit of analysis, the size of the TV audience is called households using television (HUT), or persons using television (PUT). These numbers express the absolute size of the audience at a single or average point in time.

Audience projections, used in the context of advertising, will sometimes be added to produce a number called gross audience or *gross impressions*—a summation of program or station audiences across different times. The relevant times are defined by an advertiser's schedule of spots. Table 10.1 is a simple example of how gross impressions, for women 18–49, would be determined for a commercial message that aired at 4 different times.

TABLE 10.1
Determining Gross Impressions

Spot Availability	Audience of Women 18–49
Monday, 10 a.m.	2,500
Wednesday, 11 a.m.	2,000
Thursday, 4 p.m.	3,500
Friday, 9 p.m.	1,500
Total (Gross Impressions)	9,500

Gross impressions are like GRPs, except they are expressed as a whole number rather than percentage points. They provide a crude measure of the total weight of audience exposure to a particular message or campaign. They do not take frequency of exposure or audience duplication into account. As a result, 10,000 gross impressions might mean that 10,000 people saw a message once, or 1,000 people saw it 10 times.

Ratings are the most familiar gross measures. Unlike projected audience, they express the size of the audience as a percentage of the total population, rather than a whole number. The simplest calculation for a rating, therefore, is to divide a station or program audience by potential audience. In practice, the "%" is understood, so a program with 30% of the audience is said to have a rating of 30.

The potential audience on which a rating is based can vary. Household ratings for the broadcast networks are based on all U.S. households equipped with television (TVHH). But ratings can also be based on people, or different categories of people. Local market reports have station ratings for different market areas, like DMA and metro ratings. Some national cable networks will base their ratings not on all TVHH, or even all cable households, but only on those homes that can receive a network's programming. Although there is some rationale for that, such variation can affect interpretations of the data. A ratings analyst should, therefore, be aware of the potential audience on which a rating is based.

In addition to these distinctions, there are several kinds of ratings calculations, as summarized in Table 10.2. For simplicity, everything is described in terms of television, with TV households (TVHH) as the unit of analysis. Radio ratings or TV ratings using persons as the unit of analysis would be the same, except for terminology (e.g., PUR vs. HUT).

The most narrowly defined rating is the average reported in NTI, which expresses audience size in an average minute, within a given quarter hour. That level of precision requires metering devices. As a result, this sort of rating cannot be reported for diary-based data.

Also summarized in Table 10.2 are calculations for GRPs and HUT levels. These are analogous to gross impressions and HUTs, respectively. They provide essentially the same information as those projections of audience size, but they are expressed as percentages instead of whole numbers. They are also subject to the same interpretive limitations as their counterparts. Strictly speaking, reporting HUT or PUT as percentages means they are a kind of rating. To avoid confusion, we will refer to them as such. In practice, however, these percentages are usually called HUTs or PUTs, without appending the word "rating."

Shares are the third major measure, expressing audience size as a percentage of those using the medium at a point in time. The equation for determining audience share among TV households is as follows:

$$\text{SHARE} = \frac{\text{\# OF TVHH TUNED TO STATION OR PROGRAM}}{\text{HUT LEVEL}}$$

TABLE 10.2

Ratings Computations*

Basic rating (R)	$R(\%) =$	$\dfrac{\text{TVHH watching program or station}}{\text{Total TVHH}}$
Quarter-hour rating (QH)	$QH =$	$\dfrac{\text{TVHH watching more than 5 minutes in a quarter hour}}{\text{Total TVHH}}$
Average quarter-hour rating (AQH)	$AQH =$	$\dfrac{\text{Sum of quarter-hour ratings}}{\text{Number of quarter hours}}$
Average audience rating** (AA)	$AA =$	$\dfrac{\text{Total minutes all TVHH spend watching a program}}{\text{Program duration in minutes} \times \text{total TVHH}}$
Total Audience Rating (TA)	$TA =$	$\dfrac{\text{TVHH watching program for more than 5 minutes}}{\text{Total TVHH}}$
HUT rating (HR)	$HR =$	$\dfrac{\text{Projected HUT level}}{\text{Total TVHH}}$
Gross rating points (GRP)	$GRP =$	$R_1 + R_2 + R_3 + R_4 \ldots + R_n$

*The precise method for computing a rating depends on whether the responses of sample members are differentially weighted. When they are, program audiences must be projected and then divided by the estimated population. When the responses of sample members are not weighted, or have equal weights, proportions within the sample itself determine the ratings and subsequent audience projections.
**In this computation, the number of minutes each TVHH spends watching a program is totaled across all TVHH. This is divided by the number of minutes that could have been watched, as determined by multiplying program duration in minutes by total TVHH. AA can also be reported for specific quarter hours within the program, in which case the denominator is 15 × total TVHH

The calculation of person shares is the same, with persons and PUT levels in the numerator and denominator, respectively. In either case, the rating and share of a given program or station have the same number in the numerator. The difference lies in the denominator. Because HUT or PUT levels are always less than the potential audience, a program's share will always be larger than its rating.

Like ratings, audience shares can be determined for various subsets. Unlike ratings, however, shares have limited value when buying and selling audiences. Although shares indicate performance relative to competition, they do not convey information about audience size, which is what interests advertisers. A share can only reveal information about total audience size when it is related to its associated HUT level, as shown in these two expressions:

PROJECTED PROGRAM AUDIENCE = PROGRAM SHARE × HUT

PROGRAM RATING = PROGRAM SHARE × HUT RATING

Shares can also be calculated over periods that exceed program lengths. In ratings books, shares are often reported for entire dayparts. When long-term average-share calculations are desired, the preferred method is to derive average quarter-hour (AQH) share from the average quarter-hour rating within the same daypart. The following equation summarizes how such a daypart share might be calculated with TV data:

$$\text{AQH SHARE} = \frac{\text{AQH RATING}}{\text{AQH HUT RATING}}$$

Unlike AQH ratings, it is inappropriate to calculate AQH shares from the sum of a station's share in each quarter hour divided by the number of quarter hours. Each audience share has a different denominator, and it would distort the average to give them equal weight.

Defining audience size in these ways presents interesting problems. Many occur when households are the unit of analysis. Suppose a household is watching two different programs on different sets. To which station should that home be attributed? Standard practice is to credit the household to both stations' audiences. In other words, it counts in the calculation of each station's household rating and share. However, it can only be counted once in the calculation of HUT levels. This means the sum of all program ratings could exceed the HUT rating, and the sum of all program shares could exceed 100%. This was no problem in the early days of TV, when most of these methods evolved, because most homes had one TV. But now almost three-fourths of all homes have multiple sets, and the average is more than two per home. Furthermore, it is now possible for a household to be watching several programs while simultaneously taping other programs on videotape for later viewing. Radio has long been measured on persons rather than households because of multiple sets, mostly individual listening, and much away-from-home listening.

Because households are typically collections of two or more people, household ratings tend to be higher than person ratings. Imagine a market having 100 homes, with four people in each. Suppose one person in each household were watching Station Z. Station Z would have a TVHH rating of 100 and a person rating of 25. Some programs, like family shows, do better at attracting groups of viewers, whereas others garner solitary viewers. It is, therefore, worth keeping an eye on discrepancies between household and person ratings, because differences between the two can be substantial.

Even when people are the unit of analysis, aberrations in audience size can occur. Most ratings services require that a person be in a program or quarter-hour audience for at least 5 minutes to be counted. That means it is possible for a person to be counted for two programs in a quarter hour, or to show up in several program audiences of longer duration. This creates a problem analogous to multiple-set use at the household level. When person ratings could only be derived from diaries, and audience members had to get up to change a channel, it was not much of a problem. Today, with peoplemeters tracking a population having remote controls and dozens of channel choices, the potential for viewers to be represented in more than one program audience is considerable.

Cost Calculations

The common way to extend the data reported in a ratings book is to introduce information on the cost of reaching the audience. Cost calculations are important for buyers and sellers of media audiences. Two are in wide use, both based on manipulations of gross audience measurements.

Cost per thousand (CPM)—the cost to reach 1,000 members of a target audience—is the yardstick used to compare stations or networks with different audiences and rate structures. The standard formula for computing CPM is this:

$$CPM = \frac{COST\ OF\ SPOT\ (\$) \times 1000}{PROJECTED\ TARGET\ AUDIENCE}$$

The projected target audience is expressed as a whole number. It could be the households delivered by the spot in question, men 18–49, working women, teens 12–17, and so forth. CPMs can be calculated for whatever audience is most relevant to the advertiser, as long as the ratings data can be calculated to project that audience. Occasionally, when many spots are running, it is more convenient to compute the average CPM for the schedule in the following way:

$$AVERAGE\ CPM = \frac{COST\ OF\ SCHEDULE\ (\$) \times 1000}{TARGET\ GROSS\ IMPRESSIONS}$$

CPMs are the most widely used measure of the advertising media's cost efficiency. They can be calculated to gauge relative costs within a medium or to compare different media. In print, for example, the cost of a black-and-white page or a newspaper's line rate is divided by its circulation or the number of readers it delivers. In chapter 4 we presented CPM trends across radio, television, and print media. Comparisons within a medium are easier to interpret than intermedia comparisons. As long as target audiences are defined in the same way, CPMs can reveal which spot is more cost efficient. There is less agreement on the magazine equivalent of a 30-second spot.

The electronic media have a unique form of cost calculation called cost per point (CPP). Like CPM, it is a yardstick for making cost–efficiency comparisons, except the unit of measurement is not 1,000s of audience members but ratings points. CPP is computed as follows:

$$CPP = \frac{COST\ OF\ SPOT\ (\$)}{TARGET\ AUDIENCE\ RATING}$$

An alternate method for calculating CPP can be used when many spots are being run and an average CPP is of more interest than the efficiency of one commercial. This is sometimes called the cost per gross rating point:

$$CPGRP = \frac{COST\ OF\ SCHEDULE\ (\$)}{GROSS\ RATING\ POINTS}$$

In network television, average audience ratings (AA) are preferred for CPP computations, because they more accurately express the audience size at the moment a spot is run. For ratings based on diary data, a quarter-hour rating is used. Television market reports also estimate station-break ratings by averaging quarter hours before and after the break. If that is when the spot has run, that is the most appropriate rating to use.

CPP measures are part of the everyday language of people who specialize in broadcast advertising. Station representatives, and the media buyers with whom they deal, often negotiate on a CPP basis. This measure of cost efficiency has the additional advantage of relating directly to GRPs, which are commonly used to define the size of an advertising campaign. CPPs, however, have two limiting characteristics that affect their use and interpretation. First, they are less precise than CPMs. Ratings points are rarely calculated beyond one decimal place, and must therefore be rounded. Rounding off network audiences can add or subtract tens of thousands of people from the audience, causing an unnecessary reduction in the accuracy of cost calculations. Second, ratings are based on different potential audiences. The CPP in New York is likely to be more than in Louisville, because each point represents more people. But how many more? CPMs would be easier to interpret. Even within a market, problems arise. Radio stations, whose signals cover only part of a market, should be especially alert to CPP buying criteria. While one station delivers most of its audience within the metro area, another may have an audience of equal size located mostly outside the metro. If CPPs in the market are based on metro ratings, the second station could be at an unfair, and unnecessary, disadvantage.

Comparisons

Comparing the gross measures we have just reviewed is the common form of ratings analysis. An endless number of other comparisons can be made. They might be designed to show the superiority of one station over another, the relative cost efficiency of different advertising media, the success of one program format as opposed to another, and too many others to catalog in one chapter. We can, however, provide illustrative examples useful in buying or selling time, pro-

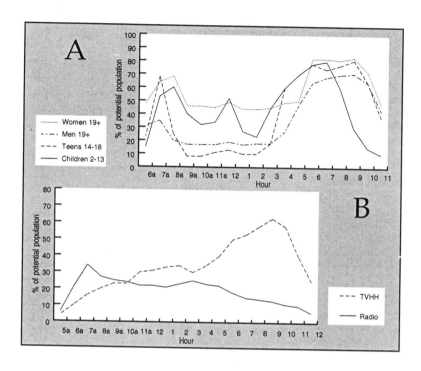

FIG. 10.1. Hypothetical audience availabilities and typical patterns of radio and television use.

gramming, or simply reaching a better understanding of the electronic media and their audiences.

One area deals with the size and composition of the available audience. Because the nature of the available audience is a powerful determinant of station or program audiences (see chap. 9, this volume), an analyst might want to scrutinize who is watching or listening at different times. This kind of analysis could certainly interest a programmer who must be cognizant of the ebb and flow of audience segments when deciding what programming to run. It might also be of value to an advertiser or media buyer who wants to know when a certain audience is most available. The most straightforward method of comparison is to graph the size of various audience segments at different hours throughout the day. So at this point we return briefly to the concept of available audiences.

The most important factor affecting the size of broadcast audiences is when people are available to listen. Work hours, school and transportation schedules, meal times, and the seasons—especially during warm weather when people are likely to be outdoors—are the strongest influences on when people are available and interested in using mass media. No regular surveys provide detailed information on such availabilities. However, several older studies can be reconstructed to give a rough idea of the availability of men, women, teens, and children throughout the day (see Fig. 10.1A).

Holidays, special events, and coverage of important news stories can alter these patterns, but as a rule, they translate directly into the patterns of media use depicted in Fig. 10.1B. Rarely does a single program or big event influence a rise in HUTs. The most famous occasions were the assassination of President Kennedy, landing and walking on the moon, and the verdict in the O. J. Simpson trial. However, important news events, like the 1991 Gulf War, often attract more viewers and listeners than usual during the daytime. Special programming or a lot of advertising and promotion might also cause a rise of 10% or more in typical HUT levels during prime time.

With few exceptions, the best indicator of how many people can and will use the media appears in the reports of when they do so. Any new program, or even new cable network, that plans to find an audience among those who are not already listening or viewing is very unlikely to be successful. New programs, formats, and program services usually divide the existing potential and available audiences into smaller pieces of the pie rather than attracting new viewers. The best evidence of this condition is the recent decline in national network share due to the increasing number of cable and DBS competitors.

A good starting point for the audience analyst is to plot when various audience segments are using a medium in a market. Radio market reports will have a section of daypart audience estimates with people using radio (PUR) levels, as well as different station audiences. Television reports estimate audiences by the quarter hour or the half hour. Figure 10.2 illustrates radio listening—at home, at work, and in cars—for 3 gender–age categories.

These data paint different pictures of radio and television use for each demographic group. Note especially the radio use by working men on the job and in their vehicles. For teens, while school is in session there is very little daytime listening but a lot at night. Older people are heavy radio users mostly at home. The distinct patterns of radio use clarify the parameters within which the programmer must operate.

Before advertisers can commit to buying time on specific stations or networks, they need to determine the most effective way to reach their target audience. This relatively simple requirement can trigger a torrent of ratings comparisons. From the time buyer's perspective, comparisons should respond to the advertiser's need to reach a certain kind of audience in a cost-efficient manner. From the time seller's perspective, the comparisons should also show his or her audiences in the best possible light. Although these two objectives are not mutually exclusive, they can cause audience analysts to view ratings data differently.

The simplest form of ratings analysis is to compare station or program audience size. This can be determined by ranking each program, station, or network

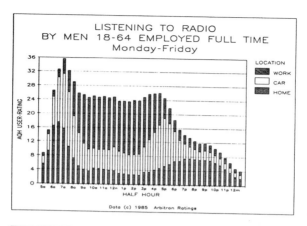

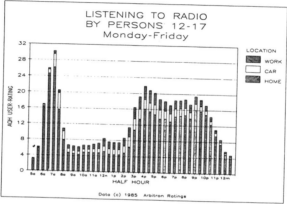

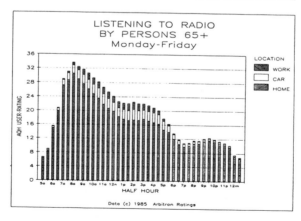

FIG. 10.2.   Comparison of radio use by location within demographic groups (based on data provided by the Arbitron Company. Reprinted with permission of Audience Research Analysis).

according to average rating. One need only glance at the trade press to see how important it is to be "number one" by some measure. Of course, it's difficult for everyone to be number one. Furthermore, buying time on the top station may not be an effective advertising expenditure. So, comparisons of sheer audience size are typically qualified by some consideration of audience composition.

The relevant definition of audience composition is usually determined by an advertiser. An avail request, for instance, will usually specify the target audience in demographics. If the advertiser has a primary audience of women ages 18–24, it would make sense for the analyst to rank programs, not by audience size, but by ratings among women 18–24. In all probability this would produce a different rank ordering of programs, and perhaps even a different number 1. For radio stations, which often specialize in a certain demographic, ranking within audience subsets can allow several stations to claim they are number one.

At this point, we should emphasize a problem in ratings analysis that troubles researchers. Analyzing or comparing subsets of the audience reduces the sample size on which those comparisons are based. It is easy for casual users to ignore or forget this because published ratings seem so authoritative. But remember that ratings estimates are subject to sampling error, which increases as the sample size decreases. The difference between being number one and number two among men ages 18–24 might be a chance occurrence, rather than a real difference. A researcher would say the difference was not statistically significant. The same phenomenon produces what people in the industry call *bounce*. It is a change in station ratings from one book to the next, resulting from sampling error rather than any real change in audience size. An analyst should question small differences, especially if they are based on small samples.

Having so cautioned, we must also point out that the business of making comparisons can be, and is, done using things other than audience size. Ratings data can be adjusted in a way that highlights audience composition, and then ranked. This may change rank orderings. Two techniques are used to make these adjustments.

Indexing is a common way to make comparisons across scores. An index number simply expresses an individual score, like a rating or CPM, relative to a standard or base value. The basic formula for creating index numbers is as follows:

$$\text{INDEX NUMBER} = \frac{\text{SCORE} \times 100}{\text{BASE VALUE}}$$

Usually the base value is fixed in time to give the analyst an indication of how some variable is changing. Current CPMs are often indexed to their levels in an earlier year. Base values have been determined in other ways, however. Suppose a program had a high rating among women 18–24 but a low rating overall. An index number could be created by using the overall rating as a base. That would make the target audience rating look strong by comparison. CPM index numbers have also been created by comparing individual market CPMs to an average CPM across markets (see Poltrack, 1983).

Thus far, we have defined target audiences only in terms of two demographic variables: age and gender. These are the segmentation variables most commonly used to specify an advertiser's audience objectives. But age and gender variables may not be the most relevant descriptors of an advertiser's target market. Income, buying habits, lifestyle, and a host of other variables might be of critical importance to someone buying advertising time. If the seller can define target audiences in those terms, it might be an effective sales tool; however, ratings books report little of this specialized information.

As noted in chapter 8, ratings services can customize ratings reports. In fact, with the widespread use of personal computers and telephone access to databases, customization has become increasingly common. It is now possible to describe audiences in ways not found on the printed page of a ratings book.

For example, ratings services keep track of the zip code in which each member of the sample lives. Zip code information is valued, because it is thought that knowing where a person lives can reveal a great deal about that individual. Inferences can be made about household incomes, occupations, ethnicity, education levels, lifestyles, and so on. As long as sample sizes are sufficiently large, these inferences will be reasonably accurate. Some companies specialize in analyzing zip code areas and grouping those with similar characteristics. This geodemography allows the definition and comparison of audience in virtually unlimited ways.

Audience comparisons alone will not necessarily convince an advertiser to buy time. As with any product, no matter how useful or nicely packaged, the question usually comes down to how much it costs. In this context, CPM and CPP comparisons are critical. Such comparisons might be designed to illuminate the efficiency of buying one program, station, or daypart as opposed to another. Table 10.3 compares CPMs for network and spot television across several dayparts, and shows how these costs have changed over time.

Although ratings usually have more sales applications than shares, share data can be useful in promoting a particular station, program, or an entire medium. Even though shares may not total 100, most people familiar with the concept of market shares expect them to, so it is common, and often effective, to represent audience shares as a pie chart. Figure 10.3, for instance, shows a series of pie charts prepared by the Cable Advertising Bureau (CAB), to dramatize the share cable services claim among various household types.

Rating and share comparisons are also useful to programmers. Using zip codes, a radio station programmer might compare ratings across geographic areas within the market. Because different formats appeal to different kinds of people, a programmer who knows the market should have some sense of where his or her listeners are likely to live. If a station places a strong signal over an area with the kind of population that should like its format but has few listeners,

TABLE 10.3

Cost-per-1000-Homes-Reached Trends for Network and Spot TV 30-second Units (1955–1997)

	1955	1960	1965	1970	1975	1980	1985	1990	1995	1997
Major Network TV										
Daytime	$0.55	$0.65	$0.75	$0.85	$1.00	$2.00	$3.10	$2.35	$3.00	$3.80
Early news	NA	NA	1.40	1.55	1.65	3.20	5.45	6.25	6.35	6.75
Prime evening	1.50	1.70	1.95	2.20	2.55	4.80	8.25	8.76	9.50	11.75
Late Evening	NA	NA	2.05	1.95	2.00	3.40	5.60	6.35	7.25	8.75
Sports[1]	NA	NA	3.00	2.95	2.60	4.50	7.30	8.75	9.85	11.15
Spot TV[2]										
Daytime	NA	NA	2.00	2.40	2.65	2.75	3.30	4.25	4.35	4.85
Early evening	NA	NA	1.25	1.65	1.75	2.80	4.05	4.85	5.45	6.65
Prime[3]	NA	NA	2.30	2.60	3.65	6.75	10.00	12.00	12.75	14.95
Late news	NA	NA	1.60	1.85	2.50	4.75	7.25	8.50	10.25	11.75
Late evening	NA	NA	1.50	1.80	2.35	3.85	5.35	6.50	6.75	8.25

[1]All-telecast average
[2]Top 100 markets
[3]Major network affiliates
Source: TV Dimensions '98, © Media Dynamics, Inc., New York, NY.

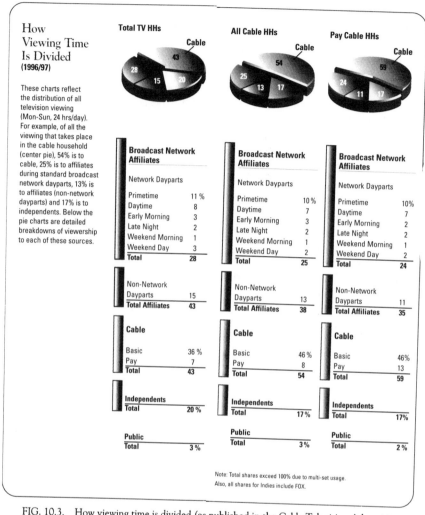

How Viewing Time Is Divided (1996/97)

These charts reflect the distribution of all television viewing (Mon-Sun, 24 hrs/day). For example, of all the viewing that takes place in the cable household (center pie), 54% is to cable, 25% is to affiliates during standard broadcast network dayparts, 13% is to affiliates (non-network dayparts) and 17% is to independents. Below the pie charts are detailed breakdowns of viewership to each of these sources.

Total TV HHs
Cable 43
28
15 20

Broadcast Network Affiliates

Network Dayparts

Primetime	11 %
Daytime	8
Early Morning	3
Late Night	2
Weekend Morning	1
Weekend Day	3
Total	28

| Non-Network Dayparts | 15 |
| Total Affiliates | 43 |

Cable

Basic	36 %
Pay	7
Total	43

Independents
| Total | 20 % |

Public
| Total | 3 % |

All Cable HHs
Cable 54
25
13 17

Broadcast Network Affiliates

Network Dayparts

Primetime	10 %
Daytime	7
Early Morning	3
Late Night	2
Weekend Morning	1
Weekend Day	2
Total	25

| Non-Network Dayparts | 13 |
| Total Affiliates | 38 |

Cable

Basic	46 %
Pay	8
Total	54

Independents
| Total | 17 % |

Public
| Total | 3 % |

Pay Cable HHs
Cable 59
24
11 17

Broadcast Network Affiliates

Network Dayparts

Primetime	10%
Daytime	7
Early Morning	2
Late Night	2
Weekend Morning	1
Weekend Day	2
Total	24

| Non-Network Dayparts | 11 |
| Total Affiliates | 35 |

Cable

Basic	46%
Pay	13
Total	59

Independents
| Total | 17% |

Public
| Total | 2 % |

Note: Total shares exceed 100% due to multi-set usage.
Also, all shares for Indies include FOX.

FIG. 10.3.   How viewing time is divided (as published in the Cable Television Advertising Bureau's *1998 Cable TV Facts*).

special promotions might be needed. One station that made such a discovery decided to place outdoor advertising and conduct a series of remote broadcasts in the areas where it was underperforming.

Radio programmers may also find it useful to represent the audience for each station in the market on a *demographic map*. This can be done by creating a 2-dimensional grid, with the vertical axis expressing, for example, the percent of males in each station's audience, and the horizontal axis expressing the median age of the audience. Once these values are known, each station can be located on the grid. The station audiences could also be averaged to map formats rather than individual stations. Local radio market reports contain the information needed to determine these values, although a few preliminary calculations are necessary.

The most difficult calculation is determining the median age of each station's audience. The median is a descriptive statistic, much like an arithmetic average. Technically, it is the point at which half the cases in a distribution are higher and half are lower. If, for example, 50% of a station's audience is younger than 36, and 50% are older, then 36 is the median age.

Determining the median age of a station's audience requires data on the size of the audience in the age categories reported by the ratings service. Table 10.4 contains that data for a single station in one daypart. It also contains estimates of men and women, to calculate the percent of males who are listening as well. The station has 43,200 listeners in an AQH. Because radio books report audiences in 100s, it is more convenient to record that as 432 in the table. The number of listeners 65+ must be inferred from the difference between the total audience 12+, and the sum of all other categories (i.e., 432 minus 408 = 24).

The median can now be located as follows: First, figure out the cumulative frequency, shown in the far right-hand column. Second, divide the size of the audience in half. In this case, it is 216 (i.e., 432/2 = 216). Third, look at the cumulative distribution and find the age category in which the 216th case falls. This table shows that 206 people are 34.5 or younger and 103 people are in the

TABLE 10.4
Calculating Median Age and Gender of Station Audience

Age Group	Male (in 00s)	Female (in 00s)	Group Frequency (in 00s)	Cumulative Frequency (in 00s)
12–17	?	?	23	23
18–24	29	50	79	102
25–34	63	41	104	206
35–44	43	60	103	309
45–54	35	27	62	371
55–64	20	17	37	408
65+	8	16	24	432
Total 12+	?	?	432	
Total 18+	198	211	409	
Percent M–F*	48%	52%		

*Because radio market reports do not ordinarily indicate gender of persons 12 to 17, the male-to-female breakdown for a station's audience must be determined on the basis of those 18 and older. In this case, there are 409(00) persons 18+ in the audience.

next oldest group. Therefore, the 216th case must be between 34.5 and 44.5. Fourth, locate the 216th case by interpolating within that age group. To do that, assume the ages of the 103 people are evenly distributed. To locate the median, move 10 cases deep into the next age group. Stated differently, we need to go 10/103 of the way into a 10-year span. That translates into 0.97 years (i.e., $10/103 \times 10 = 0.97$). Add that to the lower limit of the category—the median age is 35.47 (i.e., $34.5 + 0.97 = 35.47$).

This procedure sounds more burdensome than it is. It is simply a way to reduce a great deal of information about the age of the station's audience into a single number. Similarly, the gender of the audience is reduced to a single number by using the male–female breakdowns in each category. In the previous example, 48% of the audience was male. These two numbers could become coordinates for plotting a point on a 2-dimensional grid. Figure 10.4 shows how stations with different formats would look on a demographic map of radio stations.

Figure 10.4 is a typical array of formats and associated audiences. Formats can vary widely in terms of the type of listener they attract. An Album-Oriented Rock station and a Contemporary Hits station will both tend to have young listeners, but they typically have different appeals for young men and women. A Classical station attracts older listeners. Some music syndicators package radio formats to appeal to very specific demographics. These pronounced differences in audience composition are why it is possible for different stations to be number one with different categories of listeners.

Demographic mapping can help programmers identify holes in the market, by drawing attention to segments that are unserved by a radio station. It can also offer a different way to look at the positioning of stations in a market and how they do or do not compete for listeners. By creating maps for different dayparts, the programmer can see shifts in audience composition.

A number of cautions in the interpretation of the map should, however, be kept in mind. First, it tells the analyst nothing about the size of the potential audiences. There may be a hole in the market because there are relatively few people of a particular type. Some markets have very old populations, others do not. Similarly, the map reports nothing on the size of the station's actual audience, only its composition. Second, the analyst should remember that different types of listeners may be more valuable to advertisers and constitute a more desirable audience. This could be attributable to demographic composition or the fact that many listen exclusively to their favorite station.

Third, just because two or more stations occupy the same space on the map does not mean they will share an audience. A country-western station and a public radio station will often fall side by side on a map, but typically they have very little crossover audience. The tendency of listeners to move back and forth between stations can be more accurately studied by using the audience duplication section of the ratings book. Finally, remember that age and gender are not the only factors that might be related to station preferences. The map could

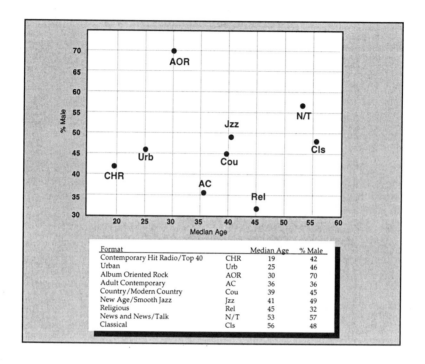

FIG. 10.4.   Demographic map of radio stations.

look quite different if ethnicity or education were among the dimensions. Just such a map can be constructed when other demographic variables, such as education and income, are available.

Median age can also be a useful way to differentiate among television program sources. Table 10.5 compares six broadcast networks on the median age of their audiences. Newer networks have programmed aggressively to younger demographics. The WB's prime-time audience has a median age of 25; UPN and Fox have successfully appealed to audiences with an average age in the low 30s. The more established networks, particularly CBS, are attracting older viewers.

Ratings comparisons are also made longitudinally, over several points in time. Most local market reports include data from previous sweeps under the heading of trends. There are many reasons for looking at audience trends. A radio programmer might want to determine how a format change had altered the composition of the station's audience, perhaps producing a series of maps, as shown in Fig. 10.4. A financial analyst might want to examine the ratings history of a particular media property. A policymaker or economist might want to study patterns of audience diversion to assess competitive positions of old and

TABLE 10.5
Prime-Time Median Age by Network*

	ABC	CBS	NBC	Fox	UPN	WB
1993	38.3	48.1	41.1	30.6		
1994	38.3	50.0	42.8	29.6		
1995	40.6	49.0	42.2	30.5	37.3	23.4
1996	40.5	51.3	40.9	32.5	34.3	25.3
1997	40.8	52.6	40.3	32.8	31.7	24.2

*Source: Fourth quarter estimates from TN Media Inc., *The Median Age Report*, January 1998. Used by permission of Steve Sternberg, Senior Partner, Director of Broadcast Research, TN Media.

new media. A social scientist might examine potential changes in the social or political impact of the media.

Because the major ratings services now produce electronic ratings books that are read by a computer, the time involved in sorting and ranking ratings data can be drastically reduced. Arbitron and Nielsen sell software packages that will manipulate their data in a variety of ways. Some private vendors have also produced software that can turn ratings data into bar graphs, pie charts, and so on. Although most of these developments are a boon to ratings analysts, a number of cautions should be exercised in either producing or consuming comparative statistics. Do not let the computational power or colorful graphics of these programs disguise what you are dealing with. Gross measures of the audience are estimates based on sample information. Keep the following points in mind:

• Be alert to the size of the sample used to create a rating or derive an audience projection. One consequence of zeroing in on a narrowly defined target audience is that the actual number of people on which estimates are based becomes quite small, which increases the sampling error. A national peoplemeter sample might be big enough to break out the audience into narrow subsets. It does not follow that local market samples, which are smaller, can provide similar target estimates of equal accuracy.

• Techniques like indexing and calculating target efficiency involve percentages of percentages, which tends to obscure the original values on which they are based. For example, comparing a 1.4 rating to a 0.7 rating produces the same index number (i.e., 200) as comparing a 14.0 to a 7.0. Sampling error, however, will be much larger relative to the smaller ratings. This means you should have less confidence in the first index value, because even slight variations in its component parts could cause it to fluctuate wildly. The fact that the second index number is more reliable is not readily apparent with this sort of data reduction.

• Keep it simple. The ability to manipulate numbers in a multitude of ways does not necessarily mean that it is a good idea. The more twists and turns in the analysis, the more likely you are to lose sight of what you are actually doing to the data, or to make conceptual or computational errors. And even if the work is flawless, more complex manipulations are harder to explain to the consumers of your research. You may understand how some special index was created, but that does not mean that a media buyer will have the time or inclination to sit through the explanation.

Prediction and Explanation

Most people schooled in quantitative research and theory are familiar with the concepts of prediction and explanation. The major reason researchers develop social scientific theory is to explain or predict the events observed in the social world. In the context of ratings research, researchers use the theories of audience behavior (developed in chap. 9) to help explain and predict gross measures of audience size and composition. But prediction and explanation are not mere academic exercises. Predicting audience ratings is one of the principal activities of industry users.

It is important to remember that all ratings data are historical, describing something that has already happened. Conversely, the buying and selling of audiences always anticipates future events. Although it is useful to know which program had the largest audience last week, what really determines the allocation of advertising dollars is an expectation of who will have the largest audience next week or next season. Hence, ratings analysts involved in sales and advertising spend a considerable portion of their time trying to predict ratings.

In the parlance of the industry, the job of predicting ratings is sometimes called pre-buy analysis (not to be confused with the pre-buy analyses done by financial planners and programmers when they evaluate a program acquisition). Each buyer and seller of advertising time must estimate the audience that will be delivered by a specific media schedule. The standard method of prediction proceeds through a 2-stage process.

In the first stage, the analyst estimates the size of the audience, as reflected in HUT or PUT levels, at the time a spot is to air. This is largely a matter of understanding audience availability, which is generally predictable (see chap. 9, this volume). It varies by hour of the day, day of the week, and week of the year. It can also be affected by extremes in the weather (e.g., snowstorms, heat waves, etc.), although these are obviously harder to know far in advance.

The simplest way to predict a future audience is to assume it will mirror what it was a year ago. This takes into account hourly, daily, and seasonal variations. A more complex procedure involves looking at HUT/PUT for a period of months or years. By doing so, the analyst may identify long-term trends or aberrations in audience levels that would affect his or her judgment about future HUT levels. A 4-year average of HUT levels for a given hour, day, or month might produce a more stable estimate of future HUTs than looking only at last year, which could have been atypical. In fact, to determine audience levels during months that are not measured, HUT levels should be interpolated by averaging data from sweeps before and after the month in question.

In the second stage, the analyst must project the share of audience that the station or program will achieve. Again the simplest approach is to assume the share will be the same as it was during the last measurement period. A number of factors can affect audience shares, and an analyst must take these into account. Programming changes can have a dramatic effect. In radio, rival stations may have changed formats making them more or less appealing to some segment of the market. In television, a competing station might be counterprogramming more effectively than in the past. Less dramatic, long-term trends might also be at work. Perhaps cable penetration has caused a gradual erosion in audience shares likely to continue in the near future. Just as in estimating HUT levels, making comparisons across several measurement periods might reveal subtle shifts that would otherwise go unnoticed.

Once total audience levels and specific audience shares have been estimated, predicting an audience rating is simple: Multiply the HUT level expected by the projected audience share. This formula is summarized as follows:

$$\text{PREDICTED RATING} = \text{ESTIMATED HUT} \times \text{PROJECTED SHARE (\%)}$$

In effect, it simply codifies the conventional wisdom expressed in Paul Klein's (1971) theory of the least objectionable program. That is, exposure is thought of as a 2-stage process in which an available audience decides which station or program to watch. The procedure to predict ratings for specific demographic subsets is the same, except the analyst must estimate the PUT level (e.g., men 18–49) and determine the program's likely share among that audience subset. In either case, there are now computer programs marketed by the ratings companies and independent vendors that perform such pre-buy analyses.

Although these formulas and computer programs are useful, remember that predicting audience ratings is not an exact science. It involves experience, intuition, and an understanding of factors that affect audience size. Unfortunately, we can only offer help in the last category. Our advice would be to consider the model of audience behavior presented in chapter 9. Systematically work your way through the structural- and individual-level factors likely to affect audience size, and begin to test them against your experience. Sometimes that will lead to modifications that just seem to work.

One of the most difficult, and high stakes, occasions for predicting ratings occurs during the upfront market in network television. Major advertising agencies and network sales executives must try to anticipate how the fall line-ups will perform. This is tricky because many programs are new, and have no track record. At least one major agency has found through experience that it can predict network ratings more accurately if it bases those predictions not on total HUT levels, but on network-only HUT levels. In other words, the first stage in the process is to estimate the number of viewers who will be watching broadcast network television. Why this results in better predictions is not entirely clear, it just seems to work.

Armed with share projections and predicted ratings for various segments of the audience, buyers and sellers negotiate a contract, with sellers inclined to be optimistic about ratings prospects and buyers tending to be more conservative. The ratings projections that each brings to the table may be colored by the need to stake out a negotiating position. Eventually a deal is struck. Because most spot buys involve a schedule of several spots, the total audience to be delivered is usually expressed in GRPs.

After a schedule of spots has run, both buyers and sellers will want to know how well they did. Just as programmers and financial managers evaluate program buys, salespeople and buyers evaluate ratings predictions through a post-buy analysis. In continuously measured markets, it is possible to know exactly how well programs performed when a spot aired. Most local markets, however, are only surveyed during certain months. Consequently, precise data on ratings performance may not be available. Table 10.6 identifies the sweeps that are traditionally used for post-buy analysis in different months. The point is to use the best available data for evaluative purposes.

With the schedule of spots in one hand and the actual ratings in the other, the schedule is re-rated. The original contract may have anticipated 200 GRPs but the audience delivered totaled 210. If true, the media buyer did better than expected. Of course the opposite could have occurred, resulting in an audience deficiency. In upfront deals, networks have traditionally made up such deficiencies by running extra spots. More often, however, it is simply the media buyer's bad luck.

Questions are often raised about the accuracy of ratings predictions. Standard practice has been to view delivered audience within +/- 10% of predicted

TABLE 10.6
Sweeps Used for Post-Buy Analysis*

February	January-February-March
May	April-May-June
July	July-August-September
November	October-November-December

*This schedule for post-buy analysis assumes the market is measured four times a year. Additional sweeps in January, March, and October would, if available, be used for post-buy analysis in January, March–April, and September–October, respectively.

levels as acceptable. Three sources of error can cause such discrepancies—forecasting error, strategic error, and sampling error. *Forecasting errors* are usually the first that come to mind. Included here are errors of judgment and prediction. For example, the analyst might not have properly gauged a trend in HUT levels or foreseen the success of a programming strategy. *Strategic errors* are deliberately introduced at the time of contractual negotiations. A researcher might honestly believe a program will deliver a 10 rating. The person selling the program, however, might believe it could be sold at 12, if a projection justified that number. To make a more profitable deal, the projection is knowingly distorted.

Sampling error can also affect the accuracy of ratings predictions and should serve as a reminder that these numbers are estimates based on sample information. As explained in chapter 7, the larger the sample on which the rating is based, the lower the associated error. Furthermore, the error surrounding small ratings tends to be rather large relative to the size of the rating itself. The same logic can be applied to a schedule of spots as expressed in GRPs. In the mid-1980s, Arbitron did an extensive study of the error (Jaffe, 1985) in GRP estimates. The principal conclusions were as follows:

- GRPs based on larger effective sample bases (ESB) had smaller standard errors. This means GRPs based on large audience segments (e.g., men 18+) are more stable than those based on smaller segments (e.g., men 18–34). It also means that larger markets, which tend to have larger samples, will generally have less error than small markets.
- The higher the pairwise correlation between programs in the schedule, the higher the standard error. In other words, when there is a high level of audience duplication between spots in the schedule, there is a higher probability of error. This happens because high duplication implies the same people tend to be represented in each program rating, thereby reducing the scope of the sample on which GRPs are based.
- For a given GRP level, a schedule with few highly rated spots was less prone to error than a schedule with many low-rated spots.
- All things being equal, the larger the schedule in terms of GRPs, the larger the size of absolute standard error, but the smaller the size of relative standard error.

As a practical matter, this means a post-buy analysis is more likely to find results within the +/–10% criterion if GRPs are based on large segments of the market and programs or stations with high ratings. A match of pre-buy predictions to post-buy ratings is less likely if GRPs are based on small ratings among small audience segments, even if forecasting and strategic error are nonexistent. As increased competition fragments radio and television audiences, and as advertisers try to target increasingly precise market segments, this problem of sampling error is likely to cause more post-buy results to fall outside the 10% range.

The method for predicting ratings described thus far is fairly straightforward, requires little in the way of statistical manipulations, and depends heavily on intuition and expert judgment. There have been, however, a number of efforts to model program ratings in the form of mathematical equations. With either approach, the underlying theory of audience behavior is the same. In attempts to model the ratings, however, many expert judgments are replaced by empirically determined, quantitative relationships.

Gensch and Shaman (1980) and Barnett, Chang, Fink, and Richards (1991) developed models that estimate accurately the number of viewers of network television at any point in time. Consistent with our earlier discussions, they discovered that audience size was not dependent on available program content, but rather a function of time of day and seasonality. Once the size of the available audience was predicted, the second stage in the process, determining each program's share of audience, was modeled independently. This, of course is analogous to the standard method of prediction in the industry.

Rust and Alpert (1984), Horen (1980), and others have concentrated on how the available audience is distributed across program options. Here factors such as lead-in effects, counterprogramming, a program's rating history, and program type are used to produce share estimates. In addition to these general ratings models, more specialized models have been tested. Litman (1979), for example, used data on the age and box office receipts of movies to predict their ratings on television.

In addition to attempts at modeling program ratings cited earlier, researchers have used correlational studies of gross audience measurements to assess the success of different programming strategies (e.g., Lin, 1995; Tiedge & Ksobiech, 1986, 1987; Walker, 1988), determine the cancellation threshold of network programs (Adams, 1993; Atkin & Litman, 1986), assess the impact of media ownership on ratings performance (Parkman, 1982), and examine the role of ratings in the evolution of television program content (McDonald & Schechter, 1988). In our judgment, these analyses represent a fertile area for further study.

RELATED READINGS

Fletcher, J. E. (1985). *Squeezing profits out of ratings: A manual for radio managers, sales managers and programmers.* Washington, D.C: National Association of Broadcasters.

Hall, R. W. (1988). *Media math: Basic techniques of media evaluation.* Lincolnwood, IL: NTC Business Books.

Rust, R.T. (1986). *Advertising media models: A practical guide.* Lexington, MA: Lexington Books.

Sissors, J. Z., & Bumba, L. (1996). *Advertising media planning* (5th ed.). Lincolnwood, IL: NTC Business Books.

Webster, J. G., & Phalen, P. F. (1997). *The mass audience: Rediscovering the dominant model.* Mahwah, NJ: Lawrence Erlbaum Associates.

11

Audience Ratings:
Analysis of Cumulative
Measures

Cumulative measures are the second kind of audience summary a ratings analyst confronts. These measures of exposure are distinguished from gross measures because they depend on tracking individual audience members over time. Although some cumulative measures are routinely reported by the ratings services, they are less common than gross measurements. Nevertheless, thoughtful analyses of cumulative measures can provide considerable insights into the nature of audience behavior and its possible effects.

CUMULATIVE MEASURES

A few of the common cumulative measurements of the audience appear in the ratings books. Several more are easily, and routinely, calculated from material contained in the books. Many other cumulative measurements are possible, but require access to the appropriate database. All are discussed here.

The most common cumulative measure of the audience is called a *cume*. A cume is the total number of different people or households who have tuned in to a station for at least 5 minutes over some longer period of time—usually a daypart, day, week, or even a month. The term cume is often used interchangeably with reach and unduplicated audience. When a cume is expressed as a percentage of the total possible audience, it is called a *cume rating*. When it is expressed as the actual number of people estimated to have been in the cume audience, it is called *cume persons*. These audience summaries are analogous to the ratings and projected audiences discussed in the previous section.

Like ordinary ratings and audience projections, variations on the basic definition are common. Cumes are routinely reported for different subsets of the audience, defined both demographically and geographically. For example, Arbitron reports a station's metro cume ratings for men and women of different age categories. Cume persons can also be estimated within different areas of the market, like the Metro and DMA. Regardless of how the audience subset is defined, these numbers express the total, unduplicated, audience for a station. Each person or household in the audience can only count once in figuring the cume, whether they listened for 8 minutes or 8 hours.

In addition to reporting cumes across various audience subsets, the ratings services will also report station cumes within different dayparts. Radio ratings books estimate a station's cume audience during morning drive time (Monday through Friday, 6:00 a.m.–10:00 a.m.), afternoon drive (Monday through Friday, 3:00 p.m.–7:00 p.m.), and other standard dayparts. Cume audiences can also be calculated for a station's combined drive-time audience (i.e., how many people listened to a station in a.m. and/or p.m. drive time).

The period over which a cume audience can be determined is constrained by the measurement technique. Radio cumes cannot exceed 1 week, because the diaries used to measure radio listening are only kept for 1 week. The same is true for television cumes in diary-only markets. Barring repeated callbacks, telephone recall techniques face similar limitations. Meter measurements, on the other hand, allow the ratings services to track cume audiences over longer periods of time.

In principle, household meters could produce household cumes, and peoplemeters could produce person cumes over any period of continuous operation (e.g., years). As a practical matter, cume audiences are rarely tracked for more than 1 month. Four-week cumes, however, are commonly reported with meter-based data. Since many TV programs air once a week, this allows a ratings user to see how widely the show is viewed over several weeks.

Two other variations on cumes are reported in radio. The first is called an *exclusive cume*, an estimate of the number of people who listen to one particular station during a given daypart. A large exclusive audience may be more salable than one that can be reached over several stations. Arbitron also reports *cume duplication*, the opposite of an exclusive audience. For every pair of stations in a market, the rating services estimate the number of listeners who are in both stations' cume audiences. It is possible, therefore, to see which stations tend to share an audience.

The various cume estimates can be used in subsequent manipulations, sometimes combining them with gross measures of the audience, to produce different ways of looking at audience activity. One common measure is *time spent listening* (*TSL*). The formula for computing TSL is as follows:

$$\text{TSL} = \frac{\text{AQH PERSONS FOR DAYPART} \times \text{NUMBER OF QUARTER HRS IN THE DAYPART}}{\text{CUME PERSONS FOR DAYPART}}$$

The first step is to determine the average quarter hour (AQH) audience for the station, within any given daypart, for any given segment of the audience. This will be a projected audience reported in hundreds. Multiply that by the number of quarter hours in the daypart. For a.m. or p.m. drive time, that is 80 quarter hours. For the largest daypart (Monday through Sunday 6:00 a.m.–Midnight), it is 504 quarter hours. This product yields a gross measure of the number of person-quarter-hours spent listening to the station. Dividing it by the number of people who actually listened to the station (the cume persons) produces the average amount of time each person in the cume spent listening to the station. At this point, the average TSL is expressed as quarter hours per week, but it is easy to translate this into hours per day, in order to make it more interpretable. Table 11.1 shows how this exercise could be done to compare several stations.

Note that the average amount of time listeners spend tuned in varies from station to station. A station would usually prefer larger to smaller TSL estimates, although it is possible that a high TSL results from only on a few heavy users, while a station with low TSLs would have very large audiences. For example, compare the first two stations listed in Table 11.1. In a world of advertiser support, gross audience size will ultimately be more important. Nonetheless, TSL comparisons can help change aggregated audience data into numbers that describe a typical listener, and so make them more comprehensible. Although TSLs are usually calculated for radio stations, analogous *time spent viewing* estimates could be derived by applying the same procedure to the AQH and cume estimates in the daypart summary of a television ratings report.

Another combination of cume and gross measurements is used to produce an assessment called *audience turnover.* The formula for audience turnover is:

TABLE 11.1

Calculating TSL Estimates Across Stations

Station	AQH Persons	$\times$ 504 Qtr Hrs	/ Cume Persons =	TSL QH per week	=	TSL HR per day
WAAA	500	252,000	3,500	72.0		2.57
WXXX	1,500	756,000	20,000	37.8		1.35
WBBB	6,500	3,276,000	40,000	81.9		2.93
WZZZ	1,000	504,000	12,000	42.0		1.5

Note. This sample calculation of TSL is based on estimated audiences Monday–Sunday from 6:00 a.m. to midnight. That daypart has 504 quarter hours.

$$\text{TURNOVER} = \frac{\text{CUME PERSONS IN A DAYPART}}{\text{AQH PERSONS IN A DAYPART}}$$

Estimates of audience turnover are intended to give the ratings user a sense of how rapidly different listeners cycle through the station's audience. A turnover ratio of 1 would mean that the same people were in the audience quarter hour after quarter hour. Although that kind of devotion does not occur in the "real world," relatively low turnover ratios do indicate high levels of station loyalty. Because listeners are constantly tuning into a station as others are tuning out, turnover can also be thought of as the number of new listeners a station must attract in a time period to replace those who are tuning out. As was the case with TSL estimates, however, the rate of audience turnover does not reveal anything definitive about audience size. A station with low cume and low AQH audiences could look the same as a station with large audiences in a comparison of audience turnover.

A third way to manipulate the cume estimates that appear in radio books is to calculate *recycling*. This manipulation of the data takes advantage of the fact that cumes are reported for both morning and afternoon drive time, as well as the combination of those two dayparts. It is therefore possible to answer the question, "Of the people who listened to a station in morning drive time, how many also listened in afternoon drive time?" This information could be valuable to a programmer in deciding on programming or promotion.

Estimating the recycled audience is a two-step process. First, the analyst determines how many people listened during both dayparts. Suppose a station's cume audience in morning drive time was 5,000 persons. Assume also that the afternoon drive time audience was 5,000. If the same 5,000 people appeared in both dayparts, the combined cume would still be 5,000, because each person can only count once. If they were entirely different groups, the combined cume would be 10,000. That would mean no one listened in both dayparts. If the combined cume fell between those extremes, say 8,000, then the number of people who listened in both the morning and the afternoon would be 2,000. This is determined by adding the cume for each individual daypart and subtracting the combined cume [persons who listen in both dayparts = (morning cume + afternoon cume) − combined morning & afternoon cume].

Second, the number of persons who listen in both dayparts is divided by the cume persons for either the morning or afternoon daypart. The following formula defines this operation:

$$\text{RECYCLING} = \frac{\text{CUME PERSONS IN BOTH DAYPARTS}}{\text{CUME PERSONS IN ONE DAYPART}}$$

This expresses the number of persons listening at both times as a percentage of those in either the morning or afternoon audience. Based on the hypothetical numbers in the preceding paragraph, 40% of the morning audience is recycled to afternoon drive time (2,000/5,000 = 40%).

Because nearly all radio stations get their largest audiences during the morning hours, programmers like to compare that figure with the number who listen at other times of the day. It may also be useful to compare whether these same listeners also tune in during the weekend, for example. In both television and radio, the promotion department can use data detailing when the most people are listening to schedule announcements about other programs and features on the station. Thus, stations hope to recycle their listeners into other dayparts—to build a larger AQH audience.

Cumulative measures can also be expressed in terms of reach and frequency. These concepts are widely used among advertisers and the people who plan media campaigns. Reach is like cume—how many different people were reached? It is the number of unduplicated audience members exposed to a particular media vehicle. Just as a broadcaster might want to know the weekly cume of his or her station, an advertiser will want to know the reach of an advertising campaign. Often that means counting exposures across different stations or networks. As is the case with cumes, reach can be expressed as the actual number of people or households exposed to a message, or it can be expressed as a percent of some universe. For instance, a media planner might talk about reaching 80% of the adult population with a particular ad campaign.

Unlike station cumes, which are usually based on 1 week's data, reach estimates generally cover a 4-week period. This enables a media buyer to compare the reach of a network schedule to monthly magazines.

Although reach expresses the number of audience members who have seen or heard an ad at least once, it does not reveal the number of times any one individual has been exposed to the message—the *frequency*. Usually, frequency is reported as the average number of exposures among those reached. A media planner might say not only that a campaign reached 80% of the population, but also that it did so with a frequency of 2.5.

Reach and frequency, both cumulative measures of the audience, bear a strict mathematical relationship to gross rating points (GRPs). That relationship is as follows:

$$\text{GRPS} = \text{REACH} \times \text{FREQUENCY}$$

A campaign with a reach of 80% and a frequency of 2.5 would generate 200 GRPs. Knowing the GRPs of a particular advertising schedule, however, does not provide precise information on the reach and frequency of a campaign. Nonetheless, the three terms are related, and some inferences about reach and frequency can be made on the basis of GRPs.

Figure 11.1 depicts the usual nature of the relationship. The left-hand column shows the reach of an advertising schedule. Along the bottom are frequency and GRPs. Generally speaking, ad schedules with low GRPs are associated with high reach and low frequency. This can be seen in the steep slope of the

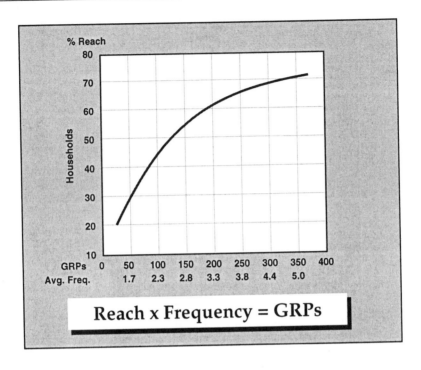

FIG. 11.1.   Reach and frequency as a function of increasing GRPs.

left-hand side of the curve. As the GRPs of a schedule increase, gains in reach occur at a reduced rate, whereas frequency of exposure begins to increase.

The diminishing contribution of GRPs to reach occurs because of differences in the amount of media people consume. People who watch a lot of TV, for example, are quickly reached with just a few commercials. The reach of a media schedule, therefore, increases rapidly in its early stages. Those who watch very little TV, however, are much harder to reach. Reaching 100% of the audience is virtually impossible. Instead, as more GRPs are committed to an ad campaign (i.e., as more commercials are run), they simply increase the frequency of exposure for heavy viewers. That raises the average frequency. Across mass audiences, these patterns of reach and frequency can be predicted with accuracy. Later in the chapter, we discuss mathematical models designed to do that.

As the preceding discussion suggests, reporting the average frequency of exposure masks variation across individuals. An average frequency of 2.5 could mean that some viewers have seen an ad 15 times and others not at all. It is often useful to consider the distribution on which the average is based. These distributions are usually lopsided, or skewed. The majority of households could be exposed to far fewer advertising messages than the arithmetic average. However, a small number of households, which presumably are the heavy viewers, might see a great many ads. In light of these distributions, advertisers often ask, "How many times must a commercial be seen or heard before it is effective?" Is one exposure enough for a commercial to have its intended effect, or even to be noticed? Conversely, at what point do repeated exposures become wasteful, or even counterproductive? There are no simple answers to these questions. The right number of exposures depends on a variety of factors, such as the number of competing messages in the marketplace or the complexity of what must be communicated. Nonetheless, many media planners seem to assume that an ad must be seen or heard at least three times before it can be effective. Such a minimum level of exposure is referred to as the *effective exposure* or *effective frequency*. This thinking imposes a conservative interpretation on ordinary measures of reach and frequency, because those who have seen a commercial fewer than three times are not "effectively" reached.

Another way to conceptualize cumulative audience behavior is in terms of *audience duplication*. Analyses of audience duplication ask, "Of the people who were watching or listening at one point, how many were also watching or listening at another point?" Those times might be broadly defined dayparts, as is the case with recycling, or brief moments, like selected minutes within different programs. In fact, audience duplication across several points in time produces the kind of reach and frequency data just described.

Studying patterns of audience duplication is one of the most powerful and illuminating techniques of analysis available to researchers. These analyses of television audience behavior have identified such patterns of duplication as inheritance effects, channel loyalty, and repeat viewing (e.g., Goodhardt, Ehrenberg, & Collins, 1987; Webster & Phalen, 1997). Unfortunately, most questions of audience duplication cannot be derived from the numbers published in a typical ratings report. To observe that one TV program has the same rating as its lead-in is no assurance that the same audience watched both. Nevertheless, if one has access to the individual level data on which the ratings are based, a variety of analytical possibilities are open.

Studies of audience duplication begin with a straightforward statistical technique called *cross-tabulation*. Cross-tabulation is described in detail in most books on research methods and is a common procedure in statistical software packages. Cross-tabs allow an analyst to view the relationship between two variables. A surveyer of magazine readership might want to identify the relationship between reader demographics and subscription (e.g., are women more or less likely than men to buy *Cosmopolitan*?). Each person's response to a question about magazine subscription could be paired with information on gender, resulting in a cross-tabulation of those variables.

When cross-tabulation is used to study audience duplication, the analyst pairs one media-use variable with another. Given diary data on a sample of 100 people, for example, an analyst could answer questions like, "Of the people who watched one situation comedy (e.g., SC1) how many also watched a second situation comedy (e.g., SC2)?" These are two behavioral variables, among a great many, contained in the data. A cross-tabulation of the two would produce a table like Table 11.2.

The numbers along the bottom of Table 11.2a show that 20 people wrote "yes," they watched SC1, whereas the remaining 80 did not watch the program. The sum of numbers in these two response categories should always equal the sample size. Along the far right-hand side of the table are the comparable numbers for SC2, again assuming that 20 people reported watching and 80 did not. The numbers reported along the edges, or margins, of the table are referred to as *marginals*. When the number of people viewing a program is reported as a percentage of the total sample, that marginal is analogous to a program rating (i.e., both SC1 and SC2 have person ratings of 20).

The key question is, did the same 20 people view both SC1 and SC2? The cross-tabulation reveals the answer in the four cells of the table. The upper left-hand cell indicates the number of people who watched SC1 and SC2. Of the 100 people in the sample, only 5 saw both programs. That is what is referred to as the *duplicated audience*. Conversely, 65 people saw neither program. When the number in any one cell is known, all numbers can be determined because the sum of each row or column must equal the appropriate marginal.

Once the size of the duplicated audience has been determined, the next problem is interpretation: Is what was observed a high or low level of duplication? Could this result have happened by chance or is there a relationship between the audiences for the two programs in question? Evaluating the data at

TABLE 11.2
Cross-Tabulation of Program Audiences

(a)			Viewed SC1		
			yes	no	total
		yes	5	15	20
Viewed SC2		no	15	65	80
		total	20	80	100
(b)			Viewed SC1		
			yes	no	total
		yes	O = 5	O = 15	20
			E = 4	E = 16	
Viewed SC2		no	O = 15	O = 65	80
			E = 16	E = 64	
		total	20	80	100

hand requires judging results against certain expectations, which are either statistical or theoretical-intuitive in nature.

The statistical expectation for this cross-tabulation is easy to determine. It is the level of duplication that would be observed if there were no relationship between two program audiences. In other words, because 20 people watched SC1 and 20 watched SC2, we would expect that a few people would see both, just by chance. Statisticians call this chance level of duplication the *expected frequency*. The expected frequency for any cell in the table is determined by multiplying the row marginal for that cell (R) by the column marginal (C) and dividing by the total sample (N): $[E = (R \times C)/N]$.

The expected frequency in the upper left-hand cell is 4 [i.e., $(20 \times 20)/100 = 4$]. Table 11.2b shows the observed frequency (O) and the expected frequency (E) for the two sitcom audiences. Comparing the two shows the duplicated audience observed is slightly larger than the laws of probability would predict (i.e., $5 > 4$). Most computer programs will also run a statistical test, like *chi-square*, to indicate whether the difference between observed and expected frequencies is statistically significant.

Audiences will often overlap from one time period to another. If 50% of the audience is watching television at one time, and 50% is watching later in the day, a percentage of the audience will be watching at both times. The statistical expectation of overlap is determined exactly as in the example just given, except as percentages. If there is no correlation between the time-period audiences, then 25% will be watching at both times just by chance [i.e., $(50 \times 50)/100 = 25$].

Audience overlap, or duplication, routinely exceeds chance, which brings the second kind of expectation into play. An experienced analyst knows enough about audience behavior to have certain theoretical or intuitive expectations about the levels of audience duplication he or she will encounter. Consider the two sitcoms again. Suppose they were scheduled on a single channel, one after the other, at a time when other stations were broadcasting longer programs. Inheritance effects would suggest a large duplicated audience. If each show were watched by 20% of the sample, it might be surprising to find anything less than 10% of the sample watching both. That is well above the statistical expectation of 4%. On the other hand, if the two shows were scheduled on different channels at the same time, it would be reasonable to expect virtually no duplication. In either case, there is good reason to expect a strong relationship between watching SC1 and SC2.

The research and theory explained in chapter 9 deal with patterns of duplication known to occur in audience behavior. Be alert, however, to the different ways in which information on audience duplication is reported. The number of people watching any two programs, or listening to a station at two different times, is often expressed as a percentage or a proportion. That makes it easier to compare across samples or populations of different sizes. However, percentages can be calculated on different bases. For each cell in a simple cross-tab, each frequency could be reported as a percent of the row, the column, or the total sample.

Table 11.3 is much like the 2 × 2 matrix in Table 11.2. In this illustration, however, the size of the SC1 audience is increased, to make things more complicated. Note that changing marginals has an impact on the expected frequencies (E) within each cell. When SC1 is viewed by 30, and SC2 by 20, E equals 6 [(30 × 20)/100 = 6]. That change affects all the other expected frequencies. For convenience, assume also that frequencies in each box were actually observed. Each can be expressed as one of three percentages or proportions. Because the sample size is 100, the duplicated audience is 6% of the total sample (T). Stated differently, the proportion of the audience seeing both programs is 0.06. It also holds that 20% (C) of the people who saw SC1 also saw SC2, or alternatively, that 30% (R) of the people who saw SC2 also saw SC1.

Different expressions of audience duplication are used in different contexts. The convention is to express levels of repeat viewing as an average of row or column percentages. Because the ratings of different episodes of a program tend to be stable, these are usually similar. This practice results in statements like, "the average level of repeat viewing was 55%." Channel loyalty is usually indexed by studying the proportion of the total sample that sees any pair of programs broadcast on the same channel (see "duplication of viewing law," this chapter). Inheritance effects are studied and reported both ways. Proportions of total audience have been used to model this kind of audience flow, whereas row and column percents are often used to report typical levels of duplication between adjacent programs.

TABLE 11.3

Cross-Tabulation of Program Audiences with Expected Frequencies
and Cell Percentages

		Viewed SC1		
		yes	no	total
	yes	E = 6	E = 14	20
		T = 6%	T = 14%	
		R = 30%	R = 70%	
Viewed SC2		C = 20%	C = 20%	
	no	E = 24	E = 56	80
		T = 24%	T = 56%	
		R = 30%	R = 70%	
		C = 80%	C = 80%	
		30	70	100

Note. In this table, E is the expected frequency, T is its percent of the total sample, R is its percent of the row total, and C is its percent of the column total.

Finally we should note that ratings users sometimes infer the existence of audience duplication without benefit of direct observation. For example, programs with low ratings may be aired more than once a day. Under such circumstances, it is not unusual for the rating from each airing to be totaled and sold as if it were a single program rating. This is done because many time buyers dislike handling tiny ratings, and also because it is assumed that no one watches the same program twice in a day, therefore, no audience duplication occurs across programs. It seems likely that as cable networks—which often repeat programming—continue to fragment the audience, this practice may increase. Whether it is based on a sound understanding of audience behavior could and should be examined.

Similarly, some ratings analysts have inferred levels of audience duplication by looking at correlations between program ratings or shares. Under this approach, it is assumed that pairs of programs with highly correlated ratings have relatively high levels of duplication and program pairs with low correlations have low levels of duplication. Researchers have examined the correlations among adjacent program audience shares (e.g., Tiedge & Ksobiech, 1986; Walker, 1988), arguing that conditions that produce high correlations indicate pronounced inheritance effects. Because no direct observation of audience duplication is made, however, such correlational data is only circumstantial evidence of audience flow. Although this approach is clearly less desirable than studying actual levels of duplication, nonetheless, it can produce useful insights into audience behavior.

Comparisons

As with gross measures of the audience, it is common to compare cumulative measures. Comparisons can provide a useful context for interpreting numbers. However, with cumulative measures, the impetus is absent for comparing every conceivable subset, indexed in every way imaginable. As a practical matter, gross measures are used more extensively than are cumulative measures in buying and selling audiences. There is less pressure to demonstrate comparative advantage, no matter how obscure. Although some cume estimates, like reach, frequency, and exclusive cumes, can certainly be useful in time sales, much of the comparative work with cumulative measures is done to realize some deeper understanding of audience behavior.

Programmers can benefit from such insights. A radio station might wish to cultivate a small but loyal audience. Perhaps the strategy is to offer a unique, or narrow, format that appeals to a limited number of people in the market. A Spanish-language station might have such an objective. If so, the programmer would want to consider not only gross measures of audience size but cumulative measures as well. Is the average TSL for the station any greater than for other formats in the market? What about audience turnover and exclusive cumes?

Table 11.4 shows how such comparisons might look by giving the average TSL, turnover ratio, and exclusive cume for stations with different formats.

For programming analysis it is especially useful to compare TSL and exclusive cume of stations with the same format, similar formats, and stations that share audiences. In the same way, it is helpful to analyze programs and personalities on one station by comparing various dayparts. TSL can also be computed to compare men and women in various age categories to determine the heaviest and lightest radio users in a specific market.

TABLE 11.4

Comparisons of Cumulative Measurements

				Audience Composition			
Format	TSL H:M	Turnover	Excl Cume	12–24	25–54	55+	At-Home
CHR (Top 40)	6:48	19	9	48	50	3	29
Urban	8:30	14	15	45	49	6	44
AOR	7:30	17	8	29	69	2	22
Adult Contemporary	6:48	18	7	19	72	10	25
Urban AC	8:30	15	9	15	69	16	44
Soft AC(lite)	7:48	16	8	11	65	24	31
Oldies	7:06	18	9	8	75	17	28
Country	8:36	14	15	16	61	24	34
Jazz	7:48	16	7	5	73	22	37
Classical	6:24	16	7	5	42	53	53
Spanish	8:42	12	11	20	62	18	53
Religious	7:30	17	13	9	58	33	53
News	6:20	20	8	3	44	54	55
Talk	8:06	16	6	3	49	48	52
Sports	6:30	20	3	7	72	22	34

Source: Arbitron data, fall 1997, analyzed and presented in James H. Duncan, Jr. *Share-to-Revenue Conversion Ratios and Format Performance Analysis*, 1998 edition. There are 1,630 stations in the sample.

Time spent listening shows the hours:minutes which an average listener spends with a given station during a week.

The turnover ratio shows the relationship between a station's weekly audience and its average quarter-hour audience—that is the ratio of the cume audience to the average audience, in this case for the entire week.

The audience composition for each format is presented for three age categories.

The at-home column shows the percent of listening at home, versus at work/office, in vehicles, or other places.

Certainly if a radio station were changing its format, the programmer would want trend data on both gross and cumulative measures. If an attempt were being made to broaden the station's format, or to position it closer to other competitors in the market, one might expect accompanying shifts in its cume audiences. Suppose a station changed from having the only AOR format in the market to being one of two classic rock stations in the market. A programmer would be well advised to monitor the exclusive and duplicated cumes of each station. Although a change in format might reduce the station's exclusive cume, if the attempt at repositioning has been successful, management should enjoy increased duplication of audience with the other rock station. Conversely, the existing rock station might find its own exclusive cume reduced. These sorts of insights can be gleaned by comparing the performance of each station over time.

Interesting analyses have also been performed on reach and time spent viewing television stations. Barwise and Ehrenberg (1988) have argued that, unlike radio, television stations rarely have small, loyal audiences. Instead, it is almost always the case that a station that reaches a small segment of the audience is viewed by that audience only sparingly. This is sometimes labeled a *double jeopardy* effect, because a station suffers not only from having relatively few viewers, but also from having relatively disloyal or irregular viewers. To demonstrate the double jeopardy effect, Barwise and Ehrenberg graphed television ratings data in both United States and the United Kingdom (see Fig. 11.2).

Along the horizontal axis is the weekly reach achieved by various types of stations, expressed as a percent of the total audience. Along the vertical axis is the average number of hours each station's audience spent viewing the station in a week. This can be determined in the same way that TSL estimates are made in radio. The slope of the curve is flat to begin with, but rises sharply as the reach increases. As a rule, low levels of station reach are associated with small amounts of time viewing. But as reach moves beyond 50%, increased reach is associated with dramatic increases in weekly time spent viewing (TSV). Furthermore, Barwise and Ehrenberg reported that the curve depicted is accurately summarized by this equation:

$$TSV = 1.8 + \frac{WEEKLY\ REACH\ \%}{100 - WEEKLY\ REACH\ \%}$$

Aside from the fact that this pattern of station reach is easy to model with an equation, the curve is interesting for what it reveals about station audiences. As is widely known, public television stations are viewed by relatively few people (i.e., they have low weekly cumes). However, contrary to what many assume, these are not PBS loyalists spending a lot of time with the station. They watch little public television in a week's time. The only exceptions that Barwise and Ehrenberg report finding are for religious and minority-language TV stations, which have audiences that are both small and loyal. Whether the double jeop-

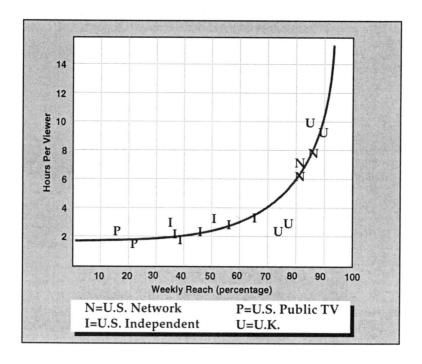

FIG. 11.2.   Channel reach and time spent viewing television
(adapted from Barwise & Ehrenberg, 1988, with permission).

ardy pattern typical of most broadcast television applies to specialized channels
in a multichannel environment, like cable, is yet to be determined.

   As noted in the discussion of audience duplication, many analyses are possible only with access to the complete ratings database. Barwise and Ehrenberg
(1988) have published analyses of television audience behavior that illustrate
some of the possibilities. A research question of considerable importance to
both programmers and theorists is whether people who watch one type of program will watch others of the same type. As a practical matter, the answer has
implications for how to manage audience flow. Beyond its applied value, however, the answer could also support or undermine different theories of program
choice that predict a demonstrable consistency of viewer preference.

   Table 11.5 offers a simple way to test whether viewers demonstrate program-
type loyalty in their choices. All programs have been categorized into one of
seven types. These are listed down the left-hand column and represented by
corresponding numbers across the top row. Viewers who watched a program in
the category listed on the left also noted how much time they spent watching

the program types listed across the top. The table shows how the average audience for each kind of program distributes the remainder of TV viewing time. The audience for an average news show spends 15% of its time watching light entertainment, 26% watching light drama, and so forth.

These data suggest there are no special patterns of program-type loyalty. People who watch one news program are unlikely to be news junkies, but rather watch as much news as everyone else. In fact, each audience segment watches about the same proportion of each program type as the other audience segments. Many viewers seem to watch a fairly wide variety of programs rather than limit their viewing to only one or two kinds.

These results have been based on analyses of audience duplication in the United Kingdom. They have yet to be fully replicated in the United States, which, with many more channels, may produce a different result. What is important to note is that data on program audience duplication can be combined and compared to produce a large and intriguing picture of exposure to program content.

Prediction and Explanation

The audience behavior revealed in cumulative measurements can be predictable—at least in the statistical sense. Because this mass behavior occurs in a stable environment over days or weeks, that behavior can be approximated with mathematical models, sometimes with great accuracy. This is certainly a boon to media planners attempting to orchestrate effective campaigns, especially be-

TABLE 11.5

Viewing of Program Types by Program Type Audiences

	Percentage of other viewing time spent watching each of seven program types below						
	1	2	3	4	5	6	7
Viewers of an average program of:							
1. Light entertainment	15	26	11	9	3	17	9
2. Light drama	15	27	12	9	3	18	9
3. Films	14	26	13	9	3	17	9
4. Sports	15	26	11	10	3	17	9
5. Drama & arts	15	26	12	9	3	18	9
6. Information	15	26	11	9	3	17	10
7. News	15	26	11	9	3	17	10
Average	15	26	12	9	3	17	9

Note. Adapted from Barwise and Ehrenberg (1988) with permission.
To read (Row 2): How does the average viewer of light drama allocate the rest of his/her viewing time?

cause actual data on audience duplication is always after the fact and often hard to come by. As a result, much attention has been paid to developing techniques for predicting reach, duplication, and frequency of exposure.

The simplest model for estimating the reach of a media vehicle is given by the following equation:

$$\text{REACH} = 1 - (1 - r)^n$$

In this equation r is the rating of the media vehicle, and n is the number of ads, or insertions, run in the campaign. When applying this equation, it is necessary to express the rating as a proportion (e.g., a rating of 20 = 0.20). Although straightforward, this reach model is limited. In the early 1960s, more sophisticated models were developed (Agostini, 1961; Metheringham, 1964) based either on binomial or beta-binomial distributions. These and other models of reach are described in detail by Rust (1986).

Most advertising agencies use computer programs to predict the reach of a media schedule based on input like GRPs. It is also common to predict reach for demographic segments of the audience, within different dayparts. Although such programs are useful, the analyst should remember these are projections, not "the truth." Baron (1988), for example, pointed out that observed levels of reach are subject to more variation than the smooth curves of a mathematical model would suggest. Therefore, deciding among media plans is foolish if based on small differences in computer projections.

Although models of reach embody some assumptions about audience duplication, to predict duplication between specific pairs of programs, it is best to employ models designed for that purpose. One of the most widely used models, called the *duplication-of-viewing law,* was developed by Goodhardt, Ehrenberg, and Collins (1987). It is expressed in the following equation:

$$r_{st} = kr_s r_t$$

In this model, r_{st} is the proportion of audience that sees both Programs s and t, r_s is the proportion seeing program s, r_t is the proportion seeing program t (i.e., their ratings expressed as proportions), and k is a constant whose value must be empirically determined. When the ratings are expressed as percentages, the equation changes slightly to:

$$r_{st} = kr_s r_t / 100$$

The logic behind the duplication of viewing law is not complicated. It is nearly the same as determining an expected frequency in cross-tabulation. If trying to predict the percent of the entire population that saw any two programs, the analyst can begin by estimating the expected frequency, which is determined by $E = (R \times C)/N$. If dealing with program ratings, it is the same as multiplying the rating of one program (s) by the rating of another (t), and dividing by 100 (the total N as a percentage). In other words, the general equation for expected frequency becomes $r_{st} = r_s r_t / 100$, when it is specifically applied to predicting audience duplication. That is exactly the same as the duplication of viewing equation, with the exception of the k coefficient.

Goodhardt and his colleagues compared the expected level of duplication with the actual level across hundreds of program pairings. They discovered that under certain well-defined circumstances, actual levels of duplication were either greater or less than chance, by a predictable amount. For any pair of programs broadcast on ABC, on different days, it was the case that audience duplication exceeded chance by about 60%. In other words, people who watched one ABC program were 60% more likely than the general population to show up in the audience for another ABC program on a different day. To adapt the equation so that it accurately predicted duplication, it was necessary to introduce a new term, the k *coefficient*. If duplication exceeded chance by 60%, then the value of k would have to be 1.6.

Values of k were determined for channels in both the United States and United Kingdom. American networks have a duplication constant of approximately 1.5 to 1.6, whereas English channels have a constant on the order of 1.7 to 1.9. These constants serve as an index of *channel loyalty*: the higher the value of k, the greater the tendency toward duplication or loyalty.

Noting deviations from levels of duplication predicted by the duplication of viewing law also serves as a way to identify unusual features in audience behavior. In effect, the law gives an empirically grounded theoretical expectation against which to judge specific observations. One important deviation from the law is inheritance effects. When the pair of programs in question is scheduled back-to-back on the same channel, the level of duplication routinely exceeds that predicted by ordinary channel loyalty. Henriksen (1985) suggested that a more flexible model of duplication, predicting both channel loyalty and inheritance effects, could be derived from models in human ecology. His model takes the form of a linear equation:

$$\log r_{st} = \log k + (b)\log r_s + (c)\log r_t$$

The duplication-of-viewing law has also been criticized for treating the kco-efficient as a constant. In fact, there is evidence that k varies considerably across individual program pairings (Chandon, 1976; Headen, Klompmaker, & Rust, 1979; Henriksen, 1985). The duplication-of-viewing law is also incapable of explicitly incorporating other factors that may affect the level of duplication between program pairs.

To address these limitations, Headen, Klompmaker, and Rust (1979) proposed using a more conventional regression equation to model audience duplication across program pairs. The equation takes the general form:

$$r_{st} = b_0 \, (b_1^{X1}) \, (b_2^{X2}) \, (b_3^{X3}) \, (b_4^{X4}) \, (r_s r_t) \, (e^u)$$

Here, r_{st} is the proportion of the population seeing programs s and t, $r_s r_t$ is the product of the programs' ratings expressed as proportions, and X_1 through X_4 are dummy variables indicating whether the programs in a pair were on the same channel, of the same type, and so forth. As the duplication-of-viewing law would suggest, $r_s r_t$ is the single best predictor of audience duplication, although other factors, including similarities in program type, add significantly to explained variation in r_{st}. It might also be noted that, when using linear regressions on data such as these, it is typically necessary to perform logarithmic transformations of the audience proportions to avoid violating the assumptions that underlie the linear model.

Webster and Phalen (1997) used a similar method of modeling to explain audience duplication between adjacent program pairs. However, they allowed each program rating (i.e., r_s and r_t) to enter the equation independently to assess the relative strength of lead-in versus lead-out effects. By doing so, they established that ratings of the earlier program in an adjacent pair explained considerably more variation than the second program rating. Overall, a model with four predictor variables explained 85% of the variation in inheritance effects.

Frequency of exposure can also be modeled. Obviously, if it is possible to predict reach on the basis of GRPs, average frequency at a certain GRP level can be determined, because the three are related. However, it is often useful to know the entire distribution on which an average frequency is based. In that way, judgments about effective exposure can be made. Consequently, models predicting an entire distribution of exposures have been developed. There are, in fact, many such models. Some are based on binomial distributions, some on multivariate extensions of beta-binomial distributions. Some require information on pairwise duplication as input, some do not. (For a full discussion of these alternatives, the reader is referred to Rust, 1986.) Moreover, the same techniques are now being applied to modeling reach and frequency on the Web (Leckenby & Hong, 1998).

Goodhardt et al. (1987) have employed one such model, based on a beta-binomial distribution (BBD), to predict what percent of the population will see a certain number of episodes in a series. Table 11.6 compares the predictions of the BBD model with actual observations for 11 episodes of the series *Brideshead Revisited*. The table indicates that 40% of the population did not watch any broadcast of the series. Seventeen percent saw one episode, 11% saw two episodes, and so forth. These data are exactly like those reported by Nielsen in its Program Cumulative Audience reports, except they extend beyond the usual 4-week time frame. The line of numbers just below the observed frequency distribution is the prediction of the BBD model. Although there are some discrepancies, the model provides a good fit to actual patterns of audience behavior.

It should be apparent by now that cumes, reach, frequency and audience duplication are different ways of expressing the same underlying audience behavior. In fact, information on pairwise duplication can be used to predict

TABLE 11.6
Observed Versus Theoretical Frequency Distribution
for Episodes of *Brideshead Revisited*

	Number of episodes seen											
	0	1	2	3	4	5	6	7	8	9	10	11
Observed frequency	40%	17%	11%	8%	4%	3%	3%	4%	2%	4%	2%	2%
Theoretical frequency	43	14	9	7	5	5	4	4	3	2	2	2

Note. Adapted from Goodhardt, Ehrenberg, and Collins (1987) with permission.

frequency distributions, and frequency distributions can be translated into analogous statements about audience duplication (Barwise, 1986).

It should also be apparent that ratings data, when properly analyzed, have the potential to answer an enormous number of questions. Certainly, these include the pragmatic concerns that prompted the creation of ratings in the first place. But, as noted in chapters 4 and 5, the data are flexible enough to address problems in public policy, economics, cultural studies, and media effects. The successful application of ratings analysis to these problems, of course, requires access to the appropriate data and an understanding of its limitations. Perhaps most important, however, it requires an appreciation of the audience behavior expressed in the ratings and the factors that shape it. Only then can analysts exploit the data for all the insights they offer.

RELATED READINGS

Barwise, P., & Ehrenberg, A. (1988). *Television and its audience.* London: Sage.
Fletcher, J. E. (1985). *Squeezing profits out of ratings: A manual for radio managers, sales managers and programmers.* Washington, DC: National Association of Broadcasters.
Goodhardt, G. J., Ehrenberg, A. S. C., & Collins, M. A. (1987). *The television audience: Patterns of viewing.* Aldershot, UK: Gower.
Rust, R. T. (1986). *Advertising media models: A practical guide.* Lexington: Lexington Books.
Sissors, J. Z., & Bumba, L. (1996). *Advertising media planning* (5th ed.). Lincolnwood, IL: NTC Business Books.
Webster, J. G. & Phalen, P. F. (1997). *The mass audience: Rediscovering the dominant model.* Mahwah, NJ: Lawrence Erlbaum Associates.

Appendix A: DMA Market Rankings

U.S. TV HOUSEHOLD ESTIMATES

DESIGNATED MARKET AREA (DMA) - RANKED BY TV HOUSEHOLDS

RANK	DESIGNATED MARKET AREA	TV HOUSEHOLDS (JAN. 1999)	% OF U.S. TV HOUSEHOLDS	CUMULATIVE % U.S. TV HOUSEHOLDS	POPULATION (JAN. 1999)	% U.S. POPULATION	CUMULATIVE % U.S. POPULATION	% TV PENE-TRATION
1	NEW YORK	6,812,540	6.854	6.854	19,148,100	7.027	7.027	98
2	LOS ANGELES	5,135,140	5.167	12.021	16,037,800	5.886	12.913	98
3	CHICAGO	3,164,150	3.184	15.204	8,904,900	3.268	16.181	99
4	PHILADELPHIA	2,667,520	2.684	17.888	7,283,500	2.673	18.854	99
5	SAN FRANCISCO-OAK-SAN JOSE	2,368,970	2.383	20.272	6,672,900	2.449	21.303	97
6	BOSTON	2,186,100	2.199	22.471	5,887,800	2.161	23.463	98
7	DALLAS-FT. WORTH	1,959,680	1.972	24.443	5,323,200	1.954	25.417	99
8	WASHINGTON, DC	1,956,160	1.968	26.411	5,333,700	1.957	27.374	99
9	DETROIT	1,846,950	1.858	28.269	4,981,800	1.828	29.203	99
10	ATLANTA	1,722,130	1.733	30.002	4,673,400	1.715	30.918	99
	SUBTOTAL	29,819,340			84,247,100			
11	HOUSTON	1,665,550	1.676	31.678	4,747,300	1.742	32.660	98
12	SEATTLE-TACOMA	1,548,200	1.558	33.235	4,102,700	1.506	34.166	97
13	CLEVELAND	1,475,820	1.485	34.720	3,871,900	1.421	35.586	99
14	TAMPA-ST. PETE (SARASOTA)	1,463,090	1.472	36.192	3,549,400	1.303	36.889	99
15	MINNEAPOLIS-ST. PAUL	1,457,130	1.466	37.658	3,921,200	1.439	38.328	99
16	MIAMI-FT. LAUDERDALE	1,418,940	1.428	39.086	3,764,700	1.382	39.710	98
17	PHOENIX	1,343,040	1.351	40.437	3,644,800	1.338	41.047	98
18	DENVER	1,230,440	1.238	41.675	3,154,600	1.158	42.205	98
19	PITTSBURGH	1,136,230	1.143	42.818	2,886,700	1.059	43.264	99
20	SACRAMNTO-STKTN-MODESTO	1,131,300	1.138	43.956	3,272,700	1.201	44.465	98
	SUBTOTAL	43,689,080			121,163,100			
21	ST. LOUIS	1,110,290	1.117	45.074	2,971,000	1.090	45.556	99
22	ORLANDO-DAYTONA BCH-MELBRN	1,072,540	1.079	46.152	2,761,700	1.014	46.569	99
23	PORTLAND, OR	993,540	1.000	47.152	2,653,900	.974	47.543	97
24	BALTIMORE	991,610	.998	48.150	2,691,300	.988	48.531	99
25	INDIANAPOLIS	955,800	.962	49.111	2,500,900	.918	49.449	99
26	SAN DIEGO	945,170	.951	50.062	2,801,200	1.028	50.477	97
27	HARTFORD & NEW HAVEN	909,930	.915	50.978	2,434,400	.893	51.370	99
28	CHARLOTTE	859,670	.865	51.843	2,268,800	.833	52.203	99
29	RALEIGH-DURHAM	834,760	.839	52.682	2,218,900	.814	53.017	98
30	NASHVILLE	811,870	.817	53.499	2,149,000	.789	53.806	98
	SUBTOTAL	53,173,370			146,614,200			

#	Market	(1)	(2)	(3)	(4)	(5)	(6)	(7)
31	MILWAUKEE	99	54.606	.800	2,180,200	54.313	.814	809,040
32	CINCINNATTI	99	55.397	.791	2,155,500	55.124	.811	805,990
33	KANSAS CITY	99	56.169	.772	2,104,100	55.931	.807	802,290
34	COLUMBUS, OH	99	56.899	.730	1,989,600	56.683	.752	747,680
35	GREENVLL-SPART-ASHEVLL-AND	98	57.602	.703	1,915,000	57.428	.744	739,850
36	SALT LAKE CITY	98	58.437	.835	2,274,300	58.139	.711	707,070
37	SAN ANTONIO	98	59.159	.723	1,969,200	58.811	.672	667,750
38	GRAND RAPIDS-KALMZOO-B.CRK	99	59.839	.680	1,853,100	59.482	.671	666,860
39	BIRMINGHAM (ANN. TUSC)	99	60.475	.635	1,731,300	60.143	.661	656,970
40	NORFOLK-PORTSMTH-NEWPT NWS	99	61.134	.660	1,797,300	60.790	.648	643,810
	SUBTOTAL				166,583,900			60,420,680
41	NEW ORLEANS	99	61.770	.636	1,733,500	61.422	.632	627,830
42	BUFFALO	99	62.377	.606	1,652,300	62.053	.631	627,020
43	MEMPHIS	98	63.007	.630	1,716,400	62.678	.625	621,170
44	WEST PALM BEACH-FT. PIERCE	98	63.552	.545	1,484,900	63.289	.611	607,360
45	OKLAHOMA CITY	99	64.130	.578	1,574,800	63.890	.601	597,780
46	HARRISBURG-LNCSTR-LEB-YORK	98	64.720	.590	1,608,200	64.486	.596	592,230
47	GREENSBORO-H.POINT-W.SALEM	99	65.265	.545	1,486,100	65.075	.588	584,500
48	LOUISVILLE	99	65.817	.552	1,504,000	65.648	.573	569,500
49	ALBUQUERQUE-SANTA FE	96	66.413	.596	1,624,900	66.218	.570	566,380
50	PROVIDENCE-NEW BEDFORD	99	66.964	.551	1,501,200	66.781	.563	559,810
	SUBTOTAL				182,470,200			66,374,660
51	WILKES BARRE-SCRANTON	98	67.498	.534	1,454,000	67.335	.554	551,050
52	JACKSONVILLE BRUNSWICK	99	68.016	.518	1,412,800	67.858	.523	520,010
53	ALBANY-SCHENECTADY-TROY	98	68.506	.490	1,334,800	68.369	.511	507,680
54	DAYTON	99	68.995	.489	1,331,600	68.877	.507	504,310
55	FRESNO-VISALIA	98	69.592	.597	1,025,600	69.382	.505	502,130
56	LAS VEGAS	98	70.071	.480	1,307,000	69.882	.500	497,020
57	LITTLE ROCK-PINE BLUFF	98	70.542	.471	1,283,600	70.369	.487	483,660
58	CHARLESTON-HUNTINGTON	98	71.010	.467	1,273,200	70.852	.483	480,330
59	TULSA	98	71.464	.454	1,237,900	71.328	.476	472,980
60	AUSTIN	98	71.915	.451	1,229,900	71.802	.474	470,970
	SUBTOTAL				195,960,200			71,364,800
61	RICHMOND-PETERSBURG	99	72.368	.453	1,235,400	72.272	.471	467,730
62	MOBILE-PENSACOLA	98	72.838	.470	1,279,600	72.738	.466	463,380
63	KNOXVILLE	98	73.262	.424	1,156,200	73.188	.449	446,510
64	FLINT-SAGINAW-BAY CITY	99	73.701	.439	1,196,100	73.635	.448	444,480
65	WICHITA-HUTCHINSON PLUS	98	74.120	.419	1,140,900	74.071	.436	433,530
66	TOLEDO	99	74.526	.406	1,106,300	74.484	.412	409,750
67	LEXINGTON	98	74.931	.405	1,103,800	74.894	.411	408,010
68	ROANOKE-LYNCHBURG	98	75.315	.384	1,045,700	75.298	.404	401,830
69	GREEN BAY-APPLETON	98	75.693	.378	1,031,100	75.686	.387	384,860
70	DES MOINES-AMES	99	76.054	.361	983,800	76.071	.386	383,510
	SUBTOTAL				207,239,300			75,608,710

229

U.S. TV HOUSEHOLD ESTIMATES

DESIGNATED MARKET AREA (DMA) - RANKED BY TV HOUSEHOLDS

RANK	DESIGNATED MARKET AREA	TV HOUSEHOLDS (JAN. 1999)	% OF U.S. TV HOUSEHOLDS	CUMULATIVE % U.S. TV HOUSEHOLDS	POPULATION (JAN. 1999)	% U.S. POPULATION	CUMULATIVE % U.S. POPULATION	% TV PENE-TRATION
71	HONOLULU	381,820	.384	76.456	1,191,800	.437	76.492	97
72	SPOKANE	378,330	.381	76.836	1,016,100	.373	76.865	96
73	OMAHA	374,830	.377	77.213	995,900	.365	77.230	99
74	SYRACUSE	371,560	.374	77.587	1,022,900	.377	77.607	98
75	SHREVEPORT	370,990	.373	77.960	1,005,400	.369	77.976	98
76	PADUCAH-C.GIRD-HARBG-MT VN	369,070	.371	78.332	949,700	.349	78.325	98
77	ROCHESTER, NY	367,510	.370	78.701	981,400	.360	78.685	99
78	TUCSON	365,210	.367	79.069	969,900	.356	79.041	97
79	SPRINGFIELD, MO	363,310	.366	79.434	945,000	.347	79.388	98
80	PORTLAND-AUBURN	351,740	.354	79.788	914,100	.335	79.723	98
	SUBTOTAL	79,303,080			217,236,500			
81	HUNTSVILLE-DECATUR,FLOR	336,350	.338	80.127	871,500	.320	80.043	99
82	CHAMPAIGN&SPRNGFLD-DECATUR	335,130	.337	80.464	882,300	.324	80.367	98
83	FT. MYERS-NAPLES	329,550	.332	80.796	819,800	.301	80.668	98
84	MADISON	316,170	.318	81.114	837,200	.307	80.975	98
85	SOUTH BEND-ELKHART	314,820	.317	81.430	855,300	.314	81.289	98
86	COLUMBIA, SC	313,930	.316	81.746	882,100	.324	81.613	98
87	CHATTANOOGA	313,820	.316	82.062	825,700	.303	81.916	98
88	CEDAR RAPIDS-WATERLOO&DUBQ	308,230	.310	82.372	820,800	.301	82.217	98
89	JACKSON, MS	301,360	.303	82.675	856,500	.314	82.531	98
90	DAVENPORT-R.ISLAND-MOLINE	300,490	.302	82.978	777,800	.285	82.817	99
	SUBTOTAL	82,472,930			225,666,000			
91	BURLINGTON-PLATTSBURGH	291,610	.293	83.271	796,700	.292	83.109	98
92	TRI-CITIES, TN-VA	290,470	.292	83.563	756,100	.277	83.387	98
93	JOHNSTOWN-ALTOONA	288,200	.290	83.853	781,300	.287	83.673	98
94	COLORADO SPRINGS-PUEBLO	282,210	.284	84.137	761,500	.279	83.953	98
95	WACO-TEMPLE-BRYAN	278,960	.281	84.418	799,500	.293	84.246	98
96	EVANSVILLE	275,740	.277	84.695	715,300	.263	84.509	99
97	YOUNGSTOWN	273,490	.275	84.970	713,800	.262	84.771	99
98	BATON ROUGE	272,050	.274	85.244	778,900	.286	85.056	99
99	EL PASO	267,990	.270	85.514	890,000	.327	85.383	98
100	SAVANNAH	265,170	.267	85.781	755,200	.277	85.660	98
	SUBTOTAL	85,258,820			233,414,300			
101	LINCOLN & HSTNGS-KRNYPLUS	255,440	.257	86.038	659,900	.242	85.902	99
102	HARLINGEN-WSLCO-BRNSVL-MCA	247,990	.250	86.287	943,300	.346	86.249	97
103	FT. WAYNE	246,470	.248	86.535	662,300	.243	86.492	99
104	SPRINGFIELD-HOLYOKE	242,120	.244	86.779	660,600	.242	86.734	98
105	GREENVILLE-N.BERN-WASHNGTN	237,720	.239	87.018	678,000	.249	86.983	98

106	LANSING	237,130	.239	87.256	654,200	.240	87.223	99
107	TYLER-LONGVIEW(LFKN&NCGD)	234,820	.236	87.493	639,500	.235	87.458	98
108	RENO	233,350	.235	87.727	620,600	.228	87.685	97
109	SIOUX FALLS(MITCHELL)	233,180	.233	87.960	617,800	.227	87.912	98
110	PEORIA-BLOOMINGTON	229,480	.231	88.191	613,900	.225	88.137	98
111	AUGUSTA	228,320	.230	88.421	639,300	.235	88.372	98
112	FLORENCE-MYRTLE BEACH	227,630	.229	88.650	623,700	.229	88.601	98
113	MONTGOMERY	227,020	.228	88.878	625,600	.230	88.831	98
114	TALLAHASSEE-THOMASVILLE	224,790	.226	89.104	627,600	.230	89.061	97
115	FARGO-VALLEY CITY	222,870	.224	89.328	587,600	.216	89.277	98
116	SANTABARBRA-SANMAR-SANLUOB	220,540	.222	89.550	648,200	.238	89.514	96
117	FT. SMITH-FAY-SPRNGDL-RGRS	220,480	.222	89.772	583,400	.214	89.728	98
118	TRAVERSE CITY-CADILLAC	217,730	.219	89.991	574,400	.211	89.939	99
119	MONTEREY-SALINAS	216,180	.218	90.209	685,100	.251	90.191	96
120	CHARLESTON, SC	215,930	.217	90.426	612,300	.225	90.415	98
121	EUGENE	208,720	.210	90.636	555,900	.204	90.619	96
122	MACON	206,710	.208	90.844	582,700	.214	90.833	98
123	LAFAYETTE, LA	200,010	.201	91.045	563,300	.207	91.040	98
124	YAKIMA-PASCO-RCHLND-KNNWCK	195,740	.197	91.242	557,300	.205	91.244	97
125	BOISE	194,520	.196	91.438	536,200	.197	91.441	98
126	AMARILLO	190,330	.191	91.629	516,600	.190	91.631	98
127	CORPUS CHRISTI	187,980	.189	91.818	565,000	.207	91.838	98
128	COLUMBUS, GA	184,320	.185	92.004	512,300	.188	92.026	98
129	LA CROSSE-EAU CLAIRE	179,460	.181	92.184	489,700	.180	92.206	98
130	BAKERSFIELD	178,940	.180	92.365	562,900	.207	92.412	98
131	COLUMBUS-TUPELO-WEST POINT	173,920	.175	92.540	474,400	.174	92.586	98
132	CHICO-REDDING	173,750	.175	92.714	464,600	.171	92.757	97
133	MONROE-EL DORADO	171,800	.173	92.887	485,200	.178	92.935	98
134	ROCKFORD	167,170	.168	93.055	441,900	.162	93.097	99
135	DULUTH-SUPERIOR	166,860	.168	93.223	423,800	.156	93.253	98
136	WAUSAU-RHINELANDER	162,870	.164	93.387	437,700	.161	93.413	99
137	BEAUMONT-PORT ARTHUR	162,800	.164	93.551	448,200	.164	93.578	98
138	WHEELING-STEUBENVILLE	157,190	.158	93.709	401,400	.147	93.725	98
139	TERRE HAUTE	156,430	.157	93.866	410,700	.151	93.876	98
140	TOPEKA	156,040	.157	94.023	419,800	.154	94.030	98
141	WICHITA FALLS & LAWTON	154,580	.156	94.179	423,200	.155	94.185	98
142	ERIE	153,510	.154	94.333	414,100	.152	94.337	98
143	MEDFORD-KLAMATH FALLS	153,370	.154	94.488	398,400	.146	94.483	96
144	SIOUX CITY	151,320	.152	94.640	403,900	.148	94.632	98
145	COLUMBIA-JEFFERSON CITY	150,850	.152	94.792	408,300	.150	94.782	98

3

231

U.S. TV HOUSEHOLD ESTIMATES

DESIGNATED MARKET AREA (DMA) - RANKED BY TV HOUSEHOLDS

RANK	DESIGNATED MARKET AREA	TV HOUSEHOLDS (JAN. 1999)	% OF U.S. TV HOUSEHOLDS	CUMULATIVE % U.S. TV HOUSEHOLDS	POPULATION (JAN. 1999)	% U.S. POPULATION	CUMULATIVE % U.S. POPULATION	% TV PENETRATION
146	JOPLIN-PITTSBURG	147,860	.149	94.941	376,700	.138	94.920	98
147	LUBBOCK	141,360	.142	95.083	404,600	.148	95.068	98
148	ALBANY, GA	140,220	.141	95.224	398,500	.146	95.214	98
149	BLUEFIELD-BECKLEY-OAK HILL	137,430	.138	95.362	357,100	.131	95.346	98
150	MINOT-BISMARCK-DICKINSON	135,250	.136	95.498	353,300	.130	95.475	99
	SUBTOTAL	94,917,320			260,158,900			
151	ODESSA-MIDLAND	134,860	.136	95.634	384,900	.141	95.616	98
152	WILMINGTON	134,080	.135	95.769	342,800	.126	95.742	99
153	ROCHESTR-MASON CITY-AUSTIN	132,280	.133	95.902	340,400	.125	95.867	99
154	BINGHAMTON	128,850	.130	96.031	345,100	.127	95.994	98
155	BANGOR	127,770	.129	96.160	337,400	.124	96.118	98
156	ANCHORAGE	123,130	.124	96.284	355,200	.130	96.248	95
157	PANAMA CITY	119,900	.121	96.405	324,200	.119	96.367	98
158	BILOXI-GULFPORT	115,310	.116	96.521	321,000	.118	96.485	98
159	ABILENE-SWEETWATER	112,760	.113	96.634	305,300	.112	96.597	98
160	PALM SPRINGS	112,680	.113	96.747	349,500	.128	96.725	98
161	SHERMAN-ADA	112,470	.113	96.861	296,700	.109	96.834	98
162	QUINCY-HANNIBAL-KEOKUK	111,820	.113	96.973	292,700	.107	96.941	99
163	SALISBURY	107,270	.108	97.081	284,000	.104	97.046	98
164	CLARKSBURG-WESTON	104,860	.106	97.186	270,500	.099	97.145	98
165	GAINESVILLE	102,790	.103	97.290	272,500	.100	97.245	97
166	IDAHO FALLS-POCATELLO	97,340	.098	97.388	300,800	.110	97.355	98
167	HATTIESBURG-LAUREL	97,280	.098	97.486	269,100	.099	97.454	98
168	UTICA	96,610	.097	97.583	264,200	.097	97.551	99
169	BILLINGS	95,000	.096	97.678	251,600	.092	97.643	97
170	MISSOULA	92,450	.093	97.771	243,400	.089	97.733	96
171	ELMIRA	91,920	.092	97.864	250,500	.092	97.825	98
172	DOTHAN	89,750	.090	97.954	239,000	.088	97.912	99
173	ALEXANDRIA, LA	87,680	.088	98.042	258,000	.095	98.007	98
174	RAPID CITY	86,110	.087	98.129	238,300	.087	98.094	98
175	WATERTOWN	85,380	.086	98.215	254,500	.093	98.188	99
176	YUMA-EL CENTRO	83,980	.084	98.300	277,800	.102	98.290	97
177	MARQUETTE	82,940	.083	98.383	218,100	.080	98.370	97
178	JONESBORO	82,090	.083	98.466	211,600	.078	98.448	97
179	LAKE CHARLES	79,050	.080	98.545	222,400	.082	98.529	98
180	HARRISONBURG	77,790	.078	98.623	214,900	.079	98.608	97

232

181	GREENWOOD-GREENVILLE	77,400	.078	98.701	239,700	.088	98.696	97
182	BOWLING GREEN	72,200	.073	98.774	191,900	.070	98.767	98
183	MERIDIAN	68,110	.069	98.842	186,100	.068	98.835	98
184	JACKSON, TN	62,870	.063	98.906	164,900	.061	98.895	98
185	GREAT FALLS	61,980	.062	98.968	170,000	.062	98.958	97
186	PARKERSBURG	61,750	.062	99.030	158,200	.058	99.016	99
187	MANKATO	59,410	.060	99.090	158,800	.058	99.074	99
188	GRAND JUNCTION-MONTROSE	58,240	.059	99.149	149,900	.055	99.129	98
189	TWIN FALLS	57,070	.057	99.206	159,100	.058	99.187	97
190	ST. JOSEPH	56,240	.057	99.263	150,400	.055	99.243	99
191	EUREKA	56,090	.056	99.319	158,400	.058	99.301	94
192	BUTTE-BOZEMAN	54,190	.055	99.373	144,000	.053	99.354	96
193	CHARLOTTESVILLE	51,140	.051	99.425	143,600	.053	99.406	96
194	LAREDO	50,940	.051	99.476	202,300	.074	99.481	98
195	SAN ANGELO	50,690	.051	99.527	142,700	.052	99.533	98
196	CHEYENNE-SCOTTSBLUF	50,180	.050	99.578	129,000	.047	99.580	99
197	LAFAYETTE, IN	49,390	.050	99.627	140,600	.052	99.632	97
198	OTTUMWA-KIRKSVILLE	48,810	.049	99.676	124,500	.046	99.678	98
199	CASPER-RIVERTON	47,690	.048	99.724	124,000	.046	99.723	98
200	BEND, OR	40,410	.041	99.765	105,300	.039	99.762	97
201	LIMA	37,760	.038	99.803	106,400	.039	99.801	99
202	ZANESVILLE	31,860	.032	99.835	85,000	.031	99.832	99
203	FAIRBANKS	28,770	.030	99.866	92,500	.034	99.866	95
204	VICTORIA	28,770	.029	99.895	83,000	.030	99.896	98
205	PRESQUE ISLE	25,730	.026	99.920	68,900	.025	99.922	98
206	JUNEAU	22,990	.023	99.944	70,300	.026	99.947	90
207	HELENA	20,970	.021	99.965	53,700	.020	99.967	98
208	ALPENA	16,610	.017	99.981	42,000	.015	99.983	98
209	NORTH PLATTE	14,450	.015	99.996	37,100	.014	99.996	98
210	GLENDIVE	4,010	.004	100.000	10,300	.004	100.000	98
	TOTAL U.S. *	99,391,780			272,488,500			

233

Appendix B:
Glossary

AAAA (American Association of Advertising Agencies): a trade association of U.S. advertising agencies.

Active audience: a term given to viewers who are highly selective about the programming they choose. Active audiences are sometimes defined as those who turn on the set only to watch favored programs and turn off the set when those programs are unavailable. See LOP, passive audience.

Adjacency: an advertising opportunity immediately before or after a specific program.

ADI (Area of Dominant Influence): a term once used by Arbitron to describe a specific market. Every county in the United States was assigned exclusively to one ADI. See DMA.

Advertising agency: a company that prepares and places advertising for its clients. Agencies typically have media departments that specialize in planning, buying, and evaluating advertising time.

Affiliate: a broadcast station that has a contractual agreement to air network programming.

AMOL (Automated Measurement of Lineups): a system that electronically determines the broadcast network programs actually aired in a local market.

ANA (Association of National Advertisers): a trade organization of national advertisers responsible for creating the first broadcast ratings service. See CAB.

AQH (Average Quarter Hour): the standard unit of time for reporting average audience estimates (e.g., AQH rating, AQH share) within specified dayparts.

ARB (American Research Bureau): a ratings company established in 1949 that was predecessor of the Arbitron Company.

Arbitron: a major supplier of local market ratings in radio.

Area probability sample: a random sample in which geographic areas are considered for selection in some stage of the sampling process. See probability sample, cluster sample.

ARF (Advertising Research Foundation): trade organization of advertising and marketing research professionals advancing the practice and validity of advertising research.

Ascription: a procedure for resolving confused or inaccurate diary entries, such as reports of listening to nonexistent stations.

Audience duplication: a cumulative measure of the audience that describes the extent to which audience members for one program or station are also in the audience of another program or station. See audience flow, channel loyalty, inheritance effect, repeat viewing, recycling.

Audience flow: the extent to which audiences persist from one program or time period to the next. See audience duplication, inheritance effects.

Audience deficiency (AD): a failure to deliver the numbers and kinds of audiences agreed to in a contract between time sellers and buyers. Sellers will often remedy audience deficiencies by running extra commercials, called make-goods.

Audience fragmentation: a phenomenon in which the audience for a medium is distributed across a large number of program services. Cable is said to fragment the television audience, resulting in a decreased average audience share for each channel.

Audience polarization: a phenomenon associated with audience fragmentation, in which the audiences for channels or stations use them more intensively than an average audience member. See channel loyalty, channel repertoire.

Audience turnover: a phenomenon of audience behavior usually expressed as the ratio of a station's cumulative audience to its average quarter hour audience.

Audimeter: Nielsen's name for several generations of its metering device used to record set tuning. See SIA.

Available audience: the number of people who are, realistically, in a position to use a medium at any point in time. It is often operationally defined as those actually using the medium (i.e., PUT or PUR levels).

Availabilities: unsold advertising time slots which are available for sale. Sometimes called *avails*.

Average: a measure of central tendency that expresses what is typical about a particular variable. An arithmetic average is usually called a *mean*. See mean, median.

Average audience rating: the rating of a station or program at an average point in time within some specified period of time. Metered data, for example, allow reports of audience size in an average minute during a television program.

Average time per page: a measure of the average time spent with a page of computer information (e.g., a Web page) across however many pages are examined in a single visit.

Away-from-home listening: estimates of radio listening that occurs outside the home. Such listening usually takes place in a car or workplace.

Banner advertising: a form of advertising on the Internet, in which a box containing the advertiser's message appears on a portion of the page being viewed. Banner advertising often allows users to connect to the advertiser's Web site.

Barter: a type of program syndication in which the cost of the programming is reduced, sometimes to zero, because it contains national or regional advertising that is sold by the syndicator.

Basic cable: the programming services provided by a cable system for the lowest of its monthly charges. These services typically include local television signals, advertiser-supported cable networks, and local access.

Birch: a research company that once provided syndicated radio rating reports in competition with Arbitron.

Block programming: the practice of scheduling similar programs in sequence to promote audience flow. See inheritance effect.

Bounce: the tendency of a station's ratings to fluctuate from one market report to the next due to sampling error rather than real changes in audience behavior. Bounce is most noticeable for stations with low ratings.

Broadband: a term describing the channel capacity of a distribution system. A common label for multichannel cable service, it is also applied to digital networks capable of delivering full motion video. See cable system.

Browser: a computer program that allows users to gain access to pages on the World Wide Web.

Buffer sample: a supplemental sample used by a rating company in the event the originally designated sample is insufficient due to unexpectedly low cooperation rates.

Cable Advertising Bureau (CAB): a trade organization formed to promote advertising on cable television.

Cable penetration: the extent to which households in a given market subscribe to cable service. Typically expressed as the percent of all TV households that subscribe to basic cable.

Cable system: a video distribution system that uses coaxial cable and optical fiber to deliver multichannel service to households within a geographically defined franchise area.

Callback: the practice in attempting to interview someone in a survey sample who was not contacted or interviewed on an earlier try. The number of callback attempts is an important determinant of response rates and nonresponse error. See nonresponse error.

Call-out research: a research design employed in radio that involves calling respondents by phone and soliciting reactions to short excerpts of songs.

CASIE (Coalition for Advertising Supported Information and Entertainment): a trade organization promoting advertising-supported media, including recommended standards for audience measurement of new media.

Cash-plus-barter: a type of barter syndication in which the station pays the syndicator cash, even though the program contains some advertising. See barter.

CATV (Community Antenna Television): an acronym for cable television, used in many early FCC proceedings.

Census: a study in which every member of a population is interviewed or measured. Every 10 years, the federal government conducts a census of the U.S. population.

Channel loyalty: a common phenomenon of aggregate audience behavior in which the audience for one program tends to be disproportionately represented in the audience for other programs on the same channel. See audience duplication, inheritance effects.

Channel repertoire: a set of channels from which a viewer chooses—typically much fewer than the number of channels available.

Circulation: the total number of unduplicated audience members exposed to a media vehicle (e.g., newspaper, station) over some specified period. See cume, reach.

Clearance: 1) the assurance given by a station that it will air a program feed by its affiliated network; 2) the sale of syndicated programs to individual markets.

Click: when the user of a Web page interacts with (i.e., clicks on) a message.

Click rate: the percentage of advertising responses as a function of the number of clicks.

Clickstream: the record of all http requests made from a browser.

Cluster sample: a type of probability sample in which aggregations of sampling units, called clusters, are sampled at some stage in the process. See probability sample.

CODE (Cable Online Data Exchange): a service of Nielsen Media Research that maintains information on the stations and networks carried on all U.S. cable systems. See cable system.

Codes: the numbers or letters used to represent responses in a survey instrument like a diary. Coding the responses allows computers to manipulate the data.

Coincidental: a type of telephone survey in which interviewers ask respondents what they are watching or listening to at the time of the call. Coincidentals, based on probability samples, often set the standard against which other ratings methods are judged.

COLRAM (Committee on Local Radio Audience Measurement): a committee of the NAB concerned with a range of local radio measurement issues.

COLTAM (Committee on Local Television Audience Measurement): a committee of the NAB concerned with local television measurement issues.

COLTRAM (Committee on Local Television and Radio Audience Measurement): a committee of the NAB which, in 1985, was divided into COLRAM and COLTAM.

Confidence interval: in probability sampling, the range of values around an estimated population value (e.g., a rating) with a given probability (i.e., confidence level) of encompassing the true population value.

Confidence level: in probability sampling, a statement of the likelihood that a range of values (i.e., confidence interval) will include the true population value.

Cooperative Analysis of Broadcasting: the first ratings company. Formed in 1930 by Archibald Crossley, it ended operations in 1946.

CMSA (Consolidated Metropolitan Statistical Area): a type of metropolitan area, designated by the U.S. Office of Management and Budget, often used by ratings companies to define a market's metro area.

Convenience sample: a nonprobability sample, sometimes called an accidental sample, used because respondents are readily available or convenient.

Correlation: a statistic that measures the strength and direction of the relationship between two variables. It may range in value from + 1.0 to − 1.0, with 0 indicating no relationship.

CPP (Cost Per Point): a measure of how much it costs to buy the audience represented by one rating point. The size of that audience, and therefore its cost, varies with the size of the market population on which the rating is based.

CPM (Cost Per Thousand): a measure of how much it costs to buy 1,000 audience members delivered by an ad. CPMs are commonly used to compare the cost efficiency of different advertising vehicles.

Cohort: a type of longitudinal survey design in which several independent samples are drawn from a population whose membership does not change over time. See longitudinal.

Common audience: the audience that visits two or more Web sites over a period of time. See audience duplication.

Cookies: unique electronic signatures placed on an Internet user's hard drive to track access to a Web site.

Counterprogramming: a programming strategy in which a station or network schedules material appealing to an audience other than the competition. Independents often counterprogram local news with entertainment.

Coverage: the potential audience for a given station or network, defined by the size of the population reached, or covered, by the signal.

Cross-sectional: a type of survey design in which one sample is drawn from the population at a point in time. See longitudinal.

Cross-tabs: a technique of data analysis in which the responses to one item are paired with those of another item. Cross-tabs are useful in determining the audience duplication between two programs. See audience duplication.

Cume: short for cumulative audience, it is the size of the unduplicated audience for a station over a specified period. When the cume is expressed as percent of the market population it is referred to as cume rating. See circulation, reach.

Cume duplication: the percentage of a station's cume audience that also listened to another station, within some specified period. See exclusive cume.

Daypart: a period of time, usually defined by certain hours of the day and days of the week (e.g., weekdays vs. weekends), used to estimate audience size for the purpose of buying and selling advertising time. Dayparts can also be defined by program content (e.g., news, sports).

Demographics: a category of variables often used to describe the composition of audiences. Common demographics include age, gender, education, occupation, and income.

Domain name level: the consolidation of multiple URLs associated with the same domain name (e.g., AOL, Yahoo, etc.) in audience research reports.

Domain consolidation level: the consolidation of multiple domain names and/or URLs associated with a main site.

DMA (Designated Market Area): the term used by Nielsen to describe specific market areas. Every county belongs to one, and only one, DMA.

Diary: a paper booklet, distributed by ratings companies, in which audience members are asked to record their television or radio use, usually for one week. The diary can be for an entire household (television) or for an individual (radio).

DST (Differential Survey Treatment): special procedures used by a ratings company to improve response from segments of the population known to have unusually low response rates. These may include additional interviews and incentives to cooperate.

Early fringe: in television, a daypart in late afternoon immediately prior to the airing of local news programs.

Editing: the procedures used by a ratings company to check the accuracy and completeness of the data it collects. Editing may include techniques for clarifying or eliminating questionable data. See ascription.

Effective exposure: a concept in media planning stipulating that a certain amount of exposure to an advertising message is necessary before it is effective. Often used interchangeably with the term effective frequency. See frequency.

ESF (Expanded Sample Frame): a procedure used by Arbitron to include in its sample frame households whose telephone numbers are unlisted. See sample frame.

ESS (Effective Sample Size): the size of a simple random sample needed to produce the same result as the sample actually used by the rating company. ESS is a convenience used for calculating confidence intervals. Also called effective sample base, or ESB.

Exclusive cume audience: the size of the unduplicated audience that listens exclusively to one station within some specified period.

FCC (Federal Communications Commission): the independent regulatory agency, created in 1934, having primary responsibility for the oversight of broadcasting and cable.

Flow texts: the succession of images actually experienced by the viewer, sometimes called viewing strips.

Format: the style of programming offered by a radio station. Common formats include MOR (middle of the road), News/Talk, and Adult Contemporary.

Frequency: in advertising, the average number of times that an individual is exposed to a particular advertising message.

Frequency distribution: a way of representing the number of times different values of a variable occur within a sample or population.

Fringe: in television, dayparts just before prime time (early fringe) and after the late news (late fringe).

Geodemographics: a type of variable that categorizes audiences by combining geographic and demographic factors, for example, organizing audiences by zip codes with similar population age and income.

Grazing: the term describing the tendency of viewers to frequently change channels, a behavior that is presumably facilitated by remote control.

Gross impressions: the number of times an advertising schedule is seen over time. The number of gross impressions may exceed the size of the population since audience members may be duplicated. See GRP

GRP (Gross Rating Point): the gross impressions of an advertising schedule expressed as a percentage of the population. GRPs are commonly used to describe the size or media weight of an advertising campaign. GRPs = Reach × Frequency.

Group quarters: dormitories, barracks, nursing homes, prisons, and other living arrangements that do not qualify as households, and are, therefore, not measured by ratings companies.

Hammocking: a television programming strategy in which an unproven or weak show is scheduled between two popular programs in hopes that viewers will stay tuned, thereby enhancing the rating of the middle program. See audience flow, inheritance effect.

Headend: the part of a cable system that receives TV signals from outside sources (e.g., off-the-air, satellite) and sends them through the wired distribution system. See cable system.

Home county: the county in which a station's city of license is located.

Home market: the market area in which a station is located.

Home station: any station licensed in a city within a given market area.

Household: an identifiable housing unit, such as an apartment or house, occupied by one or more persons. See group quarters.

HPDV (Households Per Diary Value): the number of households in the population represented by a single diary kept by a sample household. Used to make audience projections. See projected audience.

HUT (Households Using Television): a term describing the total size of the audience, in households, at any one time. Expressed as either the projected audience size, or as a percent of the total number of households.

Hyping: any one of several illegal practices in which a station, or its agent, engages in an attempt to artificially inflate the station's rating during a measurement period. Also called hyping.

IAB (Internet Advertising Bureau): a trade association promoting the Internet as an advertising medium.

Independent: a commercial television station having no affiliation with a broadcast network.

Inertia: a description of audience behavior that implies viewers are unlikely to change channels unless provoked by very unappealing programming.

Inheritance effect: a common phenomenon of television audience behavior, in which the audience for one program is disproportionately represented in the audience of the following program. Sometimes called lead-in effects, audience inheritance can be thought of as a special case of channel loyalty. See audience duplication, audience flow, channel loyalty.

In-tab: term describing the sample of households or persons actually used in tabulating or processing results.

Interview: a method of collecting data through oral questioning of a respondent, either in person, or over the telephone.

Internet: A network of computer networks around the world that makes possible services like email and the World Wide Web.

Interviewer bias: the problem of introducing systematic error or distortions in data collected in an interview, attributable to the appearance, manner, or reactions of the interviewer. See response error.

Late fringe: in television, a daypart just after the late local news (11 pm EST).

Lead-in: the program that immediately precedes another on the same channel. The size and composition of a lead-in audience is an important determinant of a program's rating. See inheritance effect.

Lead-in Effect: see inheritance effect.

Longitudinal: a type of survey designed to collect data over time. See cross-sectional.

LOP (least objectionable program): a popular theory of television audience behavior, attributed to Paul Klein, that argues people primarily watch TV for reasons unrelated to content, and they choose the least objectionable programs. See passive audience.

Make-goods: no-cost spots given to advertisers to make up for audience shortfalls.

Market segmentation: the practice of dividing populations into smaller groups having similar characteristics or interests to market goods and services more precisely. See demographics.

Maximi$er: Arbitron's computer software leased to radio stations.

Mean: a measure of central tendency determined by adding across cases and dividing that total by the number of cases. See average, median, mode.

Measure: a procedure or device for quantifying objects (e.g., households, people) on variables of interest to the researcher.

Measurement: the process of assigning numbers to objects according to some rule.

Measurement error: systematic bias or inaccuracy attributable to measurement procedures.

Media Professional: Arbitron's computer software leased to ad agencies and advertisers.

Median: a measure of central tendency defined as that point in a distribution where half the cases have higher values and half have lower values. See average, mean, mode.

Meter: a measuring device used to record the on–off and channel tuning condition of a TV set. See SIA, peoplemeter.

Metro area: the core metropolitan counties of a market area as defined by a ratings service. Metro generally correspond to MSAs.

Metro rating: a program or station rating based on the behavior of those who live in the metro area of the market. See rating.

Metro share: a program or station share based on the behavior of those who live in the metro area of the market. See share.

Mode: a measure of central tendency defined as the value in a distribution that occurs most frequently. See average, mean, median.

Mortality: a problem of losing sample members over time, typically in longitudinal survey research.

MRC (Media Rating Council): an industry organization responsible for accrediting the procedures used by ratings companies and monitoring the improvement of ratings methodologies.

Minimum reporting standard: the number of listening or viewing mentions necessary for a station or program to be included in a ratings report.

MSA (Metropolitan Statistical Area): an urban area designated by the Office of Management and Budget often used by ratings companies to define their metro areas.

MSO (Multiple System Operator): a company owning more than one cable system.

Multiset household: a television household with more than one working television set.

Multistage sample: a type of probability sample requiring more than one round of sampling. See cluster sample, probability sample.

NAB (National Association of Broadcasters): an industry organization representing the interests of commercial broadcasters.

NATPE (National Association of Television Program Executives): an industry organization of media professionals responsible for television programming.

Narrowcasting: a programming strategy in which a station or network schedules content of the same type or appealing to the same subset of the audience. See block programming.

NCTA (National Cable Television Association): an industry organization representing the interests of cable systems.

Net audience: see cume or reach.

Net weekly circulation: the cume or unduplicated audience using a station or network in a week. See cume.

Network: an organization that acquires or produces programming and distributes that programming, usually with national or regional advertising, to affiliated stations or cable systems.

Nielsen Media Research: a major supplier of national and local market television ratings.

Nonprobability sample: a kind of sample in which every member of the population does not have a known probability of selection into the sample. See convenience sample, purposive sample, quota sample.

Nonresponse: the problem of failing to obtain information from each person originally drawn into the sample.

Nonresponse error: biases or inaccuracies in survey data that result from nonresponse. See nonresponse.

Normal distribution: a kind of frequency distribution that, when graphed, forms a symmetrical, bell-shaped curve. Many statistical procedures are premised on the assumption that variables are normally distributed. See skew.

NSI (Nielsen Station Index): a division within Nielsen Media Research that issues a series of local television market ratings reports.

NSI Plus: a computerized service of NSI that allows customized analyses of audience flow, reach, and frequency.

NTI (Nielsen Television Index): a division of Nielsen Media Research that issues a series of national television network ratings.

Off-network Programs: programs originally produced to air on a major broadcast network, now being sold in syndication.

Opportunistic market: the buying and selling of network advertising time on short notice, as unforeseen developments (e.g., cancellation, schedule changes) create opportunities. See scatter market, upfront market.

O & O (Owned & Operated): a broadcast station that is owned and operated by a major broadcast network.

Overnights: the label given to ratings, based on meters, that are available to clients the day after broadcast.

Oversample: deliberately drawing a sample larger than needed in-tab to compensate for nonresponse, or to intensively study some subset of the sample.

Page views: number of Web pages viewed by users in a time period.

Panel: a type of longitudinal survey design in which the same sample of individuals is studied over time. For example, meters are placed in a panel of television households. See cross-sectional, longitudinal, trend analysis.

Passive audience: a term given to viewers who are unselective about the content they watch. Passive audiences are thought to watch TV out of habit, tuning to almost anything if a preferred show is unavailable. See active audience, LOP.

Pay cable: the programming services provided by a cable system for a monthly fee above and beyond that required for basic cable. Pay cable may include any one of several premium services like HBO, Showtime, or The Disney Channel.

PC Meter™: software developed by Media Metrix that renders a desktop computer capable of monitoring Internet use for purposes of audience measurement.

Peoplemeter: a device that electronically records the on–off and channel tuning condition of a TV set and is capable of identifying viewers. If viewers must enter that information by button pressing, the meter is called active; if the meter requires no effort from viewers, it is called passive.

Periodicity: a problem encountered in systematic sampling in which the sampling interval corresponds to some cyclical arrangement in the list.

Placement interview: an initial interview to secure the willingness of the respondent to keep a diary or receive a meter.

Pocketpiece: the common name given to Nielsen's weekly national TV ratings report.

Population: the total number of persons or households from which a sample is drawn. Membership in a population must be clearly defined, often by the geographic area in which a person lives.

Post-buy analysis: the analysis conducted after a program runs. It could refer to 1) a financial analysis to determine whether the price paid for the program was appropriate, or 2) the analysis of ratings performance to determine whether the predicted rating was correct.

Power ratio: a statistic that expresses the relationship between share of revenue and share of audience. Also called the conversion ratio, or home market share ratio.

PMSA (Primary Metropolitan Statistical Area): an urban area designated by the Office of Management and Budget used in defining ratings areas.

PPDV (Persons Per Diary Value): the number of persons in a population represented by a single diary kept by a member of a ratings sample. PPDV is used to project an audience. See projected audience.

Preempt: an action, taken by an affiliate, in which programming fed by a network is replaced with programming scheduled by the station. Certain types of commercial time can also be preempted by advertisers willing to pay a premium for the spot.

Prime time: a television daypart from 7 p.m. to 11 p.m. EST. Due to FCC regulations, broadcast networks typically feed programming only from 8 p.m. to 11 p.m. EST.

Probability sample: a kind of sample in which every member of the population has an equal or known chance of being selected into the sample. Sometimes called random samples, probability samples allow statistical inferences about the accuracy of sample estimates. See confidence interval, confidence level, sampling error.

Processing error: a source of inaccuracies in ratings reports attributable to problems inherent in the mechanics of gathering and producing the data. See ascription, editing.

Program type: a category of programming usually based on similarities in program content. Nielsen identifies more than 35 program types, used in summarizing program audiences.

Projectable: a quality describing a sample designed in such a way that audience projections may be made. See projected audience, probability sample.

Projected audience: the size of an audience estimated to exist in the population, based on sample information. See HPDV, PPDV, probability sample.

Psychographics: a category of variable that draws distinctions among people on the basis of their psychological characteristics, including opinions, interests, and attitudes.

PTAR (Prime Time Access Rule): an FCC regulation, effective from the 1970s through the early 1990s, limiting the amount of network programming that affiliates could carry during prime time, and preventing affiliates in the top 50 markets from airing off-network reruns during prime access.

PUR (Persons Using Radio): a term describing the total size of the radio audience at any point. See HUT, PUT.

Purposive sample: a type of nonprobability sample, sometimes called a judgment sample, in which the researcher uses his or her knowledge of the population to handpick areas or groups of respondents for research.

PUT (Person Using Television): a term describing the total size of the television audience, in persons, at any time. See HUT, PUR.

Qualitative ratings: numerical summaries of the audience that not only describe how many watched or listened, but their reactions including enjoyment, interest, attentiveness, and information gained.

Qualitative research: any systematic investigation of the audience that does not depend on measurement and quantification. Examples include focus groups and participant observation. Sometimes used to describe any nonratings research, even if quantification is involved, as in "qualitative ratings."

Quota sample: a type of nonprobability sample in which categories of respondents called quotas (e.g., males), are filled by interviewing respondents who are convenient. See nonprobability sample, probability sample.

RAB (Radio Advertising Bureau): an industry organization formed to promote advertising on radio.

RADAR® (Radio's All Dimension Audience Research): a syndicated ratings service for radio network audiences offered by Statistical Research, Inc.

Random Digit Dialing (RDD): in telephone surveys, a technique for creating a probability sample by randomly generating telephone numbers. By using this method, all numbers (including unlisted) have an equal chance of being called.

Random sample: see probability sample.

Rate of response: the percentage of those originally drawn into the sample who provide usable information. See in-tab.

Rate card: a list of how much a station will charge for its commercial spots. Rate cards are sometimes incorporated with ratings data in computer programs that manage station inventories.

Rating: in its simplest form, the percentage of persons or households tuned to a station, program, or daypart out of the total market population.

Ratings distortion: activity on the part of a broadcaster designed to alter the way audience members report their use of stations. See hypoing

Reach: the number of unduplicated persons or households included in the audience of a station or a commercial campaign over some specified period. Sometimes expressed as a percentage of the market population. See cume, frequency.

Recycling: the extent to which listeners in one daypart also listen in another daypart. See audience duplication.

Relative standard error: a means of comparing the amount of sampling error in ratings data to the size of different ratings. It is the ratio of the standard error to the rating itself. See sampling error.

Relative standard error thresholds: the size of a rating needed to have a relative standard error of either 25% or 50%. Often published in market reports as a means of judging ratings accuracy. See relative standard error

Reliability: the extent to which a method of measurement yields consistent results over time.

Repeat viewing: the extent to which the audience for one program is represented in the audience of other episodes of the series. See audience duplication.

Replication: a study repeating the procedures of an early study to assess the stability of results. In audience measurement, replications involve drawing subsamples from a parent sample to assess sampling error

Respondent: a sample member who provides information in response to questions.

Response error: inaccuracies in survey data attributable to the quality of responses, including lying, forgetting, or misinterpreting questions. See interviewer bias.

Rolling average: a ratings level based on the average of several successive samples. As new sample data become available, the oldest sample is dropped from the average. A rolling average is less susceptible to sampling error. See bounce.

ROS (Run of Schedule): a method of buying and scheduling ads in which the advertiser allows the station or network to run commercials at the best time that happens to be available.

Sample: a subset of some population. See probability sample.

Sample balancing: see sample weighting.

Sample frame: a list of some population from which a probability sample is actually drawn.

Sample weighting: the practice of assigning different mathematical weights to various subsets of the in-tab sample in an effort to correct for different response rates among those subsets. Each weight is the ratio of the subset's size in the population to its size in the sample.

Sampling distribution: the hypothetical frequency distribution of sample statistics that would result from repeated samplings of some population.

Sampling error: inaccuracies in survey data attributable to "the luck of the draw" in creating a probability sample.

Sampling rate: the ratio of sample size to population size.

Sampling unit: the survey element (e.g., person or household), or aggregation of elements, considered for selection at some stage in the process of probability sampling.

Scatter market: a period of time, just in advance of a given quarter of the year, during which advertisers buy network time. See opportunistic market, upfront market.

Search engine: a Web site designed to help Internet users find specific pieces of information on the World Wide Web.

Segmentation: the practice of dividing the market into subsets, often related to the needs of a marketing plan or the programming preferences of the population. See target audience.

Sets-in-use: the number of sets turned on at a given point. As a measure of audience size, it has become outdated since most households now have multiple sets. See HUT.

Share: in its simplest form, the percentage of persons or households tuned to a station or program out of all those using the medium at that time.

SIA (Storage Instantaneous Audimeter): a later version of Nielsen's original audimeter that allowed the company to retrieve electronically stored information over telephone lines.

Simple random sample: a one-stage probability sample in which every member of the population has an equal chance of selection. See probability sample.

Skew: a measure of the extent to which a frequency distribution departs from a normal, symmetrical shape. In common use, the extent to which some subset of the population is disproportionately represented in the audience (e.g., "the audience skews old").

Spill: the extent to which nonmarket stations are viewed by local audiences, or local stations are viewed by audiences outside the market.

Spin-off: a programming strategy in which the characters or locations of a popular program are used to create another television series.

SMSA (Standard Metropolitan Statistical Area): the former governmental designation of an urban area, once used by ratings companies to define local market areas. See MSA.

SRDS (Standard Rate and Data Service): a service that publishes the station rate cards and other information useful in buying commercial time. See rate card.

SRI (Statistical Research Inc.): the company that provides RADAR® and SMART audience research products, and conducts other customized audience research.

Standard deviation: a measure of the variability in a frequency distribution.

Standard error: the standard deviation of a sampling distribution. It is the statistic used to make statements about the accuracy of estimates based on sample information. See confidence interval, confidence level, relative standard error.

Station rep: an organization that represents local stations to national and regional advertisers, selling the station's time and sometimes providing research information useful in programming.

Station total area: a Nielsen term meaning the total geographic area upon which total station audience estimates are based. The total area may include counties outside the NSI area.

Statistical significance: the point at which results from a sample deviate so far from what could happen by chance that they are thought to reflect real differences or phenomena in the population. By convention, significance levels are usually set at 0.05 or lower, meaning a result could happen by chance only 5 times in 100. See confidence level.

Stratified sample: a type of probability sample in which the population is organized into homogeneous subsets or strata, after which a predetermined number of respondents is randomly selected for each strata. Stratified sampling can reduce the sampling error associated with simple random samples.

Stripped programming: a programming practice in which television shows are scheduled at the same time on 5 consecutive weekdays. Stations often strip syndicated programs.

Superstation: an independent television station whose programming is widely carried on cable systems around the country.

Sweep: in television, a 4-week period during which ratings companies are collecting the audience information necessary to produce local market reports.

Syndication: selling a standardized product to many clients. A syndicated program is available to stations in many different markets. A syndicated ratings report is also sold to many users.

Systematic sample: a kind of probability sample in which a set interval is applied to a list of the population to identify elements included in the sample (e.g., picking every 10th name).

Target audience: any well-defined subset of the total audience that an advertiser wants to reach with a commercial campaign, or a station wants to reach with a particular kind of programming.

Telephone recall: a type of survey in which a telephone interviewer asks the respondent what they listened to or watched in the recent past, often the preceding day. See coincidental.

Television household (TVHH): a common unit of analysis in ratings research, it is any household equipped with a working television set, excluding group quarters.

Theory: a tentative explanation of how some phenomenon of interest works. Theories identify causes and effects which make them amenable to testing and falsification.

Tiering: the practice of marketing cable services to subscribers in groups or bundles of channels.

Time buyer: anyone who buys time from the electronic media for purposes of running commercial announcements.

Time period averages: the size of a broadcast audience at an average point in time, within some specified period.

Total audience: all those who tune to a program for at least 5 minutes. Essentially, it is the cumulative audience for a long program or miniseries.

Trend analysis: a type of longitudinal survey design in which results from repeated independent samplings are compared over time.

TSL (Time Spent Listening): a cumulative measure of the average amount of time an audience spends listening to a station within a daypart.

Turnover: the ratio of a station's cumulative audience to its average quarter hour audience within a daypart.

TVB (Television Bureau of Advertising): an industry organization formed to promote advertising on broadcast television.

TVQ: a ratings system that assesses the familiarity and likability of personalities and programs.

UHF (Ultra High Frequency): a class of television stations assigned to broadcast on channels 14 through 80.

Unduplicated audience: the number of different persons or households in an audience over a specified period.

Unique visitors: unique Web users that visited a site over the course of the reporting period. See cume and unduplicated audience.

Unit of analysis: the element or entity about which a researcher collects information. In ratings, the unit of analysis is usually a person or household.

Universe: see population.

Unweighted in-tab: the actual number of individuals in different demographic groups who have returned usable information to the ratings company.

Unwired networks: organizations that acquire commercial time (usually in similar types of programming) from stations around the country and package that time for sale to advertisers.

Upfront market: a period of time several months in advance of the new fall television season during which networks, barter syndicators, and major advertisers agree to the sale of large blocks of commercial time for the broadcast year.

URL (Uniform Resource Locator): a standardized address locating every page on the Web. See WWW.

Validity: the extent to which a method of measurement accurately quantifies the attribute it is supposed to measure.

Variable: any well-defined attribute or characteristic that varies from person to person, or thing to thing. See demographic.

VCR (Video-Cassette Recorder): an appliance used for recording and playing videocassette tapes, now in a majority of U.S. households.

VHF (Very High Frequency): a class of television stations assigned to broadcast on channels 2 through 13.

VPVH (Viewers Per Viewing Household): the estimated number of people, usually by demographic category, in each household tuned to a particular source.

Web site: a specific location on the World Wide Web offering information, entertainment, or advertising.

Weighted in-tab: the number of individuals in different demographic groups who would have provided usable information if response rates were equivalent. See sample weighting.

Weighting: the process of assigning mathematical weights in an attempt to correct over or underrepresentation of some groups in the unweighted in-tab sample. See sample weighting.

WWW (World Wide Web): a system of protocols and programs that enables Internet users to access pages of information on computer servers around the world.

Zapping: the practice of using a remote control device to avoid commercials or program content by rapidly changing channels. Often used interchangeably with zipping.

Zipping: the practice of using the fast forward on a VCR to speed through unwanted commercials or program content. Often used interchangeably with zapping.

Bibliography
and Additional Sources

Advertising Research Foundation. (1954). *Recommended standards for radio and television audience size measurements.* New York: Author.

Adams, W. J. (1993). TV program scheduling strategies and their relationship to new program renewal rates and rating changes. *Journal of Broadcasting & Electronic Media, 37,* 465–474.

Adams, W. J., Eastman, S. T., Horney, L. J., & Popovich, M. N. (1983). The cancellation and manipulation of network television prime-time programs. *Journal of Communication, 33*(1), 10–27.

Agostini, J. M. (1961). How to estimate unduplicated audiences. *Journal of Advertising Research, 1,* 11–14.

Agostino, D. (1977). *The cable subscriber's viewing of public television: A comparison of public television use between broadcast viewers and cable subscribers within selected markets.* Bloomington, IN: Institute for Communication Research.

Agostino, D. (1980). Cable television's impact on the audience of public television. *Journal of Broadcasting, 24,* 347–363.

Agostino, D., & Zenaty, J. (1980). *Home VCR owner's use of television and public television: viewing, recording & playback.* Washington, DC: Corporation for Public Broadcasting.

Albarran, A. (1997). *Management of electronic media.* Belmont, CA: Wadsworth.

Allen, C. (1965). Photographing the TV audience. *Journal of Advertising Research, 5,* 2–8.

Allen, R. (1981). The reliability and stability of television exposure. *Communication Research, 8,* 233–256.

Alexander, A., Owers, J. & Carveth, R. (1998). *Media economics: Theory and practice* (2nd ed.). Mahwah, NJ: Lawrence Erlbaum Associates.

American Research Bureau. (1947, May). *Washington DC market report.* Beltsville, MD: Author.

Anderson, J. A. (1987). *Communication research: Methods and issues.* New York: McGraw-Hill.

Ang, I. (1991). *Desperately seeking the audience.* London, Routledge.

Arbitron. *A guide to understanding and using radio audience estimates* (annual). New York: Author.

Atkin, D., & Litman, B. (1986). Network TV programming: Economics, audiences, and the ratings game, 1971–1986. *Journal of Communication, 36*(3), 32–51.

Austin, B. A. (1989). *Immediate seating: A look at movie audiences.* Belmont, CA: Wadsworth.

Babbie, E. R. (1995). *The practice of social research* (7th ed.) Belmont, CA Wadsworth.

Babrow, A. S., & Swanson, D. L. (1988). Disentangling antecedents of audience exposure levels: extending expectancy-value analyses of gratifications sought from television news. *Communication Monographs, 55,* 1–21.

Banks, M. (1981). *A history of broadcast audience research in the United States, 1920–1980 with an emphasis on the rating services.* Unpublished doctoral dissertation, University of Tennessee, Knoxville, TN.

Banks, S. (1980). Children's television viewing behavior. *Journal of Marketing, 44,* 48–55.

Barnes, B. E., & Thompson, L. M. (1988). The impact of audience information sources on media evolution. *Journal of Advertising Research, 28,* RC9–RC14.

Barnett, G. A., Chang, H., Fink, E. L., & Richards, W. D. (1991). Seasonality in television viewing: A mathematical model of cultural processes. *Communication Research,* 18(6), 755–772.

Baron, R. (1988). If it's on computer paper, it must be right. *Journal of Media Planning, 2,* 32–34.

Barwise, T. P. (1986). Repeat-viewing of prime-time television series, *Journal of Advertising Research, 26,* 9–14.

Barwise, T. P., & Ehrenberg, A. S. C. (1984). The reach of TV channels. *International Journal of Research in Marketing, 1,* 34–49.

Barwise, T. P., & Ehrenberg, A. S. C. (1988). *Television and its audience.* London: Sage.

Barwise, T. P., Ehrenberg, A. S. C., & Goodhardt, G. J. (1979). Audience appreciation and audience size. *Journal of Market Research Society, 21,* 269–289.

Barwise, T. P., & Ehrenberg, A. S. C., & Goodhart, G. J. (1982). Glued to the box?: Patterns of TV repeat-viewing. *Journal of Communication, 32*(4), 22–29.

Bechtel, R. K. Achelpohl, C., & Akers, R. (1972). Correlation between observed behavior and questionnaire responses on television viewing. In E. A. Rubinstein, G. A. Comstock, & J. P. Murray (Eds.), *Television and social behavior: Vol. 4. Television in day-to-day life: Patterns of use* (pp. 274–344). Washington, DC: U. S. Government Printing Office.

Becknell, J. C. (1961). The influence of newspaper tune-in advertising on the size of a TV show's audience. *Journal of Advertising Research, 1,* 23–26.

Beebe, J. H. (1977). The institutional structure and program choices in television markets. *Quarterly Journal of Economics, 91,* 15–37.

Becker, L. B., & Schoenback, K. (Eds.) (1989). *Audience responses to media diversification: Coping with plenty.* Hillsdale, NJ: Lawrence Erlbaum Associates.

Benz, W. (1988). The advertiser. *Gannett Center Journal, 2*(3), 90–93.

Besen, S. M. (1976). The value of television time. *Southern Economic Journal,* 42, 435–441.

Besen, S. M., Krattenmaker, T. G., Metzger, A. R., & Woodbury, J. R. (1984). *Misregulating television: Network dominance and the FCC.* Chicago: University of Chicago Press.

Beville, H. M., Jr. (1988). *Audience ratings: Radio, television, cable* (rev. ed.). Hillsdale, NJ: Lawrence Erlbaum Associates.

Blumler, J. G. (1979). The role of theory in uses and gratifications studies. *Communication Research, 6,* 9–36.

Blumler, J. G., Gurevitch, M., & Katz, E. (1985). Reaching out: A future for gratifications research. In K. Rosengren, L. Wenner, & P. Palmgreen (Eds.). *Media gratifications research: Current perspectives* (pp. 255–273). Beverly Hills: Sage.

Boemer, M. L. (1987). Correlating lead-in show ratings with local television news ratings. *Journal of Broadcasting & Electronic Media, 31,* 89–94.

Bogart, L. (1972). *The age of television.* New York: Frederick Ungar.

Bogart, L. (1988). Research as an instrument of power. *Gannett Center Journal,* 2,(3), pp. 1–16.

Bogart, L. (1996). *Strategy in advertising: Matching media and messages to markets and motivations* (3rd ed.). Lincolnwood, IL: NTC Business Books.

Bower, R. T. (1973). *Television and the public.* New York: Holt, Rinehart & Winston.

Bower, R. T. (1985). *The changing television audience in America.* New York: Columbia University Press.

Bowman, G. W., & Farley, J. (1972). TV viewing: Application of a formal choice model. *Applied Economics, 4,* 245–259.

Boyer, P. (1988). Bewitched, bothered, and bewildered. *Gannett Center Journal, 2,*(3), 17–26.

Brotman, S. N. (1988). *Broadcasters can negotiate anything.* Washington, DC: National Association of Broadcasters.

Bruno, A. V. (1973). The network factor in TV viewing. *Journal of Advertising Research, 13,* 33–39.

Bryant, J., & Zillmann, D. (1984). Using television to alleviate boredom and stress: selective exposure as a function of induced excitational states. *Journal of Broadcasting, 28,* 1–20.

Bryant, J., & Zillmann, D. (Eds.). (1986). *Perspectives on media effects.* Hillsdale, NJ: Lawrence Erlbaum Associates.

Bryant, J., & Zillmann, D. (Eds.). (1994). *Media effects: Advances in theory and research.* Hillsdale, NJ: Lawrence Erlbaum Associates.

Buzzard, K. S. (1990). *Chains of gold: Marketing the ratings and rating the markets.* Metuchen, NJ: Scarecrow Press.

Byrne, B. (1988). Barter syndicators. *Gannett Center Journal, 2*(3), 75–78.

Cabletelevision Advertising Bureau. (1998). *Cable TV facts.* New York: Author.

Cannon, H. M. (1983). Reach and frequency estimates for specialized target markets. *Journal of Advertising Research, 23,* 45–50.

Cannon, H., & Merz, G. R. (1980). A new role for psychographics in media selection. *Journal of Advertising, 9*(2), 33–36.

Cantril, H., & Allport, G. W. (1935). *The psychology of radio.* New York: Harper & Brothers.

Carroll, R. L., & Davis, D. M. (1993). *Electronic media programming: Strategies and decision making.* New York: McGraw-Hill.

CBS. (1937). *Radio in 1937.* New York: Author.

Chaffee, S. (1980). Mass media effects: New research perspectives. In D. C. Wilhoit & H. DeBock (Eds.), *Mass communication review yearbook* (pp. 77–108). Beverly Hills, CA: Sage.

Chandon, J. L. (1976). *A comparative study of media exposure models.* Unpublished doctoral dissertation, Northwestern University, Evanston, IL.

Chappell, M. N., & Hooper, C. E. (1944). *Radio audience measurement.* New York: Stephen Daye.

Christ, W., & Medoff, N. (1984). Affective state and selective exposure to and use of television. *Journal of Broadcasting, 28,* 51–63.

Churchill, G. A. (1995). *Marketing research: Methodological foundations* (6th ed.). Fort Worth, TX: Dryden Press.

Cohen, E. E. (1989). *A model of radio listener choice.* Unpublished doctoral dissertation, Michigan State University. East Lansing, MI.

Collins, J., Reagan, J., & Abel, J. (1983). Predicting cable subscribership: Local factors. *Journal of Broadcasting, 27,* 177–183.

Comstock, G. (1989). *The evolution of American television.* Newbury Park, CA: Sage.

Comstock, G., Chaffee, S., Katzman, N., McCombs, M., & Roberts, D. (1978). *Television and human behavior.* New York: Columbia University Press.

Comstock, G., & Scharrer, E. (1999). *Television: What's on, who's watching, and what it means.* San Diego, CA: Academic Press.

Converse, T. (Speaker). (1974, May 2). *Magazine* [Television documentary] New York: CBS, Inc.

Cook, F. (1988, January). Peoplemeters in the USA: An historical and methodological perspective. *Admap,* 32–35.

Cooper, R. (1993). An expanded, integrated model for determining audience exposure to television. *Journal of Broadcasting & Electronic Media 37* (4) 401–418.

Cooper, R. (1996). The status and future of audience duplication research: An assessment of ratings-based theories of audience behavior. *Journal of Broadcasting & Electronic Media 40* (1) 96–111.

Corporation for Public Broadcasting. (1980). *Proceedings of the 1980 technical conference on qualitative television ratings: Final report.* Washington, DC: Author.

Darmon, R. (1976). Determinants of TV viewing. *Journal of Advertising Research, 16,* 17–20.

Dimling, J. (1988). A. C. Nielsen: The "gold standard." *Gannett Center Journal, 2,*(3), 63–69.

Dominick, J. R., & Fletcher, J. E. (1985). *Broadcasting research methods.* Boston: Allyn & Bacon.

Ducey, R., Krugman, D., & Eckrich, D. (1983). Predicting market segments in the cable industry: The basic and pay subscribers. *Journal of Broadcasting, 27,* 155–161.

Eastman, S. T. (1998). Programming theory under stress: The active industry and the active audience. In M. Roloff (Ed). *Communication Yearbook, 21,* 323–377.

Eastman, S. T., & Ferguson, D. A. (1997). *Broadcast/cable programming: Strategies and practices* (5th ed.). Belmont, CA: Wadsworth.

Eastman, S. T., Newton, G. D., Riggs, K. E., & Neal-Lunsford, J. (1997). Accelerating the flow: A transition effect in programming theory? *Journal of Broadcasting & Electronic Media 41* (2) 265–283.

Ehrenberg, A. S. C. (1968). The factor analytic search for program types. *Journal of Advertising Research, 8,* 55–63.

Ehrenberg, A. S. C. (1982). *A primer in data reduction.* London & New York: Wiley.

Ehrenberg, A. S. C., & Wakshlag, J. (1987). Repeat-viewing with people meters. *Journal of Advertising Research, 27,* 9–13.

Ettema, J. S., & Whitney, C. D. (Eds.). (1982). *Individuals in mass media organizations: creativity and constraint*. Beverly Hills: Sage.

Ettema, J. S., & Whitney, C. D. (Eds.). (1994). *Audiencemaking: How the media create the audience*. Thousand Oaks, CA: Sage.

Everett, S. E. (1998, July). *The "UHF Penalty" demonstrated. www. nab. org/research/webbriefs/uhfdis. html*.

Farrell, M. (1998). Spinning ratings: Reporters lack ratings understanding *Electronic Media*, 9, 4–9.

Federal Communications Commission. (1979). *Inquiry into the economic relationship between television broadcasting and cable television*. (71 F. C. C. 2d 241). Washington, DC: U. S. Government Printing Office.

Fisher, F. M., McGowan, J. J., & Evans, D. S. (1980). The audience-revenue relationship for local television stations. *Bell Journal of Economics*, 11, 694–708.

Fletcher, A. D., & Bower, T. A. (1988). *Fundamentals of advertising research* (3rd ed.). Belmont, CA: Wadsworth.

Fletcher, J. E. (Ed.). (1981). *Handbook of radio and TV broadcasting: Research procedures in audience, program and revenues*. New York: Van Nostrand Reinhold.

Fletcher, J. E. (1985). *Squeezing profits out of ratings: A manual for radio managers, sales managers and programmers*. Washington, DC: National Association of Broadcasters.

Fletcher, J. E. (1987). *Music and program research*. Washington, DC: National Association of Broadcasters.

Fournier, G. M., & Martin, D. L. (1983). Does government-restricted entry produce market power? New evidence from the market for television advertising. *Bell Journal of Economics*, 14, 44–56.

Fowler, M. S., & Brenner, D. L. (1982). A marketplace approach to broadcast regulation. *Texas Law Review*, 60, 207–257.

Frank, R. E., & Greenberg, M. G. (1980). *The public's use of television*. Beverly Hills: Sage.

Frank, R. E., Becknell, J., & Clokey, J. (1971). Television program types. *Journal of Marketing Research*, 11, 204–211.

Fratrik, M. R. (1989, April). *The television audience-revenue relationship revisited*. Paper presented at the meeting of the Broadcast Education Association, Las Vegas, NV.

Gans, H. (1980). The audience for television and in-television research. In S. B. Witney & R. P. Abeles (Eds.), *Television and social behavior: Beyond violence and children* (pp. 55–81). Hillsdale, NJ: Lawrence Erlbaum Associates.

Gantz, W., & Eastman, S. T. (1983). Viewer uses of promotional media to find out about television programs. *Journal of Broadcasting*, 27, 269–277.

Gantz, W., & Razazahoori, A. (1982). The impact of television schedule changes on audience viewing behaviors. *Journalism Quarterly*, 59, 265–272.

Garrison, G. (1939). Wayne University. In J. P. Porter (Ed.), *Journal of Applied Psychology*, 23, 204–205.

Gensch, D. H. (1969, May). A computer simulation model for selecting advertising schedules. *Journal of Marketing Research*, 6, 203–214.

Gensch, D. H., & Ranganathan, B. (1974). Evaluation of television program content for the purpose of promotional segmentation. *Journal of Marketing Research*, 11, 390–398.

Gensch, D. H., & Shaman, P. (1980). Models of competitive ratings. *Journal of Marketing Research*, 17, 307–315.

Gerbner, G., Gross, L., Morgan, M., & Signorielli, N. (1986). Living with television: The dynamics of the cultivation process. In J. Bryant & D. Zillmann (Eds.), *Perspectives on media effects* (pp. 17–40). Hillsdale, NJ: Lawrence Erlbaum Associates.

Gitlin, T. (1983). *Inside prime time*. New York: Pantheon.

Glasser, G. J., & Metzger, G. D. (1989, December). *SRI/CONTAM review of the Nielsen people meter: The process and the results*. Paper presented at the eighth annual Advertising Research Foundation Electronic Media Workshop, New York.

Goodhardt, G. J. (1966). The constant in duplicated television viewing between and within channels. *Nature*, 212, 1616.

Goodhardt, G. J., & Ehrenberg, A. S. C. (1969). Duplication of viewing between and within channels. *Journal of Marketing Research*, 6, 169–178.

Goodhardt, G. J., Ehrenberg, A. S. C., & Collins, M. A. (1987). *The television audience: Patterns of viewing* (2nd ed.). Westmead, UK: Gower.

Grant, A. E. (1989). *Exploring patterns of television viewing: A media system dependency perspective*. Unpublished doctoral dissertation, University of Southern California, Los Angeles, CA.

Greenberg, E., & Barnett, H. J. (1971). TV program diversity—New evidence and old theories. *American Economic Review, 61*, 89–93.

Greenberg, B., Dervin, B., & Dominick, J. (1968). Do people watch "television" or "programs"?: A measurement problem. *Journal of Broadcasting, 12*, 367–376.

Hall, R. W. (1988). *Media math: Basic techniques of media evaluation.* Lincoln, IL: NTC Business Books.

Headen, R. S., Klompmaker, J. E., & Rust, R. (1979). The duplication of viewing law and television media schedule evaluation. *Journal of Marketing Research, 16*, 333–340.

Headen, R. S., Klompmaker, J. E., & Teel, J. E. (1977). Predicting audience exposure to spot TV advertising schedules. *Journal of Marketing Research, 14*, 1–9.

Headen, R. S., Klompmaker, J. E., & Teel, J. E. (1979). Predicting network TV viewing patterns. *Journal of Advertising Research, 19*, 49–54.

Heeter, C., & Greenberg, B. (1985). Cable and program choice. In D. Zillmann & J. Bryant (Eds.), *Selective exposure to communication* (pp. 203–224). Hillsdale, NJ: Lawrence Erlbaum Associates.

Heeter, C., & Greenberg, B. S. (1985). Profiling the zappers. *Journal of Advertising Research, 25*(2), 15–19.

Heeter, C., & Greenberg, B. S. (1988). *Cable-viewing.* Norwood, NJ: Ablex.

Henriksen, F. (1985). A new model of the duplication of television viewing: A behaviorist approach. *Journal of Broadcasting & Electronic Media, 29*, 135–145.

Herzog, H. (1944). What do we really know about daytime serial listeners? In P. J. Lazarsfeld & F. N. Stanton (Eds.), *Radio research 1942–1943*, (pp. 23–36). New York: Duell, Sloan & Pearce.

Hiber, J. (1987). *Winning radio research: Turning research into ratings and revenues.* Washington, DC: National Association of Broadcasters.

Hill, D., & Dyer, J. (1981). Extent of diversion to newscasts from distant stations by cable viewers. *Journalism Quarterly, 58*, 552–555.

Hirsch, P. (1980). An organizational perspective on television (aided and abetted by models from economics, marketing, and the humanities). In S. B. Withey & R. P. Abeles (Eds.), *Television and social behavior* (pp. 83–102). Hillsdale, NJ: Lawrence Erlbaum Associates.

Horen, J. H. (1980). Scheduling of network television programs. *Management Science, 26*, 354–370.

Hotelling, H. (1929). Stability in competition. *Economic Journal, 34*, 41–57.

Hungerford, Aldrin, Nichols, & Carter. (1998). *The Hungerford radio revenue report: Users guide.* Grand Rapids, MI: Author.

Hwang, Hsiao-fang. (1998). *Audience and the TV networks rating games.* Unpublished manuscript, Northwestern University.

Israel, H., & Robinson, J. (1972). Demographic characteristics of viewers of television violence and news programs. In E. A. Rubinstein, G. A. Comstock, & J. P. Murray (Eds.), *Television and social behavior: Vol. 4. Television in day-to-day life: Patterns of use* (pp. 87–128). Washington, DC: U. S. Government Printing Office.

Jaffe, M. (1985, January 25). Towards better standards for post-analysis of spot television GRP delivery. *Television/Radio Age,* pp. 23–25.

Jeffres, L. W. (1978). Cable TV and viewer selectivity. *Journal of Broadcasting, 22*, 167–177.

Jeffres, L. W. (1986). *Mass media processes and effects.* Prospect Heights, IL: Waveland.

Jhally, S., & Livant, B. (1986). Watching as working: The valorization of audience consciousness. *Journal of Communication, 36*(3), 124–143.

Kaplan, S. J. (1978). The impact of cable television services on the use of competing media. *Journal of Broadcasting, 22*, 155–165.

Katz, E., Blumler, J. G., & Gurevitch, M. (1974). Utilization of mass communication by the individual. In J. G. Blumler & E. Katz (Eds.), *The uses of mass communications: Current perspectives on gratifications research* (pp. 19–32) Beverly Hills: Sage.

Katz, E., Gurvitch, M., & Haas, H. (1973). On the use of mass media for important things. *American Sociological Review, 38*(2), 164–181.

Killion, K. C. (1987). Using peoplemeter information. *Journal of Media Planning 2*(2), 47–52.

Kirsch, A. D., & Banks, S. (1962). Program types defined by factor analysis. *Journal of Advertising Research, 2*, 29–31.

Klapper, J. (1960). *The effects of mass communication.* Glencoe, IL: The Free Press.

Klein, P. (1971, January). The men who run TV aren't stupid. *New York,* pp. 20–29.

Krueger, R. A. (1994). *Focus groups: A practical guide for applied research* (2nd ed.). Thousand Oaks, CA: Sage.

Krugman, D. M. (1985). Evaluating the audiences of the new media. *Journal of Advertising, 14*(4), 21–27.

Krugman, H. E. (1972). Why three exposures may be enough. *Journal of Advertising Research, 12*, 11–14.

Kubey, R., & Csikszentmihalyi, M. (1990). *Television and the quality of life: How viewing shapes everyday experience.* Hillsdale, NJ: Lawrence Erlbaum Associates.

LaRose, R., & Atkin, D. (1988). Satisfaction, demographic, and media environment predictors of cable subscription. *Journal of Broadcasting & Electronic Media, 32*, 403–413.

Larson, E. (1992). *The naked consumer: How our private lives become public commodities.* New York: Henry Holt and Company.

Lavine, J. M., & Wackman, D. B. (1988). *Managing media organizations: Effective leadership of the media.* New York: Longman.

Lazarsfeld, P. F., & Stanton, F. N. (Eds.). (1941). *Radio research.* New York: Duell, Sloan & Pearce.

Leckenby, J. D., & Hong, J. (1998). Using reach/frequency for Web media planning. *Journal of Advertising Research, 38*, 7–20.

Leckenby, J. D., & Rice, M. D. (1985). A beta binomial network TV exposure model using limited data. *Journal of Advertising, 3*, 25–31.

LeDuc, D. R. (1987). *Beyond broadcasting: Patterns in policy and law.* New York: Longman.

Lehmann, D. R. (1971). Television show preference: Application of a choice model. *Journal of Marketing Research, 8*, 47–55.

Levin, H. G. (1980). *Fact and fancy in television regulation: An economic study of policy alternatives.* New York: Russell Sage.

Levy, M. R. (Ed.). (1989). *The VCR age: Home video and mass communication.* Newbury Park, CA: Sage.

Levy, M., & Windahl, S. (1984). Audience activity and gratifications: A conceptual clarification and exploration. *Communication Research, 11*, 51–78.

Levy, M. R., & Fink, E. L. (1984). Home video recorders and the transience of television broadcasts. *Journal of Communication, 34*(2), 56–71.

Lichty, L., & Topping, M. (Eds.). (1975). *American broadcasting: A sourcebook on the history of radio and television.* New York: Hastings House.

Lin, C. A. (1995). Network prime-time programming strategies in the 1980's. *Journal of Broadcasting & Electronic Media, 39*, 482–495.

Lindlof, T. (1995). *Qualitative communication research methods.* Thousand Oaks, CA: Sage.

Lindlof, T. R. (Ed.). (1987). *Natural audiences: Qualitative research on media uses and effects.* Norwood, NJ: Ablex.

Litman, B. R. (1979). Predicting TV ratings for theatrical movies. *Journalism Quarterly, 56*, 591–594.

Little, J. D. C. & Lodish, L. M. (1969). A media planning calculus. *Operations Research, 1*, 1–35.

LoSciuto, L. A. (1972). A national inventory of television viewing behavior. In E. A. Rubinstein, G. A. Comstock, & J. P. Murray (Eds.), *Television and social behavior: Vol. 4. Television in day-to-day life: Patterns of use* (pp. 33–86). Washington, DC: U.S. Government Printing Office.

Lowery, S., & DeFleur, M. L. (1994). *Milestones in mass communication research: Media effects* (3rd ed.). New York: Addison-Wesley.

Lu, D., & Kiewit, D. A. (1987). Passive peoplemeters: A first step. *Journal of Advertising Research, 27*(3), 9–14.

Lull, J. (1980). The social uses of television. *Human Communication Research, 6*, 197–209.

Lull, J. (1982). How families select televisions programs: A mass observational study. *Journal of Broadcasting, 26*, 801–812.

Lull, J. (Ed.). (1988). *World families watch television.* Newbury Park, CA: Sage.

Lumley, F. H. (1934). *Measurement in radio.* Columbus, OH: The Ohio State University.

MacFarland, D. T. (1990). *Contemporary radio programming strategies.* Hillsdale, NJ: Lawrence Erlbaum Associates.

MacFarland, D. T. (1997). *Future radio programming strategies: Cultivating listenership in the digital age.* (2nd ed.). Mahwah, NJ: Lawrence Erlbaum Associates.

McCombs, M. E., & Shaw, D. L. (1972). The agenda-setting function of the mass media. *Public Opinion Quarterly 36*, 176–87.

McDonald, D. G., & Reese, S. D. (1987). Television news and audience selectivity. *Journalism Quarterly, 64*, 763–768.

McDonald, D. G., & Schechter, R. (1988). Audience role in the evolution of fictional television content. *Journal of Broadcasting & Electronic Media, 32*, 61–71.

McKnight, L. W. & Bailey, J. P. (eds.). (1997). *Internet economics.* Boston: MIT Press.

McLeod, J. M., & McDonald, D. G. (1985). Beyond simple exposure: media orientations and their impact on political processes. *Communication Research, 12*, 3–33.

McPhee, W. N. (1963). *Formal theories of mass behavior.* New York: The Free Press.

McQuail, D. (1994). *Mass communication theory: An introduction.* (3rd ed.). Thousand Oaks, CA: Sage.

McQuail, D. (1997). *Audience analysis.* Thousand Oaks, CA: Sage.

McQuail, D., & Gurevitch, M. (1974). Explaining audience behavior: Three approaches considered. In J. G. Blumler & E. Katz (Eds.), *The uses of mass communications: Current perspectives on gratifications research.* (pp. 287–302) Beverly Hills, CA: Sage.

Media Dynamics, Inc. (1998). *TV Dimensions '98.* New York: Author.

Meehan, E. R. (1984). Ratings and the institutional approach: A third answer to the commodity question. *Critical Studies in Mass Communication, 1,* 216–225.

Metheringham, R. A. (1964). Measuring the net cumulative coverage of a print campaign. *Journal of Advertising Research, 4,* 23–28.

Metzger, G. (1984, February). Current audience measurement is doing the job: Meters at local level should be viewed cautiously. *Television/Radio Age,* pp. 46–47.

Miller, P. (1988). I am single source. *Gannett Center Journal 2,*(3), 27–34.

Miller, P. V. (1987, May). *Measuring TV viewing in studies of television effects.* Paper presented at the meeting of the International Communication Association, Montreal.

Morley, D. (1986). *Family television: Cultural power and domestic leisure.* London: Comedia.

Naples, M. J. (1979). *The effective frequency: The relationship between frequency and advertising effectiveness.* New York: Association of National Advertisers.

Neuman, W. R. (1991). *The future of the mass audience.* Cambridge: Cambridge University Press.

Newcomb, H. M., & Alley, R. S. (1983). *The producer's medium.* New York: Oxford University Press.

Newcomb, H. M., & Hirsch, P. M. (1984). Television as a cultural forum: Implications for research. In W. Rowland & B. Watkins (Eds.), *Interpreting television* (pp 58–73). Beverly Hills, CA: Sage.

Nielsen, A. C. (1988). Television ratings and the public interest. In J. Powell & W. Gair (Eds.), *Public interest and the business of broadcasting: The broadcast industry looks at itself* (pp. 61–63). New York: Quorum Books.

Nielsen Station Index. *Your guide to reports & services* (annual). New York: Nielsen.

Niven, H. (1960). Who in the family selects the TV program? *Journalism Quarterly, 37,* 110–111.

Noam, E. (Ed.). (1985). *Video media competition: Regulation, economics, and technology.* New York: Columbia University Press.

Noll, R. G., Peck, M. G., & McGowan, J. J. (1973). *Economic aspects of television regulation.* Washington, DC: Brookings Institution.

Ogburn, W. F. (1933). The influence of invention and discovery. In W. F. Ogburn (Ed.), *Recent social trends* (pp. 153–156). New York: McGraw-Hill.

Owen, B. M. (1975). *Economics and freedom of expression: Media structure and the first amendment.* Cambridge, MA: Ballinger.

Owen, B. M., & Wildman, S. S. (1992). *Video Economics.* Cambridge, MA: Harvard University Press.

Owen, B. M., Beebe, J., & Manning, W. (1974). *Television economics.* Lexington, MA: D. C. Heath.

Palmgreen, P., Wenner, L. A., & Rayburn, J. D. (1981). Gratification discrepancies and news program choice. *Communication Research, 8,* 451–478.

Park, R. E. (1970). *Potential impact of cable growth on television broadcasting* (R-587–FF). Santa Monica, CA: Rand Corporation.

Park, R. E. (1979). *Audience diversion due to cable television: Statistical analysis of new data.* R-2403–FCC. Santa Monica, CA: Rand Corporation.

Parkman, A. M. (1982). The effect of television station ownership on local news ratings. *Review of Economics and Statistics, 64,* 289–295.

Perse, E. M. (1986). Soap opera viewing patterns of college students and cultivation. *Journal of Broadcasting & Electronic Media, 30,* 175–193.

Peterson, R. (1972). Psychographics and media exposure. *Journal of Advertising Research, 12,* 17–20.

Phalen, P. F. (1996). *Information and markets and the market for information: An analysis of the market for television audiences.* Unpublished doctoral dissertation, Northwestern University, Evanston, IL

Phalen, P. F. (1998). The market information system and personalized exchange: Business practices in the market for television audiences. *The Journal of Media Economics, 11*(4), 17–34.

Philport, J. (1980). The psychology of viewer program evaluation. In *Proceedings of the 1980 technical conference on qualitative ratings.* Washington, DC: Corporation for Public Broadcasting.

Poltrack, D. (1983). *Television marketing: Network, local, and cable.* New York: McGraw-Hill.

Poltrack, D. (1988). The "big 3" networks. *Gannett Center Journal, 2,*(3), 53–62.

260

REFERENCES

Potter, W. J. (1996). *An analysis of thinking and research about qualitative methods.* Mahwah, NJ: Lawrence Erlbaum Associates.
Rao, V. R. (1975). Taxonomy of television programs based on viewing behavior. *Journal of Marketing Research, 12,* 335–358.
Reagan, J. (1984). Effects of cable television on news use. *Journalism Quarterly, 61,* 317–324.
Robinson, J. P. (1977). *How Americans used their time in 1965.* New York: Praeger.
Robinson, J. P., & Levy, M. R. (1986). *The main source: Learning from television news.* Beverly Hills, CA: Sage.
Rogers, E. M. (1994). *A history of communication study: A biographical approach.* New York: The Free Press.
Rosengren, K. E., Wenner, L. A., & Palmgreen, P. (Eds.). (1985). *Media gratifications research: Current perspectives.* Beverly Hills: Sage.
Rosenstein, A. W., & Grant, A. E. (1997). Reconceptualizing the role of habit: A new model of television audience activity. *Journal of Broadcasting & Electronic Media, 41* (3), 324–344.
Rothenberg, J. (1962). Consumer sovereignty and the economics of TV programming. *Studies in Public Communication, 4,* 23–36.
Rowland, W. (1983). *The politics of TV violence: Policy uses of communication research.* Beverly Hills: Sage.
Rubens, W. S. (1978). A guide to TV ratings. *Journal of Advertising Research, 18,* 11–18.
Rubens, W. S. (1984). High-tech audience measurement for new-tech audiences. *Critical Studies in Mass Communication, 1,* 195–205.
Rubin, A. M. (1984). Ritualized and instrumental television viewing. *Journal of Communication, 34*(3), 67–77.
Rubin, A. M. (1993). Audience activity and media use. *Communication Monographs, 60,* 98–115.
Rubin, A. M., & Perse, E. M. (1987). Audience activity and soap opera involvement. *Human Communication Research, 14,* 246–268.
Rubin, A. M., & Perse, E. M. (1987). Audience activity and television news gratifications. *Communication Research, 14,* 58–84.
Rust, R. T. (1986). *Advertising media models: A practical guide.* Lexington, MA: Lexington Books.
Rust, R. T., & Alpert, M. I. (1984). An audience flow model of television viewing choice. *Marketing Science, 3*(2), 113–124.
Rust, R. T., & Donthu, N. (1988). A programming and positioning strategy for cable television networks. *Journal of Advertising, 17,* 6–13.
Rust, R. T., & Klompmaker, J. E. (1981). Improving the estimation procedure for the beta binomial TV exposure model. *Journal of Marketing Research, 18,* 442–448.
Rust, R. T., Kamakura, W. A., & Alpert, M. I. (1992). Viewer preference segmentation and viewing choice models of network television. *Journal of Advertising, 21* (1), 1–18.
Rust, R. T., Klompmaker, J. E., & Headen, R. S. (1981). A comparative study of television duplication models. *Journal of Advertising, 21,* 42–46.
Sabavala, D. J., & Morrison, D. G. (1977). A model of TV show loyalty. *Journal of Advertising Research, 17,* 35–43.
Sabavala, D. J., & Morrison, D. G. (1981). A nonstationary model of binary choice applied to media exposure. *Management Science, 27,* 637–57.
Salomon, G., & Cohen, A. (1978). On the meaning and validity of television viewing. *Human Communication Research, 4,* 265–270.
Salvaggio, J. L., & Bryant, J. (Eds.) (1989). *Media use in the information age: Emerging patterns of adoption and consumer use.* Hillsdale, NJ: Lawrence Erlbaum Associates.
Schramm, W., Lyle, J., & Parker, E. B. (1961). *Television in the lives of our children.* Stanford, CA: Stanford University Press.
Schroder, K. (1987). Convergence of antagonistic traditions? The case of audience research. *European Journal of Communication, 2,* 7–31.
Schudson, M. (1984). *Advertising, the uneasy persuasion: Its dubious impact on American society.* New York: Basic Books.
Sears, D. O., & Freedman, J. L. (1972). Selective exposure to information: A critical review. In W. Schramm & D. Roberts (Eds.). *The process and effects of mass communication* (pp. 209–234). Urbana, IL: University of Illinois Press.
Sherman, B. L. (1995). *Telecommunications management: Broadcasting/cable and the new technologies* (2nd ed.) New York: McGraw-Hill.
Sieber, R. (1988). Cable networks. *Gannett Center Journal, 2*(3), 70–74.

Sims, J. (1988). AGB: The ratings innovator. *Gannett Center Journal, 2,*(3), 85–89.

Singer, J. L., Singer, D. G., & Rapaczynski, W. S. (1984). Family patterns and television viewing as predictors of children's belief's and aggression. *Journal of Communication, 34*(3), 73–89.

Sissors, J. Z., & Bumba, L. (1996). *Advertising media planning* (5th ed.). Lincolnwood, IL: NTC Business Books.

Smythe, D. (1981). *Dependency road: Communications, capitalism, consciousness, and Canada.* Norwood, NJ: Ablex.

Soong, R. (1988). The statistical reliability of people meter ratings. *Journal of Advertising Research, 28,* 50–56.

Sparkes, V. (1983). Public perception of and reaction to multi-channel cable television service. *Journal of Broadcasting, 27,* 163–175.

Spaulding, J. W. (1963). 1928: Radio becomes a mass advertising medium. *Journal of Broadcasting, 7,* 31–44.

Stanford, S. W. (1984). Predicting favorite TV program gratifications from general orientations. *Communication Research, 11,* 419–436.

Stanton, F. N. (1935). *Critique of present methods and a new plan for studying listening behavior.* Unpublished doctoral dissertation, The Ohio State University, Columbus, OH.

Statistical Research, Inc. (1975). *How good is the television diary technique?* Prepared for the National Association of Broadcasters. Washington, DC: Author.

Steiner, G. A. (1963). *The people look at television.* New York: Alfred A. Knopf.

Steiner, G. A. (1966). The people look at commercials: A study of audience behavior. *Journal of Business, 39,* 272–304.

Steiner, P. O. (1952). Program patterns and preferences, and the workability of competition in radio broadcasting. *Quarterly Journal of Economics, 66,* 194–223.

Sterling, C. H., & Kittross, J. M. (1990). *Stay tuned: A concise history of American broadcasting* (2nd ed.). Belmont, CA: Wadsworth.

Sudman, S., & Bradburn, N. (1982). *Asking questions: A practical guide to questionnaire design.* San Francisco: Jossey-Bass.

Swanson, C. I. (1967). The frequency structure of television and magazines. *Journal of Advertising Research, 7,* 3–7.

Takada, H. & Henry, W. (1993, Fall). Analysis of network TV commercial time pricing for top-rated prime time programs. *Journal of Current Issues and Research in Advertising.* 15, (2) 59–70.

Television Audience Assessment. (1983a). *The audience rates television.* Boston: Author.

Television Audience Assessment. (1983b). *The multichannel environment.* Boston: Author.

Tiedge, J. T., & Ksobiech, K. J. (1986). The "lead-in" strategy for prime-time: Does it increase the audience? *Journal of Communication, 36*(3), 64–76.

Tiedge, J. T., & Ksobiech, K. J. (1987). Counterprogramming primetime network television. *Journal of Broadcasting & Electronic Media, 31,* 41–55.

TN Media Inc. (1998, January). *The median age report.* New York: Author.

Turow, J. (1984). *Media industries.* New York: Longman.

Turow, J. (1997). *Breaking up America: Advertisers and the new media world.* Chicago: University of Chicago Press.

Urban, C. D. (1984). Factors influencing media consumption: A survey of the literature. In B. M. Compaine (Ed.), *Understanding new media: Trends and issues in electronic distribution of information* (pp. 213–282). Cambridge, MA: Ballinger.

Veronis, Suhler, and Associates. (1998). *Communications industry forecast.* New York: Author.

Vogel, H. L. (1986). *Entertainment industry economics: A guide for financial analysis.* Cambridge: Cambridge University Press.

Vogel, H. L. (1998). *Entertainment industry economics: A guide for financial analysis* (4th ed.). Cambridge: Cambridge University Press.

Wakshlag, J., & Greenberg, B. (1979). Programming strategies and the popularity of television programs for children. *Human Communication Research, 6,* 58–68.

Wakshlag, J., Agostino, D., Terry, H., Driscoll, P., & Ramsey, B. (1983). Television news viewing and network affiliation change. *Journal of Broadcasting, 27,* 53–68.

Wakshlag, J., Day, K., & Zillmann, D. (1981). Selective exposure to educational television programs as a function of differently paced humorous inserts. *Journal of Educational Psychology, 73,* 27–32.

Wakshlag, J., Reitz, R., & Zillmann, D. (1982). Selective exposure to and acquisition of information from educational television programs as a function of appeal and tempo of background music. *Journal of Educational Psychology, 74*, 666–677.

Wakshlag, J., Vial, V. K., & Tamborini, R. (1983). Selecting crime drama and apprehension about crime. *Human Communication Research, 10*, 227–242.

Walker, J. & Ferguson, D. (1998). *The broadcast television industry.* Boston: Allyn and Bacon.

Walker, J. R. (1988). Inheritance effects in the new media environment. *Journal of Broadcasting & Electronic Media, 32*, 391–401.

Wand, B. (1968). Television viewing and family choice differences. *Public Opinion Quarterly, 32*, 84–94.

Warner, C. (1993). *Broadcast and cable selling.* (updated 2nd ed.). Belmont, CA: Wadsworth.

Waterman, D. (1986). The failure of cultural programming on cable TV: An economic interpretation. *Journal of Communication, 36*(3), 92–107.

Waterman, D. (1992). "Narrowcasting" and "broadcasting" on nonbroadcast media: A program choice model. *Communication Research, 19* (1), 3–28.

Webster, J. G. (1982). *The impact of cable and pay cable on local station audiences.* Washington, DC: National Association of Broadcasters.

Webster, J. G. (1983). *Audience research.* Washington, DC: National Association of Broadcasters.

Webster, J. G. (1983). The impact of cable and pay cable television on local station audiences. *Journal of Broadcasting, 27*, 119–126.

Webster, J. G. (1984). Cable television's impact on audience for local news. *Journalism Quarterly, 61*, 419–422.

Webster, J. G. (1984, April). Peoplemeters. In *Research & Planning: Information for management.* Washington, DC: National Association of Broadcasters.

Webster, J. G. (1985). Program audience duplication: A study of television inheritance effects. *Journal of Broadcasting & Electronic Media, 29*, 121–133.

Webster, J. G. (1986). Audience behavior in the new media environment. *Journal of Communication, 36*(3), 77–91.

Webster, J. G. (1989). Assessing exposure to the new media. In J. Salvaggio & J. Bryant (Eds.) *Media use in the information age: Emerging patterns of adoption and consumer use* (pp. 3–19). Hillsdale, NJ: Lawrence Erlbaum Associates.

Webster, J. G. (1989). Television audience behavior: Patterns of exposure in the new media environment. In J. Salvaggio & J. Bryant (Eds.) *Media use in the information age: Emerging patterns of adoption and consumer use* (pp. 197–216). Hillsdale, NJ: Lawrence Erlbaum Associates.

Webster, J. G. (1990). The role of audience ratings in communications policy. *Communications and the Law, 12*(2), 59–72.

Webster, J. G. (1998). The audience. *Journal of Broadcasting & Electronic Media, 42*(2), 190–207.

Webster, J. G., & Coscarelli, W. (1979). The relative appeal to children of adult versus children's television programming. *Journal of Broadcasting, 23*, 437–451.

Webster, J. G., & Newton, G. D. (1988). Structural determinants of the television news audience. *Journal of Broadcasting & Electronic Media, 32*, 381–389.

Webster, J. G., & Phalen, P. F. (1997). *The mass audience: Rediscovering the dominant model.* Mahwah, NJ: Lawrence Erlbaum Associates.

Webster, J. G., & Wakshlag, J. (1982). The impact of group viewing on patterns of television program choice. *Journal of Broadcasting, 26*, 445–455.

Webster, J. G., & Wakshlag, J. (1983). A theory of television program choice. *Communication Research, 10*, 430–446.

Webster, J. G., & Wakshlag, J. (1985). Measuring exposure to television. In D. Zillmann & J. Bryant (Eds.), *Selective exposure to communication* (pp. 35–62). Hillsdale, NJ: Lawrence Erlbaum Associates.

Weibull, L. (1985). Structural factors in gratifications research. In K. E. Rosengren, L. A. Wenner, & P. Palmgreen (Eds.), *Media gratifications research: Current perspectives* (pp. 123–148). Beverly Hills: Sage.

Wells, W. D. (1969). The rise and fall of television program types. *Journal of Advertising Research, 9*, 21–27.

Wells, W. D. (1975). Psychographics: A critical review. *Journal of Marketing Research, 12*, 196–213.

White, B. C., & Satterthwaite, N. D. (1989). *But first these messages ... The selling of broadcast advertising.* Boston: Allyn and Bacon.

White, K. J. (1977). Television market shares, station characteristics and viewer choice. *Communication Research, 4*, 415–434.

Why's and wherefores of syndex II. (1988, May 23). *Broadcasting*, 58–59.

Wildman, S. S., & Owen, B. M. (1985). Program competition, diversity, and multichannel bundling in the new video industry. In E. Noam (Ed.), *Video media competition: Regulation, economics, and technology* (pp. 244–273). New York: Columbia University Press.

Wildman, S. S., & Siwek, S. E. (1988). *International trade in films and television programs*. Cambridge: Ballinger.

Wimmer, R. & Dominick, J. (1997). *Mass media research: An introduction (5th ed.)* Belmont, CA: Wadsworth.

Wirth, M. O., & Bloch, H. (1985). The broadcasters: The future role of local stations and the three networks. In E. Noam (Ed.), *Video media competition: Regulation, economics, and technology* (pp. 121–137). New York: Columbia University Press.

Wirth, M. O., & Wollert, J. A. (1984). The effects of market structure on local television news pricing. *Journal of Broadcasting, 28*, 215–224.

Wober, J. M. (1988). *The use and abuse of television: A social psychological analysis of the changing screen*. Hillsdale, NJ: Lawrence Erlbaum Associates.

Wober, J. M., & Gunter, B. (1986). Television audience research at Britain's Independent Broadcasting Authority, 1974–1984. *Journal of Broadcasting and Electronic Media, 30*, 15–31.

Wulfemeyer, K. T. (1983). The interests and preferences of audiences for local television news. *Journalism Quarterly, 60*, 323–328.

Zeigler, S. K., & Howard, H. (1991). *Broadcast advertising: A comprehensive working textbook* (3rd ed.) Ames, IA: Iowa State University Press.

Zenaty, J. (1988). The advertising agency. *Gannett Center Journal, 2*(3), 79–84.

Zillmann, D. (1988). Mood management through communication choices. *American Behavioral Scientist, 31*(3), 327–340.

Zillmann, D., & Bryant, J. (Eds.). (1985). *Selective exposure to communication*. Hillsdale, NJ: Lawrence Erlbaum Associates.

Zillmann, D., Hezel, R. T., & Medoff, N. J. (1980). The effect of affective states on selective exposure to televised entertainment fare. *Journal of Applied Social Psychology, 10*, 323–339.

Author Index

Note: Numbers in *italics* indicate pages on which full bibliographical entries appear.

A

Adams, W. J., 208
Agostini, D., 224
Albarran, A., *34, 52, 67*
Alexander, A., 67
Alley, R. S., *50*
Allport, G., 70
Alpert, M. E., 208
Anderson, J. A., *126*
Ang, I., *12*
Atkin, D., *50*, 208

B

Babbie, E., *126*
Bailey, J. P., 67
Barnett, G. A., 208
Baron, R., 224
Barwise, P., *184, 221, 222, 223, 227*
Besen, S. M., 66, 67, 79
Beville, H., *10, 12*, 88, 98, 109, *126, 157*
Bloch, H., 66
Blumler, J. G., 166
Bogart, L., 9
Bower, R. T., *184*
Bower, T. A., *126, 157*
Bryant, J., 74, *80, 184*
Bumba, L., 208, *227*
Buzzard, K. S., 98

C

Cantril, H., 70
Carroll, R. L., *50*
Carveth, R., 67
Chandon, J. L., *225*
Chang, H., 208
Chappell, M. N., 85, 98
Churchill, G. A., *126*
Collins, M. A., *176, 184, 215, 224, 226, 227*
Comstock, G., *184*
Converse, T., 40

D

Davis, D. M., *50*
DeFleur, M. L., *80*
Dominick, J. R., 4, *12, 126*
Duncan, J. H., Jr., 220

E

Eastman, S. T., *50*
Ehrenberg, A. S. C., *176, 184, 215, 221, 222, 223, 224, 226, 227*
Ettema, J. S., *12*, 50, 98
Evans, D. S., 66, 67
Everett, S. E., 78

265

Subject Index

sports, 16
time frame for, 16–17
upfront market, 16–17
television stations, 22–24
avail requests, 24
Designated Market Area (DMA), 23
post-buy analysis, 24
station representative, 24
Advertising agency, 235
Advertising Research Foundation (ARF)
defined, 236
and research methods, 115
Affiliate, 235
American Association of Advertising Agencies
(AAAA)
defined, 235
and ratings business, 83
American Medical Association (AMA), 72
American Research Bureau (ARB)
defined, 236
and ratings business, 87–88, 91, 92
America Online (AOL), 27
Applied research, 1–2
as action research, 2
in electronic media, 2
methodological, 2
in print media, 2
Arbitron
defined, 236
development of, 92, 95
financial analysis, 52, 53, 55
Maximi$er, 46, 48, 146, 243
Media Professional, 146
defined, 243
radio ratings, 38
research products, 140–146
Area of Dominant Influence (ADI), 235
Area probability sample, 236
Ascription
defined, 236
and research products, 129
Association of Local Television Stations
(ALTV), 72
Association of National Advertisers (ANA)
defined, 235
and ratings business, 83
Audience behavior
audience factors, 168–173
awareness, 172
group viewing, 172
individual, 172–173
preferences, 172
structural, 168–173
cumulative measures, 160
cume, 160
frequency, 160
gross measure comparison, 161–162

reach, 160
unduplicated audience, 160
economic theory, 165–166
audience fragmentation, 166
gross measures, 159–160
Cost Per Point (CPP), 160
Cost Per Thousand (CPM), 160
cumulative measure comparison,
161–162
Gross Rating Point (GRP), 159–160
media choice theories, 162–167
economic, 165–166
selective-exposure, 166
uses/gratifications, 166–167
working, 163–164
media exposure measures
comparison of, 161–162
cumulative, 160
gross, 159–160
time factor, 159
media factors, 173–179
cable television, 178–179
channel repertoire, 178–179
coverage, 174–176
grazing, 177
individual, 177–179
library use, 177
network clearance, 175
program scheduling, 176
remote-control devices, 177
structural, 174–177
subscriptions, 178
time-shifting, 177
VCR usage, 177–178
model of, 179–184
sample scenario, 182–184
overview, 158–159
selective-exposure theory, 166
understanding of, 167–179
audience factors, 168–173
individual determinants, 167, 172–173,
177–179
media factors, 173–179
structural determinants, 167, 168–171,
173t, 174–177, 179t
uses/gratifications theory, 166–167
working theory, 163–164
active audience, 164
Least Objectionable Program (LOP),
164
passive audience, 164
Audience Deficiency (AD), 236
Audience duplication
and advertising, 30
defined, 236
and ratings analysis, 215–219
cross-tabulation, 215–218

duplicated audience, 216
expected frequency, 217
Audience flow
defined, 236
and scheduling, 49
Audience fragmentation
and audience behavior, 166
defined, 236
Audience measurement business, *see also specific companies*
contemporary, 92–98
development of
diaries, 90–92
interviews, 86–88
meters, 88–90
roster-recall method, 87
telephone coincidental, 84–85
telephone recall, 84–85
telephones, 83–86
overview, 81–83
toll broadcasting, 82
Audience polarization, 236
Audience research
administrative vs. critical
administrative, 2–3
critical, 2, 3
applied vs. theoretical
action research, 2
applied, 1–2
methodological research, 2
theoretical, 2
commercial, 7–9
characteristics of, 8–9
limitations of, 9
and statistical thinking, 8–9
quantitative vs. qualitative, 3–5
ethnography, 4–5
focus group, 4
industry meanings of, 4
methods in, 3–4
qualitative, 3
quantitative, 3
ratings, 4
ratings
defined, 10, 247
importance of, 4, 10–12
origination of, 10–11
syndicated vs. custom, 5–7
call-out research, 5
custom, 5, 7
hook, 5
maintenance research, 5, 7
primary research, 7
program analyzer, 5
secondary analysis, 7
syndicated, 5, 6t, 7
Audience turnover

defined, 236
and ratings analysis, 211–212
Audimeter
defined, 236
and ratings business, 88–89
and research methods, 119–120
Audit Bureau of Circulation (ABC), 26
Audits of Great Britain (AGB), 95–96
Automated Measurement of Lineups (AMOL)
defined, 235
and research products, 131
Availabilities
and advertising, 24
defined, 236
Available audience
defined, 236
and ratings analysis, 193–194, 195f
Avail requests, 24, 236
Average audience rating, 237
Average measure, 236
Average Quarter Hour (AQH)
defined, 235
and ratings analysis, 190
and research products, 141, 150
Average time per page, 237
Average unit rate, 57
Awareness, 172
Away-from-home listening, 237

B

Banner advertising, 26
defined, 237
Barter syndication
and advertising, 20–22
all-barter, 20
cash-plus-barter, 20
defined, 237
Basic cable, 237
Birch Radio
defined, 237
and ratings business, 95
Block programming
defined, 237
and scheduling, 49
Bounce
defined, 237
and ratings analysis, 196
Broadband, 237
Browser, 237
Buffer sample
defined, 237
and research methods, 111
Bureau of Applied Social Research (Columbia University), 70
Buyer-graphics, 32, 33f

C